Information and Computer Science

Information and Computer Science

Edited by
Fiona Hobbs

www.willfordpress.com

www.willfordpress.com

Published by Willford Press,
118-35 Queens Blvd., Suite 400,
Forest Hills, NY 11375, USA

ISBN: 978-1-68285-446-4

Cataloging-in-Publication Data

Information and computer science / edited by Fiona Hobbs.
    p. cm.
Includes bibliographical references and index.
ISBN 978-1-68285-446-4
1. Information science. 2. Computer science. I. Hobbs, Fiona.
Z665 .I54 2018
020--dc23

For information on all Willford Press publications
visit our website at www.willfordpress.com

Contents

Preface

The implementation of computers and other networking and storage devices for processing, retrieving and transmitting data is known as information technology. Database administration, information security, network architecture, etc. are some of the main sectors where information technology is used. SQL servers, real-time order entry software, customer relationship management and enterprise resource planning systems, etc. are some of the major software used in information technology management. This book consists of contributions made by international experts. The topics covered in this book offer the readers new insights in the field of computer science and information technology.

After months of intensive research and writing, this book is the end result of all who devoted their time and efforts in the initiation and progress of this book. It will surely be a source of reference in enhancing the required knowledge of the new developments in the area. During the course of developing this book, certain measures such as accuracy, authenticity and research focused analytical studies were given preference in order to produce a comprehensive book in the area of study.

This book would not have been possible without the efforts of the authors and the publisher. I extend my sincere thanks to them. Secondly, I express my gratitude to my family and well-wishers. And most importantly, I thank my students for constantly expressing their willingness and curiosity in enhancing their knowledge in the field, which encourages me to take up further research projects for the advancement of the area.

Editor

High Quality - Low Computational Cost Technique for Automated Principal Object Segmentation Applied in Solar and Medical Imaging

Sofyan M. A. Hayajneh[1], AbdulRahman Rashad[1], Omar A. Saraereh[1,2] & Obaida M. Al-hazaimeh[3]

[1] Faculty of Engineering, Isra Univeristy, Amman, Jordans

[2] Faculty of Engineering, The Hashemite University, Amman, Jordan

[3] Faculty of Informatics, AlBalqa Applied University, Salt, Jordan

Correspondence: Sofyan M. A. Hayajneh, Faculty of Engineering, Isra Univeristy, PO 11622, PO box: 22, Amman, Jordan. E-mail: sofyan.hayajneh@iu.edu.jo

Abstract

The objective of this paper is to introduce a fully computerized, simple and low-computational cost technique that can be used in the preprocessing stages of digital images. This technique is specially designed to detect the principal (largest) closed shape object that embody the useful information in certain image types and neglect and avoid other noisy objects and artifacts. The detection process starts by calculating certain statistics of the image to estimate the amount of bit-plane slicing required to exclude the non-informative and noisy background. A simple closing morphological operation is then applied and followed by circular filter applied only on the outer coarse edge to finalize the detection process. The proposed technique takes its importance from the huge explosion of images that need accurate processing in real time speedy manner. The proposed technique is implemented using MATLAB and tested on many solar and medical images; it was shown by the quantitative evaluation that the proposed technique can handle real-life (e.g. solar, medical fundus) images and shows very good potential even under noisy and artifacts conditions. Compared to the publicly available datasets, 97% and 99% of similarity detection is achieved in medical and solar images, respectively. Although it is well-know, the morphological bit-plane slicing technique is hoped to be used in the preprocessing stages of different applications to ease the subsequent image processing stages especially in real time applications where the proposed technique showed dramatic (~100 times) saving in processing time.

Keywords: medical fundus images, solar images, image preprocessing, morphological bit-plane slicing.

1. Introduction

1.1 Image Processing Stages

Digital image processing and analysis is among rapidly growing technologies. It encompasses a wide-ranging field of applications in our everyday life. Medical, solar, industrial, text recognition, biometrics and graphics, are just examples of hundreds of possible applications of image processing (Solomon and Breckon 2011). Although every single application needs a well-designed approach to parse and extract the required useful information and, most of these approaches can be categorized under a single or multi major aspects that include but are not limited to: image visualization, sharpening, enhancement, recognition, retrieval, segmentation and /or restoration, etc. (Gonzalez and Woods 2002).

The modified algorithms to handle the aspects and applications almost follow a semi-schematic route that includes the following phases (Gonzalez and Woods 2002), and the contribution of such modified method almost fall in one or more of these phases.

1. Image preprocessing.

2. Image enhancement.

3. Feature segmentation.

4. Post-Processing.

5. Features classification

The proposed work in this paper is aimed to contribute on the first phase to make the preprocessing in certain applications faster (i.e. less computational) while improving the outcomes accuracy of the subsequent phases. This technique will be applied, tested and evaluated on digital images in two fields (namely, solar imaging and medical fundus images). A brief review about the processing of these images will be highlighted in the reminder of this section. While the motivation, methodology, results, evaluation and conclusions of the proposed technique will be pronounced and shown in the next sections.

1.2 Solar Images

Solar imaging techniques are usually implemented to extract numerical features that provide efficient representation of solar features, solar activities or general regions of interest in the different types of publicly available solar images. The integration of advanced image processing techniques with solar physics concepts can positively improve the ability of knowledge extraction and increase the ability to predict forthcoming solar activities that may have serious impacts on our daily life (Qahwaji, Green et al. 2011).

MDI-magnetogram is an example of solar images that draw a lot of researchers' attention because they depicts information about the whole solar magnetic activity which is thought to be the main driver of almost all other solar activities (Stöhr and Siegmann 2007). The important information (knowledge) in these images are in the solar disk that shows different indications (e.g. sunspots, active regions, prominence, filaments) about the magnetic activity.

The processing of this and other types of solar images such as MDI- continuum, Calcium II K-line, H-alpha, etc. starts by the detection of the main solar disk and removing any possible surrounding noise and textual information (e.g. date, time, directions, instrument name, and wavelength). Figure 1 shows examples of these images.

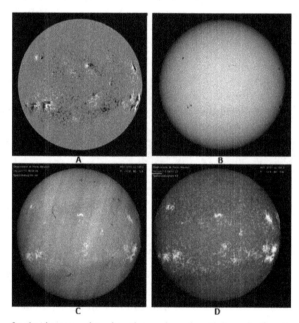

Figure 1. Different types of solar images showing the main solar disk and other textual descriptions. Images Courtesy (www.sdo.gsfc.nasa.gov/data/, www.bass2000.obspm.fr)

1.3 Medical Fundus Images

Fundus images are acquired by special medical camera to create a photograph of the inner surface of the eye including the retina, optic disc, macula, vessels and fovea (Yannuzzi, Ober et al. 2004). Fundus images are used by ophthalmologists to detect many different medical signs such as hemorrhages, exudates, cotton wool spots, blood vessel abnormalities and pigmentation (Akram and Rubinstein 2005). Manual examination (Ophthalmoscopy) is a tedious and time consuming process; yet no conclusive decisions can be made on spot without resorting to further inspecting using Fundus photographs. With the current technological advancement in image processing, it is possible to carry out rigorous hands free diagnosis that lowers the cost and the work load done by ophthalmologists for manual examination.

There are many medical research centers that publicly provide datasets of fundus images at different sizes for different subjects. The most common datasets are DIARETDB0 (Kauppi, Kalesnykiene et al. 2006), DIARETDB1 (Kauppi, Kalesnykiene et al. 2007), DRIVE (Staal, Abràmoff et al. 2004), Figure 2. The processing of these images starts by the segmentation of the retinal disk and removing the noisy background that can affect the subsequent features (e.g. optic disk, vessels) extraction (Jaafar, Nandi et al. 2010, Akram 2012).

The following section states the problem under investigation and the motivation of the work. While in section 3, the proposed technique is presented. The proposed technique implementation, accuracy and time efficiency are discussed and evaluated in section 4. Finally, the presented work is concluded in section 5.

2. Problem Statement and Motivation

As the amount of available solar and medical images is growing, there is a growing need for new approaches (i.e. systems and tools) to ease the analysis and knowledge extraction from these images. Such approaches must provide a real-time fully automated solutions while providing high accuracy outcomes and diagnosis that converge with the specialists' ones.

In the processing of the previously described images, solar disk and retina disk segmentation (mask) is considered to be the first phase of any proposed approach. This phase is important to:

1. Exclude the non-informative noisy background.

2. Reduce computational costs.

3. Improve result, where values of the noisy background are not included in the subsequent analysis such as statistic-based and training techniques in the sake of feature detection.

4. Determine some other parameters such as area and radius of the disk for further analysis.

5. Reduce the amount of information to be transferred in the case of cloud-based computing services (i.e. SaaS).

6. Unify the processing of different image types. As an example, the available datasets use a variety of instruments (i.e. cameras) to acquire the images, hence the noise and artifacts levels are not unified neither define.

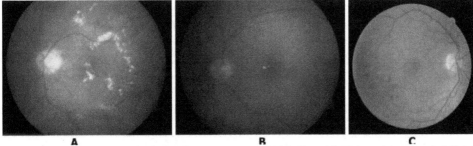

Figure 2. Different types of medical Fundus images. (Strutz 2001, Kauppi, Kalesnykiene et al. 2006, Kauppi, Kalesnykiene et al. 2007)

Some of these images suffer a pixel noise, bad illumination and/or backgrounds artifacts. Also, Pixel noise is focused around the edges of main disk (i.e. solar or retina disk) and on the black background which isn't really black (very low intensities are perceived as black by human eye).

Figure 3 illustrates the later fact by plotting the profile for a certain row in a retinal image. Using local or global thresholding based techniques to estimate and mask the background is often challenged by these problems. As a result of the presence of pixel noise and noisy background, the resulting mask from thresholding requires further refinement. Those obstacles are often overcome by applying a combination of morphological operations and filters on the foreground mask in order to refine it.

A region of interest based approach is used in (Zharkova, Ipson et al. 2003) to detect the solar limb. This approach starts by estimating the solar disk intensity by computing the mean intensity of a small rectangle located at the image center. Then a histogram analysis is performed to estimate the thresholding value that separates the disk from the background. A region filling algorithm and an iterative Canny edge detector is then applied to mark pixels within the solar disk and to complete the disk detection process.

In (Qahwaji and Colak 2005), the filling algorithm in (Qahwaji and Green 2001) is used to detect the largest closed shape object (i.e. Solar disk). This algorithm is mainly implemented by the 1) morphological hit-miss transform (HMT) which is used for the edge detection and noise removal, and the 2) morphological watershed transform (WST) which is used to analyze the image. As mentioned above, this step is important because it removes textual and non-solar information that may be superimposed on the original acquired image.

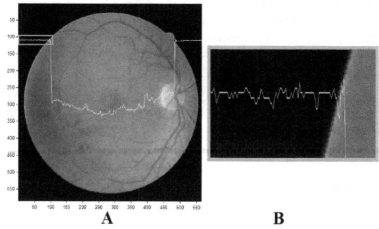

Figure 3. (A) Retinal image and (B) a zoomed background profile (along row = 100) showing that the background is not purely black

A series of gray-scale erosion, gradient transformation and thresholding is used to detect the solar limb (disk) in (Curto, Blanca et al. 2008). A 3×3 structuring element (SE) is used to implement the erosion step, followed by subtracting the original image form the eroded one to achieve the eroded gradient transformation which strengthen the edges intensities. As a consequent, applying a thresholding technique will be easier.

In (Akram 2012), retinal disk segmentation is achieved by implementing a local mean and variance based method applied on non-overlapping blocks of the HSI version of an equalized and filtered fundus image. In each block, the mean and the standard deviation is calculated to decide whether the block is a part of the background or the retina disk. In the subsequent phases, the refinement techniques results in the removal of some other parts that contain useful information about the retina health. This approach is also used in (Marrugo and Millan 2011) but reinforced by a principle component analysis (PCA) model to enhance the detection of the foreground objects and avoid any bias to the background region.

In (Garaibeh, Ma'mon et al. 2014), the extraction of retina disk is achieved by applying an edge detection filter followed by a contour-based detection algorithm where the detection starts by defining suitable locations followed by completing the contour to fit a circle arc in the regions of discontinuity.

A growing region based retina disk segmentation is performed in (Giancardo 2011) by scaling the image to an empirically chosen level to reduce the computational costs. Four seeds (chosen to be at corners with a certain offset from the borders) were used to implement the growing region algorithm based on three criteria. Then the image is rescaled back to its original size. This approach leads to less computational cost but in expense of quality loss.

To conclude, the above referenced works achieved the main disk (Sun or Retina) segmentation using different high computational cost approaches. Also, these approaches need to estimate some other important parameters to apply the proposed approaches, such details can be found on these references.

In this piece of work, we present a simpler but efficient disk segmentation approach. The proposed technique is aimed to separate the solar or retina foreground (disk) from the background using a simple, low-computational, non-adaptive and non-iterative approach without going through complex filters, while maintaining a very high accurate results.

3. Proposed Methodology

Bit planes based noise suppression techniques are often used for still images compression (Strutz 2001, Pandian and Sivanandam 2012), and in other applications such as retinal blood vessels localization (Fraz, Barman et al. 2012). Through our investigations, we found that bit planes elimination along with simple morphological operations can be utilized in foreground estimation for solar and retinal disks. The success of the proposed technique will contribute for any system in the field of the above two possible application.

A bit plane of a digital discrete signal (such as image) is a set of bits corresponding to a given bit position in each of the binary numbers representing the signal. As an example, from

Figure 4, we can see that the least 3 significant bit planes (

Figure 4 G, H, I) of a retinal image do not encode much useful visual information; rather they seem rich with pixel noise.

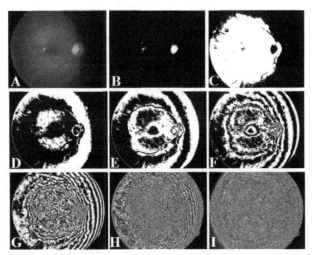

Figure 4. An example of applying the bit plane splitting on a retinal image. A: original fundus image. B-I: Single bits slicing contribution from MSB (B) to LSB (I).

The proposed technique starts by checking whether the original image is colored RGB (e.g. Fundus retinal images) or gray-scaled (e.g. MDI magnetogram) one. In the case of RGB images, a conversion from RGB to HSI color space is performed according to equations (1), (2), (3), then the rest of the proposed technique is applied on the I (Intensity) channel. Using the HSI color space makes it easier to remove noise and it is by definition closer to the human perception (Jain, Kasturi et al. 1995). It is noteworthy that only equation (1) is considered in our implementation because it represents the I channel value directly. In the case of gray scaled image, the subsequent processing is performed directly, Figure 5.

$$I = \frac{R + G + B}{3} \tag{1}$$

$$S = 1 - \frac{\min(R, G, B)}{I} \tag{2}$$

$$H = \begin{cases} \cos^{-1}\left[\dfrac{(R - G/2 - B/2)}{\sqrt[2]{R^2 + G^2 + B^2 - RG - RB - GB}}\right] & ; G \geq B \\ 360 - \cos^{-1}\left[\dfrac{(R - G/2 - B/2)}{\sqrt[2]{R^2 + G^2 + B^2 - RG - RB - GB}}\right] & ; G < B \end{cases} \tag{3}$$

where R, G and B represent the Red, Green and Blue channels of the colored image.

The next step is the slicing level estimation which is achieved by considering the four corners of the original image in a histogram based process. The histogram of the four corners are computed, then the average of the pixels above the 10th and below the 90th percentiles points of the cumulative distribution is calculated and considered to be the bit-plane slicing level (SL). A pixel-wise ANDing operation is then applied with the binary representation of SL, and all pixels with zero results are considered to be part of the background.

As an example, it is found by that keeping the 5 most significant bit planes of the retinal image and combining them while discarding the 3 least significant bit planes will maintain the image's disk main structure while removing the vast majority of pixel noise (especially those around the edges) as well as the low intensities on the background. Majority of pixel noise put out of the way and black background made really black, applying a global thresholding at zero intensity yields a relatively fine mask. Followed by erosion and dilation morphological operations will remove the very small amount of noise pixels remaining and fills the gaps within the main disk area.

This approach requires neither complex statistical computations nor mathematical computations of the total image; rather employs a single logical AND operation on binary level to discard the least significant bit planes. Moreover, the resulting mask requires much less refinement computation. Figure 6 shows the goodness of the proposed technique segmentation even before applying morphological operations. Applying a circular edge detector with centers *only* on the outer coarse segmentation is found to enhance the coarse segmentation accuracy without dramatically increase the computational time costs.

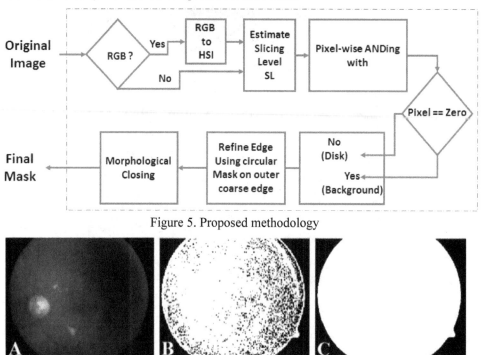

Figure 5. Proposed methodology

Figure 6. Compare (B) (Akram 2012) technique with (C) proposed technique applied on (A) retinal image from DIARETDB1 dataset. Both before applying any morphological operations

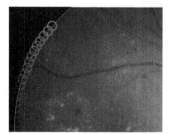

Figure 7. Applying a circular window on the outer coarse pixels to refine the segmentation

4. Results and Evaluations

4.1 Accuracy Performance

Usually, the evaluation of an algorithm is done by comparing the new results with certain ground truths. To evaluate the proposed technique in this paper, the SOHO/MDI magnetogram and Drive datasets were used. These specific datasets are used in the evaluation for many reasons (contain different illumination levels and verities, contain different noise levels, contain a ground truth to evaluate and contain different artifact such as textual tagging in the case of solar images).

4.1.1 Solar MDI Images

Solar images: Each MDI solar image is provided in both formats (GIF and FITS). Each FITS file contains a header that describes many parameters of the corresponding MDI image, these parameters include the center, radius and area of the solar disk. Also, the background area in the FITS files are represented by a not a number (NaN) symbol. These parameters along with the spatial location of the detected disk will be compared to the results of the proposed technique when applied to the corresponding .GIF image. It is noteworthy that multiple MDI GIF images are provided daily; so that it is important to match exactly the same GIF and FITS files for the same day for the sake of evaluation.

The proposed technique is implemented using MATLAB without using the predefined functions, which means that the proposed algorithm and the ones under comparison were built using basic MATLAB statements to avoid any effect of these predefined functions. Table 1 compares the results obtained by applying the proposed technique on some MDI GIF examples with that provided in the corresponding FITS files. Three types of errors are calculated according to equations (4), (5) and (6):

$$Error(Area) = \left| \frac{ProposedArea - FITSArea}{FITSArea} \right| \times 100\% \tag{4}$$

$$Error(Raduis) = \left| \frac{ProposedRaduis - FITSRaduis}{FITSRaduis} \right| \times 100\% \tag{5}$$

$$Error(Center) = \left| \frac{\sqrt[2]{(ProposedXc - FITSXc)^2 + (ProposedYc - FITSYc)^2}}{\sqrt[2]{(FitsXc)^2 + (FitsYc)^2}} \right| \times 100\% \tag{6}$$

where FITSArea, FITSRaduis, FITSXc and FITSYc represent, respectively, the area, radius, center's x-axis coordinates and center's y-axis coordinates of the provided mask in FITS files. While, ProposedArea, ProposedRaduis, ProposedXc and ProposedYc represent the area, radius, center's x-axis coordinates and center's y-axis coordinates of the calculated mask using the proposed technique which are calculated as follows:

- *Area*: is calculated by summing up the number of foreground pixels after applying the proposed technique.

- *Center*: is calculated using the centroid (center of mass) method (Baxes 1994). Where ProposedXc and ProposedYc are calculated according to equations (7) and (8) respectively.

- *Radius*: is calculated by averaging the distances from the center towards the four mask ends along the quadratic directions.

$$ProposedXc = \frac{sum\ of\ mask\ pixels'x\_coordinates}{Area} \tag{7}$$

$$ProposedYc = \frac{sum\ of\ mask\ pixels'Y\_coordinates}{Area} \tag{8}$$

It is clear that the proposed technique shows a very high accuracy performance; the highest error achieved for the three defined types of errors is .88% (less than 1%); this means more than 99% similarity. It is worth mentioning that a 1% to 2% oblateness is exist in some solar GIF images; which results in disagreements between the calculated parameters and the corresponding provided in the FITS files headers (Zharkova, Ipson et al. 2003).

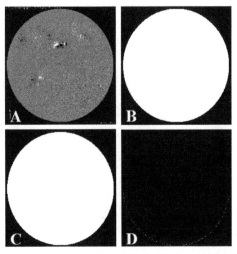

Figure 8. Example of MDI-magnetogram image. B: Provided FITS mask for A. C: Proposed technique applied on A. D: difference between B and C

4.1.2 Medical Fundus Images

The Drive dataset (Staal, Abràmoff et al. 2004) provides publicly 40 fundus images and their corresponding manually labelled masks. These available masks will be compared to the masks resulted by applying the proposed technique on the same corresponding images. Figure 9 shows an example to compare the result of the proposed technique applied on a fundus image and the corresponding mask provided by Drive dataset. Table 2 compares the masks obtained by applying the proposed technique on 15 randomly selected Drive fundus images with the corresponding masks provided by Drive dataset (i.e. ground truth). The above types of errors (equations (4), (5) and (6)) are used again in the evaluation. It is clear that the proposed technique shows a very high accuracy performance; the highest error achieved for the three error types is 2.98%; this means a similarity that exceeds 97%.

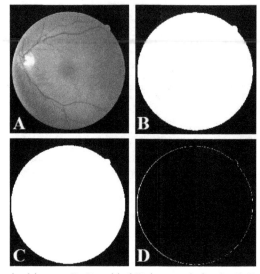

Figure 9. Example of Fundus retinal image. B: Provided Drive mask for A. C: Proposed technique applied on A. D: difference between B and C

Table 1. Comparison between the proposed technique and the FITS files masks

	FITS DATA				Proposed Technique				Error (100%)		
MDI-Mag Date	Area Pixels	Radius Pixels	Center_X Pixels	Center_Y Pixels	Area Pixels	Radius Pixels	Center_X Pixels	Center_Y Pixels	Area	Raduis	Center
2010.12.15	772396	495.8	512.5	512.5	771773	496.0	513.0	511.0	0.08	0.03	0.22
2010.12.11	771592	495.6	512.5	512.5	771062	495.5	513.0	512.0	0.07	0.02	0.10
2010.11.16	763426	493.0	512.9	511.9	762887	493.0	508.0	513.0	0.07	0.01	0.70
2010.10.30	756411	490.7	512.5	512.5	755835	490.5	516.0	512.0	0.08	0.04	0.49
2010.10.29	756068	490.6	512.5	512.5	755543	490.5	513.0	513.0	0.07	0.01	0.10
2010.09.19	740113	485.4	512.5	511.6	739652	485.0	514.0	513.0	0.06	0.08	0.28
2010.09.03	735233	483.8	512.5	511.7	734739	484.0	515.0	513.0	0.07	0.05	0.39
2010.08.20	731774	482.6	512.5	511.8	731278	483.0	511.0	513.0	0.07	0.08	0.27
2010.08.05	728778	481.6	512.5	511.9	728284	482.0	511.0	513.0	0.07	0.08	0.26
2010.07.23	726696	481.0	512.5	512.0	726236	481.0	513.0	512.0	0.06	0.01	0.07
2010.07.08	725033	480.4	512.5	512.0	724540	480.0	510.0	512.0	0.07	0.09	0.34
2010.06.24	724489	480.2	512.4	512.0	723989	480.0	512.0	512.0	0.07	0.05	0.06
2010.06.03	726039	480.7	512.5	512.5	725558	481.0	509.0	512.0	0.07	0.06	0.48
2010.05.22	728399	481.5	512.5	512.5	727929	482.0	512.0	512.0	0.06	0.10	0.09
2010.04.21	738565	484.9	512.6	512.2	738092	485.0	514.0	513.0	0.06	0.03	0.23
2010.03.15	756252	490.6	512.7	512.0	755747	490.0	519.0	513.0	0.07	0.13	0.88
2010.02.24	765185	493.5	512.7	511.8	764671	493.5	515.0	513.0	0.07	0.00	0.36
2010.02.23	765633	493.7	512.7	511.8	765064	493.5	513.0	513.0	0.07	0.03	0.17
2010.01.27	773980	496.4	512.7	511.6	773496	496.5	512.0	512.0	0.06	0.03	0.11
2010.01.17	775082	496.7	512.7	511.6	774557	496.5	511.0	512.0	0.07	0.04	0.25

Table 2. Comparison between the proposed technique and the Drive images' masks

DRIVE Image	Drive Data				Proposed Technique				Error (100%)		
	Area Pixels	Radius Pixels	Center_X Pixels	Center_Y Pixels	Area Pixels	Radius Pixels	Center_X Pixels	Center_Y Pixels	Area	Raduis	Contor
DRIVE_02	225087	268.0	302.0	268.0	228277	270.0	298.0	278.0	1.42	0.75	2.67
DRIVE_04	227577	270.0	293.0	270.0	227927	270.0	294.0	281.0	0.15	0.00	2.77
DRIVE_05	227693	270.0	300.0	270.0	227986	270.0	299.0	282.0	0.13	0.00	2.98
DRIVE_08	225248	268.0	298.0	268.0	228022	270.0	298.0	278.0	1.23	0.75	2.50
DRIVE_11	227814	270.0	298.0	270.0	228104	270.0	299.0	278.0	0.13	0.00	2.00
DRIVE_15	227394	269.0	301.0	269.0	227734	269.0	300.0	279.0	0.15	0.00	2.49
DRIVE_18	227612	270.0	301.0	270.0	227925	270.0	297.0	278.0	0.14	0.00	2.21
DRIVE_21	225600	268.0	299.0	268.0	227981	270.0	299.0	278.0	1.06	0.75	2.49
DRIVE_24	227726	270.0	296.0	270.0	228056	270.0	297.0	276.0	0.14	0.00	1.52
DRIVE_27	227826	270.0	294.0	270.0	228122	270.0	296.0	276.0	0.13	0.00	1.58
DRIVE_30	227259	270.0	300.0	270.0	227605	270.0	298.0	279.0	0.15	0.00	2.28
DRIVE_32	224944	268.0	297.0	268.0	227893	270.0	299.0	276.0	1.31	0.75	2.06
DRIVE_35	227646	270.0	296.0	270.0	227964	270.0	296.0	276.0	0.14	0.00	1.50
DRIVE_37	227186	269.0	296.0	269.0	227494	270.0	295.0	276.0	0.14	0.37	1.77
DRIVE_39	227460	270.0	300.0	270.0	227750	270.0	299.0	282.0	0.13	0.00	2.98

4.2 Processing Time Validation

Besides achieving a high accuracy records, in this validation, the ability of the proposed technique to reduce the processing time is investigated. The proposed technique is applied on different retinal image from different datasets (DIARETDB0, DIARETDB1, and DRIVE) and the CPU processing time is noted for each image and recorded. The technique in (Akram 2012), which is considered the simplest technique in literature, is applied on the same images and the corresponding processing time is recorded.

Table 3 shows the CPU time for coarse background estimation (Proposed technique and (Akram 2012) technique), the first 5 images of each of the databases (DIARETDB0, DIARETDB1, and DRIVE) were processed three times on each technique. The mean time for the three runs was calculated as well as the average of those means. It is easily noted fromTable 3 that the proposed technique reduces the processing time dramatically.

Table 3. Comparison between the proposed technique and Akram's technique applied on different images of different datasets

	AKRAM				PROPOSED			
	Run1 Time (ms)	Run2 Time (ms)	Run3 Time (ms)	Mean Time (ms)	Run1 Time (ms)	Run2 Time (ms)	Run3 Time (ms)	Mean Time (ms)
	DIARETDB0							
IMAGE 1	100.11	98.57	97.84	98.84	0.8266	0.8809	1.3800	1.0292
IMAGE 2	103.38	101.53	103.43	102.78	0.8236	0.8219	0.7740	0.8065
IMAGE 3	105.26	105.11	103.20	104.52	0.8236	0.8553	0.8228	0.8339
IMAGE 4	105.27	105.91	101.04	104.07	1.3749	0.8886	0.8472	1.0369
IMAGE 5	104.90	106.00	101.73	104.21	0.7954	0.8745	0.8258	0.8319
AVERAGE				102.88				0.9077
	DIARETDB1							
IMAGE 1	100.87	98.38	99.11	99.45	0.8514	1.3988	1.3040	1.2102
IMAGE 2	98.06	99.34	98.34	98.58	1.1029	0.8818	0.8296	0.9381
IMAGE 3	97.79	98.91	97.32	98.00	0.8780	1.1906	0.8771	0.9819
IMAGE 4	99.09	98.57	98.63	98.76	0.7984	0.8395	0.8219	0.8199
IMAGE 5	98.86	97.54	99.75	98.72	0.8202	0.8172	0.8527	0.8301
AVERAGE				98.70				0.9560

	DRIVE							
IMAGE 1	19.26	19.48	19.69	19.48	0.3319	0.3203	0.3408	0.3310
IMAGE 2	19.31	19.41	19.23	19.32	0.3336	0.3113	0.3092	0.3180
IMAGE 3	18.88	19.01	19.06	18.98	0.3079	0.3053	0.3036	0.3056
IMAGE 4	18.90	19.13	19.22	19.08	0.3122	0.3023	0.3665	0.3270
IMAGE 5	19.32	19.15	19.25	19.24	0.3250	0.3182	0.3203	0.3212
AVERAGE				19.22				0.3206

To ensure that the proposed algorithm shows the same goodness and computational time saving despite the existence of severe abnormalities and despite their shapes in images, the proposed algorithm is applied on all images of DIARETDB0, DIARETDB1, and DRIVE datasets. It is difficult to show the segmentation results, while Figure 10 shows the CPU processing time using the proposed technique and Akram's technique applied on all images contained in DIARETDB0, DIARETDB1, and DRIVE. This CPU processing time validation was performed on an Intel i7 4700mq (4 physical cores, 8 logical cores) supported by 8 GB DDR3 RAM 1600MHZ operated by a 64-bit WINDOWS 7

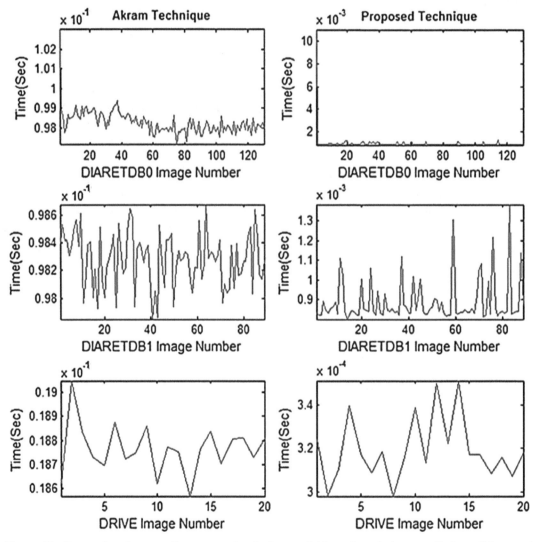

Figure 10. Comparison between the proposed technique and Akram's technique applied on all images in DIARETDB0, DIARETDB1 and DRIVE datasets

5. Conclusions

In this paper, we have utilized the concept of bit-plane splitting to detect the large principal objects in some types of solar and medical images. The proposed technique revealed high quality results compared to other techniques that utilized iterative, adaptive, and complex edge detection techniques. The proposed technique is implemented on MATLAB operates on a Windows based platform. 99% and 97% similarity were achieved when the proposed method is applied and compared to solar MDI-magnetogram and medical Fundus retinal images. This high degree of accuracy is achieved while reducing the processing time dramatically.

This piece of work represents single part of our ongoing research in solar and medical fundus image processing. It is aimed that we can keep maintaining the subsequent phases of processing by keep eye on the simple adopted approach (i.e. bit-split slicing) along with other simple refinement, detection and classification techniques rather than complex ones of high computational cost. Also, further visualization and representation can be made making use of the state of the art utilization of cloud-based services (Hayajneh 2015).

References

Akram, I., & Rubinstein, A. (2005). Common retinal signs: An overview. Optometry Today.

Akram, U. (2012). Retinal image preprocessing: Background and noise segmentation. TELKOMNIKA *Indonesian Journal of Electrical Engineering.*

Baxes, G. A. (1994). Digital Image Processing: Principles and Applications. New York, NY, John Wiley & Sons.

Curto, J., Blanca, M., & Martínez, E. (2008). Automatic sunspots detection on full-disk solar images using mathematical morphology. *Solar Physics, 250*(2), 411-429. http://dx.doi.org/10.1007/s11207-008-9224-6.

Fraz, M. M., Barman, S. A., Remagnino, P., Hoppe, A., Basit, A., Uyyanonvara, B., Rudnicka, A. R., & Owen, C. G. (2012). An approach to localize the retinal blood vessels using bit planes and centerline detection. *Computer Methods and Programs in Biomedicine, 108*(2), 600-616. http://dx.doi.org/10.1016/j.cmpb.2011.08.009

Garaibeh, N. Y., Ma'mon, A., & Al-Jarrah, M. (2014). Automatic Exudate Detection Using Eye Fundus Image Analysis Due to Diabetic Retinopathy. *Computer and Information Science, 7*(2), 48. http://dx.doi.org/10.5539/cis.v7n2p48

Giancardo, L. (2011). Automated fundus images analysis techniques to screen retinal diseases in diabetic patients, Université de Bourgogne.

Gonzalez, R. C., & Woods, R. E. (2002). Digital image processing.

Hayajneh, S. (2015). Cloud Computing SaaS Paradigm for Efficient Modelling of Solar Features and Activities. *International Journal of Cloud Applications and Computing (IJCAC), 5*(3), 20-34. http://dx.doi.org/10.4018/IJCAC.2015070102.

Jaafar, H. F., Nandi, A. K., & Al-Nuaimy, W. (2010). *Detection of exudates in retinal images using a pure splitting technique.* Engineering in Medicine and Biology Society (EMBC), 2010 Annual International Conference of the IEEE, IEEE. http://dx.doi.org/10.1109/IEMBS.2010.5626014

Jain, R., Kasturi, R., & Schunck, B. G. (1995). Machine vision. New York, McGraw-Hill.

Kauppi, T., Kalesnykiene, V., Kamarainen, J. K., Lensu, L., Sorri, I., Raninen, A., Voutilainen, R., Uusitalo, H., Kälviäinen, H., & Pietilä, J. (2007). The DIARETDB1 Diabetic Retinopathy Database and Evaluation Protocol. BMVC.

Kauppi, T., Kalesnykiene,V., Kamarainen, J. K., Lensu, L., Sorri, I., Uusitalo, H., Kälviäinen, H., & Pietilä, J. (2006). *DIARETDB0: Evaluation database and methodology for diabetic retinopathy algorithms.* Lappeenranta University of Technology.

Marrugo, A. G., & Millan, M. S. (2011). Retinal image analysis: Preprocessing and feature extraction. *Journal of Physics*: Conference Series, IOP Publishing. http://dx.doi.org/10.1088/1742-6596/274/1/012039

Pandian, A. P., & Sivanandam, S. N. (2012). Hybrid Algorithm for Lossless Image Compression using Simple Selective Scan order with Bit Plane Slicing. *Journal of Computer Science, 8*(8), 1338-1345. http://dx.doi.org/10.3844/jcssp.2012.1338.1345

Qahwaji, R., & Colak, T. (2005). Automatic detection and verification of solar features. *International Journal of Imaging Systems and Technology, 15*(4), 199-210. http://dx.doi.org/10.1002/ima.20053

Qahwaji, R., & Green, R. (2001). Detection of closed regions in digital images. *The International Journal of Computers and Their Applications, 8*(4), 202-207.

Qahwaji, R., Green, R., Hines, E., & Global, I., (2011). Applied Signal and Image Processing: Multidisciplinary Advancements, Information Science Reference.

Solomon, C., & Breckon, T., (2011). Fundamentals of Digital Image Processing: A practical approach with examples in Matlab, John Wiley & Sons.

Staal, J., Abràmoff, M. D., Niemeijer, M., Viergever, M. A., & van Ginneken, B. (2004). Ridge-based vessel segmentation in color images of the retina. *Medical Imaging, IEEE Transactions on, 23*(4), 501-509.

Stöhr, J., & Siegmann, H. C. (2007). Magnetism: from fundamentals to nanoscale dynamics, Springer.

Strutz, T. (2001). Fast Noise Suppression for Lossless Image Coding.

Yannuzzi, L. A., Ober, M. D., Slakter, J. S., Spaide, R. F., Fisher, Y. L., Flower, R. W., & Rosen, R. (2004). Ophthalmic fundus imaging: Today and beyond. *American Journal of Ophthalmology, 137*(3), 511-524.

Zharkova, V., Ipson, S., Zharkov, S., Benkhalil, A., Aboudarham, J., & Bentley, R. (2003). A full-disk image standardisation of the synoptic solar observations at the Meudon Observatory. *Solar Physics, 214*(1), 89-105. http://dx.doi.org/10.1023/A:1024081931946

2

A Proposed Assessment Criterion for E-Learning Sites Evaluation: An Experts' Opinion

Hayel Khafajeh[1] & Issam Jebreen[1]

[1] Faculty of Information Technology, Zarqa University, Jordan

Correspondence: Issam Jebreen, Faculty of Information Technology, Zarqa University, Jordan. E-mail: Hayelkh@zu.edu.jo/ijebreen@zu.edu.jo

The research is financed by Deanship of Research and Graduate Studies in Zarqa University/Jordan

Abstract

An increasing growth in the number of e-learning sites at universities and other educational institutions led to necessary of develop and adopt a standards element to assess these sites to ensure efficiency, rival, and educational quality. Therefore, this study proposed an assessment criterion to evaluate the e-learning sites as a guide for decision-makers in order to purchase and development e-learning sites in which these assessment criterions are commensurate with the learning process. An experts' opinion from universities professors who specialize in the field of teaching in different Jordan universities have been considered in order to develop a proposed assessment criterion, the result shows that the assessment criterion to evaluate the e-learning sites has twenty six criterion under five main categorizes namely: website design, and scientific knowledge content, technical elements, operational elements and finally with credibility of information sites. Given that the proposed assessment criterion to evaluate e-learning sites is guide for students, teachers, owners and developers about the benefits of e-learning sites.

Keywords: e-learning site, assessment criterion, decision-making

1. Introduction

Learning process aims to spread knowledge about the specific topic through interactive and interesting environment. Teachers convey their knowledge in both types (implicit and explicit) using some learning techniques (Nokelainen, 2006). Improves learning process conditions and environment to transfer both types knowledge will be enhancing learning process then that achieve education goals. Hence, intervene and usage of the information revolution and e-learning approach provides an improvement and solution to the problems experienced by the traditional learning approach such as the absence of students from their lessons, and increasing population growth and individual differences that makes a computer-based educational software and e-learning assistant outstanding teachers and the education approach itself either. These software applications aim to help and support teachers rather to replace them. However, the evaluation of educational software and e-learning is an important factor that impact on the learners' knowledge and teachers. Therefore, it is necessary to adopt a standards element to assess these sites to ensure efficiency, rival, and educational quality.

Several researchers have therefore approached the analysis of e-learning sites as website design, and scientific knowledge content, technical elements, operational elements and finally with credibility of information sites. Some have argued that the website design aspects of e-learning sites and scientific knowledge content are such importance that they often overshadow the substantial learning complexities (Sharlin & Bartus, 2009; Tarafdar & Zhang, 2005). The use of poor e-learning sites has often been identified as one of the major factors that can jeopardize the success of a learning process and its objectives. Meanwhile, researchers have also recognized that following appropriate e-learning sites contributes to the success of learning process. For example, Veeramani (2010) stated that credibility of information sites is key factors when it comes to the success of learning process. There is a general critical consensus that evaluation of e-learning sites a very important role in the success or failure of learning process.

Other study by Stewart et al, (2004) developed a tool that enabled the lecturers to evaluate the quality of the courses on the e-learning. The study results suggested seven categorizes namely (hyperlinks and navigation, class procedures and expectations, technical issues, appearance of Web pages, online applications, content delivery, and instructor and peer interaction) that contains fifty-nine items in which lecturers were able to determine the quality of the e-learning courses. Bernard et al. (2004) recommended four factors to assess the achievements of e-learning namely general beliefs e-learning, and confidence in the abilities of pre-requisites, and autonomy and initiative, and the desire to interact. Kay and Knaack (2008) suggested student rating scale development to examine educational objects. The results showed that the student rating scale development will be a valid tool for measuring the three constants: learning, quality and commitment of the learning object.

However, most of e-learning studies have been focus on evaluate e-learning sites from perspective of the learning objects, it is not possible to improve learning process until areas that need improvement in an organization's current standards element to assess e-learning sites have been identified. In other words, the lack of an assessment criterion to evaluate the e-learning sites as a guide for decision-makers in order to purchase and development e-learning have been little mentioned in literature especially from the experts' opinion. Meanwhile, the solution for improving learning process and to assess e-learning sites will be different in each sites and educational institutional; it has been found that a one-size-fits-all approach does not work in such a scenario.

One core question that remains, despite the work done in previous studies, is: what are the experts' opinions of purchase and development e-learning sites? This study set out to understand assessment criterion to evaluate the e-learning sites in terms of purchase and development e-learning sites. The rest of this paper is organized as follows: in Section II we provide a review of previous literature relevant to the concept of e-learning and its assessment; in Section III we describe our research method; in Section IV we present our findings and discussion (the cross elements between e-learning sites and its assessment), in Section V delivers our conclusion and considers future work.

2. Research Method

The purpose of the present study is to understand the phenomenon of e-learning sites evaluation. Many researchers in the field of software engineering and information systems suggest that the best way to understand the phenomenon "evaluation of e-learning sites" practices is to observe and interpret the experiences of the participants involved in the process. One group of participants in universities is professors and doctors who are using e-learning sites to teach and interact with their students. These participants may possibly understand and agree among themselves upon the assessment criterion usage in order to evaluate e-learning sites. This study focuses particularly on participants' perspectives regarding assessment criterion usage in order to evaluate e-learning sites.

Two universities have participated in this research with 10 is professors and doctors who are using e-learning sites to teach and interact with their students from both universities, University 1 and 2 was established in 1997 and 1994 in which has 200 employees and 250 for university 2. The services they offer include undergraduate degree and master degree.

Table 1. Background of the participants

Position	Uni 1	Uni 2
Experience (Years)		
Less than 3 years	2(40%)	1(20%)
3 to 10 years	2(40%)	2(40%)
11 to 20 years	1(20%)	2(40%)
Experience (Position)		
Assistant Prof	2(40%)	1(40%)
Associate Prof	2(40%)	3(60%)
Professor	1(20%)	1(20%)

Table 1 shows the background of the participants who were participated in this study. The total number of participants was 10from both universities. The participants included assistant prof, associate prof, and full professor. All of the professors had a total experience of 11-20 years in the field. However, only 30% of the participants in both universities had less than 3 years' experience. Most of associate prof had over 11 years' experience in the field.

In the last decade focus group interviews have become a commonly used technique to collect qualitative data by asking the participants about their perceptions, beliefs, opinions, or attitudes regarding a concept, idea, service, or product (Krueger & Casey, 2008). While social research typically adopts direct observation, focus groups are more appropriate for studies of attitudes and experiences. The communication between participants in the focus group allows the researcher to gain access to various areas for studies, sampling, and raises unexpected issues for exploration (Krueger & Casey, 2008). Focus groups are used as a self-contained method as well as in addition to other research methods, like in-depth interviews (Krueger & Casey, 2008).

Furthermore, group interviews may facilitate the discussion of taboo topics, reveal the opinions common to the group, and encourage people whose experiences are similar to discuss these experiences, when they might have been unwilling to discuss them otherwise. Some research has shown that group discussions generate more criticism than individual interviews (Krueger & Casey, 2008).

Before conducting a focus group, we identified the major objectives of the meeting and developed the main questions relevant to the research questions. The discussion session normally lasted an hour or an hour and a half. To plan the session, we needed to schedule a time when all the participants could attend. The universities' conference rooms were used, which allowed all of the participants to see each other. The main ground rules we followed during a focus group were to remain focused on the research topic while the discussion flowed and evolved, to maintain momentum, and to achieve closure of questions. The focus group meeting agendas always included: welcoming the participants, reviewing the agenda and goals of the meeting, explaining the means of recording the session, introduction, conducting a questions and answers period, and wrapping up. During the main part of the session, we might sit back and listen to the discussion. Later on, we might encourage the participants to conduct a discussion in more of a debate style, and to encourage different opinions to be voiced. We worked to facilitate equal participation of all the members, giving each person time to answer the question and to voice their opinion on the matter. To avoid having one or two people dominate the discussion, a round-table rule should be introduced as one of the ground rules at the beginning of a session.

Focus group discussions held presented in the table 2. We had 4 such meetings with participants. Some of these were audio recorded and some were not. The main point of the focus groups was to discuss the participants' perspective about the phenomenon of "e-learning sites evaluation". The participants also discussed the users' interaction strategies during the usage of e-learning sites.

Table 2. Focus group topics

Focus Groups Topics	Questions
Design	What do you think about eLearning site design?
	Do you think design has any impact on the use of e-learning site, if yes how, if no why?
Content	Electronic content elements clearly related to the quality of the website?
	What do you think about the validate and accuracy of the information presented on e-learning site?
Technical elements	- What are the elements that must be available in educational software so that the user can access the website?
	- How it can be treated Website individual differences among users?
Operational elements	What do think about e-learning site operational?
	Do site operational impact users, if yes how and why?
	What are the operational elements must be available in e-learning site?
Credibility	What do think about e-learning site credibility?
	Do site credibility impact users, if yes how and why?
	What are the credibility elements must be available in e-learning site?

3. Analysis Method Selection

The literature regarding qualitative research methods places great emphasis upon the methods used to go out and collect or generate data, but less emphasis upon the analytical techniques that can be used to interpret these data.

So whilst different approaches might be taken when conducting qualitative research, there are also requirements that there should be some consistency between methods, methodology and analysis, in order to demonstrate narrative story being told. At the same time, in order for the research to be credible to the reader, the reader needs to be led toward what the researcher thinks are most significant about the research findings (Gregor, 2006; Denzin, 2000). The importance of these findings must be made "transparent" and choices and assumptions made by the researcher made explicit in relation to the methodological perspective Klein & Myers 2001). For example, if a researcher is a positivist and tends to use deductive method reasoning, they'll tend to do "this". If they are an interpretivist and tend to use inductive method reasoning, they'll tend to do "that". A wide range of literature documents the underlying assumptions and procedures associated with analyzing qualitative data, including the evaluation of data and data analysis strategies, and inductive and deductive approaches.

4. Results & Discussion

The results discussed in this section were obtained by our summarizing and synthesizing the findings we derived from the data collected during focus groups held with participants. During the focus groups we aimed to collect information from the participants regarding what are their opinions about assessment criterion to evaluate the e-learning sites. Table 3 shows the assessment criterion for each categorize they should be concerned to evaluate the e-learning sites.

Table 3. Assessment criterion for each categorize

Categorize	Assessment Criterion
Design	Ease movement from page to page
	The use of colors, sounds, movements and images
	Readability of the texts and the ease of finding information
	Person enjoyment by browsing and viewing
	Consistency between the colors, fonts and background thread
	Clarity in the chain lessons of logical sequence and linkages built
Content	Suitable title for content
	Information is accurate, objective, useful and sound
	Use of educational activities, useful exercises for target class, and constantly evolving and commensurate with the cognitive levels of users
	The presence of diversity in the presentation of content to achieve the principle of individual differences among the educated.
	The availability of the suspense elements, attract attention, creativity and challenge learners' abilities. The possibility of learning by play and entertaining
	The existence of an interactive dialogue between the software and learners
	It provides link to various sources of knowledge in the teaching areas
Technical elements	Site must provide users log file that show their activates and Users must be authorized to use the site.
	Site should Contains tools determine the level of knowledge of the user
	Site allows the user to choose and control the lesson.
	Site allows the user to return to revise certain parts of a particular lesson
Operational elements	Effective Feedback about online test
	Site performance.
	Effective and necessary links to the site.
	Available help tools to solve technical, writing, and learning problems
Credibility	Show the release date and it was last modified
	The information displayed is based on references and sources of credit
	E-mail is available for someone site owner or his representative
	All images, graphics, texts have names and addresses can be referenced
	The martial quality on the site

After the data had been analyzed inductively to produce the findings reported in this section, we sent emails to both participants in order to validate our data analysis. We have 9 responded out of 10 participants. The instructions for the participants stated: "We are interested in understanding which assessment criterion to evaluate the e-learning sites. For each criterion shown in the following tables place a tick in the column (from strongly disagree (0) to strongly agree (4)) that indicates whether you either personally think or witnessed someone else that use criterion to evaluate the e-learning sites".

We compared the assessment criterion to evaluate the e-learning sites marked in order to note similarities and differences between our data analysis and the participants' answers as well as to develop a formulas evaluation model for e-learning site, as shown in Table 4 and Table 5. we adopted an acceptable matching level and compared what the participants' said with what we had originally found in focus group, in order to display whether the two forms of results matched or not. Table 4 shows design category as examples of our result validation.

Table 4. Design category– result validation

Categorize	Assessment Criterion	Strongly Agree (4)	Agree (3)	Neutral (2)	Disagree (1)	Strongly Disagree (0)
Design	Ease movement from page to page	7	1	1	---	---
	The use of colors, sounds, movements and images	6	2	1	---	---
	Readability of the texts and the ease of finding information	5	4	---	---	---
	Person enjoyment by browsing and viewing	8	1	---	---	---
	Consistency between the colors, fonts and background thread	6	1	2	---	---
	Clarity in the chain lessons of logical sequence and linkages built	4	5	---	---	---
	The formats of files upload	1	2	2	3	1

As shown in Table 4, our results were validated from the original focus group sessions with participants. For example, 'Ease movement from page to page', and 'Consistency between the colors, fonts and background thread' were found as assessment criterion during our focus group analysis and was confirmed by participant's validation. However, 'the formats of files upload' was found as assessment criterion during our focus group analysis but was not confirmed by participant's validation. The general result of the validation process carried out by means of the checklist was that the viewpoints the participants held of the assessment involved in e-learning sites had an approximately 86% similarity with our own view of the process. Therefore, the findings made through our analysis of focus group were validated by the participants at a rate of about 80-90%.

Table 5 shows a proposed formulas evaluation model for e-learning sits in which each criterion has 4 points and each category has the sum of points for its assessment criterion. The table 5 shows the maximum point's criterion, and grades achieved for each category.

The results indicate those different assessment criterions are used for different purposes during the evaluation of e-learning sites. For instance, design of e-learning sites criterions were indicated by participants from the perspective of usability (Chiu et al, 2005). Given that, our study was perceived usability from software design perspective as ease movement from page to page, the use of colors, sounds, movements and images, readability of the texts and the ease of finding information, and person enjoyment by browsing and viewing. In contrast, the study by Chiu et al (2005) was perceived usability from learning perspective as "It is easy for me to become skillful at using the e-learning service", "Using the e-learning service can improve my learning performance". Our results suggest that continuance intention of participants and satisfaction are achieved by perceived software design usability of e-learning sites.

Table 5. Formulas evaluation model for e-learning sits

Categorize	Number of Criterion (NC)	Maximum Marks (MM)	The amount of degrees' verification (DV)	The percentage of grades achieve
Design	6	24	$D1=\sum_{i=1}^{NC}$ Criterion $*$ ScoreMark	D1/MM *100
Content	7	28	$D2=\sum_{i=1}^{NC}$ Criterion $*$ ScoreMark	D2/MM *100
Technical elements	4	16	$D3=\sum_{i=1}^{NC}$ Criterion $*$ ScoreMark	D3/MM *100
Operational elements	4	16	$D4=\sum_{i=1}^{NC}$ Criterion $*$ ScoreMark	D4/MM *100
Credibility	5	20	$D5=\sum_{i=1}^{NC}$ Criterion $*$ ScoreMark	D5/MM *100

Formula of overall site evaluation (SE)

$$SE = \frac{\sum_{i=1}^{5} D_i}{\sum MM} \times 100\%$$

The results imply that content of e-learning sites seem to be indicated by participants in order to identify negative critical incidents of e-learning sites. Our result indicated that suitable title for content, information is accurate, objective, useful and sound, and use of educational activities, useful exercises for target class, and constantly evolving and commensurate with the cognitive levels of users, and the presence of diversity in the presentation of content to achieve the principle of individual differences among the educated, the availability of the suspense elements, attract attention, creativity and challenge learners' abilities. the possibility of learning by play and entertaining, the existence of an interactive dialogue between the software and learners, it provides link to various sources of knowledge in the teaching areas are an important assessment criterions from participants' perspective as perhaps one that could have an impact on the progress and outcomes of the teaching process Lin, 2011). In contrast, the study by Lee (2010) has evaluated content of e-learning sites from the perspective of concentration that adopted from the study of Moon and Kim as e-learning web site provides the service needs, feel comfortable in using the functions and services provided by the e-learning web site, the e-learning web site provides complete information, and the e-learning web site provides information that is easy to comprehend. One possible explanation for our result is that our data analyses driven from the perspective of software develop and chosen rather than from teaching process. Furthermore, the developing and choosing e-learning sites incorporates a set of progress activities that require different assessment criterions such as a software quality, and elements. These activities may improve the participants' experience of developing and choosing e-learning sites.

5. Conclusion and Future Works

To conclude, the development of an information system involves knowing what to create and how to create it. Understanding what an e-learning sites needs to improve demands on assessment of these sites. This is widely considered to be a challenging process in the development and chosen of the e-learning sites, and the evaluation of e-learning sites has long been considered an important topic in the literature on information systems. Prior research has identified wrong evaluation of e-learning sites as a major contributor to the failure of the efficiency, rival, and educational quality.

In various studies, the issues of assessment criterion to evaluate the e-learning sites have been found to effect execution of development and chosen of the e-learning sites; thus, much of the literature on e-learning investigates how to evaluate the e-learning sites. Having reviewed the literature on this topic, we conclude that there is a significant relationship between assessment criterion to evaluate the e-learning sites and the development and chosen of the e-learning sites. Moreover, the understanding of assessment criterion to evaluate the e-learning sites improves decision-makers vision of what the e-learning sites can provide.

References

Bernard, R. M., Brauer, A., Abrami, P. C., & Surkes, M. (2004). The development of a questionnaire for predicting online learning achievement. *Distance Education, 25*(1), 31-47.

Chiu, C. M., Hsu, M. H., Sun, S. Y., Lin, T. C., & Sun, P. C. (2005). Usability, quality, value and e-learning continuance decisions. *Computers & Education, 45*(4), 399-416.

Denzin, N. K. (2000). Interpretive ethnography. *Zeitschrift für Erziehungswissenschaft, 3*(3), 401-409.

Gregor, S. (2006). The nature of theory in information systems. *Mis Quarterly, 30*(3), 611-642.

Kay, R. H., Knaack, L., & Vaidehi, V. (2008). A multi-component model for assessing learning objects: The learning object evaluation metric (LOEM). *Australasian Journal of Educational Technology, 24*(5), 574-591.

Klein, H. K., & Myers, M. D. (2001). A classification scheme for interpretive research in information systems. Qualitative Research in IS: Issues and Trends, 218-239.

Krueger, R. A., & Casey, M. A. (2008). Focus groups: A practical guide for applied research: SAGE Publications, Incorporated.

Lee, M. C. (2010). Explaining and predicting users' continuance intention toward e-learning: An extension of the expectation–confirmation model. *Computers & Education, 54*(2), 506-516.

Lin, K. M. (2011). E-Learning continuance intention: Moderating effects of user e-learning experience. *Computers & Education, 56*(2), 515-526.

Nokelainen, P. (2006). An empirical assessment of pedagogical usability criteria for digital learning material with elementary school students. *Educational Technology & Society, 9*(2), 178-197.

Sharlin, M., Tu, E., & Bartus, T. (2009). Guide to Creating Website Information Architecture and Content. Princeton University.

Stewart, I., Hong, E., & Strudler, N. (2004). Development and validation of an instrument for student evaluation of the quality of web-based instruction. *The American Journal of Distance Education, 18*(3), 131-150.

Tarafdar, M., & Zhang, J. (2005). Analysis of critical website characteristics: A cross-category study of successful websites. *Journal of Computer Information Systems, 46*(2), 14-24.

Veeramani, M. (2010). E-learning: A conceptual framework. *International Journal of Educational Research and Technology, 1*(2), 20-24.

3

A Cloud-Based Adaptive Disaster Recovery Optimization Model

Omar H. Alhazmi[1]

[1] Department of Computer Science, Taibah University, Medina, Saudi Arabia

Correspondence: Omar H Alhazmi, Department of Computer Science, Taibah University, Medina, Saudi Arabia. E-mail: ohhazmi@taibahu.edu.sa

Abstract

Disaster recovery and business continuity plans are essential to make sure businesses keep on going. However, many small and medium businesses feel that these plans can cost them a lot. Moreover, the issues of cost and operation overhead prevent them from having solid disaster recovery plans. However, with the spread of cloud computing and pay-as-you-go and pay-for-what-you-use models, issues of operational overhead and expensive investment in extra storage and extra infrastructure are significantly minimized. On the other hand, as it becomes more affordable, businesses want to make sure they get the most optimal solution for minimum cost and overhead. In this work, we propose an adaptive cloud-based disaster recovery model that will be flexible in protecting data and applications with different plans by considering changes in risk levels and at the same time managing the costs and billing issues associated with the cloud. Therefore, this suggests an adaptive model to manage resources on the go while keeping costs as planned with the best possible protection.

Keywords: disaster recovery plan, disaster recovery as a service, business continuity

1. Introduction

1.1 Introduction to Disaster Recovery Optimization

Business Continuity Plans and Disaster Recovery Plans are becoming standard requirements as part of any organization's IT department, sometimes as a government regulation and sometimes as a standard, for example, ISO 22301 (ISO, 2011) for business continuity and ISO 24762 for disaster recovery (ISO & IEC, 2008). Hence, this is the case in big organizations because they realize the benefits; moreover, they have the capacity to dedicate some of their resources to this purpose. However, many medium and small businesses (SMBs) believe that cost is too high. A study by Semantic shows that 57% of small businesses and 47% of medium businesses do not have a disaster recovery plan (Semantic, 2011). Recently, a study by Cisco and Fortune showed that about 49% of small businesses owners do not have disaster recovery plan, fearing extra costs of remote sites and operational overhead (Cisco, 2015). Fortunately, advances in cloud computing and pay-as-you-go plans made startup costs significantly lower; thus, more medium and small organizations are able to afford disaster recovery plans than at any time before. However, SMBs need to plan their budgets to make sure that they spend funds in the best optimized way.

1.2 Importance of Disaster Recovery Optimization

We need to provide SMBs some adaptive model to cover their disaster recovery and business continuity and at the same time direct the resources in the right direction and stick with a pre-assigned limited budget.

In order to design a suitable disaster recovery plan (DRP) for a SMB, a business analyst must make a cost-benefit analysis of the technology used; for example, how much does one hour of downtime cost? How much does the loss of 1MB of data cost? How much can the business tolerate? If the business has more than one application or database, each might need separate analysis. Moreover, the indirect costs of downtime and loss of data should also be considered, such as loss of reputation, loyalty and customer confidence. Hence, the outcome will be setting the right recovery time objective (RTO) and recovery point objective (RPO). These can be set for the whole system or, even better, for each independent part of their system.

1.3 Related Work

When cloud computing became an important option for organizations, the cloud providers offered different forms, such as platform as a service (PaaS), infrastructure as a service (IaaS), or software as a service (SaaS).

However, not until later was disaster recovery as a service introduced and discussed by researchers such as (Wood et al. 2010), where they have shown how the cloud can be an excellent alternative for disaster recovery sites. Others (Alhazmi & Malaiya, 2013) have compared co-location disaster recovery and cloud-based disaster recovery. Now the term disaster recovery as a service (DRaaS) is becoming a common type of cloud service.

The issue of optimizing resources and trying to find the best allocation with some constraints is not a new topic. For example, (Buyya et al. 2001) has proposed an algorithm to allocate heterogeneous resources on the global grid. They have considered a time-budget constrained model. Also, recently, (Wientraub & Cohen, 2015) have proposed a combination of IaaS, PaaS and SaaS to optimize resource allocation. Moreover, (Manikandaprabhul & Senthil, 2013) have discussed some dynamic provisioning plans to reduce cost based on reserving resources by using on-demand vs. pre-reserved resources. They have shown some promising results. However, their models are based on multi-service providers and are for generic cloud resource allocation, while our work is specifically for disaster recovery purposes and our model does not take service providers into account.

(Banu & Saravanan, 2013) have proposed a two-phase algorithm to allocate resources at minimum cost and improved quality of service in the cloud. With similar objectives, (Poobalan & Selvie, 2013) have proposed better management of resources by utilizing an optimal cloud resource provisioning algorithm (OCRP). All have considered the pre-reserved and the on-demand options provided by infrastructure as a service (IaaS) cloud providers. The service providers offer the pre-reserved option, which costs less but needs to be reserved earlier. However, the on-demand option is more expensive but more convenient by not requiring prior reservation.

1.4 The Proposed Model

In this work, we present an adaptive cost optimizing algorithm based on a constraint of cost or budget and some other factors given by the user.   However, the business is responsible for setting their RPO and RTO and also for identifying potential risks and changing levels of risk over time, which is sometimes predictable and can be set according to alerts and external threats, such as weather, or internal threats, such as scheduled maintenance. Here, the optimization model will allocate more resources and increase protection during these periods; this makes the optimization model flexible.

The goal of this model is to have a flexible adaptive optimization disaster recovery model that manages the resources according to some quality of service goals, financial limitations and internal and external threats, yet is applicable and practical and has very little management overhead. Moreover, the proposed model is vendor independent and can be applied to various cloud service providers, not limited to some billing and service plans. Therefore, in its current form it is generic and can be tailored to the specific needs of a SMB with some changes to accommodate the requirements of cloud service providers (CSPs).

In the following section which will give the main parameters, inputs, outputs of the model and the main algorithm. Next, in section 3, the optimization model is simulated using a scenario to illustrate how the model works, how it can be applied, and what will happen in a real operational environment; finally, in section 4 we will present a conclusion and remarks about the advantages and disadvantages of the model, identify strengths and limitations of the model, suggest possible improvements and briefly discuss some future research directions.

2. The Adaptive Cloud Based Disaster Recovery Model

Here, we preview the proposed model; in the next section we will preview the parameters used in the model; in section 2.2 we will preview the outline; and in section 2.3, the algorithm is previewed.

2.1 The Main Factors

Here we are going to overview the factors that impact the proposed system, which are: Criticality levels, Risk levels, Disaster Recovery tiers and Cost. Here we shall explain each factor.

The first factor is *criticality level,* which represents the level of importance of the data or an application. It can be assigned to a certain segment of data or an application. This is usually based on the business need and business analysis. The analysis should set the required Recovery Time Objective (RTO) and Recovery Point Objective (RPO). For simplification, we will assume three levels of criticality (high, medium and low); and segments with higher level of criticality have more priority when they are allocated in the cloud.

The second factor is *risk level.* A study by (Qurium, 2013) shows that although disaster recovery is often associated with natural disasters, nature is only responsible for about 5% (See Table 1), while the other 95% are mainly due to hardware and software failures and human errors. This can be helpful for system administrators to take care of their disaster recovery system during specific periods of time, particularly during software and hardware installations, upgrades and reconfiguration. With increased risks during these times, an optimized disaster recovery system can be elevated to allocate more resources during these times than during other times and thus utilize resources more efficiently.

Table 1. Ranking of Causes of Outages (Qurium, 2013)

Cause Rank	Cause	Percentage
1	Hardware failure	55%
2	Human error	22%
3	Software failure	18%
4	Natural	5%

Here, we will also assume that risk changes over time and we can assume three levels of risk (high, medium and low). The risk level of a disaster happening can be determined, although some natural disasters come without warning, such as earthquakes or fires. However, some of them come with a short notice, like floods and storms, which can be predicted by weather forecasts. Moreover, some disasters actually happen during prescheduled system upgrades and system maintenance. Those are ideal for this system because by raising the risk level during these activities, more resources are allocated to protect the data in a better way. Here, Figure 1 shows a hypothetical change of risk level over time:

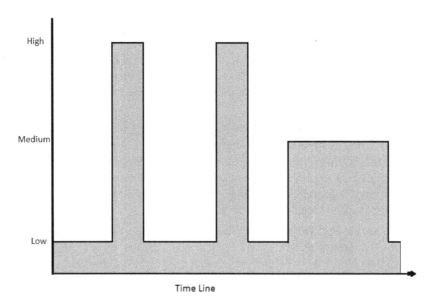

Figure 1. Risk level changes over a period of time

The third factor is the disaster recovery tier. There are several disaster recovery tier schemes previewed in (Alhazmi & Malaiya, 2012). However, in the cloud, we can prefer a scheme designed for the cloud; hence, we will choose Firdhous' (Firdous, 2014) classification of Disaster Recovery as a Service (DRaaS). Firdhous has proposed three levels of DRaas: CDDRaaS, WMDRaaS and HTDRaaS. However, Firdhous does not give full descriptions for these levels; thus, we are defining these levels using (Carroll, 2013).

Table 2. Firdhous classification (Firdhous, 2014)

DRaaS Level	Description	RTO	RPO
No DRaaS	No disaster recovery	-	
Cold site (CDDRaaS)	Only data is backed up; recovery systems need to be installed and configured and data needs to be loaded	Hours to days	Hours to days
Warm site (WMDRaaS)	Systems are preloaded and preinstalled preconfigured; however, data is not fully or partially	Minutes to hours	Minutes to hours

	ready		
Hot site (HTDRaaS)	Disaster recovery system is fully mirrored with the original system and fully synchronized and ready to take over operation	Less than 5 minutes	Less than 5 minutes

The fourth factor is *cost,* a main constraint here, because many small businesses don't want to spend more on extra storage and recovery systems. A study conducted by Forrester has shown that cost prevents many SMBs from owning a disaster recovery; for example, 49% worry about cost of a remote site, while 46% are concerned about cost of extra hardware in the recovery site. Moreover, 42% answered that the cost of implementation of a DR system is the main reason they don't have one (Cisco, 2015). Hence, the cost constraint is very important. Cloud technology and DRaaS could reduce the upfront cost and allow more companies and small businesses to own disaster recovery systems.

2.2 The Cloud-Based Adaptive Disaster Recovery Optimization Model (CBADROM)

The Cloud-Based Adaptive Disaster Recovery Optimization Model (CBADROM) assumes that data can be divided into independent segments so for each S_i (S_1, S_2, S_3, ..., S_n), there is a criticality level associated with it. Based on business analysis and business need, these levels can be in m levels (C_1, C_2, ..., C_m) (see Table 4) and there are also *k* risk levels for the whole system. Moreover, the cost is strongly linked to the disaster recovery tiers and the billing policy of the disaster recovery service provider. In other words, CBADROM takes four inputs: two direct inputs which are cost and current level of risk, and two inputs that need configuration, which are criticality/risk/disaster recovery tier matrix (see Table 3) and segment criticality map (see Table 4). Figure 4, illustrates the model's main outlines and how the components interact.

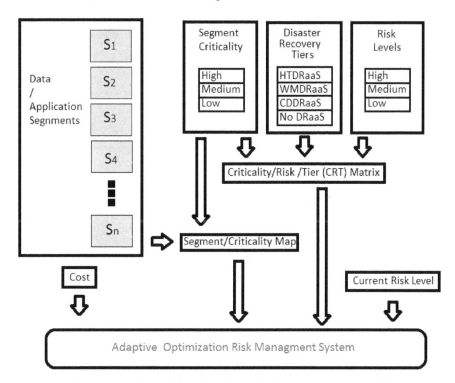

Figure 2. Outline of the Cloud-based Disaster Recovery Model

The CRT matrix (see Table 3) suggests multiple modes of operation and resource scheduling based on risk. We will assume the role of a business owner and build a criticality requirement table. This should be built by the business analyst to reflect the actual business needs of an organization. Table 3, below, shows an example of how a system analyst must build a criticality/risk tier for each criticality level and risk level, the desired recovery time objective (RTO) (how much time does the system need to recover) and a recovery point objective (RPO) (how much data loss can be tolerated). This can be achieved by analyzing loss impact on the business and must take into account direct, indirect, short term and long term impacts. After the CRT is built, segments must be given

24

Information and Computer Science

the appropriate criticality level (Table 4).

Table 3. Criticality/Risk Matrix/Tier matrix

Risk Level	Segment Criticality Level		
	Low	Medium	High
Low	CDDRaaS	CDDRaaS	WMDRaaS
Medium	CDDRaaS	WMDRaaS	HTDRaaS
High	WMDRaaS	HTDRaaS	HTDRaaS

2.3 The Cloud-Based Adaptive Disaster Recovery Optimization Model (CBADROM) Algorithm

The algorithm is given in Figure 3, below. The four inputs are shown in the top box. The main part is also shown on the bottom part. The system will call allocate_all() every period of time; here, the default is one day. It can be extended or shortened as desired.

Input Disaster_recovery_tiers RC [risk_levels] [criticality_levels],
Segment [num_segments], cost, risk; *// the four factors*
Output Allocated[num_segments] [tier]; *// the allocation matrix*

Main( )
Begin
    //each 24 hours the resources will be allocated based on current risk level
While (TRUE)
    Begin
    Risk ← Current_Risk_level; *// current risk level for the day*
    //defined by user or external factors
    Allocate_All (Risk, Cost, RC, Segment); *// allocate the DR system on the cloud*
    wait_for_one_day (); *// wait for some time default:24 hours*
    end while
end

Figure 3. The main algorithm

Figure 4 shows the algorithm for the functions. Cost() will estimate the cost of allocating a segment on a specific tier, based on size. Allocate_all() will go on all segments, starting with the higher criticality level, and allocate them based on this priority and then to the lower criticality level and so on. Of course, all of this is based on criticality-risk-tier matrix and segment-criticality map.

Into Cost(Segment S,Tier T)
Begin
Return Segment.size*T.cost_per_gigabyte;// return the actual cost
end

```
Int Allocate_All ()
Begin
for j← 1 to 3 // for criticality level 3 to 2 to 1
        for i ← 0 to num_segments     //for all segments 0 to i
                Begin
                    if (Segment[i]. Criticality ==j)
                       result = Allocate (Segment[i], RC [Risk, Segment[i]. Criticality]);
                       if (result == 0) return 0; //if can not allocate , fail
                end for
Return (number_of_segments);
// this will allocate segment i to the appropriate disaster recovery tier
End

Allocate (segment S, Tier)
Begin
   If (Budget-Cost (S,Tier) < 0 ) return 0 //   if budget is too low return fail
   Else Budget ← Budget – Cost (S,T); //deduct the cost from budget
           return 1;
End
//allocated and cost deducted from Budget
```

Figure 4. Functions to be called by the main program

3. Applying the Cloud-based Disaster Recovery Optimzation Model

Here we examine a hypothetical scenario, as an assumption we will consider the criticality-risk-tier matrix given by Table 3. We shall see that if the company decides to spend only $100 for disaster recovery, the company has a set of systems and applications; their business analyst determined that their system can be divided into six segments as shown in Table 4. They assigned different a criticality level for each segment, and the size of each segment is also shown in the last column.

Table 4. A hypothetical system for simulation

Segment	Criticality	Size (Gb)
S_1	High	50
S_2	Low	80
S_3	Low	20
S_4	Medium	40
S_5	High	40
S_6	Medium	60
	Total	290

This company has obtained a list of prices from their cloud service provider (CSP), along with its RTO/RPO specifications, all illustrated in Table 5:

Table 5. Sample pricing for cloud-based disaster recovery system

DRaaS Level	Price	RTO	RPO
No DRaaS	0.00$	-	
Cold site (CDDRaaS)	0.03$ per day	Hours to days	Hours to days
Warm site (WMDRaaS)	0.05$ per day	Minutes to hours	Minutes to hours
Hot site (HTDRaaS)	0.09$ per day	Less than 5 minutes	Less than 5 minutes

From Tables 3, 4, and 5, we have produced Table 6, which shows the daily cost of the whole system for different risk levels.

Table 6. Applying the Criticality-Risk on the given example

Segments	Size(Gb)	Low Risk Cost (GB/day)	Segment cost($)	Medium Risk Cost (GB/day)	Segment cost($)	High Risk Cost (GB/day)	Segment cost($)
S_1	50	0.09	4.5	0.09	4.5	0.09	4.5
S_2	80	0.03	2.4	0.03	2.4	0.05	4
S_3	20	0.03	0.6	0.03	0.6	0.05	1
S_4	40	0.03	1.2	0.05	2	0.09	3.6
S_5	40	0.09	3.6	0.09	3.6	0.09	3.6
S_6	60	0.03	1.8	0.05	3	0.09	5.4
Total disaster recovery cost per day		14.1		16.1		22.1	

The company's analyst decides that for some reason risk will be medium on the third day and high on the fifth day and for all other days it is low.

Figures 5 and 6, show how the model allocates the appropriate disaster recovery tier to the segment based on the criticality/risk matrix given in Table 3. Here is the scenario:

- Days 1 and 2 are low risk days; therefore, S1 and S5 are allocated to HTDRaaS while S2, S3, S4 and S6 are allocated to CDDRaaS.

- In day 3, risk is elevated to medium. Based on the criticality/risk matrix in Table 4, only S4 and S6 need to be upgraded to WMDRaaS, while the rest of them stay unchanged.

- In day 4, risk is demoted to low, causing the downgrade of S4 and S6 back to CDDRaaS.

- In day 5, risk is elevated again but this time to high, causing an upgrade to S4 and S6 to HTDDRaaS and S2 and S3 to WMDRaaS.

- In day 6, risk is demoted to low, causing a downgrade of S2, S3, S4 and S6 to CDDRaaS.

- In day 7, the funds are about to finish (the balance is only about $5.40), causing a downgrade to most of the segments. Only S1 is allocated at the cost of $4.50; here, the remaining balance is too low, so the model had to skip S5, S4, S6 and then S2, to allocate only S3, as it is the first segment that is allocatable with the available funds.

Given this scenario in Figures 5 and 6, it is clear that the company needs to allocate more funds to disaster recovery to avoid the drop in the disaster recovery service that occurred on the seventh day. This occurred due to the lack of planning of the system but can be remedied by increasing the planning from one day to a longer period of time, thus avoiding the drop of DR for all segments.

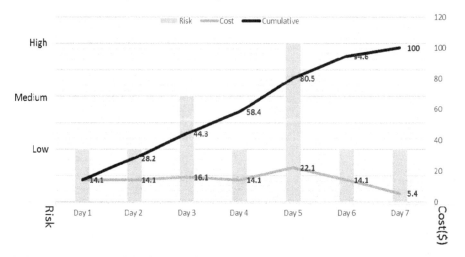

Figure 5. The bars represent the risk, the gray shows the daily cost, and the black shows the cumulative cost

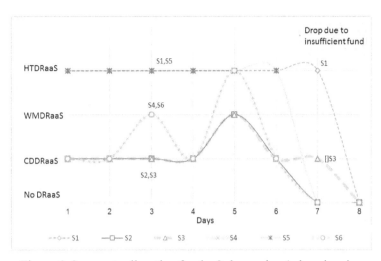

Figure 6. Segments allocation for the 8-days using 1-day planning

For the previous example, we have used day-by-day planning, and we have seen that at the seventh day most segments could not be allocated and on the eight day all of them – even critical segments – are left without coverage. Therefore, we shall try a four-day allocation system. We expect that this way, the results will change and the most critical segments will be favored over others. Let us repeat the scenario but with four-day planning (see Figure 7):

- The first four days will cost a total of $58.40 to allocate all segments. Thus, the remaining balance is $41.60.

- The estimated cost of the next four days is 22.10+14.10+14.10+14.01= $64.40, which is too high; therefore, the most critical parts will be allocated first.

- The first critical job S1 will be allocated for four days, costing 4.5*4=$18. The remaining balance is 41.60-18=$23.60.

- The next highly critical job S5 will be allocated, costing $14.40 for the four days; here the remaining balance will be 23.60-14.40=$9.40.

- Then, the system will look at the next job S4 which costs 1.20*3+2=$5.60 and will be allocated for four days. The remaining balance will drop to 9.40-5.60=$3.80.

- Then, the system will go to S6, only to discover that the needed amount is $8.40 while the balance is enough for two days at a low tier: 3.80-3.60=$0.20.

- Here, we notice that S2 and S3 are not allocated anymore for the second through   fourth days because they have low criticality status, as illustrated by Figure 7.

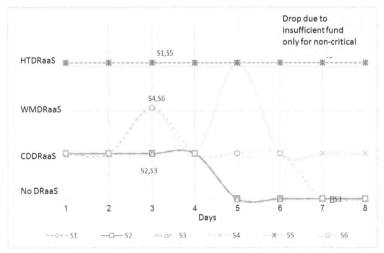

Figure 7. Segment Allocation using 4-day planning

4. Conclusions

Cloud computing has given the area of disaster recovery boost, as it has significantly reduced the upfront costs and thus increased interest in disaster recovery systems. Moreover, it has given disaster recovery systems more flexibility and made them dynamic and scalable. However, for small and medium businesses the issue of cost is still a concern, especially in times of slow economies. Here, we have presented a model to optimize resources based on available budget constraints. The model needs a business strategy as an input, which is the criticality-risk-tier matrix and segment-criticality map, cost and current risk, in order to manage resources in real time and give more priority to critical resources and change allocation based on changing risk levels.

We have demonstrated how the model can be applied on some hypothetical use case examples, and we have shown that the system prioritizes segment allocation based on criticality and that the system successfully re-allocates segments based on changes in risk levels. The success of the model is based on the correct business analysis and representing the analysis on the criticality-risk-tier matrix correctly, because this matrix is the main reference for the model and shows business priorities.

We have tested the model with two modes, a one-day planning mode and a four-day planning mode. We have found that longer term planning causes the model to enforce priorities more strictly and shorter term planning is quite the opposite.

Further work needs to be done; for example, the model can be implemented and tested in a simulation or experimental environments. Furthermore, longer term planning is a good area for experiments. Moreover, the model should be tested in a real environment and feedback should be collected and analyzed.

References

Alhazmi, O. H., & Malaiya, Y. K. (2013). *Evaluating Disaster Recovery Plans Using the Cloud*, Proc. Reliability and Maintainability Symposium (RAMS 2013), 37-42.

Alhazmi, O. H., & Malaiya, Y. K. (2012). *Assessing Disaster Recovery Alternatives: On-site, Colocation or Cloud*, Proc. 23rd IEEE Int. Symposium on Software Reliability Engineering Workshop, pp. 19-20.

Banu, U., & Saravanan, K. (2013). Optimizing the Cost for Resource Subscription Policy in IaaS Cloud. *International Journal of Engineering Trends and Technology, 6*(5). 296-301.

Buyya, R., Murshed, M., & Abramson, D. (2001). *A Deadline and Budget Constrained Cost Time Optimisation Algorithm for Scheduling Task Farming Applications on Global Grids*, in Int. Conf. on Parallel and Distributed Processing Techniques and Applications, pp.

Carroll, B. (2013). The Three Stages of Disaster Recovery Sites. Retrieved from http://www.seguetech.com/blog/2013/11/20/three-stages-disaster-recovery-sites

Cisco (2015). Are SMBs Taking Disaster Recovery Seriously Enough, white paper. Retrieved from http://www.cisco.com/c/dam/en_us/solutions/trends/open_network_environment/docs/draas-whitepaper.pdf

Firdhous, M. (2014). *A Comprehensive Taxonomy for the Infrastructure as a Service in Cloud Computing*, Fourth International Conference on Advances in Computing and Communications (ICACC), pp.158-161, 27-29 Aug. 2014.

ISO & IEC 24762 (2008). Guidelines for Information and Communications Technology Disaster Recovery Services. Retrieved from http://www.iso.org/iso/catalogue_detail?csnumber=41532

ISO 22301 (2012). International Standard Organization: Business Continuity. Retrieved from http://www.iso.org/iso/news.htm?Refid=Ref1602

Manikandaprabhu1, M., & Senthil, R. S. (2013). *Resource Provisioning Cost of Cloud Computing by Adaptive Reservation Techniques*, International Journal of Computer Trends and Technology, Volume 4, Number 5. Pp. 1118-1124.

Poobalan, A., & Slevi, V. (2013). Optimization of Cost in Cloud Computing Using OCRP Algorithm. *International Journal of Engineering Trends and Technology, 4*(5), 2105-2107.

Qurium (2013). Disaster Recovery Report, Q1-2013, White paper. Retrieved from http://oneclick.quorum.net/rs/position2quorum/images/Disaster-recovery-report-Q1-2013-1031.pdf

Symantic (2011). SMB Disaster Recovery Preparedness: Global Results. Retrieved from http://www.symantic.com/about/news/resources.jsp

Wientraub, E., & Cohen, Y. (2015). Cost Optimization of Cloud Computing Services in a Networked

Environment. *International Journal of Advanced Computer Science and Applications, 6*(4), 148-157.

Wood, T., Cecchet, E., Ramakrishnan, K. K., Shenoy, P., Van Der Merwe, J., & Venkataramani, A. (2010). *Disaster Recovery as a Cloud Service: Economic Benefits & Deployment Challenges*, 2nd USENIX Workshop on Hot Topics in Cloud Computing, p8.

4

Human Identification Based on Geometric Feature Extraction Using a Number of Biometric Systems Available

Eman Fares Al Mashagba[1]

[1] Zarqa University, Jordan

Correspondence: Eman Fares Al Mashagba, Computer Sciences Department, Zarqa University, Zarqa, Jordan. E-mail: efaris@zu.edu.jo

Abstract

Biometric technology has attracted much attention in biometric recognition. Significant online and offline applications satisfy security and human identification based on this technology. Biometric technology identifies a human based on unique features possessed by a person. Biometric features may be physiological or behavioral. A physiological feature is based on the direct measurement of a part of the human body such as a fingerprint, face, iris, blood vessel pattern at the back of the eye, vascular patterns, DNA, and hand or palm scan recognition. A behavioral feature is based on data derived from an action performed by the user. Thus, this feature measures the characteristics of the human body such as signature/handwriting, gait, voice, gesture, and keystroke dynamics. A biometric system is performed as follows: acquisition, comparison, feature extraction, and matching. The most important step is feature extraction, which determines the performance of human identification. Different methods are used for extraction, namely, appearance- and geometry-based methods. This paper reports on a review of human identification based on geometric feature extraction using several biometric systems available. We compared the different biometrics in biometric technology based on the geometric features extracted in different studies. Several biometric approaches have more geometric features, such as hand, gait, face, fingerprint, and signature features, compared with other biometric technology. Thus, geometry-based method with different biometrics can be applied simply and efficiently. The eye region extracted from the face is mainly used in face recognition. In addition, the extracted eye region has more details as the iris features.

Keywords: biometric, human identification, geometry-based

1. Introduction

The term biometric is derived from the Greek words bio, which means "life," and metric, which means "the measure of." Biometrics is the automated use of unique and measurable characteristics to establish or verify an identity based on some special biometric features derived from physiological and behavioral characteristics (Tiwari, Chourasia, & Chourasia, 2015; Jayaram & Fleyeh, 2013; Mäkinen & Raisamo, 2008; Vaidya, 2015).

However, verification and identification are interchangeably used in the literature for biometric recognition (Mir, Rubab, & Jhat, 2011). Identification and verification have distinct meanings. Verification refers to 1:1 matching, which indicates that a person is claiming his/her identity from the system and then having been verified himself/herself. Identification refers to 1:m matching, which refers to a situation where the user does not know who he/she is or is not to claim his identity, but presents his/her biometric to match with the entire database (K. P. 2011; Himanshu, S. 2013). A biometric system includes all the hardware, associated software, firmware, and network components required for the biometric matching process.

(Erno et al., 2008) found that biometrics can enhance the high assurance to a system, particularly when tied with one or two other forms of verification. These "multimodal" forms of authentication (e.g., passwords together with speech, speech together with gesture, or passwords together with speech and eye features) allow the potential for significant state of security and privacy enhancement.

A biometric authentication system is a satisfactory solution to authentication problems. However, biometric authentication has disadvantages (K. P., 2011; Mali & Bhattacharya, 2013). This process requires user skills. Users should know how to position their fingers, faces, and eyes to be read. Biometrics cannot reduce the cost of current and established authentication methods. Businesses will not implement such security systems because of their technical complexity and high cost. Biometrics requires much data of an individual to be stored. These systems are not always reliable because a person changes over time, such as when the eyes turn puffy or when the voice of a person changes when the person is ill. The voice of a person changes with flu or throat infection or in the presence of too much noise in the environment. This method may not authenticate properly a person's fingers that had become rough because of work. Thus, a machine may have difficulty in identifying a person precisely. Several methods for retinal scan are invasive, i.e., a laser light (or other coherent light source) is directed through the cornea of the eye and uses an infrared light source to highlight the biometric pattern. This process can damage an individual's eye (K. P. 2011; Mali & Bhattacharya, 2013).

Biometric recognition system is performed as follows:

1. Acquisition. Acquisition devices capture a sample. For example, a digital device is used to collect data. A finger is placed on a plate for finger reader device. The face, gait, ear, or hand may be recorded by a video or camera device and an audio device for speech.

2. Comparison. The template then compares the acquired data from a sample.

3. Feature Extraction. Features are extracted from the sample using different techniques.

4. Matching. The acquired feature set is compared against the template set in the database. The results will show whether the identity of a user is authenticated.

The requirements for certified features are described as follows (Vaidya, 2015; K. P. 2011; Wu, Zhuang, Student, Long, Lin & Xu, 2015; Tiwalade., Francis &. Idachab, 2011; Duquenoy, Carlisle & Kimppa, 2008):

1) Universality. The features should be universal among each individual, which can be used to identify a person. A feature is not appropriate for classification if the feature cannot be extracted from each individual.

2) Individuality. The feature should be effectively discriminated among individuals.

3) Stability. The feature should be stable and remain unchanged over a long period, i.e., regardless of age and environment

4) Collectability. The feature should be measured quantitatively, which has a remarkable effect on the applications. An approach based on a feature with high collectability, such as vision-based application, is suitable for real-time or online applications. The approach based on a feature with lower collectability can only be used in complex or offline applications.

This paper represents a review of human identification based on geometric feature extraction using several biometric systems available, after-study papers, articles, conference paper, and from our experiments in previous works in this field. The rest of this review paper is organized as follows. The biometric technology is discussed in section 2. Tables based on various aspects, such as geometric features, are compared, and the results are concluded in section 3.

2. Biometric Technology

Biometric qualities in information technology can be split into two main categories, namely, physiological or behavioral biometrics (Shradha et al., 2015; Jayaram & Fleyeh, 2013; Mir, S. Rubab & Jhat, 2011; Kaur, Singh, Kumar, 2014; Singh & Singla, 2013; Alsaadi 2015; Mali & Bhattacharya, 2013; Moustakas, Tzovaras & Stavropoulos, 2010; K. P. 2011).

2.1 Physiological Biometrics

Biometrics is relatively a stable human physical characteristic based on the direct measurements of a part of the human body. Fingerprint, face, iris eye, *Ear*, and hand or palm scan recognition belong to this group. This measurement is unchanging and unalterable without significant duress. Different techniques are used to extract these features, such as appearance- or geometry-based techniques. Our current investigation is focused on geometric feature extraction using several biometric systems available.

2.1.1 Fingerprint Geometry

The fingerprint is the pattern of ridges and valleys at the tip of a finger and used to personally verify a person (Mir et al, 2011). Local and global geometric features are extracted. Fingerprint global features are identified by the local orientation of fingerprint ridges, i.e., the orientation field curves. These features occur in the form of a core and/or a delta and are normally at the central region of the fingerprint. These features are referred to as singularities. A core is the area around the center of the fingerprint loop, and a delta is the area where the fingerprint ridges triangulate. The fingerprint local features are attributes that provide the minute details about the fingerprint pattern. These features are known as the minutiae, which include ridge endings, ridge bifurcations, and, although uncommon, the islands. These minutiae constitute the uniqueness of every human fingerprint pattern. The local features have an important role to play in a fingerprint-matching problem because of their detailed nature given that the key to the matching problem is each fingerprint (Ishmael et al. 2009; S. Msiza, Leke-Betechuoh, V. Nelwamondo & Msimang, 2009).

The enhanced data from the proposed methods (Khazaei & Mohades, 2007; Poulos, Magkos, Chrissikopoulos & Alexandris, 2003) are submitted to specific segmentation (datasets) using computational geometric algorithms implemented via Matlab. Thus, onion layers (convex polygons) are created from these datasets. The smallest layer of the constructed onion layers is isolated from the fingerprint in vector form, which will be referred to as the referenced polygon. This characteristic is supposed to be stored in a reference database for subsequent verification. The proposed feature extraction can be used for accurate and secure fingerprint verification because the proposed feature extraction is based on a specific area in which the fingerprint exhibits a range of dominant brightness value. The proposed method promisingly allows very small false acceptance and false rejection rates because it is based on specific segmentation. Biometric applications will gain universal acceptance in digital technologies only when the number of false rejections/acceptances approach zero.

The crop region is defined as the region of interest (w × w) around a base point of an input fingerprint image. The width of the region of interest of an image depends on the resolution of the input image. In this system, the region of interest is considered using the number of similar pixels around the base point. Maximum curvature of the concave ridges is defined as the base line and base point. The coordinate of this point is represented as (xo, yo). The base line is the horizontal line across the base point. In addition, the base point is used to align input and enrolment fingerprints. Rotation metrics is used to align the input and template images. Fingerprint alignment is performed to make both images have the same orientation. α is the difference in the orientation between the template and input images. The crossing number (CN) is used to extract minutiae points. Rutovitz's definition of CN for pixel p is as follows (Valarmathy & Kumar, 2012):

$$C(p) = \left(\frac{1}{2}\right)\sum_{i=1}^{8}|p_i - p_{i+1}|$$

(2)

where P (i) is the neighborhood of P, which has a binary value of 0 or 1.

2.1.2 Face Geometry

The face is the commonly used biometric characteristic to recognize a person (Bakshe & Patil, 2014). The geometry-feature-based approach analyzes local features, such as nose and eyes, and their geometric relationships (Bakshi & Singhal, 2014). Image processing techniques extract feature points, such as eyes, nose, and mouth, and then these points are used as input data for application. Geometry-based technique features are extracted using the sizes and relative positions of important components of images. In this technique, the direction and edges of important component is first detected under the first method, and then feature vectors are built from these edges and direction (Bakshi et al., 2014). Detecting edges, directions of important components, or regional images contain important components to build feature vectors from these edges and directions.

Filters, such as Canny filter, were used to detect the eye or/and mouth image region; whereas transforms methods, such as Hough transform, were used to detect the eyes and to perform gradient analysis. (Kim, Lim & Mi-Hye Kim, 2015) presented a method to detect image regions that contain eyes and mouth in face color images. To detect image regions containing the left eye, the right eye, and the mouth, they first used a filter technique and threshold to change the images to binary images followed by a connected region algorithm to detect image regions containing the eyes and the mouth. Then, calculated the feature vector, which is called a "component feature vector". The bounding box location of feature segments obtained in the previous step is used to calculate the heights and widths of the left eyebrow, left eye, right eyebrow, right eye, nose, and mouth. The distances between center of the left eye and the eyebrow, the right eye and the eyebrow, and the mouth and the nose were calculated. Thus, the following 15 parameters were obtained and considered as feature vectors: height of the left eyebrow; width of the left eyebrow; height of the left eye; width of the left eye; height of the right eyebrow; width of the right eyebrow; height of the right eye; width of the right eye; height of the nose; width of the nose; height of the mouth; width of the mouth; distance between the center of the left eyebrow and the left eye; distance between the center of the right eyebrow and the right eye; and distance between the center of nose and mouth (Kim et al., 2015).

In previous research (Mashagba, E. F., 2016), geometric-based features were extracted by using ellipse mathematical definition and properties. Global features were calculated for a video sequence frame from the ellipse for the face region, horizontal center (Xo), and vertical center (Y0) of the detected face, where a and b are the semi-major and semi-minor axes (half of the major and minor axes of the ellipse), respectively. The area is enclosed by an elliptical area. The two foci (the term "focal points" are also used) of an ellipse are two special points, F1 and F2, on the ellipse's major axis and are equidistant from the center point. The sum of distances from any point P on the ellipse to the two foci is constant and equal to the major axis (PF1 + PF2 = 2a), denoted as eccentricity. The eccentricity of an ellipse, which is denoted by ε or e, is the ratio of the distance between the two foci to the length of the major axis, that is, e = 2f/2a = f. The ratio of the dimension and four-quadrant inverse tangent (arctangent) of the real parts of the semi-major axis (a) and semi-minor axis (b) are calculated. The distance from the center C to either focus is f = ae, which can be expressed in terms of the major and minor radii (Mashagba, E. F., 2016).

2.1.3 Hand or Palm Geometry

Hand geometry refers to the geometric structure of the hand, which consists of the lengths and widths of fingers, and width of a palm, among others. Palm print is the region between the wrist and fingers. Palm print features, such as ridges, singular points, minutia points, principal lines, wrinkles, and texture, can be used for personal verification (Mir et al., 2011).

(Mathivanan, Palanisamy & Selvarajan, 2012) located the local minima and the local maxima points, which correspond to fingertips and finger valleys. In addition, they identified the orientation of each finger, as well as four points on the finger contour (two points each on both sides of the fingertip), at fixed distances from the fingertip. Two middle points are computed for corresponding points on either side and are joined to obtain the finger orientation. Points at the center and bottom parts of the finger are not considered for the estimate of orientation, as certain fingers are found to be non-symmetric at these parts. Once finger orientation and fingertip valley points are determined, extracting a rectangular ROI from the fingers is a straightforward test. Similarly, based on the two finger valley points (between little-ring and middle-index fingers), a fixed ROI can be extracted. Hand-geometry features are extracted from the version of the gained intensity images of the hand. Features considered in their work include finger lengths, finger widths at equally spaced distances along the finger area, and finger perimeters.

The feature extraction module extracts the features of hand geometry; the handprint features are calculated by using the reference point as follows (Poonam & Sipi, 2013):

a) Tip point of all fingers, including the thumb

b) Starting reference point and ending reference point.

c) Centroid of the hand

d) Major axis length

e) Minor axis length

f) Perimeter

The hand contour was obtained from the black-and-white image. The Cartesian coordinates of the hand contour were converted to polar coordinates (radius and angle), with the center of the hand base being considered as the coordinate origin. The peaks of the radius were located at the finger ends, and the minima of the radius show the valleys between fingers. To obtain the exterior base of the index and little fingers, the slope of the line going from the valley of the index heart fingers to that of the ring–little finger valley was determined. The exterior of the thumb is identified as the intersection of the contour and the line going from the heart–ring finger valley to the index–thumb finger valley. Once the most important points of the hand were located, the geometric features were determined by means of measures. The geometrical features of the index, middle, and ring fingers were used. The little and thumb fingers were not used because of the non-uniform illumination of the region in their system. The geometric feature vector was immediately obtained once the ends and valleys between fingers have been detected. Each finger was characterized as a triangle. The three vertices of the triangle are the end and the two side valleys of the finger. Approximately 40 wide measures to the index, middle, and ring fingers were obtained. The first 20% of the finger was discarded to solve the problem of rings. Three different measure vectors were independently obtained for each finger. The three vectors characterize each user and were combined at the score level (Aythami, Miguel, Francisco, Jesús & Carlos, 2008).

In this module, various hand geometric features finger length, finger width, palm length, palm width, and hand length. To find these features, fingertips, valley points, and landmark points were identified, and the features were then extracted (Mandeep & Amardeep, 2015).

An algorithm for feature extraction was created in MATLAB programming environment and based on counting pixel distances in specific areas of the hand. Given that the system uses special surface with pegs to fix the appropriate position of the hand, the pixel distance of the given measurement can be obtained. The algorithm looks for white pixels between two given points and computes a distance by using geometrical principles. The result is a vector of 21 elements (Peter & Dušan,2007):

Widths: each of the fingers is measured in three different heights. The thumb finger is measured in two heights.

Heights: the height of all fingers and thumb is obtained.

Palm: two measurements of palm size.

By scanning the pixels at the bottom of the image from left to right, the left-most pixel of the hand image, S1, and the right-most pixel, E1, are located. The reference point is the middle point between S1 and E1. The next step involves finding all fingertips and valley points of the hand. The distances between the reference point and each contour point of the hand, from S1 to E1, are measured by Euclidean distance (Nidhi, Vipul, Neelesh & Pragya, 2013), where (x,y) is a point in the contour and (xr, yr) is the reference point. Comparing the distances with those of other neighbor points on the hand contour in some distances, the fingertips are the points with the most distances and the least valley points. The result positions of fingertips and valley points are marked as circles. The extracted features used in the research are the lengths of each finger, the widths of each finger at three locations, and the width of the palm. A total of 21 features were utilized. These features can be found as follows. Finger baselines: the finger baselines of a middle finger and a ring finger are obtained by connecting the valley points, which are on both sides of that finger. The baselines are the lines linked between two valley points. Finger lengths: Finger lengths are obtained by measuring the distances from the fingertips to the middle points of the finger baselines. Finger widths: Finger widths are the widths of a finger measured at three locations. The first is measured at the middle of the finger length; the second at the one-third, and the last at the two-thirds of the finger length. Palm width: Palm width is the distance from b1 to b2 in the database [Nidhi et al., 2013].

2.1.4 Iris and Retina Geometry

The iris image I(x,y) is remapped from raw Cartesian coordinate to polar coordinates I (r,θ), where r radius lies in the unit interval (0,1). The normalization step exactly reduces the distortion of the iris caused by pupil movement and simplifies subsequent processing ((Bhawna & Shailja, 2010; Roselin, chirch & Waghmare,. 2013).

The geometric characteristics are classified as follows (Poonguzhali & Ezhilarasan, 2015): pupil-based features, collarette-based features, and iris-based features.

Pupil-based feature: The pupil is defined to be circular or round but is not an actual circle. Therefore, the geometrical properties of the circle can identify the pupil, and the features can be used for recognition. The following are pupil-based features (Poonguzhali & Ezhilarasan, 2015):

• pupil roundness (PR)

• pupil largeness (PL)

• pupil smoothness (PS)

PR: Roundness measurement requires tracing the iris at 360 °C; hence, the consistency of the diameter can be measured at a number of orientation points on the iris. In general, roundness is defined as a measure of sharpness at the corners and the edges of a circle. This measure is related with sphericity and compactness of the circle. In simple terms, the radii around the iris are measured at regular intervals. The roundness feature is calculated based on the diameter at various orientations, where the ratio between the maximum value and the minimum value is calculated at horizontal (h), vertical (v), left (l), and right (r) at 0°, 45°, 90°, and 135°, respectively (Poonguzhali & Ezhilarasan, 2015).

PL: The largeness of the pupil is described based on the radius of the pupil. As the pupil is not an actual circle the general diameter calculation of distance from the center to any point on the pupil is insufficient. The diameter is calculated at eight directions on the pupil at 0° (horizontally), 90° (vertically), 30°, 45°, 75°, 120°, 135°, and 165°. Hence, PL is defined according to (Poonguzhali et al., 2015).

PS: The smoothness of the iris can be represented according to the curvature of the circle. The curvature (K) of the circle is defined as the reciprocal of the radius (Poonguzhali & Ezhilarasan, 2015):

Collarette-based feature: The collarette area is insensitive to pupil dilation and not affected by the eyelid or the eyelash. The collarette is concentric with the pupil, and the radius of the area is restricted within a certain range. The collarette can be defined as a snaky scalloped line that splits the iris ancillary zone and ciliary zone. The collarette is restricted to the inner half of the iris and contains ether radial spokes or dots. Given that collarette-based features cannot be detected directly from the iris, the collarette should be detected first, and the geometric measures should then be computed. The proposed method uses the adjusted angle zigzag sampler to detect the collarette. In the given image, the collarette along the line is detected. Here, the height of the collarette is denoted as hs (x), where s is the sampler at the location x along the axis (Poonguzhali & Ezhilarasan, 2015).

Collarette roundness (CR): As the collarette feature is extracted from the iris, the next step is determining the geometric feature of the collarette. The roundness feature of the collarette is computed as the ratio between the maximum and minimum values of the six diameters of the collarette (Poonguzhali & Ezhilarasan, 2015).

Collarette iris ratio (CIR): The CIR is computed based on the diameter of the iris. The diameter of iris is nearly 10–11 mm. The collarette occupies one-third of the iris and is approximately 1.5 mm away from the pupil. Hence, the distance of the collarette and the iris diameter (ID) is calculated at eight points, where the iris is divided into equal space ordinates regarding the polar coordinates. The distance is computed for each intersection point on the edge of the iris, and the CIR is computed (Poonguzhali & Ezhilarasan, 2015).

Iris-based feature: In the proposed work, the geometric feature of iris is used for recognition rather than the texture features of iris. The following are the iris geometric features used for recognition (Poonguzhali & Ezhilarasan, 2015):

- Iris Roundness

- ID

2.1.5 Eye Geometry

Tracing the boundaries of the eyes is important, as finding the outline of the eyes makes computational localization of the position of the irises easier. Several calculations were performed on images to detect the actual position of the iris. The fine eye region is detected at the second stage after the face region is marked in face detection; and then eye features, namely, two eye corners and an iris circle, are extracted from this region at the final stage (Namrata & M.S. Burange 2016). According to my previous experiment in this field, the eye is extracted as a face part and is mainly used in face recognition. In addition, more details are extracted as iris features for identification purposes.

2.1.6 Ear Geometry

The shape of the ear and the structure of the cartilaginous tissue of the pinna are distinctive (Asmaa, Kareem & Elmahdyc, 2015). The ear offers an ideal solution in human identification. As ears can be seen, their images are easy to capture, and the ear structure does not change. The boundary of binary images is obtained. The ear is next to the face and able to provide valuable additional information to supplement facial images (Mudit, Ajinkya & Sagar, 2015). The largest object is detected, and the minimum Euclidean distance between every pixel and all pixels was obtained. Finally, the matrix is sorted, four distances are obtained, and the centroid of the largest object and the mean of ear image are considered as feature values to ensure uniqueness between ear images. Seven extracted values for the feature vector include the following (Mudit et al., 2015):

Distance 1 (D (1)).

Distance 2 (D (Size (D) / 2).

Distance 3 (D (Size (D) / 3).

Distance 4 (D (Size (D) / 4).

X coordinate of the centroid

Y coordinate of the centroid

Mean is calculated

where X is the mean of the image and N is the number of pixels (Asmaa et al., 2015).

Feature extraction conducted in the following two stages:

1. Shape and edge detection.

2. Euclidian distances and angles of triangle detection.

The proposed approach can detect ears of different shapes. Ear shapes include are round, oval, triangular, and rectangular. If the obtained shape matches, then other feature vectors, such as Euclidian distances and angle of a triangle, are compared, and the maximum feature vector of a person is matched for human identification

(Luaibilafta, R., 2013).

2.2 Behavioral Biometrics

Behavioral biometrics reflects an individual's psychological makeup, although physical traits, such as size and gender, exert a major influence. This approach is based on data derived from an action performed by the user and thus ultimately measures the characteristics of the human body. This approach includes signature/handwriting, gait, voice, gesture, and keystroke dynamics that measure the time spacing of typed words (Mir et al., 2011).

2.2.1 Signature/Handwriting Geometry

The first established biometric verification technique in society is the handwritten signature (Mir et al., 2011). The total distance that the pen travelled on the hand-written signature is extracted, and the Euclidean distance of all the points are as follows: xi is the coordinate in the x direction, and yi is the coordinate in the y direction; speed vx and vy express the functions of time; xm is the coordinate in the x direction, and ym is the coordinate in the y direction; tm is the time of movement; vx is the speed at point tm in direction x, and vy is the speed at point tm in direction y. Acceleration values ax and ay can be calculated at different speeds and represent the acceleration at point tm in the x and y directions. Tk is the total time of the hand-written signature. The total time, stroke length, and the time for lifting the pen can vary for different signatures of the same user. These features oscillate about the average and variance, thus possibly symbolizing the biometric features of a person. Two time-related features are the total signature time T and the time down ratio Tdr, which is the ratio of pen-down time to the total time. By considering ad hoc parameters, such as speed, acceleration, and pen-downs, a simple system can be improved. The improvement referred to by the biometric handwritten system involves minimizing the rate of false acceptance and false rejection (Syed et al2015).

Geometric global and local features are extracted separately as follows (Dakshina, Phalguni & Jamuna, 2010):

Width: For a binary signature image, width is the distance between two points in the horizontal projection. The width must contain more than 3 pixels of the image.

Height: Height is the distance between two points in the vertical projection and must contain more than 3 pixels of the image for a binary image.

Aspect ratio: Aspect ratio is defined as width-to-height ratio of a signature.

Horizontal projection: Horizontal projection is computed from both binary and skeletonized images. The number of black pixels is counted from the horizontal projections of binary and skeletonized signatures.

Vertical projection: A vertical projection is defined as the number of black pixels obtained from vertical projections of binary and skeletonized signatures.

Area of black pixels: The area of black pixels is obtained by counting the number of black pixels in the binary, thinned, and HPR signature images separately.

Normalized pixels are found by dividing the area of black pixels by the area of signature image (width × height) of the signature. The normalized area of black pixels is calculated from binary, thinned, and HPR images.

Center of gravity: A signature image is obtained by adding all x, y locations of gray pixels and dividing them by the number of pixels counted. The resulting two numbers (one for x and other for y) is the location of the center of gravity.

Maximum and minimum black pixels: The maximum and minimum black pixels are counted in the horizontal projection over smoothened horizontal projection. These values are the highest and the lowest frequencies of black pixels in the horizontal projection, respectively.

Global baseline: The vertical projection of the binary signature image shows one peak point, and the global baseline corresponds to this point; otherwise, the global baseline is considered as the median of the two outermost maximum points. Global baseline is defined as the median of the pixel distribution. The upper and lower edge difference between smoothened and original curves of the vertical projection above the baseline and under the baseline is known as the upper and lower edge limits, respectively.

Middle zone: The middle zone is the distance between upper and lower edge limits. Each signature image is divided into 25 equal grid regions.

The local features for each grid region are considered as global features. Both feature sets are combined into a feature vector and then used as input to classifiers (Dakshina et al., 2010).

The feature vector is extracted as follows (Pallavi & Salokhe, 2015):

Maximum horizontal and vertical histograms: The horizontal histogram is calculated by going through each row of the signature image and counting the number of black pixels. The row with the maximum number of black pixels is recorded as the maximum horizontal histogram.

Centers of mass: The signature image is split in two equal parts, and the center of mass is determined for individual parts.

The normalized area of signature is the ratio of area of signature image to the area of signature enclosed in a bounding box. The area of a signature is the number of comprising pixels.

The aspect ratio is the ratio of width of signature image to the height of the image. The value is considered because the width or height of person's signature may vary, but its ratio remains approximately equal.

Tri-surface feature: Two different signatures may have the same area. Therefore, to increase the accuracy of the features, three surface features are used. Here, a signature is divided into three equal parts, and the area for each part is calculated.

The sixfold surface feature divides a signature in three equal parts, and the bounding box was found for each part. Then, the center of the mass for each part was calculated. A horizontal line was drawn passing through the center of mass of each part, and the area of signature above and below the center of mass within a bounding box is calculated, yielding six features (Pallavi et al., 2015). The new proposed features include Walsh coefficient of pixel distribution, code word histogram based on clustering technique (Vector Quantization), spatial moments of code word, grid and texture features, and successive geometric centers of depth 2 (Pallavi et al., 2015).

2.2.2 Gait Geometry

The gait is a particular manner of moving in lower body joints. New biometrics aims to recognize people via the style of human walking, which contain physiological or behavioral individuality of humans (Sajid, Zhongke, Abdul & Hafeez, 2013; Mashagba, E. F., 2015).

A triangle is formed from extracted joints (hip knee and ankle) data from the motion file (BVH file), and the triangle area of each frame is computed. First, the joint parameter values of each frame of the hip joint during walking are computed.

The main motive of triangle formulation is to compute the area of a triangle and ultimately compute the average area from the computed areas of each frame triangle of a subject via the statistical method that was described (Sajid et al., 2013).

The features of interest points are used in extracting motion parameters from the sequence of gait figures to show human gait patterns. The feature is represented as joint angles and vertex points, which are used together for gait classification. For gait feature extraction, the width and height of the human silhouette are measured. The dimension of the human silhouette, joint angle, angle velocity, and gait velocities from body segments are calculated as gait features. The horizontal coordinates of each body points are calculated (Nyo Nyo Htwe & Nu War, 2013).

Gait parameters, such as cadence, are the number of steps taken in a time. Two steps are involved in a single gait cycle, and the cadence is a measure of half-cycles. The cycle time is also known as the "stride time," in seconds: cycle time (s) = 120/cadence (steps/min). Walking speed is the distance covered in a given time. The instantaneous speed varies from one instant to another during the walking cycle, whereas the average speed is the product of the cadence and the stride length. The cadence, in steps per minute, corresponds to half-strides per 60 s or full strides per 120 s. The speed can be calculated by using the following formula: speed (m/s) = stride length (m) × cadence steps/min/120. If cycle time is used in place of cadence, the calculation becomes considerably more straightforward: speed (m/s) = stride length (m)/cycle time (s). Walking speed thus depends on two-step lengths, which depend to a large extent on the duration of the swing phase on each side. When pathology affects one foot more than the other, an individual will usually try to spend a shorter time on the "bad foot" and correspondingly longer time on the "good foot." Shortening the stance phase on the "bad" foot means bringing the good foot to the ground sooner, shortening both the duration of the swing phase and the step length on that side. Thus, a short step length on one side means problems with a single support on the other side (Ashutosh, Vipin, Y. K Jain & Surender, 2011).

The trajectories of gait figure contain the general gait, such as stride length, cycle time, and speed, and provide a basic description of the gait motion. The number of frames determines the period of the gait motion during one gait cycle in image sequence, and the frame rate of the SOTON database was 25 frames/s, where the stride length can be directly estimated from the physical dimensions of the image plane. The coordinates of the forward displacements of gait figures during one gait cycle determine the stride length. In addition, the kinematic parameters are usually characterized by the joint angles between body segments and their relationships to the events of the gait cycle. In the gait figures, the joint angles can be determined from the coordinates of the body points. By definition, the joint angles are measured as one joint relative to another, so the relative angles in each joint are derived from the extracted angle values. In normal walking, the torso of a human body can be considered to be almost vertical. Thus, the relative hip angle is identical to that of the extracted value, and the relative knee angle can be defined from the extracted hip angle and knee angle. The trajectories of the gait figure contain numerous kinematic characteristics on human movement, including linear and angular position, their displacements, and time derivatives. Joint angles were efficiently interpolated by trigonometric–polynomial functions (Jang-Hee & Mark, 2011).

In previous work (Mashagba.E. F., 2015; Mashagba.E. F, Mashagba. F & Nassar, 2014), the x and y coordinates of the hip joint were used to calculate the thigh angle segment. In addition, knee and ankle coordinates were used to calculate the shank angle segment. For each frame low limb joint and segment, kinematic features were partly extracted to form the gait motion trajectories. The feature vectors of gait motion parameters were extracted from each frame by using image segmentation methods and were categorized into five categories (Mashagba. E. F. et al., 2014). Two of these categories were used to form gait motion trajectories. Category one: Gait angle velocity: angle velocity hip, angle velocity knee, and angle velocity thigh and shank. Category two: Gait angle acceleration: angle acceleration hip, angle acceleration knee, and angle acceleration thigh and shank for each image sequence (Mashagba, E. F., 2015).

2.2.3 Voice Geometry

Speaker/voice verification combines physiological and behavioral factors to produce speech patterns that can be captured by speech processing technology. Inherent properties of the speaker, such as fundamental frequency, nasal tone, cadence, and inflection, among other, are used for speech authentication. Speaker recognition systems are classified as text-dependent (fixed text) and text-independent (free text). Text-dependent systems perform better than text-independent systems because of the foreknowledge of what is said can be exploited to align speech signals into more discriminate classes. By contrast, text-dependent systems require a user to repronounce several specified utterances, which usually contain the same text as the training data (G. Chiţu, M. Rothkrantz, Wiggers & C. Wojdel, 2007).

The following features are used for the final evaluation (Michalevsky & Talmon, 2010):

Mel Frequency Cepstral Coefficients

2) Pitch statistics (mean, variance, minimum, and maximum) and pitch derivative statistics

3) Voiced/unvoiced frame percentage

Both the combination of all features and separate features were attempted. Other features that were omitted in the final evaluation include the following:

1) Zero-crossing rate

2) Short-time energy

2.2.4 Gesture Geometry

Gesture recognition is primarily concerned on analyzing the functionality of human mind. The major aim of gesture recognition is to recognize specific human gestures and use these gestures to communicate information or for device control ([Ithm Karthik, Manoj, M.V.V.N. & Naveen, 2010). Gesture is the use of motions of the limbs or body as a means of expression or communicating a meaning or emotion. Gestures include body movements (e.g., palm-down and shoulder-shrug) and postures (e.g., angular distance). Face and body gestures are two of the several channels of nonverbal communication that arise together. Messages can be expressed through face and gesture (Hatice, Massimo& Tony, 2004) and often occur in conjunction with speech. Thus, representative gestures that can replace speech are not considered gestures. In noisy situations, humans depend on access to more than one modality; thus, nonverbal modalities come in to play. Listeners rely on gestural cues when speech is ambiguous or in a speech situation with certain noises (Hatice et al., 2004).

The use of YUV Skin Color Segmentation followed by CAMSHIFT algorithm will facilitate effective detection and tracking, as the centroid values can easily be obtained by calculating the moments at each point. As the hand is the largest connected region, then the hand was segmented from the body. Afterward, the position of the hand centroid is calculated in each frame by first calculating the zeroth and first moments and then using this information to calculate the centroid. Then, different centroid points are joined to form a trajectory. This

Human Identification Based on Geometric Feature Extraction Using a Number...

39

trajectory shows the path of the hand movement; thus, the hand tracking procedure is determined. For the nose detection and tracking system, edge detection techniques yield comparatively better results and detect the nose for faces at various angles (Ith et al., 2010).

In this thesis (Mashagba E. F, 2010), hand and face gesture are used to automate sign language. By extracting the hand and face regions in each frame, the position, angle, and velocity are tracked to extract feature vectors that classify the sign.

2.2.5 Keystroke Dynamics Geometry

Keystroke dynamics is not what you type but how you type (Alsultan & Warwick, 2013; Shivshankar & Priyanka, 2015). During typing, the user types in text, as usual, with no kind of extra work. The original idea of using keystroke patterns for user identification purposes originated from identifying the sender of Morse code on a telegraph machine, where operators have been able to identify the sender of a message by the rhythm, pace, and syncopation of the received taps (Shivshankar 7 Priyanka, 2015). The manner by which user data is collected in free-text keystroke systems differs considerably from that of fixed-text systems in how a user is normally monitored for a period, such as a duration of several days for example. From all typing data collected during this time, the system infers the typing pattern that the user typically follows and stores the data as the user database. The time for typing single letters or combinations of letters, such as di-graphs or tri-graphs, involve even longer combinations in the free-text keystroke systems. However, a condition includes a particular letter or combination of letters in the template, which should be typed often enough during the enrolment phase. This condition renders the mean and standard deviation as statistically sound. Timing features (Alsultan & Warwick, 2013; Shivshankar & Priyanka, 2015; Giot, Mohamad El-Abed & Rosenberger, 2009) are calculated by using the press and release times of every key that the user types. These data are processed in a specific manner before being stored in the user's profile. The use of keystroke dynamics has been investigated previously as a more useable authentication alternative. Researchers have focused on the research conducted on free-text keystroke systems and its ability to provide continual identity verification during the whole time that the user is using the system (Alsultan & Warwick, 2013; Shivshankar & Priyanka, 2015).

Features such as keystroke latency, duration of key hold, and typing rate are extracted as follows (Shivshankar & Priyanka, 2015):

1) Session time is the total time spent by the user on the system. Session time is calculated by computing the difference between the starting time and user response times. Session time: Starting time – User response time.

2) Keystroke latency is the time interval between the key release of the first keystroke and the key press of the second keystroke. However, the latency of longer n-graphs (n > 2) is defined as the time interval between the down key events of the first and last keystrokes that compose the n-graph.

3) Held time (or dwell time) is the time (in milliseconds) between a key press and a key release of the same key.

4) Sequence is a list of consecutive keystrokes. For example, "REVIEW" is a sequence. A sequence can be of any length (minimum two). In this example, the sequence is a valid English word, but this need not be the case. Thus, "REV" and "IEW" are also valid sequences from the same keystroke

Stream. A length–2 sequence is called a digraph, a length–3 sequence is a trigraph, and so on. Therefore, a general sequence is an n-graph.

5) Typing speed is the total number of keystrokes or words per minute. Typing speed could be an indicator of different emotions.

Two features were extracted during the keystroke: keystroke duration and keystroke latency. Keystroke duration is the interval of time that a key is pressed and liberated. Keystroke latency is the interval of time between pressing two consecutive keys. The interval of time to liberate a key and press the key successor is known as flight time or dwell time. Flight time is the time between releasing the key and pressing the next key, whereas dwell time is the time taken to press a key (Pavithra & Sri Sathya, 2015).

3. Conclusion

Biometric technologies have recently played an important function as a suitable method of identification. These technologies have been proposed for high-security professional applications but are now applied as a major part of developing online applications, offline applications, standalone security systems, use for human interaction to non-traditional network-based delivery systems, and ability to verify a human being remotely.

In this work, we focus in geometry features extraction techniques, the most important issues in these techniques are the emphases in the choosing a appropriate geometry features that can identification human being, where this can be achieved by conducted several experiments with different geometry features. Another issues is security applications need to use multi biometric type.

The most existing techniques using geometric features,it not real time recognition so we need to focus in this point to propose suitable online applications.

In this work, we established a comparison between different biometrics. The following table compares several biometric technologies from the point of the geometric feature extraction in different research. From the following tables, we can see that geometry-based methods with different biometrics are applied simply and efficiently. According to previous experiments, the eye region is extracted as face part for use mainly in face recognition. In addition, the extracted eye region shows more detail in comparison with iris features. We can see that certain biometric technologies, such as fingerprint and signature, present more geometric features than other biometric technologies, as shown in the table below.

Table 1. Comparisons between different biometrics

Biometric Technology	Features	Research
	• Global features (Core, Delta) • Local features (ridge endings, ridge bifurcations, and islands)	(Ishmael et al., 2009)
	• Onion layers (convex polygons) are created from data sets. The smallest layer (convex polygon) of the constructed onion layers is isolated from the fingerprint in vector form.	(Khazaei et al.,2007; Poulos et al., 2003).
	• Extract feature points such as eyes, nose, and mouth. The direction and edges from the points are detected, and then feature vectors are built from the edges and direction.	(Bakshe & Patil, 2014)
	• Image regions that contain eyes and mouth are detected. Thus, a total of 15 parameters are considered as feature vectors: height of the left eyebrow, width of the left eyebrow, height of the left eye, width of left eye, height of right eyebrow, width of the right eyebrow, height of the right eye, width of the right eye, nose height, nose width, mouth height, mouth width, distance between the center of the left eyebrow and the left eye, distance between center of the right eyebrow and the right eye, and distance between the center of the nose and the mouth	(Kim et al., 2015)
	• Horizontal center • Vertical center • Semi-major axes • Semi-minor axes • Eccentricity • Area	(Mashagba, E. F.,2016)
	• Finger lengths • Finger widths at equally spaced distances along the finger area • Finger perimeters • Tip point of all fingers, including thumb • Starting reference point and ending reference point	(Mathivanan et al., 2012)
	• Centroid of the hand • Major axis length • Minor axis length • Perimeter	(Poonam & Sipi, 2013)

• Geometrical features of the index, middle, and ring fingers. Each finger is characterized as a triangle. The three vertices of the triangle are the end and the two side valleys of the finger. Approximately 40 wide measures to the index, middle, and ring fingers were taken.	(Aythami et al., 2008)
• Extracted: finger length, finger width, palm length, palm width, and hand length	(Mandeep & Amardeep, 2015)
• Widths: each of the fingers is measured in three different heights. Thump finger is measured in two heights.	
• Heights: the heights of all fingers and thumb are obtained	(Peter & Dušan,2007)
• Palm: two measurements of palm size	
• Finger baselines	
• Finger length.	
• Finger width	(Nidhi et al., 2013)
• Palm width	
• Distance 1 (D (1))	
• Distance 2 (D (Size (D) / 2)	
• Distance 3 (D (Size (D) / 3)	
• Distance 4 (D (Size (D) / 4)	(Asmaa et al., 2015)
• X-coordinate of centroid	
• Y-coordinates of centroid	
• Calculated mean	
• Feature vectors, such as Euclidian distances and angles of a triangle	(Luaibilafta, 2013)
• The iris region, Cartesian coordinates, polar coordinates, coordinates of the pupil, and iris boundaries along the θ direction, the mean, variance, standard deviation of the circles, and pixel correlation	(Bhawna et al., 2010; Roselin, et al., 2013)
• Pupil-based features (pupil roundness, pupil largeness, and pupil smoothness).	(Poonguzhali & Ezhilarasan, 2015)
• Collarette-based features (collarette iris ratio and collarette pupil ratio).	
• xi is the coordinate in direction x	
• yi is the coordinate in direction y	
• Speed vx and vy express the functions of time	
• tm is the time of movement	
• vx is the speed at point tm in direction x	
• vy is the speed at point tm in direction y.	(Syed et al., 2015)
• Acceleration ax and ay can be calculated with different speeds and the acceleration at point tm in directions x and y	
• Tk, total time of the hand-written signature; total time, stroke length, the time for lifting the pen	
• The position of the hand centroid is calculated in each frame	
• Different centroid points are joined to form a trajectory. This trajectory shows the path of the hand movement	(Mashagba E.F et al., 2010)
• Extraction of hand and face region in each frame	
• Position	
• Angle	
• Velocity to extracted feature vector	

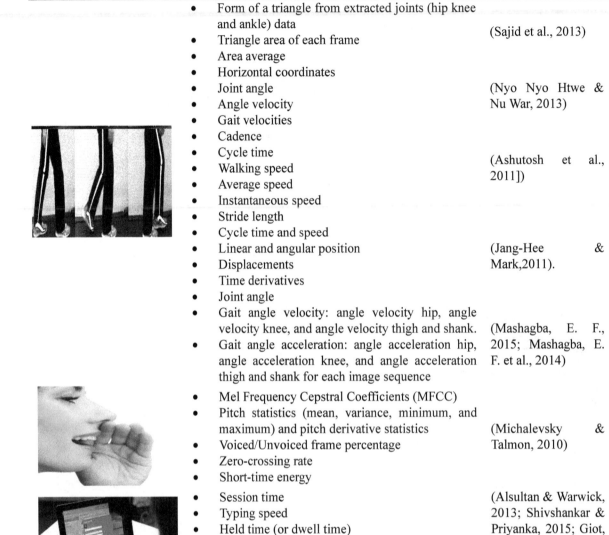

• Form of a triangle from extracted joints (hip knee and ankle) data • Triangle area of each frame • Area average • Horizontal coordinates	(Sajid et al., 2013)
• Joint angle • Angle velocity	(Nyo Nyo Htwe & Nu War, 2013)
• Gait velocities • Cadence • Cycle time • Walking speed • Average speed • Instantaneous speed • Stride length • Cycle time and speed	(Ashutosh et al., 2011])
• Linear and angular position • Displacements • Time derivatives • Joint angle	(Jang-Hee & Mark,2011).
• Gait angle velocity: angle velocity hip, angle velocity knee, and angle velocity thigh and shank. • Gait angle acceleration: angle acceleration hip, angle acceleration knee, and angle acceleration thigh and shank for each image sequence	(Mashagba, E. F., 2015; Mashagba, E. F. et al., 2014)
• Mel Frequency Cepstral Coefficients (MFCC) • Pitch statistics (mean, variance, minimum, and maximum) and pitch derivative statistics • Voiced/Unvoiced frame percentage • Zero-crossing rate • Short-time energy	(Michalevsky & Talmon, 2010)
• Session time • Typing speed • Held time (or dwell time) • Sequence • Keystroke latency	(Alsultan & Warwick, 2013; Shivshankar & Priyanka, 2015; Giot, Mohamad El-Abed & Rosenberger, 2009)
• Keystroke duration • Keystroke latency: flight time and dwell time	(Pavithra & Sri Sathya, 2015)

References

Alin, G., Chiţu, L., Rothkrantz, J. M., Pascal, W., & Jacek, C. W. (2007). Comparison between Different Feature Extraction Techniques for Audio-Visual Speech Recognition. *Journal on Multimodal User Interfaces*, 7–20.

Alsaadi, I. M. (2015). Physiological Biometric Authentication Systems Advantages, Disadvantages and Future Development: A Review. *International Journal of Scientific & Technology Research*, 285-289.

Arun, R., & Anil, K. J. (2007). Human Recognition Using Biometrics: An Overview. *Annals of Tellecommunications*, 11-35.

Arwa, A., & Kevin, W. (2013). Keystroke Dynamics Authentication: A Survey of Free-Text Methods. *IJCSI International Journal of Computer Science Issues*, 1-10.

Ashutosh, K., Saini, V., Jain, Y. K., & Dhiman, S. (2011). A Review of Gait Cycle and Its Parameters. *IJCEM International Journal of Computational Engineering & Management*, 78-83.

Asmaa, S. A., Kareem, D., Kamal, A., Ghanyb, D, & Hesham, E. (2015). Human Ear Recognition Using Geometrical Features Extraction. *International Conference on Communication, Management and Information Technology* (pp. 1-9). Elsevier B.V.

Aythami, M., Miguel, A., Ferrer, Francisco, D., Jesús, B., Alonso, C., & Travieso, M. (2008). Contact-Free Hand Biometric System For Real Environments. 16th European Signal Processing Conference (Eusipco 2008). Lausanne, Switzerland: Eurasip.

Bhawna, C., & Shailja, S. (2010). Analysis of Statistical Feature Extraction For Iris Recognition System Using Laplacian of Gaussian Filter. *International Journal of Applied Engineering Research, Dindigul,* 528-535.

Dakshina, R., Kisku, Phalguni, G., & Jamuna, K. S. (2010). Offline Signature Identification by Fusion of Multiple Classifiers Using Statistical Learning Theory. Ournal: Corr.

Eman, A. M. (2010). Automatic Isolated-Word Arabic Sign Language Recognition System Based on Time Delay Neural Networks.

Eman, A. M., Feras, A. M., & Mohammad, N. (2014). Simple And Efficient Marker-Based Approach In Human Gait Analysis Using Gaussian Mixture Model. *Australian Journal of Basic and Applied Sciences,* 137-147.

Erno, M., & Roope, R. (2008). An Experimental Comparison of Gender Classification Methods. *Pattern Recognition Letters,* 1544–1556.

Gagandeep, K., Gurpreet, S., & Vineet, K. (2014). A Review on Biometric Recognition. *International Journal of Bio-Science and Bio-Technology,* 69-76.

Hamzeh, K., Ali, M. (2007). Fingerprint Matching and Classification Using an Onion Layer Algorithm of Computational Geometry. International Journal of Mathematics and Computers In Simulation, 26-32.

Hatice, G., Massimo, P., & Tony, J. (2004). Face and Body Gesture Recognition for aVision-Based Multimodal Analyzer. *Australian Computer Society, Inc. Darlinghurst, Australia,* 19-28.

Himanshu, S. (2013). A Comparison Based Study on Biometrics for Human Recognition. *Iosr Journal of Computer Engineering* (Iosr-Jce), 22-29.

Htwe, N. N., & War, N. (2013). Human Identification Based Biometric Gait Features Using Msrc. *International Journal of Advanced Research in Computer Engineering & Technology (IJARCET),* 1879-1885.

Ishmael, S., Msiza, B., Leke-Betechuoh, F. V., & Nelwamondo, N. M. (2009). *A Fingerprint Pattern Classification Approach Based on the Coordinate Geometry of Singularities.* Proceedings of the 2009 Idée International Conference on Systems, Man, and Cybernetics (pp. 516-523). San Antonio: Idée.

Ith, C., Karthik, R., Shastry, M., Ravindran, M. V. V. N., & Srikanth, S. N. (2010). Survey on Various Gesture Recognition Techniques for Interfacing Machines Based on Ambient Intelligence. *International Journal of Computer Science & Engineering Survey(IJCSES),* 31-42.

Jang-Hee, Y. M., & Nixon, S. (2011). Automated Markerless Analysis of Human Gait Motion for Recognition and Classification. *Etri Journal,* 259-266.

Jayaram, M. A., & Hasan, F. (2013). Soft Computing In Biometrics: A Pragmatic Appraisal. *American Journal of Intelligent Systems,* 105-112.

Kalyani, M., & Samayita, B. (2013). Comparative Study of Different Biometric Features. *International Journal of Advanced Research in Computer and Communication Engineering,* 2776-2784.

Konstantinos, M., Dimitrios, T., & Georgios, S. (2010). Gait Recognition Using Geometric Features and Soft Biometrics. *Signal Processing Letters, Idée, 17*(4), 367-370. http://dx.doi.org/10.1109/Lsp.2010.2040927

Luaibilafta, R. (2013). Geometric Ear Recognitionbased on Neural Network. *Journal of College of Education for Pure Science,* 7-13.

Mandeep, K. A., & Amardeep, S. (2015). A Survey of Hand Geometry Recognition. *International Journal of Advance Research in Computer Science and Management Studies,* 312-318.

Mashagba, E. F. (2015). Human Identification By Gait Using Time Delay Neural Networks. *Computer and information Science,* 56-63.

Mashagba, E. F. (2016). Real Time Gender Classification Using Face.

Mathivanan, B., Palanisamy, V., & Selvarajan, S. (2012). Multi Dimensional Hand Geometry Based Biometric Verification And Recognition System. *International Journal of Emerging Technology and Advanced Engineering,* 348-354.

Mir, A. H., Rubab, S., & Jhat, Z. A. (2011). Biometrics Verification: A Literature Survey. *Journal of Computing And Ict Research,* 67-80.

Mir, A. H., Rubab, S., & Jhat, Z. A. (2011). Biometrics Verification: A Literature Survey. *Journal of Computing and Ict Research,* 67-80.

Mudit, M., Ajinkya, R., Sagar, G., & Dalv, J. (2015). Human Ear Recognition Using Geometric Features. *International Advanced Research Journal in Science, Engineering and Technology*, 122-125.

Namrata, V., Khope, M., & Burange, S. (2016). A Review on Implementation of Real Time Image Processing For A Human Eye Computer Interaction System. *International Journal on Recent and Innovation Trends in Computing and Communication,* 205 - 208.

Nidhi, S., Vipul, S., Neelesh, D., & Pragya, M. (2013). Hand Geometry: A New Method For Biometric Recognition. *International Journal of Soft Computing and Engineering (IJSCE),* 192-196.

Pallavi, V. H., & Salokhe, B. T. (2015). Offline Handwritten Signature Verification Using Neural Network. *Journal of Information, Knowledge and Research in Electrical Engineering,* 449-453.

Pavithra, M., K. & Sathya, B. S. (2015). Continuous User Authentication Using Keystroke Dynamics. M. Pavithra et al., *(IJCSIT) International Journal of Computer Science and Information Technologies,* 1922-1925.

Penny, D., Carlisle, G., & Kai, K. (2008). Biometrics, Human Body, And Medicine: A Controversial History. *Italy: Emilio Mordini, Centre for Science, Society and Citizenship.*

Peter, V., & Dušan, L. (2007). Using of Hand Geometry in Biometric Security Systems. *Using of Hand Geometry in Biometric Security Systems,* 82-87.

Poonam, R., & Dubey, S. (2013). Hand Geometry Recognition System Using Feature Extraction. International *Journal of Advanced Research in Computer Engineering and Technology (IJARCET),* 2064-2067.

Poonguzhali, N., & Ezhilarasan, M. (2015). Identification Based On Iris Geometric Features. *Journal of Applied Sciences,* 792-799.

Poulos, M., Magkos, E., Chrissikopoulos, V., & Alexandris, N. (2003). *Secure Fingerprint Verification Based on Image Processing Segmentation Using Computational Geometry Algorithms.* In Proceedings of the Iasted International Conference Signal Processing Pattern Recognition & Application (pp. 308-312). Rhodes Island, Greece: Acta Press.

Prachi, P. B., Saurabh, M., & Maanak, G. (2014). Biometrics: 21st Century Technology of Authentication And Security. *International Journal of Advanced Research in Computer Science and Software Engineering,* 189-196.

Rahul, C., Bakshe, A., & Patil, M. (2014). Hand Geometry Techniques: Review. *International Journal of Modern Communication Technologies & Research (IJMCTR)*, 14-20.

Romain, G., Mohamad, E. A., Christophe, R. (2009). Greyc Keystroke: A Benchmark for Keystroke Dynamics Biometric Systems. Idée International Conference on Biometrics: Theory, Applications and Systems (Btas 2009) (P. 6). Washington, United States. Idée Computer Society.

Sajid, A., Wu, Z. K., Zhou, M. Q., Abdul, R., & Hafeez, A. (2013,). *Human Identification Based on Gait Joints Area Through Straight Walking View.* Proceedings of 2013 3rd International Conference on Computer Engineering and Bioinformatics, (pp. 13-19). Bangkok, Thailand.

Shivshankar, R., & Priyanka, V. (2015). Objective of Keystroke Dynamics for Identifying Emotional State. Shivshankar Rajput. *(IJCSIT) International Journal of Computer Science and Information Technologies, 44,* 632-636.

Shradha T., Chourasia, J. N., & Vijay, S. C. (2015). International Journal of Innovative Research In Advanced Engineering (IJIRAE), 2349-2163.

Sukhdeep, S., & Sunil, K. S. (2013). A Review On Biometrics And Ear Recognition Techniques. International *Journal of Advanced Research in Computer Science and Software Engineering,* 1624-1630.

Syed, F., Zaidi, A., & Mohammed, S. (2015). Biometric Handwritten Signature Recognition. Metadata by Citeseerx Is Licensed Under Cc By-Nc-Sa 3.0.

Tiwalade, O., Majekodunmi, F., & Idachaba, E. (2011). A Review Of The Fingerprint, Speaker Recognition, Face Recognition and Iris Recognition Based Biometric Identification Technologies. *Proceedings of the World Congress on Engineering.* London, U. K.

Tripathi, K. P. (2011). A Comparative Study of Biometric Technologies with Reference to Human Interface.

International Journal of Computer Applications, 0975 – 8887.

Urvashi, B., & Singhal, R. (2014). A Survey On Face Detection Methods And Feature Extraction Techniques Of Face Recognition. *International Journal of Emerging Trends & Technology in Computer Science (IJETTCS),* 233-237.

Vaidya, M. G. (2015). A Study Of Biometrics Technology Methods and Their Applications- A Review. *International Journal of Innovation In Engineering and Technology,* 235-240.

Valarmathy, S., & Satheesh, K. P. (2012). Svm-Bdt Based Intelligent Fingerprint Authentication System Using Geometry Approach. *International Journal of Computer Network and Security (IJCNS),* 62-67.

Vanaja, R., Chirchi, E., & Waghmare, L. M. (2013). Feature Extraction And Pupil Detection Algorithm Used For Iris Biometric Authentication System. *International Journal of Signal Processing, Image Processing and Pattern Recognition,* 141-160.

Wu, Y. X., Zhuang, Y., Long, X., Lin, F., & Xu, W. Y. (2015). Human Gender Classification: A Review. *Idée Sensors Journal,* 1-12.

Yan, M., & Ronen, T. N. D. (2010). Speech-Singing Discrimination Using Geometric Methods.Project.

Yong-Ki, K., Jong, G. L., Kim, Mi-Hye (2015). Comparison of Lip Image Feature Extraction Methods for Improvement of Isolated Word Recognition Rate. *Advanced Science and Technology Letters,* 57-61.

5

Mobile Network Planning Process Case Study - 3G Network

Saed Tarapiah[1], Shadi Atalla[2], Kamarul Faizal Bin Hashim[3] & Motaz Daadoo[4]

[1] Telecommunication Engineering Department, An-Najah National University, Nablus, Palestine

[2] College of Information Technology (CIT), University of Dubai, Dubai, UAE

[3] College of Information Technology (CIT), University of Dubai, Dubai, UAE

[4] Computer Systems Engineering, Palestine Technical University (Kadoorie), Tulkarm, Palestine

Correspondence: Shadi Atalla, College of Information Technology (CIT), University of Dubai, Dubai, UAE
E-mail: s.tarapiah@najah.edu/satalla@ud.ac.ae/kbinhashim@ud.ac.ae/m.daadoo@ptuk.edu.ps

Abstract

Third Generation cellular networks (3G) were developedwith the aimof offering high data rates up to 2Mbps and 384Kbps for stationary and mobile users respectively which allows the operators to offer a multimedia connectivity and other data services to the end customers. In this work we apply techniques to design a 3G radio network, in particular we study the planning and implementation in developing countries, and state of Palestine as a case study. In order to carry a 3G radio network planning for a selected regions, wemust followa roadmap consists of set of phases; First of all, wemust determine the region under study on the digitized map in order to obtain some useful information, such as the area distribution; thus using digital maps gives a good clearness for areas classification, land use, land terrain, heights, vectors, etc. Also we must forecast subscriber profile to perform coverage and capacity dimensioning process to achieve nominal cell plan. This paper work studies Nablus as one of the major Palestinian cities. then, subscriber forecast profile is applied in order to calculate the service traffic demand, the capacity and and coverage requirements, this study is carried in corporation withWataniya which is one of the leading mobile telecommunication service provider in Palestine. For Nablus city we've found that 28 sites are required to be installed to meet the given capacity requirements, on the other hand 46 sites are for coverage. At this point we should make decision about how many site will be implemented. In general we have to select number of sites relative to coverage requirement; so to serve Nablus city by 3G services we should implement 46 sites. At final stage, we have to be sure that our proposed 3G network is suitable not only for the first year of running the 3G services over the deployed network, our design takes into consideration the growth of subscribers number and their demands, so periodically, the networking administrators and the network planning department, assess the network current status and upgrade the network to meet the future demands.

Keywords: 3G, Network Planning, Mobile Communication, Radio Network

1. Introduction

Cellular technology evolution has been started since 1950s, and the first commercial systems came in the late 1970s. Where cellular networks can be classified into different generations, namely, First Generation, Second Generation [**GSM**], Third Generation [**3G**] and Fourth Generation [**4G**]. In this paper we study the planning phases in order to upgrade the mobile operator network, to build a third generation in parallel with the current deployed second generation network. Many earlier works have been conducted regarding the 3G radio network planning i.e. [**book3G**], our study is related to the 3G planning and implementation for Nablus city, as one of the major Palestinian cities. The planning process have some main attributes and factors such as subscriber profile forecasting and the calculation of the service traffic demand, in addition to the capacity coverage requirements. This paper ends up with a proposed for an applicable 3G network to be deployed in the selected cities.

1.1 Motivation for Carrying Out this Research

It is worth to know that the Palestinian cellular network operators are still working on GSM/GPRS/EDGE (Global System for Mobile Communications/ General Packet Radio Service/ Enhanced Data Rates of GSM Evolution) that offers voice service and non matured data services. Nowadays, Palestinian subscribers are demanding more data communication services and aligned with the international subscribers demand. As figure 2 represents that GSM is already covered almost all over the world.

The telecommunication operators and providers followed accordingly. Third Generation is the next step for Palestinian, the implementation of the 3G in Palestine, is still not approved by the Palestinian MTIT (Ministry of Telecommunication and Information Technology) [MTIT]; that is typically due to political issues between Israel and Palestine. in all cases, the demand for 3G services become crucial, we have to be ready and have a study and road-map for the upgrading to 3G network, thus we are ready once the local mobile operators has got the permission to implement and run the 3G network service.

while figure 2 depicts the coverage of different mobile communication technologies; 2G, 3G and LTE (Long-Term Evolution) [LTE] based on the world map coverage for year 2015 [MAPWorld] [MAPVerizon], where we focus on the 2G and 3G technology coverage in the middle-east area.

As a result, we selected this topic to be aligned with the coming data evaluation in Palestine. This study will be very useful for the current operators to upgrade for the 3G network.

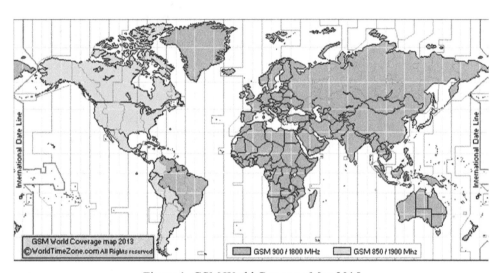

Figure 1. GSM World Coverage Map 2015

2. Literature Review and RelatedWork

In this paper, we outline the "3G Radio Planning Design" in order to plan and design UMTS/3G (Universal Mobile Telecommunications System) network in Palestine. It provides design requirements and assumptions (e.g. service quality, link budgets, etc) that should be used for planning a UMTS network; the Radio network design process is outlined keeping in mind that Radio design will be an overlay on the existing 2.75G GSM network. Palestinian telecommunication mobile operators upon getting the approval and the permission to implement the 3G mobile technology, they have to design and deploy a UMTS network across all regions that will be capable of providing voice and packet data (including High Speed Packet Access HSPA) services to meet the rapidly data demand. The design will be an overlay on the existing GSM networks in Palestine to keep the current available infrastructure for the operational companies and to keep the utilization of current 2.75G services.

2.1 Third Generation Evolution

The wireless voice services started by the first generation circuit switched analogue service, which was for voice only; this technology did not provide SMS (Short Message Services) or other data services. Upgrading from first generation to Second digital system Generation (2G); this transition was posted due to several services provided by 2G technologies such as: data storing, coping, encryption and compression, and permits data transmission without loss be supporting error correction. Many other several cellular and wireless data services are provided in 2G networks, such as internet access, with speeds up to 14.4.kbps as a theoretical value. In addition, voice quality improved, even though, 2G is also circuitswitched, but this generation still not meets the required data rates and throughput compared with the demanded data volumes.

The Second generation technologies 2G, includes GSM (Global System for Mobile Communication) that is based on both time division multiple access mechanism (TDMA), and frequency division multiple access mechanism(FDMA), where a sectrum is divided into small slices, as well each slice is divided in time to multimple time slices, where users are allocated in turn to specific spectrum slice, and specific time slice as well.

Moving from 2G to 2.5G technologies, GSM/GPRS [GSM] [GPRS]; GPRS (General Packet Radio Services), that is a data-oriented technology extending the GSM voice services where GPRS theoretical can provide up to 200Kbps; which made an introduction to another revolutionary change. An enhanced GPRS is also introduced and named as EDGE which provides more data rate. The Third Generation cellular networks (3G) were developed with the aim of offering high speed data and up to 2 Mbps in the served areas or more which allow the operators to offer a multimedia connectivity and other data services to the end customers. A few technologies are able to fulfill the mentioned data rate such as CDMA (Code Division Multiple Access), UMTS and others. High Speed Packet data Access (HSPA) has been an upgrade to Wideband Code Division Multiple Access (WCDMA) networks used to increase packet data performance. The required

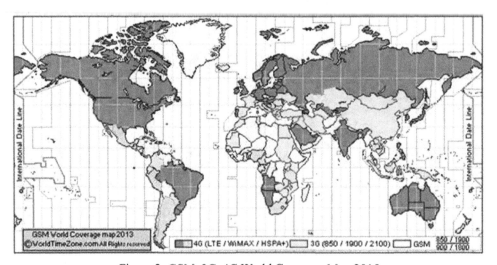

Figure 2. GSM, 3G, 4G World Coverage Map 2015

downloads and data volume demand has been recently increased per user. The HSDPA (High Speed downlink Packet Access) is developed to provide more data rates and up to 14.4Mbps to meet the users demand. HSDPA using different telecommunication techniques to increase the down-link data flow by developing different modulation and using MIMO (Multiple-Input and Multiple-Output)technology [MIMO].

Moreover, the upgrading to the Fourth Generation system 4G means that more data demand going to be booming during the coming decades, the fourth generation which called LTE (Long Term Evolution) is developed to meet the rapidly data demand.

The 4th generation still not utilizing major part in the market share due to the lack of devises that can support the LTE (Orthogonal Frequency-DivisionMultiple Access OFDMA) [OFDMA] technique and the existing network infrastructure required.

Nowadays, the LTE still supporting the data services only and not the voice, but it is in the process and development to support the voice also, after that, it will be called as "advanced LTE". The LTE can support more than 100 Mbps depends on the network structure and spectrum used.

2.2 Related Work

The first case study of 3G network in Europe, including the design and implementation was undertaken in Isle of Man, as the Manx Telecom 3G project [wu2015optimization], where all design and planning decisions were based on consideration of the desired end user experience, considering network quality, service coverage and performance of new data applications. Moreover, many other related works have been carried to study the 3G mobile network planning, where Guo et al., 2003 in [guo2003coverage] have studied the coverage and capacity calculations for 3G mobile network planning, where The planning process aims to allow the maximum number of users sending and receiving adequate signal strength in a cell. Moreover, the work carried in [amaldi2008radio] [tarapiah2015radio] has shown that the network planning process does not depend only on the signal prediction, moreover, it is not appropriate to depends on the classical second system generation in terms of formulas and parameters. Notwithstanding,mathematical programmingmodels for supporting the decisions on where to install new base stations and how to select their configuration (antenna height and tilt, sector orientations, maximum emission power, pilot signal, etc.) are discussed in [amaldi2008radio] [tarapiah2015common] which finds a trade-off between minimizing costs as well maximizing the covered area. In general the model take into consideration signal-quality constraints and requirements in both directions uplink and downlink, in addition to the power control mechanism and the pilot signal. More sophisticated work has been run, to automate the cellular planning process of the 3G network as being stated in [skianis2013introducing] [tarapiah2015advanced], some more important factors can be taking into consideration during the planning process, besides the coverage plan, and capacity pan, the Quality of Service QoS, resource utilization, and economical aspects have been considered in the work in [wu2015optimization]. In this work, we are going to state and describe full and complete methodology, design steps,and calculations for mobile planning of 3G network, on top of existing 2G network, for a given Palestinian city as a case study.

3. ResearchMethodology

This paperwork has been conductedwith the cooperationwithWataniyaMobile [WATANIYAH], The paperwork focuses on and discussing three major aspects of radio network planning and design which are: coverage, capacity, and Quality of Service (QoS). The designed methodology is requiring an advanced tools and procedure to accomplish the mentioned parties of the planning. WataniyaMobile offers the radio network planning tools to be used in their Head Quarter (HQ) and to support the idea and the techniques of capacity design and calculation, the QoS in theWCDMA [WCDMA] technology directly linked to the coverage and capacity design. To perform a complete 3G radio network design, we configured the radio planning tools to meet paper target and scope, the work include filling and configuring 3G radio capacity sheet to calculate and automate the capacity planning, moreover, to be more close to the actual design which started with nominal design, we did an actual site survey in addition to visit some selected sites of the designed ones based on the radio planning guidelines i.e. to match between the nominal and the actual sites location. At the end, we formulate the design based on the mentioned required important steps which include the coverage, capacity, and QoS steps. This will include the sub-actions like the propagation model, link budget calculations,... etc.

4. Design Procedure and Analysis

The process of designing the radio network is considered as one of the most important and crucial issue in the wireless design since it depends on many variables related to the land terrain, population density, allocated spectrum, and the target itself. The design process for any wireless system could have some common steps like the check list matrix, where figure 3 states the simple flow that will be followed during the planning and design for the 3G network, the design process can be enumerated as:

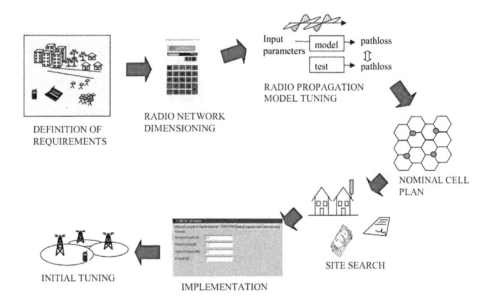

Figure 3. Radio Network Design Process

1. Definition of the Requirements: The first stage of the design process is to define the target required of the design, this stage holds surveying for an optimal solution and identifying the required tools and data to in order to start the designing and planning task i.e coverage percentage, forecasted number subscribers, subscriber traffic profile, ...e.t.c.

2. Radio Network Dimensioning: The next step, involves starting data mining, and to calculate the required capacity and equipments and tolls to meet the forecasted demand.

3. Radio Propagation Model Tuning: This stage concerns looking for the most important service Key Performance Indicators KPIs which is the coverage footprint, where the WCDMA coverage prediction depends on the loaded traffic, we have to allocate the mentioned step two traffic per sector to the tool in order to have better accuracy in the coverage prediction. The propagation model is one of the most important steps to be tuned and suitable for the land terrain to have the efficient coverage prediction.

4. Nominal Cell Planning: The planning tool is used to create a nominal cell plan by using the engineering sense and the tools features. The tools will support the engineering decision with many plots analysis related to the coverage, spectrum, and interference.

5. Site Survey: The cell planner, and site hunters, identify the suitable and applicable sites location that fits the radio coverage requirements. The site leasing/rental issues and the construction obstacles are also taken into consideration at this stage.

6. Implementation: This step includes all the sub-steps that are required for nominal cell planning. Whereas, planning tools could be used to evaluate many related parameters such as cell parameters, handover cell candidates, as well as the best location from Site Survey step,Antenna, RBS type, feeders,...etc are to be selected in this phase.

7. Initial Tuning: This step considers performing the drive test of the selected target area, where there are some available drive tests tools which can be applied in this stage, the outcomes and findings of the related target area measurements will be used further in order to tune the network to achieve the intended KPIs based on the design requirements.

4.1 Requirements Definition

The design requirements of the radio network include coverage, capacity and QoS, those requirements are related to different area types: dense urban, urban, suburban and rural during the design assumptions. In addition to these main area types, roads have to be considered due to their importance in the service continuity and traffic volume.

4.1.1 Area and Population

Most WCDMA networks are rolled out in phases, where for each phase of the network the number of km-square of each area classification (Dense Urban, urban, sub-urban, and rural and road) in addition to the subscribers distribution per area have to be defined and determined. Starting with Nablus city, and by using the digitized map that is typically supported by any planning tools (TEMS [TEMS] Cell planner are used in this project-it is a Swedish tool). The used digital map is created from high resolution satellite in 2015 and have 2 meter resolution which can be described as an accurate digital map, the used map have Palestinian land terrain, elevations, land use (urban, sub urban etc) and vectors (roads, main streets,...), figure 4 shows an example of Nablus city based on the available and the digital map in use for the land use purposes.

Table 1. Nablus city areas classification

Category	In Km-Square
Seasonal water bodies	0.01
Low tree	3.79
Open	9.23
Industrial/commercial	0.98
Buildings	0.02
Urban	1.03
Dense urban	0.92
Dense urban high	0.68
Suburban low	0.8

Suburban high	0.76
Residential	1.11
Open in urban	0.02
Parks	0.01
Agriculture	1.19

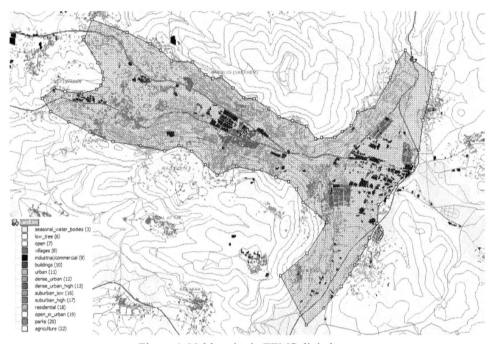

Figure 4. Nablus city in TEMS digital map

As per the digital map filtering, the area to be used for the planning issues will be 20.57 Km-square which could be classified as mentioned in the digital as stated in table 1.

According to statistics of the Palestinian Central Bureau of Statistics in 2015, Nablus city has 187,839 people, so we expect that the number of population in 2018 to be around 205,000 people based on the population growth in west-bank/Palestine. The design assumption is targeting to serves 30% of the population as a market share which means we will end up with 60,000 subscribers at the end of 2018.

4.1.2 Required Equipments

This section enumerates the required equipments for the implementation of the proposed 3G network, as being described:

1. Radio Base Station (RBS) Main remote Solution A Main Remote solution, optimized to deliver high radio performance for efficient cell planning in a wide range of indoor and outdoor applications. The Main Remote Radio Base Station, in which each Remote Radio Unit (RRU) is located near an antenna, reduces feeder losses and enables the system to use the same high-performance network features at lower output power, thereby lowering power consumption and both capital and operational expenditure. The Main Remote concept is designed to support all technologies in virtually any combination. The main Remote Solution is divided into a Main Unit (MU) and multiple Remote Radio Unit (RRU) that are connected to the MU through optical fiber cables. Where figure 5 shows RBS MU, Remote Radio Unit RRU and RBS 3-sector site respectively.

Figure 5. Ericsson RBS MU, RRU and 3-sector site respectively

2. Remote Radio Unit Remote Radio UnitWCDMA (RRUW) and Remote Radio Unit Standard (RRUS) are designed to be installed close to the antennas, and can be either wall or pole mounted. The RRUW has got WCDMA capability, and it is Multi Standard Radio (MSR) capable, that means RRUS is capable of running GSM, WCDMA and LTE on the same RRU hardware. The unit configuration can be done by software reload. The RRUS hardware is prepared for running mixed mode configurations, where RRUW and RRUS sustainable average output power is 60 Watt, for very large coverage and high capacity requirements. Dual band configurations are also supported by connecting RRUW or RRUS for different frequency bands to the same MU. The RRUW and RRUS contain most of the radio processing hardware. The main parts of the RRU are the followings:

• Transceiver (TRX)

• Transmitter (TX) amplification

• Transmitter/Receiver (TX/RX) duplex

• TX/RX filtering

• Voltage StandingWave Ratio (VSWR) support

• Tower Mounted Amplifier (TMA) and Remote Electrical Tilt (RET) support.

• Optical interface

Table 2. Antenna Specification

Frequency Range	1910 2170 MHz
Gain	17.2 dBi
Front to Back Ratio	more than 25 dB
Electrical Down Tilt (RET)	0-10 degrees

3. Optical Interface Link The RRU are connected to theMU through optical fiber cables, where units can be connected to each other in several different ways depending on the site setup. The RBS can supports the followings:

• Star connection of the RRU, where each RRU is connected to the MU.

• RRUWand RRUS can support cascade connections, where only one fiber cable is connected between theMU and one of the RRU, while other RRUs are then connected to each others, this solution reduces the length of the optical fiber cable needed and can be used in multiple applications when the RRU are located far away from the MU.

4. Antenna Configuration The antenna configuration recommended being able to configure different setups to cope with the strategic installation and keeping the existing infrastructure (co-located GSM and UMTS). All antenna configurations assume that the number of antenna ports available equals the number of feeder lines that can be installed. During the design we select antennas with specifications according to the project need and

selected area as stated in table 2

4.1.3 Traffic Requirements

Considering both area and population requirements, the traffic requirements will vary depending on the area type (dense urban, urban, sub-urban, rural and road). Whereas the percentage of subscribers using each service is used to calculate "Average Subscriber Traffic Profile" as stated in the followings:

1. Speech Traffic Requirements: The subscriber Busy Hour (BH) traffic profile for speech must be calculated from the given requirements in terms of:

• Busy Hour Call Attempts (BHCA).

• Call Mean Hold Time (MHT).

• Grade of Service\Blocking Probability (GOS\P b).

while, assuming the existence of 50,000 subscribers in 3G network which will use speech service, the average subscriber traffic profile is equal to: (50,000/60,000)*100%=83%

2. Speech Traffic Requirements calculation: By assuming that BHCA = 0.5 and MHT = 3 min = 0.05 hours. Traffic (Nablus) = BHCA X MHT. Traffic (Nablus) = 0.5 X 0.05 = 0.025 E = 25 mE. Average Subscriber Speech Traffic = 25 X 83% = 20.75 mE.

3. CS64 Traffic Requirements: The subscriber Busy Hour (BH) traffic profile for CS64 is to be calculated based on the following given requirements in terms of:

• Busy Hour Call Attempts (BHCA).

• Call Mean Hold Time (MHT).

• Grade of Service\Blocking Probability (GOS\P b).

While, assuming that 10,000 subscribers to be exists in 3G network which will use CS64 service, the average subscriber traffic profile is to equal: (10,000/60,000)*100%=17%

and by assuming that BHCA = 0.1, and MHT = 6 min (= 0.1 hours). Traffic (Nablus) = BHCA X MHT. Traffic (Nablus) = 0.1 X 0.1 = 0.01 E = 10 mE. Average Subscriber Speech Traffic = 10 X 17% = 1.7 mE.

Table 3. Network Requirements

Service	Dense Urban	Subscribers using Service
Speech BHCA	0.5	83%
Speech MHT	3 min	83%
Speech Speech GOS	2%	83%
CS64 BHCA	0.1	17%
CS64 MHT	6 min	17%
CS64 GOS	2%	17%
R99 PS UL Traffic [Kbyte\h]	6	67%
R99 PS DL Traffic [Kbyte\h]	60	67%

4. PS Traffic Requirements: The term "PS Traffic" is used to distinguish between Third Generation Partnership Project (3GPP) Release 99 (R99 or UMTS) data services which have a maximum rate of 384 kbps and High Speed data services that employs High Speed Downlink and Uplink Packet Access channels (HSDPA/HSUPA) [HSDPA]. The subscriber Busy Hour (BH) traffic profile for R99 PS have to be calculated from the given requirements in terms of:

• Uplink Traffic Volume [Kbyte\h].

• Downlink Traffic Volume [Kbyte\h].

when, assuming that 40,000 subscribers in 3G network will use PS R99 service, the average subscriber traffic profile is equal to:

(40,000/60,000)*100%=67%

5. R99 PS Traffic Requirements:

This requirement is already given in Kbyte\h, and we assumed that the uplink traffic is 10% of the downlink.

Average Subscriber R99 DL PS Traffic = 60 X 67% = 40.2 Kbyte\h. Average Subscriber R99 UL PS Traffic = 6 X 67% = 4.02 Kbyte\h.

4.2 Radio Network Dimensioning

During the design, we use Ericsson Radio Network Proposal Tool (RNPT) to perform R99 dimensioning and preparing the Bill of Quantity (BoQ), which details the hardware required to implement the radio network design, this information can be used for pricing purpose. We can summarize this process into the following steps:

Step 1 Calculating the limitation on the capacity on basis of the maximum allowed traffic load on both directions; uplink and downlink.

Step 2 Based on the available given number of sites, compute and determine the actual cell load on both directions; uplink and downlink.

Step 3 Calculating the interface margin at uplink (B IUL) and ensure it is greater than 0 dB.

Step 4 Calculating the required power at the Common Pilot Channel (CPICH) at the reference point (C (PICH,ref)) take into consideration, that the power must be less than 10% of the nominal power at the reference point (P (nom,ref)).

Step 5 Calculating the total power at the reference point (P (tot,ref)) and check that it must be less than 75% of nominal power at the reference point (P (nom,ref)).

Step 6 Calculating the required power at themaximumtransportDedicated Channel (DCH) at the reference point (P (DCH,ref)), where the calculated power must be ess than 30% of the nominal power at the reference point (P (nom,ref)).

Table 3 states the network requirements for Nablus city, based on the output and findings from the R99 dimensioning process, where the maximum load should not exceed 70% and 76% uplink and downlink direction respectively.

4.2.1 Dimensioning Process Step 1 (Capacity)

based on the RNPT Cell Load Calculator on the "Tools" sheet, the findings show that the maximum number of users supported 70% uplink load as shown in figure 6,

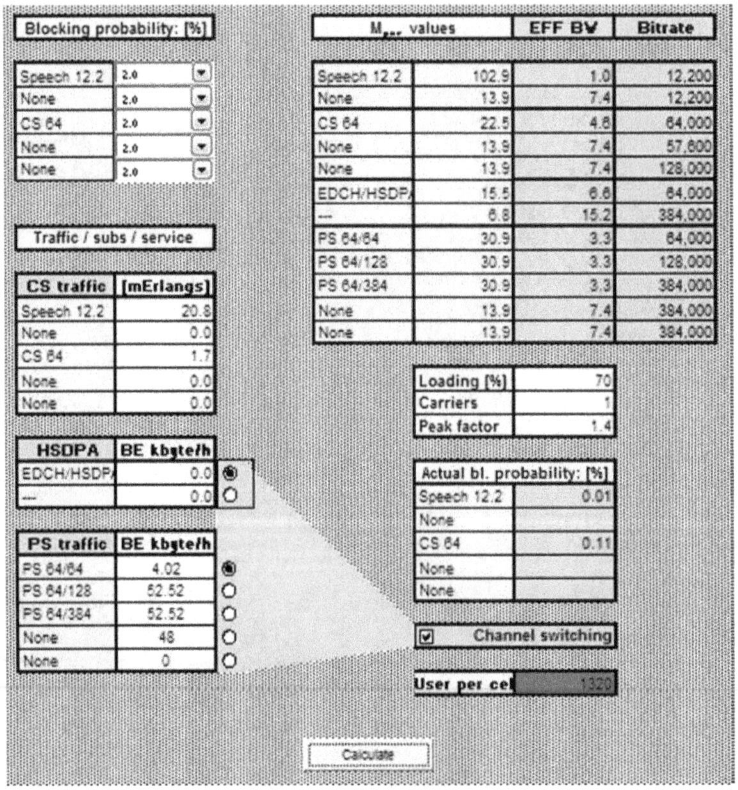

Figure 6. Number of Uplink Capacity Sites

where the outputs states 1320 subscribers per cell, thus in order to serve 60,000 subscriberswhichmeans that 60,000\1320 = 45 cells or 45\3 = 15 sites. The number of subscribers supported in the downlink at 76% load can also be calculate using the RNPT cell load calculator as shown in figure 7,

where the findings show that 1335 subscriber per cell, thus in order to serve 60,000 subscribers thismeans that 60,000\1335 = 45 cells or 45\3 = 15 sites. Based on capacity requirements at least 15 sites or 45 cells are required each for serving 60,000 subscribers.

4.2.2 Dimensioning Process Step 2 (Cell Load -15 sites)

Estimating the uplink and downlink cell load based on the number of subscribers, this can be performed by entering and increasing the input parameter load values until the targeted required number of subscribers per sector is produced as shown in figure 8,

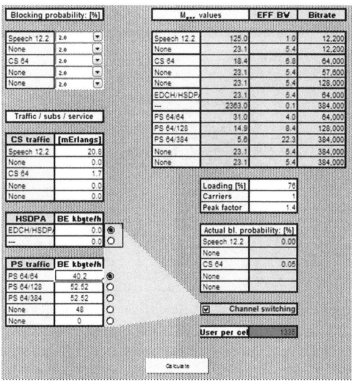

Figure 7. Number of Downlink Capacity Sites

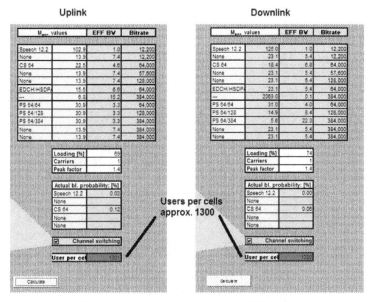

Figure 8. Uplink and Downlink Cell Load

when 15 sites is defined, the uplink load is 69% and the downlink load is 74%.

4.2.3 Dimensioning Process Step 3 (UL Interface 15 sites)

in order to find the uplink interface margin, the cell range must be performed earlier based on the formula 1.

$$R = \sqrt{\frac{8 \times CoverageArea}{15.59 \times N_{sites}}} \left[KM\right]$$

$$R = \sqrt{\frac{8 \times 20.57}{15.59 \times 15}} = 0.84 \left[KM\right]$$

(1)

Moreover, cell range can be used to determine the maximum uplink interference margin, as well the guaranteed load as depicted in figure 9

Service type	Speech 12.2
Thermal noise power density	-174.0
Noise figure	1.3
Eb/No	4.3
User rate	15600
RBS Sensitivity	-126.45
Cell range	0.84
BS antenna height	25
MS antenna height	1.5
Okumura - Hata: A parameter	155.1
a(Hm)	0.00
a (a + b log10(d)) [d in km]	134.00
b (a + b log10(d)) [d in km]	35.22
Attenuation A	135.78
Attenuation B	3.57
Pathloss	133.07
Results of selected services	
Maximum interference margin	0.43
Equivalent R99 Load	9.48
Requested R99 Load	

Figure 9. Maximum Uplink InterferenceMargin-1

Site Number Iteration (Increased from 15 to 28): Unfortunately, the maximum interference margin is 0.43 dB ¿ 0, but the uplink load here is less than 69%, thus we have to increase the number of sites, where the uplink load increases, the cell range decreases. So, by increasing the number of sites in in the earlier dimensioning process phases, we will have a number of sites equal to 28 sites and a cell range of 0.61 Km, also the load increase to 71.15% and the maximum interference margin will be 5.4 dB ¿ 0 as shown in figure 10

Service type	Speech 12.2	
Thermal noise power density	-174.0	
Noise figure	1.3	
Eb/No	4.3	
User rate	15600	
RBS Sensitivity	-126.45	
Cell range	0.61	
BS antenna height	25	
MS antenna height	1.5	
Okumura - Hata: A parameter	155.1	
a(Hm)	0.00	
a (a + b log10(d)) [d in km]	134.00	
b (a + b log10(d)) [d in km]	35.22	
Attenuation A	135.78	
Attenuation B	3.57	
Pathloss	128.11	
Results of selected services		
Interference margin	Not selected	Not
Maximum interference margin	5.40	
Equivalent R99 Load	71.15	

Figure 10. Maximum Interference Margin-2

4.2.4 Dimensioning Process Step 4 (CPICH Power 28 sites)

The CPICH power can be calculated using the tools as shown in figure 11,

DL MARGIN	15.1
Max. power at syst. Ref. Point	9.6
DL Interference margin	4.3
Received Signal Code Power (dBm)	-116.3
CPICH power [dBm]	26.9
CPICH power [W]	0.5
Average CCH power [W]	1.24
Peak CCH power [W]	2.85
CPICH power / Ptotal ref.	5.12%
Average CCH power / Ptotal ref.	13.02%
Peak CCH power / Ptotal ref.	29.89%

Figure 11. CPICH Power

it is clear that at the range of 0.61 Km, the CPICH power test passes, that the CPICH power is less than 10%.

4.2.5 Dimensioning Process Step 5 (Total Power 28 sites)

The total downlink power calculation can be performed using the "DL total power calculations" for the calculated cell range and load, as stated in figure 12.

DL load	14
DL Mpole	125.0
DL Number of cells	3
Area factor	0.6495
gamma (C/I)	0.0075
Noise (No*W*NF)	5.453E-14
Attenuation A	135.78
Attenuation B	3.57
Tabulated integral (phi)	1.083
SHO	1.108
H (noise term)	2.377E-15
Used average CCH power	1.24
Total DL power	2.95
Selected Total DL power	2.95
Maximum total DL power [W]	2.95
Maximum total DL power [dBm]	34.70
Max. total DL power / Ptotal ref.	30.87%

Figure 12. Total Downlink Power

It is clear to notice that the total power downlink power is less than 75% of the nominal power at the reference point (P (nom,ref)).

4.2.6 Dimensioning Process Step 6 (Maximum DCH Power 28 sites)

The maximum DCH power calculation can be performed using the "DL DCH power calculations" for the calculated cell range and load as depicted in figure 13,

DL DCH power calculations	
Maximum DL DCH power [W]	0.52
Maximum DL DCH power [dBm]	27.16
Max. DL DCH power / Ptotal ref.	5.44%

Figure 13. Maximum Downlink DCH Power

as this stage represents the last step in the dimensioning, the maximum DL DCH power is less than 30% of the nominal power at the reference point (P (nom,ref)). So we will end up with number of sites equal to 28 sites, with a cell of range around 0.61 Km.

4.3 Radio Propagation Model Tuning

The 3rd Generation Partnership Project (3GPP [3GPP]) and Third Generation Partnership Project 2 (3GPP2) industry alliances jointly developed channel models that are to be used for the evaluation of cellular systems with multiple antenna elements. The models are defined for three environments, namely urban microcells, urban macrocells, and suburban macrocells. The model is a mixed geometrical stochastic model that can simulate a cellular layout including interference, where as one of the most important steps is to tune the propagation model in order to get the best model parameters, that fit the land terrain to have the efficient coverage prediction, during the cell planning process, radio cell planning tool is used to predict the radio coverage by means of propagation models, for a particular site configuration. Different propagation models are considered according to the different environments and site configurations. The Algorithm 9999 model [R9999] is without knife-edge and spherical earth loss contribution implemented by Ericsson and based on the Okumura-Hatamodel [hata] which is the best suited for large cell coverage (distances up to 100 km) and it can extrapolate predictions up to the 2GHz band. This model has been proven to be accurate and is used by computer simulation tools. The earlier mentioned propagationmodel is the one adopted byWataniyaMobile. Themodel tuning (model calibration) is performed in order to obtain more reliable radio propagation predictions. Measured and predicted signal strength samples are compared, and the mean error between them is minimized.

4.4 Coverage and Nominal Cell Planning

The service footprint and availability is the most important key Performance Indicators (KPIs) in any wireless technology, this KPI determine if the end customer can access the network or not. In order to meet the design required coverage area, we have to classify and study the areas aspects i.e. population, building types, land terrain, ... all the mentioned issues need advanced tools to automatically iterate the calculations. In this work, we used advanced tools to support our network design goals which are provided byWataniyaMobile for the target of this study. The tools can predictmost of the required engineering analysis i.e. technology coverage, equipment infrastructure configurations, and required and accepted level of signal noise. Thus, in order to cover Nablus city with 3G services, we end up with 46 sites., where figure 14, and figure 15 represent the coverage sites distribution using cell planning tool and Google Earth software respectively:

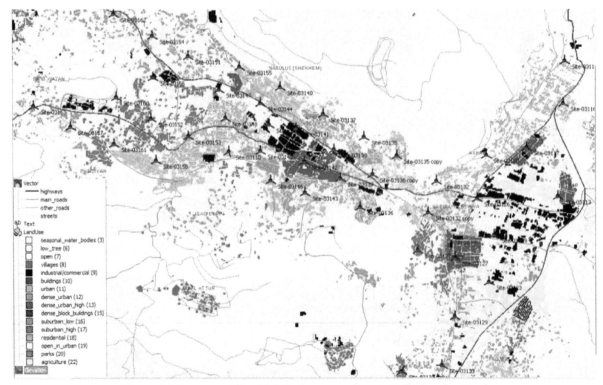

Figure 14. Coverage Sites Distribution according to Cell Planning Tool

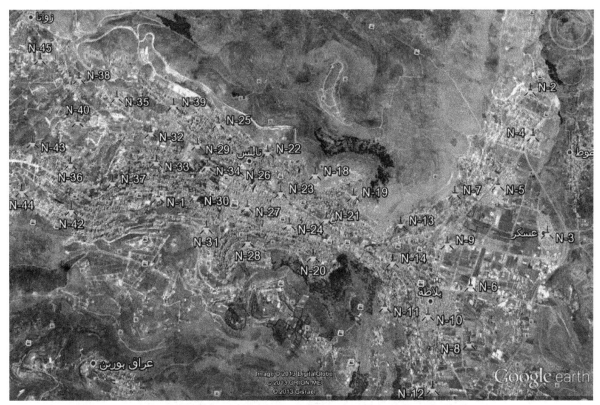

Figure 15. Coverage Sites Distribution according to Google Earth

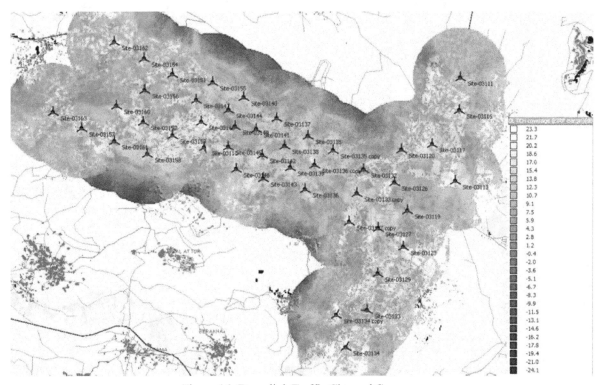

Figure 16. Downlink Traffic Channel Coverage

Various coverage plots and analysis can be prepared by cell planning tool to ensure that our plan meets the requirements; Where figure 16,17,and 18 represent each of downlink traffic channel coverage, handover and downlink total interference respectively.

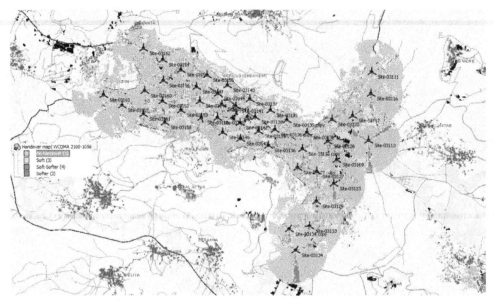

Figure 17. Hanover

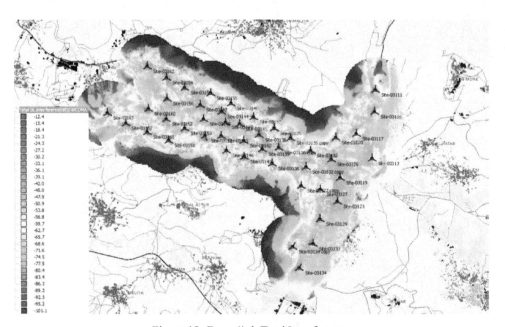

Figure 18. Downlink Total Interference

4.5 Site Search and Survey

After designing the radio nominal points, the ideal scenario is to install the sites based on the exact location outcome from the planning tool, but in reality it usually it differs due to the geographical constraints, streets, houses, and some other environmental factors, thus site survey is to to be performed which translates the ideal solution to be an actual solution, and mostly we will shift or move the nominal points into near points due to ground obstacles i.e. leasing problem, nominal points locates in a middle of major street, not accessible piece of lands, no electricity, or any other arising constraints that may appear in site. Continuous refining and re-planning tasks will be accomplished during the site survey to maintain the major coverage objectives. The basic concepts of the "Site Survey" are very simple, where it intends to indicate one or more points as possible candidates, as shown in figure 19which in fact represent the selected site number 34 to visit.

Figure 19. Site Number 34 at Nablus City

More alternative sites is preferred to be considered, which allow a better margin for trading in the area responsible for this engagement. This is because, may be the first indicated point has many problems to be installed in that location such as the proprietary owner do not want to allow the operator to use his proprietary or any other constrains transmission problems, unavailability of infrastructure,.. etc. In order to avoid these constraints, the "Site Survey" stage will be conducted together with the areas of RF, Transmission, and Infrastructure, Contract.

4.5.1 Required Equipments for Site Survey

There is not a mandatory rule about what equipment to have in the site, but here's a little "Check List" with the main equipment desired. As always, everything depends on what is needed, as it may depend the 'Survey' type, Region,... etc. We could use during our work in the site survey the followings:

1. GPS [GPS] In order to define the geographical location based on the longitude and latitude coordinates in addition to altitude, a Global Positioning System GPS device is used in the site, where figure 20 shows the GPS device used in the selected sute 34.

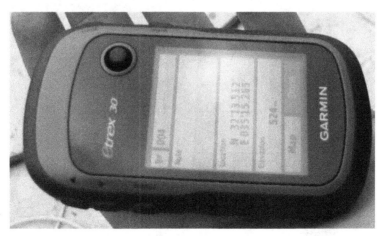

Figure 20. GPS Device

2. Camera usually in the site, some photos are required, especially to have the panorama view of 360 degree, the

captured photos may be used for further analysis. the photos is illustrative, and various other factors must be taken into account in this decision, but in general, not having a limited vision, and get a macro view always helps to get the best result. 21 shows 360 degrees divided by 30 to 30 degrees photos for N-34 site chosen as nominal point.

Figure 21. 30 to 30 degrees photos for N-34 site.

3. Compass In order to determine the orientation of azimuths, a compass with north orientation is used as depicted in Figure 22.

Figure 22. Compass-North Direction/0 degree

5. Conclusions

Advances in technology have lead to massive data communications, telecommunication operators need to cope with this evolution; so new technologies are being applied to satisfy customers need. 3G is one of the candidate technologies that supplies customers with high data rate and throughput. Several phases are considered to apply 3G radio design in any region, first of all, a region must be determined to be subjected to study on the digitized map in order to obtain some useful information such as the area distribution; this gives a good clearness for areas classification, land terrain, heights, vectors, and some other parameters. Therefore, propagation model is determined and defined along with the link budget, capacity and coverage calculations, as a result of this process; the nominal cell planning is produced. The design of the network architecture have to capable to accommodate with increasing population and subscriber data demands, so the network can be upgraded to maintain it services and sustainability.

References

Amaldi, E., Capone, A., & Malucelli, F. (2008). Radio planning and coverage optimization of 3G cellular networks. *Wireless Networks, 14*(4), 435-447.

Briers, M., & Hutchings, D. (2002, May). *Europe's first 3G network: a case study in design and implementation.* In 3G Mobile Communication Technologies, 2002. Third International Conference on (Conf. Publ. No. 489) (pp. 1-4). IET.

Chaudhury, P., Mohr, W., & Onoe, S. (1999). The 3GPP proposal for IMT-2000. *Communications Magazine, IEEE, 37*(12), 72-81.

Dahlman, E., Parkvall, S., Skold, J., & Beming, P. (2010). *3G evolution: HSPA and LTE for mobile broadband.* Academic press.

Garg, V. K., & Rappaport, T. S. (2001). *Wireless network evolution: 2G to 3G.* Prentice Hall PTR.

Goodman, D. J., & Myers, R. A. (2005, June). *3G cellular standards and patents.* InWireless Networks, Communications and Mobile Computing, 2005 International Conference on (Vol. 1, pp. 415-420). IEEE.

Guo, L., Zhang, J., & Maple, C. (2003). *Coverage and Capacity calculations for 3G mobile network planning.* proc. PGNET2003, June, 16-17.

Halonen, T., Romero, J., &Melero, J. (Eds.). (2004). *GSM, GPRS and EDGE performance: evolution towards 3G/UMTS.* John Wiley & Sons.

Holma, H., & Toskala, A. (Eds.). (2007). HSDPA/HSUPA for UMTS: High speed radio access for mobile communications. John Wiley & Sons.

Holma, H., & Toskala, A. (Eds.). (2009). *LTE for UMTS-OFDMA and SC-FDMA based radio access.* John Wiley & Sons.

Hosein, P. A. (2002). *QoS control for WCDMA high speed packet data.* In Mobile and Wireless Communications Network, 2002. 4th InternationalWorkshop on (pp. 169-173). IEEE.

Khan, F. (2009). *LTE for 4G mobile broadband: Air interface technologies and performance.* Cambridge University Press.

Medeisis, A., & Kajackas, A. (2000). *On the use of the universal Okumura-Hata propagation prediction model in rural areas.* In Vehicular Technology Conference Proceedings, 2000. VTC 2000-Spring Tokyo. 2000 IEEE 51st (Vol. 3, pp. 1815-1818). IEEE.

Misra, P., & Enge, P. (2006). *Global Positioning System: Signals, Measurements and Performance Second Edition.* Lincoln, MA: Ganga-Jamuna Press.

Mouly, M., Pautet, M. B., & Foreword By-Haug, T. (1992). *The GSM system for mobile communications.* Telecom publishing.

MTIT. (2016). *Ministry of telecommunication and information technology palestine.* Retrieved from http://www.mtit.pna.ps/arv/index.php?p=home

Skianis, C. (2013). Introducing automated procedures in 3G network planning and optimization. *Journal of Systems and Software, 86*(6), 1596-1602.

Stuber, G. L., Barry, J. R., Mclaughlin, S. W., Li, Y., Ingram, M. A., & Pratt, T. G. (2004). Broadband MIMO-OFDM wireless communications. *Proceedings of the IEEE, 92*(2), 271-294.

Tarapiah, S., Aziz, K., & Atalla, S. (2015). Radio ResourceManagement in Heterogeneous Networks, FunctionalModels and Implementation Requirements. *International Journal of Computer Applications, 127*(16), 1-4.

Tarapiah, S., Aziz, K., & Atalla, S. Common Radio Resource Management Algorithms in Heterogeneous Wireless Networks with KPI Analysis. *International Journal of Advanced Computer Science & Applications, 1*(6), 53-58.

Tarapiah, S., Aziz, K., Atalla, S., & Tarabeih, Y. (2014). Advanced Radio Resource Management Solutions for Multi-Access Wireless and Mobile Technologies.

TEMS¢ Investigation (2015). *TEMS¢ Investigation.* Retrieved from http://www.ascom.com/nt/en/index-nt/tems-products-3/tems-investigation-5.htm#overview

Verizon Coverage Maps. (2016). *GVerizon Coverage Maps - 2G, 3G and 4G LTE Coverage Map — OpenSignalMaps - OpenSignal.* Retrieved from http://opensignal.com/network-coverage-maps/verizon-coverage-map.php

Wataniya Mobile powered by Blue Technology and Development (2016). *Wataniya Mobile, member of ooredoo group.* Retrieved from http://www.wataniya.ps/en/

WorldTimeZone. (2016). *GSM World Coverage Map- GSM Country List by frequency bands.* Retrieved from http://www.worldtimezone.com/gsm.html

Wu, Y., & Pierre, S. (2007). Optimization of 3G radio network planning using tabu search. *Journal of Communication and Information Systems, 22*(1), 32-40.

Yelen, S., Seker, S. S., & Kunter, F. C. (2010, May). *Radio propagation path loss prediction of UMTS for an urban area.* In Electromagnetic Field Computation (CEFC), 2010 14th Biennial IEEE Conference on (pp. 1-1). IEEE.

6

Mobile Cloud Computing: Offloading Mobile Processing to the Cloud

Currently, there is a new set of services being widely implemented in the computer field that are able to perform computing-intensive tasks remotely with a lower cost of energy consumption on the mobile system and a shorter response time, namely, Cloud Computing Services.

1.1 Android Mobile OS

Android, one of the most popular mobile operative systems powers hundreds of millions of mobile devices around the world. The mobile OS utilizes a Linux based kernel; it implements its permission based security model and most of its code is under Apache License. Unlike on other mobile operating systems like Apple's iOS, Palm's WebOS or Symbian, Android applications are written in Java and run in virtual machines (Brahler, 2010). Therefore, Android has a broad Java library support (Java.io, Java.security, Java.net, Java.sql). In addition, Android uses its own VM; the Dalvik VM, see Figure 1. The Dalvik VM manages garbage collection, memory in a per-app cap size and allows sharing core libraries through a methodology called The Zygote. The Zygote is an approach that enables both sharing of code across VM instances and providing fast startup time of new VM instances. The Zygote design assumes that there are a significant number of core library classes and corresponding heap structures used across many applications. Generally, these core library classes are read-only and are therefore a good candidate for preloading and sharing across processes. In other words, this is data and classes that most applications use but never modify. These characteristics are exploited to optimize sharing of this memory across processes (Ehringer, 2010).

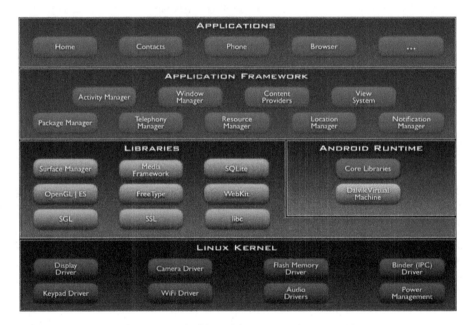

Figure 1. Android Architecture (eLinux, 2011)

1.2 Amazon EC2

Amazon EC2 is an IaaS cloud service that provides resizable computing capacity in Amazon Web Services Cloud (AWS). EC2 allows launching as many virtual machines as needed, configure security and networking, and manage storage. EC2 enables to scale up or down to handle changes in requirements or spikes in popularity, reducing needs to forecast traffic, see Figure 2. Amazon EC2 provides a web-based interface that allows users to configure their environment, virtual machines, operative systems, memory, storage and even the data center location so virtual machines can be deployed closer to the service target. Amazon EC2 also supports several instance types including micro, high CPU, high memory, cluster GPU, cluster compute, high memory cluster and high I/O instances (Bhagavathi, 2013).

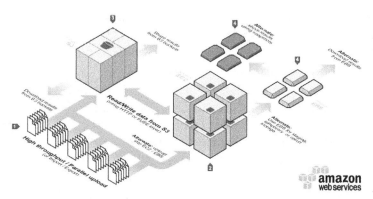

Figure 2. Amazon Web Services Architecture (Amazon AWS, 2013)

1.3 Microsoft Windows Azure

Azure is an Internet-scale cloud computing and services platform hosted in datacenters created by Microsoft Corp. An open and flexible cloud platform that provides a web-based console that allows user to create and manage cloud services, virtual machines as well as to configure networking, create security policies, administer storage, replication and so on, see Figure 3. It delivers a 99.95% monthly SLA and enables to build and run highly available applications without focusing on the infrastructure (Microsoft, 2013). A significant difference between Amazon EC2 and Windows Azure is that Azure has built in a network load balancer and resiliency to hardware failure.

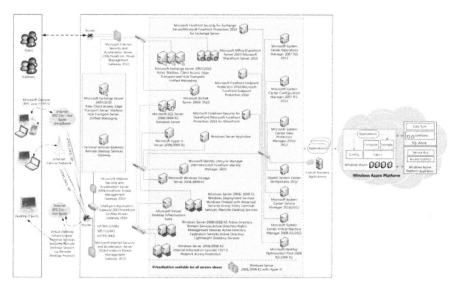

Figure 3. Microsoft Windows Azure Architecture (Azure, 2013)

In this paper, we evaluate offloading two different workloads to two public cloud-computing platforms; Amazon EC2 and Microsoft Windows Azure as well as it is evaluated the performance when using Wi-Fi and 4G as communication links. On the cloud platform sides, small, medium and large VM instance types were created on both Amazon EC2 and Microsoft Windows Azure for performing these workloads and collecting information on response times and energy consumption on a mobile phone.

The remaining sections in the paper discuss the related works in section II, our experimentation in section III followed by results discussion in section IV and conclusions in section V.

2. Motivation and Related Work

2.1 Efficiency of Mobile Clients in Cloud Computing

Miettinen *et al.* in 'Energy efficiency of mobile clients in cloud computing' discussed the potential saving of mobile clients energy when offloading certain mobile workloads to the cloud. They also discussed the trade-off between energy consumed by computation and the energy consumed by the additional communication. They showed how the trade-offs are highly sensitive to the exact characteristics of the workload and data communication patterns.

2.2 Benefits of Offloading Mobile Computation

Kumar *et al.* in 'Cloud Computing for Mobile Users: Can Offloading Computation Save Energy?' stated that mobile cloud computing can enhance the computing capability of mobile systems and it is a possible solution for extending battery. They also discuss some factors in which mobile cloud computing may not be beneficial: privacy and security, and reliability and dependency on the wireless network and the cloud service.

2.3 Advances in Mobile Cloud Computing

Mirzoev *et al.* in 'Advances in Mobile Cloud Computing' stated that current mobile devices run high computation applications that tend to head up and drain battery power sooner. Additionally, they discussed that by allowing mobile devices to offload heavy processing to cloud systems, they can mimic traditional computer performance and enable devices to use less battery power, increase uptime and improve response times. Therefore, this computer framework dramatically improves the overall mobile computing experience.

2.4 Virtual Cloud Computing Provider for Mobile Devices

Huerta-Canepa *et al.* presented the guidelines for a framework to create virtual mobile cloud computing providers. They showed the feasibility of a new scheme of sharing mobile resources to perform common workloads among different mobile users. The power of this approach increases when there is a high availability of nearby devices with common goals/activities.

3. Methodology

3.1 Workloads

We used two different workloads on three different experiments in order to determine their suitability to be offloaded to the cloud. Since the decision whether or not offload processing to the cloud depends mainly on two different workload characteristics; see Figure 4. We designed one light-communication / intensive-computation and one intensive-communication / intensive-computation workload.

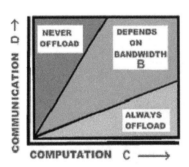

Figure 4. Decision graph with variables Computation (C) and Bandwidth (B). (Kumar, 2010)

We executed three experiments, collected data and analyzed it in order to determine the suitability of offloading intensive-computation workloads to cloud computing providers.

3.2 Light-Communication/Intensive-Computation Workload

In this study, the Android app calculates the next prime number of a given Java long number (64KB) on both, phone and cloud platforms. The algorithm used locally is the same used on the Java server application running on the both cloud providers.

This workload was designed due the data to be transmitted to the cloud has not significant size, but computing a next prime number of a large number it is a computing-intensive process. Response times and energy consumption measures were collected in order to be compared and analyzed.

3.3 Intensive-Communication/Intensive-Computation Workload

In this study, a text file was generated by a developed Java application. The file structure consists in 16-characters alphanumerical indexes randomly generated next to their pairs a regular Java integer number ordered ascending. The Android app performs a sequential search algorithm which finds the matching pair for a given file index in this big text file on both phone and clouds platforms. The 16-characters alphanumeric file indexes were intentionally created to make the processing of comparing the given index to each file index a more computing-intensive process.

This workload was designed due the data to be transmitted to the cloud or performed locally is more communication-intensive as well as computing-intensive. Response times and energy consumption measures were collected in order to be compared and analyzed.

3.4 Methodology

This research evaluated the performance on a mobile device; a Samsung S3 phone, and two different cloud computing providers; Amazon EC2 and Microsoft Windows Azure as platforms for data-intensive computation. The study performs and analyzes three experiments in order to determine the suitability of offloading certain workloads to the cloud. This research is done by obtaining response times and energy consumption on the mobile device when performing two different kinds of workloads; light-communication / intensive-computation and intensive-communication / intensive-computation. These studies reflect what workload characteristics are more suitable to offload to the cloud.

3.4.1 Local vs. Remote Processing Comparison

In this study, the mobile app performed both workloads locally on the Android mobile phone as well as it offloaded them to three different VMs sizes on both Amazon EC2 and Windows Azure. Response times and energy consumption measurements were both collected while performing local and remote processing.

Based on these measurements, T-Test statistical analysis was performed in order to determine what kinds of workloads are more suitable to be offloaded to the cloud.

The mobile phone specifications and Cloud Computing providers VMs specifications are shown in Table 1, 2 and 3.

Table 1. Android Mobile Phone

Mobile OS	Memory	Battery	Processor
Android 4.1.2	1 GB	10.74	Quad Core 1.4Ghz

Table 2. Amazon EC2

Instance	Memory	Processor*
Small	1.6 GB	1 EC2 Compute Unit
Medium	3.7 GB	5 EC2 Compute Unit
Large	15 GB	2 EC2 Compute Unit

Table 3. Windows Azure

Instance	Memory	Processor*
Small	1.75 GB	1 EC2 Compute Unit
Medium	3.5 GB	5 EC2 Compute Unit
Large	7 GB	2 EC2 Compute Unit

Note. *1 EC2 Compute Unit provides the equivalent CPU capacity of a 1.0-1.2 GHz 2007 Opteron or 2007 Xeon processor

3.4.2 Mobile Memory Saturation Breakpoint

The goal of this study was to find a breakpoint where the mobile app could not handle workloads due their size exceeds the app memory heap size assigned by the Dalvik VM. This was performed by varying intensive-communication / intensive-computation workloads to a large VM on Amazon EC2 using both Wi-Fi and 4G. The workloads consisted in different data file size (1MB, 10MB, 25MB, 42.5MB and 45MB)

3.4.3 Amazon EC2 vs. Microsoft Windows Azure

The goal of this study was to compare response times and energy consumption measurements collected by offloading mobile workloads to Amazon EC2 and Microsoft Windows Azure. Based on these measurements,

T-Test statistical analysis was performed in order to determine what cloud platform performed better.

3.5 Metrics

Response times were measured in milliseconds for each experiment. Locally speaking, it is time it took the mobile app while performing the assigned task. Remotely, it is the time it took from offloading the assigned workload, processing it and obtaining the result back from the cloud provider. The final response time measurements are an average of performing the experiment five times under similar conditions in order to obtain a more accurate value.

Energy consumption values were measured in mAh for each experiment. Locally speaking it is the energy consumed by the app while performing the assigned task. Remotely, it is the energy consumed by the app when offloading the assigned workload, processing it and obtaining the result back from the cloud provider. The final energy consumption measurements are an average of performing the experiment five times under similar conditions in order to obtain a more accurate value.

4. Results Analysis and Discussion

The previous studies captured fair amount of data for analysis, comparison and to determine what kinds of workloads are more suitable to be offloaded to more powerful computing platforms. A statistical analysis was performed on the obtained results using the T-TEST.

In the first study, T-TEST consumed two datasets as inputs; one for Local execution and one for Amazon EC2 or Windows Azure for both response times and energy consumptions on each VM size.

In the second study, T-TEST consumed two datasets as inputs; one for Amazon EC2 and one for Windows Azure for both response times and energy consumptions on each VM size. The result of this test is a p-value where $p < 0.05$ indicates statistically significant difference between data sets.

4.1 Local vs. Remote Processing Comparison

4.1.1 Light Communication / Intensive Communication

While most of the p values are not significant ($p > 0.05$) for overall data set when comparing local computation with Amazon EC2 and Azure, there is a significant difference in computing time and energy consumption when the workload is more computing-intensive. This is supported by collected data as well as for the plotted graphics, as seen in Figures 5 and 6. The reason is that there is a communication penalty in response times and energy consumption when offloading this kind of workload to both cloud computing platforms using Wi-Fi or 4G. Results indicated that it is up to 28 times faster and it saves up to 37 times more energy on the mobile phone when the workload is more computing-intensive and it is offloaded to either cloud platform, see Table IV.

The results indicate the suitability of the cloud for computing-intensive workloads.

Table 4. Local vs. Remote Processing Comparison-Light-Communication/Intensive-Computation Response times and Energy consumption results

Workload	Response Times	Energy Consumption
Light-Communication	Up to 28 times faster	Up to 37 times more energy saving

4.1.2 Intensive Communication / Intensive Communication

Most of the p values are significant ($p < 0.05$) for overall data set when comparing local computation with Amazon EC2 and Azure. Only when using 4G and small virtual machines the P-values are not significant due this poor configuration. Therefore, there is a significant difference in computing time and energy consumption when offloading this kind of workloads, see Figures 7 and 8. After using Wi-Fi and a large VM on EC2, the response time is up to 1.6 times faster and there is a 53% of energy saving on the mobile device, See Table V.

The results indicate the suitability of the cloud for computing-intensive workloads.

Table 5. Local vs. Remote Processing Comparison - Intensive-Communication/Intensive-Computation Response times and Energy consumption results

Workload	Response Times	Energy Consumption
Intensive-Communication	Up to 1.6 times faster	Up to 53% more energy saving

4.2 Mobile Memory Saturation Breakpoint

After offloading a varying intensive-communication / intensive-computation workload to Amazon EC2 using Wi-Fi and 4G, a breakpoint found shows that there are certain workload sizes not suitable to be offloaded due loading them into memory could exceed the assigned memory heap size causing that the app crashes. After transmitting different file sizes, the results show that the app performs well when transmitting file sizes below 42.5 MB over any communication link, see Figure 9. When trying to transmit files over 42.5 MB the app misbehave; it crashes due it reaches its memory heap size. Moreover, when the app tries to allocate more memory the Android memory manager kills the app throwing an *out of memory error.* Therefore, the memory heap size assigned by the Dalvik VM for an app is a very important factor when deciding to offload certain workload.

Additionally, it is vital to clarify that heap size is device-dependent and the Dalvik VM increases it on demand until it reaches its maximum assigned memory size. Although it is possible to manually set the maximum heap size in runtime it is strongly not recommended due it may degrade the overall system performance as well as turn other apps to become unstable.

4.3 Amazon EC2 and Microsoft Windows Azure

While most of the p values are not significant (p>0.05) for overall data set when comparing Amazon EC2 to Microsoft Windows Azure, there is a slightly significant difference in computing time and energy consumption when offloading to Amazon EC2, see Figures 10, 11, 12 and 13.

Based on the previous measurements, Microsoft Windows Azure response times are slightly higher than the ones on Amazon EC2. Therefore, it also means that energy consumption tends to be higher when performing processing on Microsoft Windows Azure.

4.4 Wi-Fi vs. 4G

After collecting and analyzing all the previous response times and energy consumption measures offloading workloads to both cloud providers using Wi-Fi and 4G, the outcome was that Wi-Fi produces significant better response times and saves more energy compared to using 4G for the two different   intensive-communication workloads on both cloud computing platforms, see Table VI . The reason is that transmission time over Wi-Fi takes less than transmitting over 4G.

Table 6. Wi-Fi vs. 4G Response times and Energy consumption averages results

	Response Times	Energy Consumption
Light-Communication	Wi-Fi 1.6 times faster	Wi-Fi 19% Energy Saving
Intensive-Communication	Wi-Fi 1.8 times faster	Wi-Fi 48% Energy Savings

5. Conclusions

This paper benchmarked the benefits in response times and energy consumption when offloading mobile computing-intensive workloads to Amazon EC2 and Windows Azure using Wi-Fi and 4G network technologies. Therefore, two different workloads impacting the possible decision were used to determine the suitability of offloading processing.

5.1 Local vs. Remote Processing Comparison

There appeared to be a significant benefit in response time and energy consumption when processing computing-intensive workloads on the cloud due these remote platforms can be performed them faster no matter the trade-off between energy consumed by computation and the energy consumed by communication. Additionally, it is vital to remark that the workload size is a determining factor when deciding whether or not offloads, no due the transmission time, but for the constraint given for the assigned memory heap size that doesn't allow allocating more memory than the assigned by the Dalvik VM per app. Although it is possible to manually set the maximum heap size in runtime it is strongly not recommended due it may degrade the overall system performance as well as turn other apps to become unstable.

5.2 Amazon EC2 vs. Microsoft Windows Azure

While the T-Test statistical analysis didn't determine any significant difference between Amazon EC2 and Windows Azure for overall data set there appeared to be slightly better response time and energy consumption in Amazon EC2 compared to Windows Azure.

5.3 Wi-Fi vs. 4G

There appeared to be that Wi-Fi produces significant better response times and saves more energy compared to using 4G for the two different intensive-communication workloads on both cloud computing platforms. The reason is that transmission time over Wi-Fi takes less than transmitting over 4G.

For future work this research can be taken as base to execute similar tests on different cloud providers, more powerful VMs, mobile devices, mobile OS, and more computing-intensive workloads. This research can also be used as reference for developing a middleware interface that automatically and transparently makes the decision whether or not offload mobile processing using the conclusions of this research as start point.

Acknowledgement

This research was supported by the FIS Distinguished Professorship Award in Computer and Information Sciences awarded to Dr. Sanjay Ahuja.

References

Amazon, A. W. S. (2013). *Large Scale Computing & Huge Data Sets*. Retrieved October 3, 2013, from http://media.amazonwebservices.com/architecturecenter/AWS_ac_ra_largescale_05.pdf

Bhagavathi, K. (2013). *Performance Evaluation of Data-Intensive Computing in the Cloud*. Cloud Commons Online.

Brahler, S. (2013). *Analysis of the Android Architecture*. Retrieved September 4, 2013, from http://os.ibds.kit.edu/downloads/sa_2010_braehler-stefan_android-architecture.pdf

Ehringer, D. (2010). *The Dalvik Virtual Machine Architecture*. Retrieved September 8, 2013, from http://show.docjava.com/posterous/file/2012/12/10222640-The_Dalvik_Virtual_Machine.pdf

Elinux. (2011). *Android Architecture*. Retrieved September 21, 2013, from http://elinux.org/Android_Architecture

Huerta, C., & Dongman, L. (2010). *A Virtual Cloud Computing Provider for Mobile Devices*. ACM Workshop on Mobile Cloud Computing & Services: Social Networks and Beyond. MCS'10, 2010, San Francisco, California, 2010.

Kumar, K. (2010). *Cloud Computing for Mobile Users: Can Offloading Computation Save Energy?* Retrieved June 16, 2011, from http://ieeexplore.ieee.org/stamp/stamp.jsp?arnumber=05432121

Mandeep, K. (2015). *A Review on Mobile Cloud Computing: Issues, Challenges and Solutions*. Retrieved January 17, 2016, from http://www.ijarcce.com/upload/2015/june-15/IJARCCE%208.pdf

Microsoft. (2013). *Microsoft Azure*. Retrieved September 12, 2013, from http://www.windowsazure.com/en-us/overview/what-is-windows-azure

Miettinen, A. P. (2010). *Energy efficiency of mobile clients in Cloud Computing*. Nokia Research Center. Retrieved June 10, 2011, from http://research.nokia.com/files/hotcloud10_miettinen_nurminen.pdf

Mirzoev, T. (2015). *Advances in Mobile Cloud Computing*. Retrieved January 17, 2016, from http://v1.wcsit.org/media/pub/2015/vol.5.no.7/Advances%20in%20Mobile%20Cloud%20Computing.pdf

Ranganathan, P. (2010). *Recipe for Efficiency: Principles of Power-Aware Computing*. Retrieved June 24, 2011, from http://delivery.acm.org/10.1145/1730000/1721673/p60-ranganathan.pdf?ip=66.177.3.238&CFID=330

Appendix A

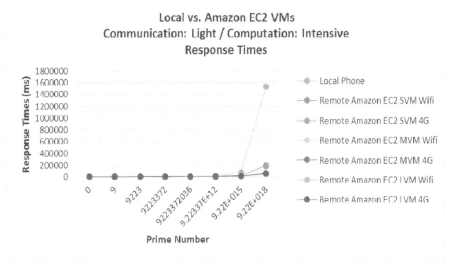

Figure A1. Local vs. Amazon EC2 – Light-Communication Response times

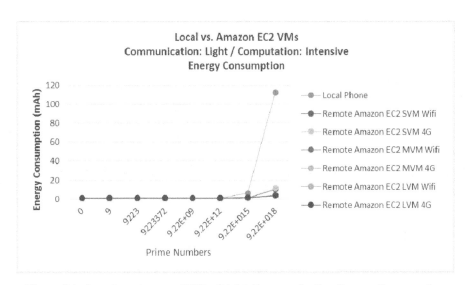

Figure 2A. Local vs. Amazon EC2 – Light-Communication Energy Consumption

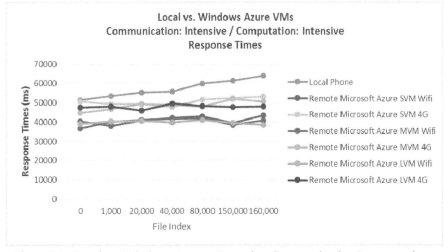

Figure 3A. Local vs. Windows Azure – Intensive-Communication Response times

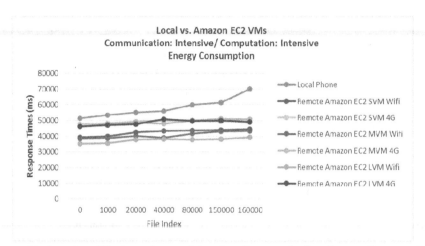

Figure 4A. Local vs. Windows Azure Intensive-Communication Energy Consumption

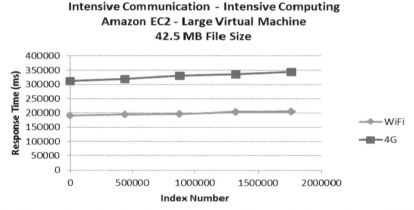

Figure 5A. Mobile Memory Saturation Breakpoint – Intensive-Communication on Amazon EC2 Large VM. 42.5 MB file execution

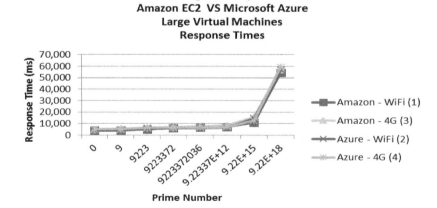

Figure 6A. Amazon EC2 vs. Windows Azure – Light-Communication Response time

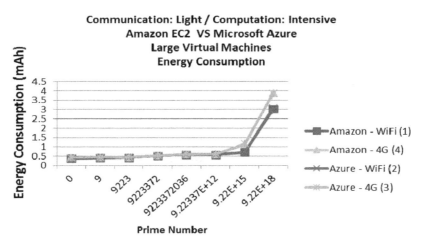

Figure 7A. Amazon EC2 vs. Windows Azure – Light-Communication Energy Consumption

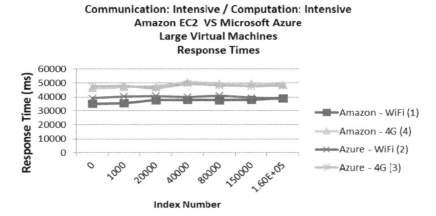

Figure 8A. Amazon EC2 vs. Windows Azure – Intensive-Computation Response time

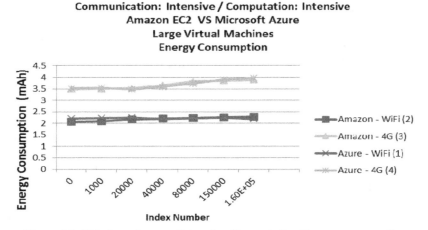

Figure 9A. Windows Azure – Intensive-Computation Energy consumption

7

Smart Parking Guidance Using Optimal Cost Function

Mohamed S. Farag[1], M. M. Mohie El Din[1] & H. A. El Shenbary[1]

[1] Department of Mathematics, Faculty of Science Al-Azhar University, Egypt

Correspondence: Mohamed S. Farag, Department of Mathematics, Faculty of Science, Al-Azhar University, Nasr city, 11884, Cairo, Egypt. E-mail: mohamed.s.farag@azhar.edu.eg

Abstract

The industrialization of the world, increase in population and mismanagement of the available parking space has resulted in parking problems. There is a need for an intelligent and reliable system which can be used for searching the unoccupied parking facility, to reduce the cost of leasing people and for better use of resources for car-park owners. This paper introduces an algorithm to increase the efficiency of the current smart-parking system. The main objective of this algorithm is helping users automatically to find an unoccupied parking lot with least cost based on a new performance metrics to calculate the parking cost. Considering the distance between the User and Parking, Distance between Parking and services area, Percent of free spaces in each car park and Cost of parking for a time t. Matlab software was used to compute the cost function and to save an optimal parking space upon a request by the user. The experimental results show that the proposed cost function helps improve the probability of optimal parking with least cost.

Keywords: smart parking, Internet of Things, cost function, Intelligent Transportation Systems

1. Introduction

The industrialization of the world, slowdown city development, increase in population and mismanagement of the free parking lots has resulted in parking problems. There is a need for an intelligent and reliable sys-tem which can be used for searching the unoccupied parking facility. Smart Parking System is a part of an Intelligent Transportation Systems (ITS) (Faheem, Mahmud, Khan & Zafar, 2013). Nowadays, the general method of finding a free parking lot is manual where the user usually finds a space in the street depending on luck and experience. This process waste effort, time and may lead to the worst case of parking failure. The aforementioned reasons encourage the user to find a predefined car park with high capacity, but this is not a preferred solution. In the last decades, a lot of researches were made in this point in order to solve the problem of parking management. The design smart parking system was introduced and implemented trying to solve the parking problem (Shiyao, Ming, Chen & Na, 2014). This system is com-posed of ZigBee network, which sent pressure information to PC through a coordinator and then update database. The application use internet to get the parking information, and use advantages of Web service to gather all the scattered parking information to bring convenience to the user who want to get a parking position. An Intelligent Parking Assistant (IPA) architectural model developed in (Barone, Giur, Siniscalchi, Morgano & Tesoriere, 2014). In this IPA the only authorized users can reserve a parking space. For users to be authorized, they should register on the IPA website. A parking lot is shown as reserved for a period (for ex. 20 mins). If the authorised user did not arrive at the given period, he will be informed that reservation is expired and this parking lot is shown as free parking lot. Parking guidance information systems were provided to minimize parking search traffic by dynamically monitoring avail-able parking and directing drivers to a vacant parking spot. An intelligent parking management system using wireless sensor networks was developed in (Tang, Zheng & Cao, 2006). The wireless sensors were deployed into a car park space to detect and show the occupation of a parking lot. The data collected by the sensors were sent periodically to a database. This database is used for finding vacant parking lots and knowing occupation rate which can generate statistic reports about the parking status. Due to the lake of space, a lot of research tends to a multi-level parking idea. A multi-level parking is introduced as a building with number of floors for the cars to be parked. A multi-level parking can serve a lot of cars in a limited space. In (Reza, Ismail, Rokoni & Sarkar, 2012), authors constructed a prototype of a multi-level parking assistance system based on the facility of image processing techniques. Image processing was used for detecting car plate numbers. Template matching method was used in order to recognize plate characters. After recognizing plate numbers, it is compared with the list of plate numbers in the system database. The authors in (Bonde, Shende, Gaikwad, Kedari & Bhokre, 2014) aims to minimize the human intervention in parking by automating the process of car parking. They proposed a design of an Automated Parking System commanded by an Android application to organize the number of cars to be parked. There is two sub architectures (Car Control Unit and Parking Control Unit). The Parking Control Unit is commanded by the Android device having the Android application. The Parking unit is responsible for the movement of the car. Multi-level smart parking system architecture was proposed in (Ismail, Reza, Rokoni & Sarkar, 2012; Rokoni, Ismail, Reza & Sarkar, 2011). An image processing techniques also introduced to monitor and identify the vehicles. They used Optical character recognition (OCR) to identify the illegal cars. OCR is the electronic translation of scanned images of typewritten, handwritten or printed text into machine text. OCR is widely used to convert books and documents into electronic les. The OCR technique has several steps like enhancement, segmentation, feature extraction and classification (Lotufo, Morgan & Johnson, 1990; Tavsanoglu & Saatci, 2000). The concept of Internet of Things (IoT) begins with things which have identity communication devices. This de-vices could be controlled, or monitored using computers connected through internet (Khanna & Anand, 2016). A smart parking system using IoT to reduce parking hazards and helps to minimize emitting greenhouse gases, increase the security of these smart parking (Ramaswamy, 2016; Juliadotter, 2016). IoT enables smart parking system using the system of interconnected Distance Sensor, Pi Camera devices together. This hardware were used in collecting data and transmit it to cloud storage, to enable commuters to get a parking lot in less time to save fuel and ultimately producing excessive CO2 emission. In (Mainetti, Palano, Patrono, Stefanizzi & Vergallo, 2014), authors present a heterogeneous network of the integration of Ultra-High Frequency (UHF) Radio, Frequency Identification (RFID) and IEEE 802.15.4 Wireless Sensor Network (WSN) devices which can be deployed in any outdoor parking. This System could collect information from the parking like occupancy of the parking lots and guide the driver to the nearest vacant space. Also, the application has an NFC-based e-wallet system enabling users to pay for the parking fee. The remainder of this paper is organized as follows. Section 2 outlines the architecture of the proposed smart parking system. Section 3 presents the experimental results. Finally, conclusion and future work are given in Section 4.

2. Proposed Method

This paper present a parking system architecture based on the least cost function. A mathematical model for the system operation is delivered. The system aimed to guide the user for an optimal parking space with least cost. Figure 1 show the design of the parking area surrounded by service places and streets.

There exist 4 gates for entrance, 4 gates for exit, 4 parking places and 10 services area. Matrix A denote the distance between the Entrance Gates G_i and the parking places p_j

$$A = \begin{pmatrix} 4 & 6 & 6 & 2 \\ 2 & 4 & 6 & 6 \\ 6 & 2 & 4 & 6 \\ 6 & 6 & 2 & 4 \end{pmatrix} \tag{1}$$

and the matrix B define the distance between the parking place P_i and Service area S_j.

$$B = \begin{pmatrix} 4 & 4 & 8 & 8 & 7 & 7 & 4 & 3 & 3 & 3 \\ 7 & 3 & 3 & 7 & 6 & 2 & 2 & 2 & 6 & 3 \\ 8 & 8 & 3 & 4 & 3 & 2 & 2 & 5 & 5 & 3 \\ 4 & 7 & 7 & 3 & 2 & 6 & 3 & 5 & 2 & 2 \end{pmatrix} \tag{2}$$

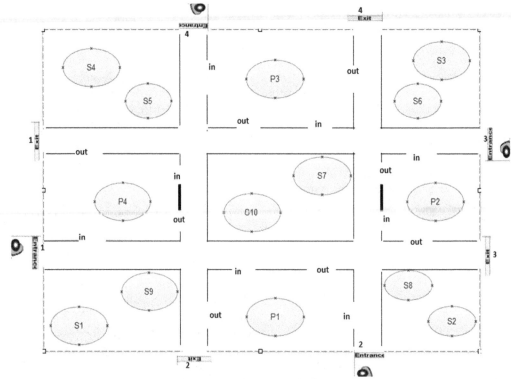

Figure 1. Architecture of Parking

Figure 2 show what happen when a new car reach an entrance gate. If a new car arrives at an entrance gate, the user should sent information to the system in order to get the optimal parking. The User sends the entrance gate number and the service number which he will go to it after parking.

The system collects this information and then computes the cost function to get the optimal parking number. After the system guide the user to the optimal parking according to least cost function, the system update the parking expected number.

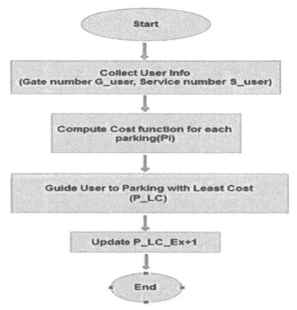

Figure 2. Steps of Collecting Data at Parking Entrance

The proposed Cost function,

$$\text{Cost\_P}_i = a_1*D(G\ User; P_i)+a2*D(P_i; S\_User)+a3*(n\_P_i)+a4*(P_i*cost). \tag{3}$$

where Cost P_i is the cost of the User parking in Parking number i,

D(G_User; P_i) is the distance between the user entrance gate and the parking number i, D(P_i, S_User) is the distance between the parking number i and the user service place, n_P_i is the number of free slots in the parking number i and P_i_cost is the cost of money of the parking number i. a_1, a_2, a_3 and a_4 are parameters which can be defined according to experimental results. After computing the cost function for all Parking places, the user is guided to the

parking which has the minimum cost. Figure 3 is a flow chart that views how to get the optimal parking according to the given Cost function equation.

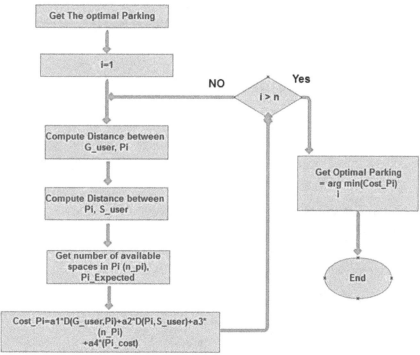

Figure 3. Flow chart of computing Least Cost Function

3. Experimental Results and Discussion

In order to view the efficiency of the proposed method, Matlab was used for setup the model and simulate the parking system. We determined the parameter of the system execution as the cost function. If we minimized this cost, we will reduce the other costs like fuel, monetary, distance the user walk, traffic congestion and environmental pollution costs. An optimal cost value reach to a good system performance. The parameters with the least cost value will be considered as the optimal solution and will be used as a proposal to apply a similar model indeed. In the simulation, we used 100, 200, 300, 400, and 500 cars that arrived at the parking. Both the inter-arrival time

of cars and the time which car spent in the parking were randomly selected. In (HAM, TSAI, Nguyen, Dow & Deng, 2015) the author did not use the percent of free parking spaces in the cost function, which leads them to introduce a method for forwarding the vehicle to another parking if the current parking is full. We think it must not allow the user to reach a full park. The system must guide the user to the correct park (park with free space) at first time, So we introduce the cost function depends in to 4 parameters. We added the parameter of Percent of free spaces in the parking, and the cost of the parking. Also, if any Parking is full, we make the cost function of this parking equal infinity, in order not to guide the user to a full parking. Now there exist 4 car parks with the capacities P_1 = 120 spaces, P_2 = 170, P_3 = 200, P_4 = 120, P_1_cost=7, P2_cost=5, P_3_cost=9 and P_4_cost=10. The Cost Function depends on 4 parameters (a_1, a_2, a_3 and a_4). We make a lot of experiments, to determine the optimal parameter values, which make the cost function value smaller as much as possible. These parameters subject to the equation

$$a_1 + a_2 + a_3 + a_4 = \text{Constant:} \tag{4}$$

Table 1 show the result of some experiments in case of 100 cars served. The cost function is determined according to different parameter values. The parameter value (2, 5, 1, and 2) gives least cost.

Table 1. Effect of Parameters value on Cost Function in case of 100 cars served

a_1	a_2	a_3	a_4	Number of cars served	Average Cost func-tion value
3	3	3	1	100	6.771
5	2	1	2	100	6.847
2	5	1	2	100	6.533
3	3	1	3	100	7.4183

Table 2 show the result of some experiments in case of 300 cars served. The parameters values were changed, it is shown that parameter value (2, 5, 1, and 2) gives least cost.

Table 2. Effect of Parameters value on Cost Function in case of 300 cars served

a_1	a_2	a_3	a_4	Number of cars served	Average Cost func-tion value
3	3	3	1	300	6.672
5	2	1	2	300	6.920
2	5	1	2	300	6.352
2	2	4	2	300	7.3097

Table 3 show the result of some experiments in case of 500 car served. The parameters values were changed, it is shown that parameter value (2, 5, 1, and 2) gives least cost.

Table 3. Effect of Parameters value on Cost Function in case of 500 cars served

a_1	a_2	a_3	a_4	Number of cars served	Average Cost func-tion value
3	3	3	1	500	6.672
5	2	1	2	500	6.920
2	5	1	2	500	6.352
2	2	4	2	500	7.3097

Table 4. Least Cost Function in different numbers of car parking

a_1	a_2	a_3	a_4	Number of cars served	Average Cost func-tion value
2	5	1	2	100	6.533
2	5	1	2	200	6.407
2	5	1	2	300	6.352
2	5	1	2	400	6.386
2	5	1	2	400	6.331

Table 4 show the best parameter values that increase the average cost function in different cases on number of cars served. After a lot of experiments on different value of parameters and from the above results, it is clear that the value ($a_1 = 2$; $a_2 = 5$; $a_3 = 1$; $a_4 = 2$) minimize the cost function to the optimal value.

4. Conclusion and Future Work

In this paper we proposed a method to improve performance of the parking process. This method depended on minimizing the cost function, which reduce the cost of moving to the parking space, cost of moving from parking to destination service and monetary to pay. The proposed architecture has been successfully simulated. The results show that our method significantly reduces the average cost value. The simulation of our system is considered as an optimal solution when most of the vehicles successfully found a free parking space with least cost. In our future study, we will use image processing techniques in order to detect free slots and car plate number to increase the security of our system.

References

Barone, R. E., Giur, T., Siniscalchi, S. M., Morgano, M. A., & Tesoriere, G. (2014). Architecture for parking management in smart cities, Insti-tution of Engineering and Technology(IET). *Intelligent Transportation System, 8*(5), 445-452.

Bonde, D. J., Shende, R. S., Gaikwad, K. S., Kedari, A. S., & Bhokre, A. U. (2014). Automated car parking system commanded by android application. *International Journal of Computer Science and Information Technologies (IJCSIT), 5*(3), 3001-3004.

Faheem, S. A., Mahmud, G. M., Khan, M. R., & Zafar, H. (2013). A survey of intelligent car parking system. *Journal of Applied Research and Technology, 11*, 714-726.

Ham, T. H., Tsai, M., Nguyen, D. B., Dow, C., & Deng, D. (2015). A cloud-based smart-parking system based on internet of things technologies. *The journal for rapid open access publishing, 3*, 1581-1591.

Ismail, M. F., Reza, M. O., Rokoni, A. A., & Sarkar, M. A. R. (2012). *Design and development of an advanced vehicle parking system.* International Conference on Informatics. Electronics and Vision (ICIEV) IEEE, 458- 463.

Juliadotter, N. V. (2016). Hacking smart parking meters, International Confer-ence on Internet of Things and Applications (IoTA), Maharashtra Institute of Technology, Pune, India,191-196.

Khanna, A., & Anand, R. (2016). Iot based smart parking system, International Conference on Internet of Things and Applications (IoTA),Maharashtra Institute of Technology, Pune, India, 266-270.

Lotufo, R. A., Morgan, A. D., & Johnson, A. S. (1990). Automatic number plate recognition, Inst. Elect. Eng. Colloquium on Image Analysis for Transport Applications, 1- 6.

Mainetti, L., Palano, L., Patrono, L., Stefanizzi, M. L., & Vergallo, R. (Sept. 2014). Integration of rfid and wsn technologies in a smart parking system, 22nd International Conference on Software, Telecommunications and Computer Networks (SoftCOM), 104-110.

Ramaswamy, P. (2016). Iot smart parking system for reducing green house gas emission, Fifth International Conference on Recent Trends in Information Technology, IEEE, 1-6.

Reza, M. O., Ismail, M. F., Rokoni, A. A., & Sarkar, M. A. R. (2012). Smart parking system with image processing facility. International Journal of Intelligent Systems and Applications, 3, 41-47.

Rokoni, A. A., Ismail, M. F., Reza, M. O., & Sarkar, M. A. R. (2011). De-velopment of an image processing based container traff control system, International Conference on Mechanical, Automotive and Aerospace Engineering-ICMAA, 10-13.

Shiyao, C., Ming, W., Chen, L., & Na, R. (2014). *The research and implement of the intelligent parking reservation management system based on zigbee technology.* IEEE Sixth International Conference on Measuring Technology and Mechatronics Automation, 741-744.

Tang, V., Zheng, Y., & Cao, J. (2006). An intelligent car park management system based on wireless sensor networks. *International Symposium on Pervasive Computing and Applications,* 65-70.

Tavsanoglu, V., & Saatci, E. (2000). *Feature extraction for character recog-nition using gabor-type filters implemented by cellular neural networks.* IEEE International Workshop on Cellular Neural Networks and their Applications, IEEE, 63-68.

8

System Architecture for Approximate Query Processing

Francesco Di Tria[1], Ezio Lefons[1] & Filippo Tangorra[1]

[1] Dipartimento di Informatica, Università Aldo Moro, Bari, Italy

Correspondence: Francesco Di Tria, Dipartimento di Informatica, Università degli Studi di Bari Aldo Moro, via Orabona 4, 70125 Bari, Italy. E-mail: francesco.ditria@uniba.it; ezio.lefons@uniba.it; filippo.tangorra@uniba.it

Abstract

Decision making is an activity that addresses the problem of extracting knowledge and information from data stored in data warehouses, in order to improve the business processes of information systems. Usually, decision making is based on On-Line Analytical Processing, data mining, or approximate query processing. In the last case, answers to analytical queries are provided in a fast manner, although affected with a small percentage of error. In the paper, we present the architecture of an approximate query answering system. Then, we illustrate our ADAP (Analytical Data Profile) system, which is based on an engine able to provide fast responses to the main statistical functions by using orthogonal polynomials series to approximate the data distribution of multi-dimensional relations. Moreover, several experimental results to measure the approximation error are shown and the response-time to analytical queries is reported.

Keywords: approximate query processing, OLAP, data warehouse, Business Intelligence tool, ADAP system

1. Introduction

The increasing importance of data warehouses (DWs) in information systems is due to their capacity of allowing decision makers to perform the extraction of knowledge and information by means of On-Line Analytical Processing (OLAP) and data mining techniques (Chaudhuri, Dayal, & Ganti, 2001).

At present, there are three logical models for the development of a DW: (a) Relational OLAP model (ROLAP), that resides on the relational technology, (b) Multidimensional OLAP model (MOLAP), that uses multi-dimensional arrays for storing data; and (c) Hybrid OLAP model (HOLAP), which adopts both ROLAP and MOLAP technologies (Golfarelli & Rizzi, 1998a; Golfarelli, Maio, & Rizzi, 1998b).

In DWs built over the relational technology, analytical processing involves typically the computation of summary data and the execution of aggregate queries. This kind of queries needs to access all the data stored in the database and, on large volumes of data, the computation of aggregate queries leads to a long answering time. Although the availability and the use of indexes (usually, bitmaps and B-trees), materialized views, summary tables, and statistical data profiles can drastically reduce the response time to OLAP applications, operations often take hours or days to complete, due to the processing of extremely large data volumes (Di Tria, Lefons, & Tangorra, 2014).

The alternative to the scan of huge amounts of data in data warehouses provides approximate query answering when applications can tolerate small errors in query answers (Sassi, Tlili, & Ounelli, 2012). The goal of this approach is to achieve interactive response times to aggregate queries. Really, in the most decisional activities, it is unnecessary to have exact answers to aggregate queries if this requires expensive time; it suffices to obtain (reasonably accurate) approximate answers and good estimates of summary data provided that fast query responses are guaranteed. Moreover, initial phases of data analysis involved by drill-down or roll-up query sequences can take advantages of sacrificing the accuracy of fast answers for this allows the analyst to explore quickly many possibilities or alternatives (scenarios) of analysis.

Here, our contribution is the definition of the system architecture, which supports the main processes involved in the approximate query processing. Furthermore, the ADAP system is presented, which implements the system architecture using a methodology based on orthonormal series. The underlying method allows summarizing information about the data distribution of multi-dimensional relations using few computed data. These data, that are easily updated when the data distribution in the DW changes, allow to execute the main aggregate user queries without accessing the DW and to obtain answers in constant time for their execution does not depend on the cardinality of the relations.

The paper is organized into the following sections. Section 2 contains an overview about traditional and emerging methodologies for approximate query processing. Section 3 explains the architecture of ADAP, our system devoted to approximate query processing. Section 4 presents the architecture and the features of this system. Section 5 reports the experimental evaluation of this system in reference to a real context of analysis. Finally, Section 6 concludes the paper with some remarks.

2. Background

The most popular methodologies that represent the theoretical basis for the approximate query processing are founded on the following approaches.

Summary tables: materialized tables that represent pre-computed aggregate queries (Abad-Mota, 1992; Gupta, Harinarayan, & Quuas, 1995). The impossibility to get summary tables for all possible user queries is the limit of this approach.

Wavelet: process that computes a set of values, or *wavelet coefficients*, which represent a compact data synopsis (Chakrabarti, Garofalakis, Rastogi, & Shim, 2000; Sacharidis, 2006).

Histogram: synthetic histograms used to store the data frequencies in a relation (Ioannidis & Poosala, 1999; Cuzzocrea, 2009). User's queries are translated into equivalent ones that operate on histograms via a new algebra that has the same expressivity power of SQL operators.

Sampling: collection of random samples of large volumes of data (Cochran, 1977; Chaudhuri, Gautam, &Vivek, 2007). Gibbons *et al.* (1998a, 1998b) introduced two new sampling-based methodologies: concise samples and counting samples. A concise sample is a technique according to which values occurring more than once can be represented by pairs ⟨*value, count*⟩. Counting samples allow counting the occurrences of values inserted into a relation after they have been selected as sample points. The authors also provide a fast algorithm to update samples as new data arrive. This methodology is advantageous because it offers accurate answers and it is able to store more sample points than other sampling-based techniques, using an equal amount of memory space. In order to improve the accuracy of the OLAP queries, that always involve relationships among the central fact table and the dimensions tables via foreign keys, Acharya, Gibbons, Poosala, & Ramaswamy (1999) proposed the computation of a small set of samples for every possible join in the schema, so to obtain join synopses that provide random and uniform samples of data.

Sketch: summary of data streams that differs from *sampling* in that *sampling* provides answers using only those items which were selected to be in the sample, whereas the sketch uses the entire input, but is restricted to retain only a small summary of it. As an example, the cardinality of a dataset is computed exactly, and incremented or decremented with each insertion or deletion, respectively (Cormode, Garofalakis, Haas, & Jermaine, 2011; Khurana, Parthasarathy, & Turaga, 2014).

Orthonormal series: this well-known method to analytically approximate continuous functions, is used in the OLAP environments to approximate the probability density function of multi-dimensional relations. To this end, a set of coefficients is computed that can be then used to perform quick statistical operations, such as *count*, *sum* and *average*, in the context of very large databases. Usually, polynomial series (Lefons, Merico, & Tangorra, 1995) or trigonometric series are used. Systems using cosine series are described to approximate the data selectivity (Yan, Hou, Jiang, Luo, & Zhu, 2007) and to compute range-sum queries (Hou, Luo, Jiang, Yan, & Zhu, 2008). However, the coefficients to be generated are different for those two cases. Consequently, the cosine method is very ineffective practically.

All these methodologies perform a data reduction process (Cormode *et al.*, 2011; Furtado & Madeira, 1999) and, basically, they apply to mono-dimensional cases. However, all they provide extensions to multi-dimensional cases and are, therefore, relation-oriented. Further approaches have been proposed for managing also data stored in large XML files (Palpanas & Velegrakis, 2012).

Other approaches have recently been proposed, some of them do not perform a data reduction. Examples of this kind of methodologies are based on (a) *Graph-based model*, which creates a graph that summarizes both the join-distribution and the value-distribution of a relational database (Spiegel & Polyzotis, 2006); (b) *Genetic programming*, where a starting query is re-written in order to minimize the elaboration costs and maximize the accuracy (Peltzer, Teredesai, & Reinard, 2006); (c) *On-line processing*, which shows a preview of the final answer to each aggregate query, by continuously providing an estimate of it during the elaboration (Jermaine, Arumugam, Pol, & Dobra, 2008); (d) *Sensornet*, which consists of a network of wireless sensors that collects discrete data of continuous phenomena (Deshpande, Guestrin, Madden, Hellerstein, & Hong, 2004); and (e)

Locally Closed World Assumption, where queries against partially complete databases are answered in polynomial time using a deductive database (Cortés-Calabuig, Denecker, Arieli, & Bruynooghe, 2007).

3. Approximate Query Answering System

In this Section, the architecture of an approximate query answering system is presented. The proposed system is an OLAP tool that collects and processes the data stored in a data warehouse, in order to produce fast answers in analytical processing. To this end, in the following we explain the main processes supported by approximate query answering systems.

1) *Data reduction.* The preliminary step is devoted to calculate the data synopsis, which represents a concise representation of the data warehouse. The system also generates and stores metadata, which provide useful information about the DW schema—tables, fields, and data types,—and especially which tables have been effectively reduced. Only the reduced datasets are available in the next approximate query processing and can be used for analyses purposes, instead of accessing real data.

2) *Approximate query processing.* The main step is devoted to perform the computations of the aggregate functions in approximate way, by using the stored previously reduced data. The analytical queries are formulated on the basis of the fact-tables, measures, dimensions, and aggregate functions selected by the user. The system also allows the user to set a selection condition on the values of the chosen attributes; this condition represents the criteria adopted to narrow the interval of data to be analyzed. The output of the processing is a scalar value that represents the approximation of an aggregate value. In addition, the system provides also methods to execute queries directly on the real data of the DW. This usually happens when the user deals with critical factors or when it is necessary to obtain deeper levels of refinement in query answering.

The data flow related to these two processes is depicted in Figure 1.

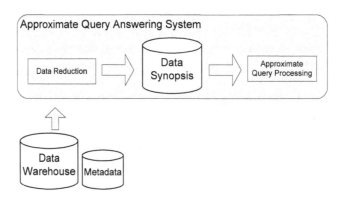

Figure 1. Data flow in approximate query processing

3.1 System Architecture

The architecture of approximate query answering systems, supporting the main processes in query processing, is illustrated in Figure 2.

This classic three-level architecture is composed of the following components:

Presentation Layer comprises the user interface components. The main users are the *administrator*, who manages the data reduction process, and the *analyst*, who executes the approximate query processing.

   (i) *Administration* is the input component used by the administrator to select the DW and set the data reduction parameters. It receives the metadata of the DW and presents them to the user. Metadata consist of table's names, field's names, and so on. Only the first time the users access the DW, a set of tables must be selected, in order to define which of them are fact tables, and which of them are dimension tables. Users must also choose which attributes are to be involved in multi-dimensional analyses. Once the user selects the parameters of data reduction, the system stores these metadata (*i.e.*, selected attributes and fact tables) in the DS database and then starts generating the data synopsis on selected attributes.

   (ii) *Analysis Environment* is the input component used by the analyst to define and submit the analytical queries returning fast and approximate answers. First, this component loads the metadata that define which fact tables and attributes are available for multi-dimensional analysis. Thanks to the metadata, users are able to express queries at a high level of abstraction. Then, they only have to set the kind of analysis—*real* or *approximate*—they want to perform. A real analysis consists of executing the query directly on the DW, so to get the exact value as query answer, with possibly high response-time. An approximate analysis is based only on the data synopses stored in the DS database. This kind of query gets a very fast query answer in constant response-time with a small percentage error. In general, a query can be formulated by simply selecting a fact table, an attribute and an aggregate function. Optionally, a user can define criteria to narrow the data on which to perform the analytical processing.

(iii) Reports Browser is the non-graphical output component that shows the result of a computation, representing the query answer. It first retrieves from the *Analysis Environment* the parameters of the user query and then redirects it to the appropriate engine. It reports the computed results—approximate value or real one—along with the response time in milliseconds. Moreover, it allows the user to print the result or to save it in HTML format. It must be integrated with Microsoft Office, as it should be also able to export the result in MS Excel.

Application Layer includes the business components that implement the basic processes of the approximate query processing.

(i) DW Manager is the component that interacts with the DW via the *DB Bridge*, in order to extract both data and metadata and distribute them to other components. To clarify this concept, it extracts the metadata of the selected DW and distribute them to the *Administration* component to start the data reduction process. Similarly, it performs a read-access to the DW and distribute the dataset containing the data necessary for the generation of a data synopsis to the *DS Manager* component. For the *Reports Browser*, it provides real analyses, by translating the query into SQL statements and executing them against the DW.

(ii) DS Manager is the basic component that executes a twofold task: the generation of the data synopsis and its extraction during the approximate query analysis. As already stated, when it stores the reduced data in the DS database, it also stores further metadata about the used DW (*i.e.*, which tables and attributes of the DW the user selected for the multi-dimensional analysis). These metadata will be used later by the *Analysis Environment* component. In the generation process, it takes the data stored in the DW and generates the data synopsis, according to data reduction parameters on the set of attributes specified by the user. It requires a reading-access to the DW and performs a writing-access to the Repository via the *DB Bridge* component. Notice that this component implements the data reduction process on the basis of the underlying methodology.

(iii) Approximate Query Engine is the most important component that executes analytical queries in an approximate way. To this end, it performs a read-access to the DS database to load the data synopsis relative to tables and attributes involved in the user query. Finally, it executes the query very quickly, using only that data synopsis. This component implements the query processing according to the adopted methodology. To evaluate the performance of these engines, metrics have been defined recently to measure the answering time and approximation error (Di Tria, Lefons, & Tangorra, 2012, 2015).

Data Layer contains the components for the management of the system databases.

(i) DB Bridge is the component that manages the physical connections towards the databases. As it must ensure access independence from the database technology, it is based on an ODBC connection for general purpose. Its task is to handle both the Data Warehouse, that represents the read-only data source, and the system repository, where all the computed data are stored. The data extracted from the Data Warehouse are the data stored in tables, and the metadata (*e.g.*, table's names, field's names, and data types) providing information about the data model of the Data Warehouse itself.

3.2 Metadata Representation

The meta-model depicted in Figure 3 describes the structure we defined for representing the metadata needed by approximate query answering systems. Such a meta-model is based on the standard meta-models provided in the CWM (Object Management Group [OMG], 2003). The figure reports the main classes and relationships for creating standard metadata that can be effectively used by Approximate Query Answering systems, in order to trace the data reduction process and to support analytical processing.

It is worth noting that this meta-model depends on (a) the CWM Relational meta-model, which is devoted to define the metadata for describing the data warehouse logical model, and (b) the CWM Core meta-model, which creates meta-objects representing descriptors to be attached to each model element (that is, an element of the database being modelled).

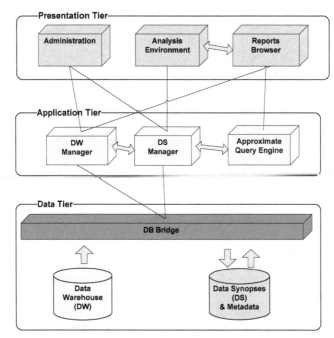

Figure 2. Architecture of the approximate query answering system

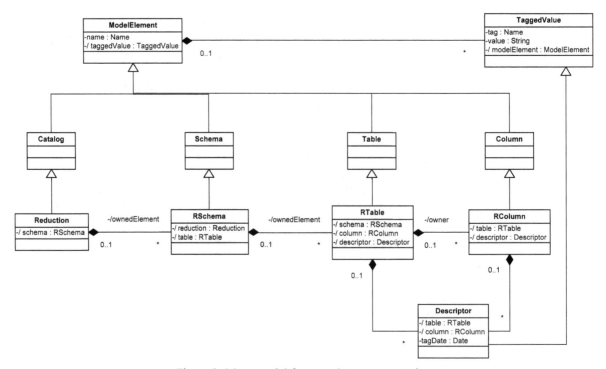

Figure 3. Meta-model for metadata representation

The main classes are summarized in Table 1. According to the meta-model, each element of the target system is represented by a meta-object. The steps for the creation of the meta-objects are:

- In order to represent the physical database, a meta-object of the class *Reduction* is created. The name of this object is the Data Source Name (DSN) used for the physical connection to the database;

- For each relational schema chosen for the data reduction, a meta-object of the class *RSchema* is created. This object has the same name as the relational database and a reference to the catalogue of membership;

- For each table of a relational schema chosen for the data reduction, a meta-object of the class *RTable* is created. This object has the same name as the table and a reference to the schema of membership;

- For each column of a table chosen for the data reduction, a meta-object of the class *RColumn* is created. This object has the same name as the column of that table and a reference to the table of membership; and

- If a table or a column must be tagged, then a meta-object of the class *Descriptor* is created. The name of this new object is unconstrained. Furthermore, it presents reference to the model element of membership.

Table 1. Meta-model classes

Class	Definition
ModelElement	Element that is an abstraction drawn from the system being modelled.
TaggedValue	Information attached to a model element in the form "tagged value" pair; that is, *name = value*.
Catalogue	Unit of logon and identification. It also identifies the scope of SQL statements: the tables contained in a catalogue can be used in a single SQL statement.
Schema	Named collection of tables. It collects all tables of the relational schema (*i.e.*, the logical database).
Table	Data structure representing a relation.
Column	Data structure representing the field of a relation.
Reduction	Class representing a process of reduction of the data stored in a relational database.
RSchema	Class representing a relational schema chosen for the data reduction.
RTable	Class representing a table chosen for the data reduction.
RColumn	Class representing a column whose data have been reduced.
Descriptor	Tag that can be attached to any element of the model.

4. The ADAP System

In dell'Aquila, Lefons, & Tangorra (2004), we faced the necessity to integrate the approximate query processing in a Web-based Decision Support System. In this section, we present the system used for the approximate query answering. The system uses the 'Canonical Coefficients' methodology that is based on orthonormal series. This methodology represents the theoretical base of the software tool presented here. In detail, the methodology is based on the statistical data profile, which serves to summarize information about the multi-dimensional data distribution of relations, and uses the polynomial approximation provided by Legendre orthogonal series.

The software that implements this methodology is the so-called *Analytical Data Profiling* (ADAP) System. ADAP is an OLAP tool, whose features are to collect, to organize, and to process large data volumes stored in a DW, in order to obtain statistical data profiles to use for approximate query processing. The data profile offers a way to compute aggregate functions fast as an alternative to accessing the DW.

The Canonical Coefficients is the data synopsis calculated by ADAP in the data reduction process on the basis of the algorithm given in Lefons *et al.* (1995), according to a *degree of approximation* and relative to the set of attributes specified by the user. When ADAP needs to calculate/update the Canonical Coefficients, it executes read-only access to the DW.

The query result is obtained in constant time, since it does not depend on the cardinality of the tables of the DW, but it relies only on the Canonical Coefficients, whose cardinality is known *a priori*.

Moreover, the software has been developed according to a modular design, in order to allow the add-in of other features, not yet implemented. It represents the OLAP tool that allows users to perform approximate query processing on a DW, managed by an OLAP Server. The ADAP system implements the three-layer architecture depicted in Figure 2.

ADAP generates three kinds of chart: lines, histograms, and gauge charts. A graphic representation of the output consists of the visualization of a chart that allows the user to easily interpret query answers.

Really, the cost for the computation of the canonical coefficients is very high. For this reason, an extended, distributed architecture of ADAP includes a parallel algorithm to compute the Canonical Coefficients (dell'Aquila, Di Tria, Lefons, & Tangorra, 2010).

As concerns the metadata, ADAP stores information about which tables have been reduced and what approximation degree of Legendre series has been utilized, along the min-max values of domains of the relation attributes.

4.1 User Interface

Figure 4 shows the user interface of ADAP that allows administrators to define which tables and columns are to be involved in the data reduction. First of all, an ODBC connection must be established. Then, the administrator can analyze the schema of the selected database, that is, the list of tables' names and their columns' names. At this point, the administrator has only to select the table and to choose its opportune columns to be considered for data reduction.

Once the input data are specified, the data reduction process generates the set of canonical coefficients, according to the approximation degree chosen by the user. The computed coefficients are then stored in the repository managed by ADAP.

ADAP system needs to trace also (a) the minimum and the maximum of each column, and (b) the number of rows of each table, as these data will be used by the algorithms performing the analytical processing based on approximate responses.

Finally, based on the list of which data have been reduced and then effectively available for approximate query processing, the user can create queries and execute them in order to obtain (approximate) query answers (*cf.*, the query processing interface in Figure 5).

4.2 Advanced Features

In addition to the fundamental features related to the basic methodology, ADAP has the following further features:

SQL Generator

When the user requires real values instead of approximate ones, ADAP traduces the aggregate query into an SQL instruction and passes it to the DBMS that manages the DW. The kind of queries supported by ADAP is of the following form, expressed according to the Backus-Naur Form:

```
    <aggregate query> ::= SELECT <aggregate function> FROM <relation>
                          WHERE <conditions>;
 <aggregate function> ::= <function>(<field>)
          <function> ::= SUM | AVG | COUNT
          <relation> ::= table_name
             <field> ::= field_name
        <conditions> ::= <condition> | <conditions> <logical operator> <conditions>
         <condition> ::= <field> | <relational operator> <comparison term>
   <comparison term> ::= numeric_constant
 <relational operator> ::= <= | >=
    <logical operator> ::= AND | OR
```

Dashboard

For providing support in decision making on the basis of a set of *key performance indicator*s (Scheer & Nüttgens, 2000), the *Report Browser* component is equipped with a dashboard creator. The dashboard is a useful Business Intelligence tool, able to represent data in a very synthetic way, that contains all the elements really necessary for the business performance reporting process (Palpanas, Chowdhary, Mihaila, & Pinel, 2007). In the user interface, the indicators are visualized with a graphical support, represented by gauges, lines, and histograms charts. A gauge is a chart that shows a single scalar value, aggregated on an interval. A red traffic light indicates whether this value is out of a predetermined range, meaning that it represents a critical value. Histogram is a chart that shows a set of aggregate values. A lines chart is used for monitoring the trend of a value in a given period of time. The graphical user interface of the dashboard is shown in Figure 6.

Figure 4. Administration interface

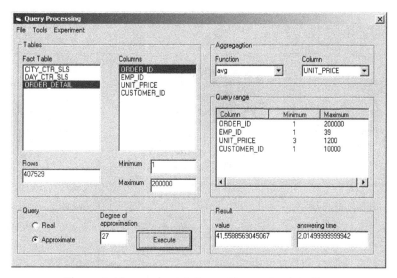

Figure 5. (Approximate) Query Processing interface

5. Experimental Set-Up

The data warehouse chosen for the experimentation is the multi-dimensional database distributed with the MicroStrategy Business Intelligence Platform. It contains real data about a fictitious e-commerce company, that sells retail electronics items, books, music and film CDs. The historical data stored in the database cover years 2002 to 2003. For the case study, we considered the relation *order_detail*, whose logical schema is shown in Figure 7. It is a fact table containing data about the sold items, and its cardinality is about 400 000 records.

For the analytical process, we defined the following three metrics as business indicators:

1) *sum(unit_price)*,
2) *avg(unit_price)*,
3) *count(orderID)*,

and we chose to aggregate the data of the fact table according to the following three dimensions:

1) *order*,
2) *employ*,
3) *customer*.

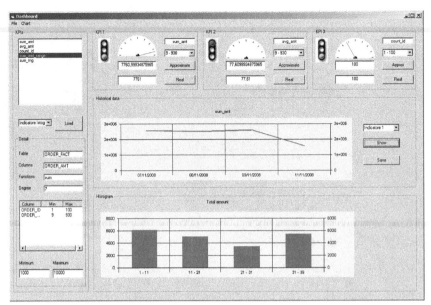

Figure 6. ADAP Dashboard

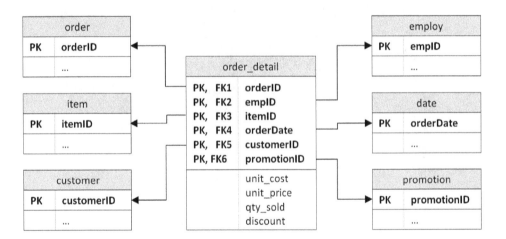

Figure 7. Part of the logical schema of the experiment DW

Accordingly, the Canonical Coefficients have been generated on the schema R(*orderID*, *empID*, *customerID*, *unit_price*), corresponding to a view on the *order_detail* relation.

5.1 Experimental Plan

We divided the experiment into three sections I, II and III: in each section, we calculated the three metrics, for a total of nine launches (*see*, Table 2). In the first section, we created the queries generating random intervals on *orderID*. In the second section, we generated random intervals on *orderID* and *empID*. In the third section, we generated random intervals on *orderID*, *empID*, and *customerID*.

Random intervals were generated according to given widths. For example, if *min*(*orderID*) = 1 and *max*(*orderID*) = 50, then possible random intervals, which accord to the chosen widths, are shown in Table 3. Note that, in the first row, (3, 48) is an interval of width equals to the 90% of the original interval.

For each launch, we calculated:

- the error between the real value and the approximate one, and
- the difference between the response time for obtaining the real value and that for the approximate value

by varying the interval width and the approximation degree.

Table 2. Experimental plan

Experiment	aggregation/grouping Attribute	metrics		
		SUM (*unit_price*)	AVG (*unit_price*)	COUNT (*orderID*)
Section I	*orderID*	*cf,* Figure 8a	*cf,* Figure 8b	*cf,* Figure 8c
Section II	*orderID, empID*	*cf,* Figure 9a	*cf,* Figure 9b	*cf,* Figure 9c
Section III	*orderID, empID, customerID*	*cf,* Figure 10a	*cf,* Figure 10b	*cf,* Figure 10c

Table 3. Random interval sample

Width (%)	Absolute width	Random interval (*inf, sup*)
90	45	(3, 48)
80	40	(2, 42)
70	35	(6, 41)
60	30	(20, 50)
50	25	(17, 42)
40	20	(12, 32)
30	15	(29, 44)
20	10	(26, 36)
10	5	(19, 24)

Given an aggregate function and one or more attributes, the pseudo-code of Algorithm 1 describes a single query launch, where each query is repeated z times.

Algorithm 1. Query launch (pseudo-code)

```
W = {90%, 50%, 10%}  // set of the width
maxdegree = 27        // approximation degree
z = 100               // number of repetitions of the query

for each x in W
    for i = 1 to maxdegree
        for j = 1 to z
            generate a random interval of width x for the selected field(s)
            calculate real_v as the real value
            calculate real_t as the response time for the real value
            calculate appr_v as the approximate value
            calculate appr_t as the response time for the approximate value
        next j
        calculate δ_v as the mean value of (real_v - appr_v)
        calculate δ_t as the mean value of (real_t - appr_t)
    next i
next x
```

5.2 Experimental Results

Each experiment consists of a query launch that calculates the mean relative error and the mean response time, at the varying of three kinds of query range width (namely 90%, 50%, and 10%) and the approximation degree 1 to 27. Therefore, for each query launch, two charts had produced and each chart shows the trend of three functions.

Figure 8a reports the charts of the relative error and response time of the first experiment relative to the first metrics *sum(unit_price)* and random query ranges generated on the (domain of) attribute *orderID*. This experiment shows that the first function—the one related to the 90% width—has a very low relative error, even if a low degree of approximation is used. On the other hand, the relative error tends to increase as the interval width decreases. In fact, for the interval width of 10% (that is, the third function), the degree of approximation must be greater than 10 in order to obtain good approximate answer to queries.

Figure 8a also reports the trend of the response time calculated as the difference between the time required for obtaining the real answer and the response time for the computing the approximate one. The chart shows that the difference tends to decrease in favour of the real value as the degree of approximation increases. In fact, the higher the degree, the more coefficients are (loaded and) used by the system for computing answers. Moreover, the third function has lower response times than the others because it corresponds to a low selectivity factor and, then, the query optimizers of DBMSs allow performing a strong filtering of data before the computation starts (Jarke & Koche, 1984). As a consequence, the response time difference between the real value and the approximate one is lower than usual whenever the interval width is small.

The results of the first experiment were confirmed by the similar second one, relative to the metrics *avg(unit_price)*. In fact, Figure 8b shows that the performance of the AVERAGE algorithm is quite similar to the SUM algorithm as concerns both the relative error and the response time.

relative error: (*real* − *approx*)/*real*   Δ-response time: (time$_{real}$ − time$_{approx}$) sec.   (*)

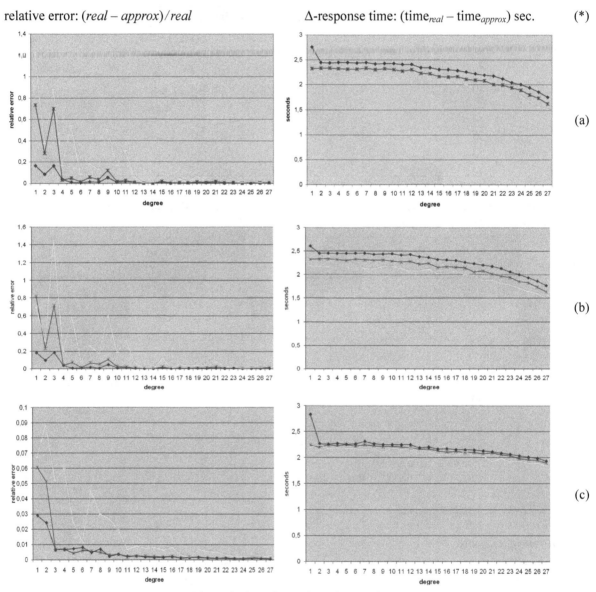

Figure 8. Experimental results: Section I

(*) *Legend.*
    Aggregation by (*orderID*) attribute.
    Interval width: ━◆━ 90%,   ━✳━ 50%,   ──── 10%.
    Metrics: (a) SUM(*unit_price*); (b) AVG(*unit_price*); (c) COUNT(*orderID*).

In the third similar experiment, the metrics measured was *count(orderID)*. This experiment, summarized in Figure 8c, shows that the relative error in the computation of the COUNT algorithm is generally very low, although the third function reports an error considerably greater than the others. The response time chart is coherent with the previous ones.

The next three experiments measured the same metrics respectively, but involved the generation of random intervals on both attributes *orderID* and *empID*, and they are summarized in Figure 9. The charts in Figures 9a-b highlight that both SUM and AVERAGE algorithms determined very high relative errors whenever the interval width is small. This trend did not change even if a high degree of approximation is used. Approximate values were only acceptable in case of wide interval widths and approximation degrees greater than 8. The response time charts showed that the distances among the three functions are more evident, because the query optimizers work well as concerns the selectivity of two (or more) attributes. However, the response time for approximate answers is lower than for the real ones, since the functions were not negative.

relative error: $(real - approx)/real$ Δ-response time: $(time_{real} - time_{approx})$ sec.   (*)

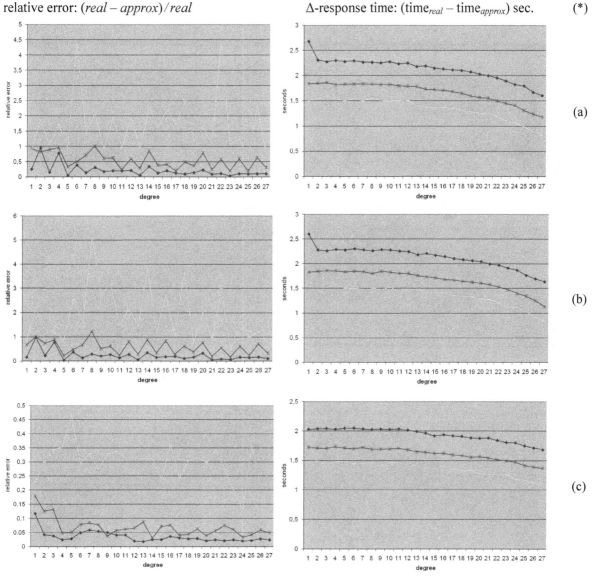

Figure 9. Experimental results: Section II

(*) *Legend.*
      Aggregation by (*ordered, empID*) attributes.
      Interval width: ⬥ 90%,   ✳ 50%,   10%.
      Metrics: (a) SUM(*unit_price*); (b) AVG(*unit_price*); (c) COUNT(*orderID*).

As concerns the COUNT algorithm, the charts in Figure 9c showed that the relative error is quite acceptable in every case, although the third function had always the greatest relative error. The response time was in line with the previous ones.

At last, the next three experiments regarded the same three metrics, but involved the generation of random intervals on attributes *orderID*, *empID*, and *customerID*. As concerns the relative error, the charts of Figure 10 confirmed the results of the previous experiment. On the other hand, relative to the response time of the SUM and the AVERAGE algorithms, Figures 10a-b showed that the function is negative when the interval width is 10% and the degree of approximation is greater than 19. The negative function means that the response time of the approximate answer is greater than the one of the real value. On the other hand, the chart in Figure 10c showed that the approximation degree should be greater than 24 for the COUNT algorithm in order to have a negative function.

relative error: (*real – approx*) / *real*   Δ-response time: (time$_{real}$ – time$_{approx}$) sec.   (*)

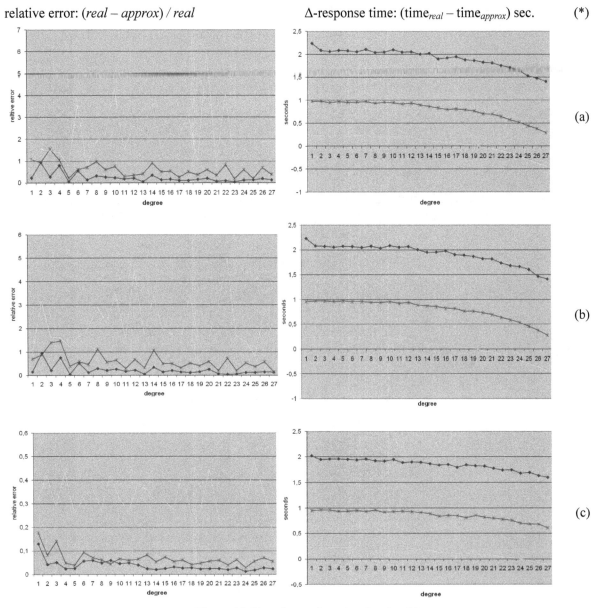

Figure 10. Experimental results: Section III

(*) *Legend.*
    Aggregation by (*ordered, empID, customerID*) attributes.
    Interval width: ◆ 90%, ✳ 50%, ─── 10%.
    Metrics: (a) SUM(*unit_price*); (b) AVG(*unit_price*); (c) COUNT(*orderID*).

To summarize, the evaluation of the system allows us to state that the best performance is gained with analytical queries relative to intervals with wide ranges. In this case, a low degree of approximation suffices and, therefore, the response time is very low. Furthermore, *sum* and the *average* functions exhibit the same trend, but the *count* function always performs better than the others two.

6. Conclusions

In this paper, we have presented the architecture of approximate query answering systems, showing also the meta-model for the representation of metadata. This meta-model is general and methodology-independent. Therefore, it is possible to apply the architecture and the meta-model to every methodology by only creating both the opportune components and necessary metadata.

Furthermore, we have presented the ADAP system, which implements this architecture. The system methodology is based on orthonormal series. Then, the data synopsis is represented by a set of polynomials coefficients and the approximate query engine adopts the Canonical Coefficients methodology.

The system can be used in decision making process as a tool able to perform analytical processing in a fast manner. Experimental results showed that generally the approximation error relies in an acceptable range and that the ADAP approximate query answering system can effectively be considered a valid OLAP tool, whenever decision makers do not need total precision in answers but prefer to obtain reliable responses in short times. In this way, response times remain almost constant as they do not depend on the cardinality of the DW tables but only on that of the computed synopses, whose cardinality is known *a-priori*.

References

Abad-Mota, S. (1992). Approximate query processing with summary tables in statistical databases. In A. Pirotte, C. Delobel, & G. Gottlob (Eds.), *Advances in Database Technology: Proceedings of EDBT '92* (pp. 499-515). Lecture Notes in Computer Science, vol. 580. http://dx.doi.org/10.1007/BFb0032451

Acharya, S., Gibbons, P. B., Poosala, V., & Ramaswamy, S. (1999). Join synopses for approximate query answering. *SIGMOD '99: Proceedings of the 1999 ACM SIGMOD International conference on Management of data, 28*(2), 275-286. http://dx.doi.org/10.1145/304181.304207

Chakrabarti, K., Garofalakis, M., Rastogi, R., & Shim, K. (2000). Approximate query processing using wavelets. *Proceedings of the 26th VLDB conference* (pp.111-122). Cairo, Egypt. http://research.microsoft.com/pubs /79079/wavelet_query_processing.pdf

Chaudhuri, S., Das, G., & Narasayya, V. (2007). Optimized stratified sampling for approximate query processing. *ACM Transactions on Database Systems, 32*(2). http://dx.doi.org/10.1145/1242524.1242526

Chaudhuri, S., Dayal, U., & Ganti, V. (2001). Database technology for decision support systems. *Computer, 34*(12), 48-55. http://dx.doi.org/10.1109/2.970575

Cochran, W. G. (1977). *Sampling Techniques.* John Wiley & Sons.

Cormode, G., Garofalakis, M., Haas, P. J., & Jermaine, C. (2011). Synopses for massive data: Samples, histograms, wavelets, sketches. *Foundations and Trends® in Databases, 4*(1-3), 1-294. http://dx.doi.org /10.1561/1900000004

Cortés-Calabuig, A., Denecker, M., Arieli, O., & Bruynooghe, M. (2007). Approximate query answering in locally closed databases. In R. C. Holte, & A. Hawe (Eds.), *Proceedings of the 22nd National conference on Artificial intelligence, vol.1,* 397-402. https://www.aaai.org/Papers/AAAI/2007/AAAI07-062.pdf

Cuzzocrea, A. (2009). Histogram-based compression of databases and data cubes. In J. Erickson (Ed.), *Database Technologies: Concepts, Methodologies, Tools, and Applications,* 165-178. http://dx.doi.org/10.4018/978-1 -60566-058-5.ch011

dell'Aquila, C., Di Tria, F., Lefons, E., & Tangorra, F. (2010). A Parallel Algorithm to Compute Data Synopsis. *Wseas Transactions on Information Science and Applications, 7*(5), 691-701. http://www.wseas.us/e-library /transactions/information/2010/89-536.pdf

dell'Aquila, C., Lefons, E., & Tangorra, F. (2004). Approximate query processing in decision support system environment. *Wseas Transactions on Computers, 3*(3), 581-586. http://citeseerx.ist.psu.edu/viewdoc /summary?doi=10.1.1.363.2342

Deshpande, A., Guestrin, C., Madden, S. R., Hellerstein, J. M., & Hong, W. (2004). Model-driven data acquisition in sensor networks. *Proceedings of the 30th VLDB conference* (pp. 588-599). Toronto, Canada. http://db.csail.mit.edu/madden/html/vldb04.pdf

Di Tria, F., Lefons, E., & Tangorra, F. (2012). Metrics for approximate query engine evaluation. *SAC '12 Proceedings of the ACM Symposium on Applied Computing* (pp. 885-887). http://dx.doi.org/10.1145

/2245276.2245448

Di Tria, F., Lefons, E., & Tangorra, F. (2014). Big data warehouse automatic design methodology. In W. C. Hu, & N. Kaabouch (Eds.), *Big Data Management, Technologies, and Applications* (pp. 115-149). Hershey, PA: Information Science Reference. http://dx.doi.org/10.4018/978-1-4666-4699-5.ch006

Di Tria, F., Lefons, E., & Tangorra, F. (2015). Benchmark for approximate query answering systems. *Journal of Database Management (JDM), 26*(1), 1-29. http://dx.doi.org/10.4018/JDM.2015010101

Furtado, P., & Madeira, H. (1999). Analysis of accuracy of data reduction techniques. In M. Mohania, & M. A. Tjoa (Eds.), *Proceedings of the First International conference on Data Warehousing and Knowledge Discovery* (pp. 377-388). Lectures Notes in Computer Science, vol. 1676. http://dx.doi.org/10.1007/3-540-48298-9_40

Gibbons, P. B., Poosala, V., Acharya, S., Bartal, Y., Matias, Y., Muthukrishnan, S., ... Suel, T. (1998a). AQUA: System and techniques for approximate query answering. *Tech. Report*, 1998. Murray Hill, New Jersey, U.S.A.. http://citeseerx.ist.psu.edu/viewdoc/download?doi=10.1.1.207.344&rep=rep1&type=pdf

Gibbons, P. B., & Matias, Y. (1998b). New sampling-based summary statistics for improving approximate query answers. *Proceedings of the 1998 ACM SIGMOD International conference on Management of data* (pp. 331-342). Seattle, Washington, United States. http://dx.doi.org/10.1145/276305.276334

Golfarelli, M., & Rizzi, S. (1998a). A methodological framework for data warehousing design. *DOLAP '98 Proceedings of the 1st ACM International workshop on Data warehousing and OLAP* (pp. 3-9). http://dx.doi.org/10.1145/294260.294261

Golfarelli, M., Maio, D., & Rizzi, S. (1998b). The dimensional fact model: A conceptual model for data warehouses. *International Journal of Cooperative Information Systems, 7*(2-3), 215-247. http://dx.doi.org/10.1142/S0218843098000118

Gupta, A., Harinarayan, V., & Quaas, D. (1995). Aggregate-query processing in data warehousing environments. *Proceedings of the 21st VLDB conference* (pp.358-369). Zurich, Switzerland. http://www.vldb.org/conf/1995/P358.PDF

Hou, W.C., Luo, C., Jiang, Z., Yan, F., & Zhu, Q. (2008). Approximate range-sum queries over data cubes using cosine transform. In S. S. Bhowmick, J. Küng, & R. Wagner (Eds.), *Proceedings of the 19th International conference on Database and Expert Systems Applications* (pp. 376-389). Lecture Notes in Computer Science, vol. 5181. http://dx.doi.org/10.1007/978-3-540-85654-2_35

Ioannidis, Y., & Poosala, V. (1999). Histogram-based approximation of set-valued query answers. *Proceedings of the 25th VLDB conference* (pp. 174-185). Edinburgh, Scotland. http://www.madgik.di.uoa.gr/sites/default/files/vldb99_pp174-185.pdf

Jarke, M., & Koche, J. (1984). Query optimization in database systems. *ACM Computing Surveys, 16*(2), 111-152. http://dx.doi.org/10.1145/356924.356928

Jermaine, C., Arumugam, S., Pol, A., & Dobra, A. (2008). Scalable approximate query processing with the DBO engine. *ACM Transactions on Database Systems, 33*(4). http://dx.doi.org/10.1145/1412331.1412335

Khurana, U., Parthasarathy, S., & Turaga, D. (2014). FAQ: Framework for fast approximate query processing on temporal data. *Proceedings of the 3rd International workshop on Big Data, Streams and Heterogeneous Source Mining: Algorithms, Systems, Programming Models and Applications,* BigMine 2014 (pp.29-45). New York City, USA. http://dx.doi.org/10.1145/1412331.1412335

Lefons, E., Merico, A., & Tangorra, F. (1995). Analytical profile estimation in database systems. *Information Systems, 20*(1), 1-20. http://dx.doi.org/10.1016/0306-4379(95)00001-K

Object Management Group (OMG), *Common Warehouse Metamodel (CWM) specification, vers. 1.1, vol. 1,* OMG, Needham, MA USA, 2003. http://www.omg.org/spec/CWM/1.1/PDF/

Palpanas, T., & Velegrakis, Y. (2012). dbTrento: the data and information management group at the University of Trento. *ACM SIGMOD Record, 41*(3), 28-33. http://dx.doi.org/10.1145/2380776.2380784

Palpanas, T., Chowdhary, P., Mihaila, G., & Pinel, F. (2007). Integrated model-driven dashboard development. *Information Systems Frontiers, 9*(2-3), 195-208. http://dx.doi.org/10.1007/s10796-007-9032-9

Peltzer, J. B., Teredesai, A., & Reinard, G. (2006). AQUAGP: Approximate query answers using genetic programming. *Proceedings of the 9th European conference on Genetic Programming* (pp. 49-60). Lecture

Notes in Computer Science, vol. 3905. http://link.springer.com/chapter/10.1007%2F11729976_5

Sacharidis, D. (2006). Constructing optimal wavelet synopses. In T. Grust *et al.* (Eds.), *Current Trends in Database Technology: Proceedings of EDBT 2006* (pp. 97-104). Lecture Notes in Computer Science, vol. 4254. http://dx.doi.org/10.1007/11896548_10

Sassi, M., Tlili, O., & Ounelli, H. (2012). Approximate query processing for database flexible querying with aggregates. In A. Hameurlai, A. Küng, & J. Wagner (Eds.), *Transactions on Large-Scale Data- and Knowledge-Centered Systems V* (pp. 1-27). Lecture Notes in Computer Science, vol. 7100. http://dx.doi.org/10.1007/978-3-642-28148-8_1

Scheer, A. W., & Nüttgens, M. (2000). ARIS Architecture and reference models for business process management. In W. Aalst, J. Desel, & A. Oberweis (Eds.), *Business Process Management* (pp. 376-389). Lecture Notes in Computer Science, vol. 1806, 2002. http://dx.doi.org/10.1007/3-540-45594-9_24

Spiegel, J., & Polyzotis, N. (2006). Graph-based synopses for relational selectivity estimation. *SIGMOD '06 Proceedings of the 2006 ACM SIGMOD International conference on Management of data* (pp. 205-216). http://dx.doi.org/10.1145/1142473.1142497

Yan, F., Hou, W. C., Jiang, Z., Luo, C., & Zhu, Q. (2007). Selectivity estimation of range queries based on data density approximation via cosine series. *Data & Knowledge Engineering, 63*(3), 855-878. http://dx.doi.org/10.1016/j.datak.2007.05.003

9

Transforming Governance through Mobile Technology in Developing Nations

Simon M Karume[1]

[1] Department of Computing and Informatics , Laikipia University, Nyahururu, Kenya

Correspondence: Simon M Karume, Department of Computing and Informatics , Laikipia University, Nyahururu, Kenya. E-mail: smkarume@gmail.com

Abstract

Increasing penetration of mobile broadband as opposed to fixed broadband in developing nations like Kenya has spurred an extra ordinary uptake of mobile phones in these countries. This has presented a mobile opportunity to public institutions to devise innovative ways of providing access to public information and delivering services. This paper seeks to demonstrate the role played by mobile broadband technology transform governance by providing access to public information and services. A desk methodology was used to gather secondary data related to adoption of mobile phones as a tool for delivering government services in Kenya. Findings indicate that increasing penetration of broadband technology resulted to increased number of government services offered via mobile phones.

Keywords: connectivity, fixed broadband, mobile broadband, e-Governance, m-Governance, m-Opportunity

1. Introduction

Contrary to fixed broadband whose penetration rate has remained low in developing nations, mobile broadband has penetrated rapidly resulting to speedy uptake of mobile phone (ITU, 2012; ITU & OECD, 2011). This scenario provides a splendid opportunity for public institutions in developing nations to offer more responsive public services by innovatively exploiting mobile applications and solutions. For instance, Kenya, which has historically been limited by poor communications infrastructure, that has in turn inhibited social improvement and economic growth, has realized noteworthy progress in mobile broadband penetration. This has resulted to rapid adoption of mobile phones leading to a rise in its use in various sectors other than for social life (Crandall, 2011).

Mobile phones are an important consideration for development because of the benefits offered such as mobility and security to owners (Donner, 2004). Due to their unique characteristics of working using the radio spectrum, mobile phones do not need to rely on physical infrastructure such as phone wires and roads and base-stations can be powered using their own generators in places where there is no electrical grid. Mobile phones only require basic literacy, and therefore are accessible to a large portion of the population (Masuki et al., 2010). Since mobile phones are progressively more affordable to the population of lower strata, they can therefore be used as a mechanism for ensuring greater participation of the groups in the process of development (Rashid & Elder , 2009). In addition, mobile phone coverage has been associated with developments in the job market. The CCK, 2008 recommended that the rise of formal employment in the private and telecommunication sector from by 130% between 2003 and 2007 may be associated with mobile phone penetration (CCK, 2008).

2. Problem Statement

Electronic governance is recognized as an effective tool to bring about 'simple, moral, accountable, responsive and transparent' (SMART) governance (Heeks, 2001; Budhiraja, 2003). However, electronic governance has not proven to be the ultimate solution to governance challenges in Africa since infrastructure required for the connection is largely fixed broadband which is expensive to the low strata population (Harris, 2004). Furthermore penetration rate of fixed broadband has remained low thereby presenting an opportunity for mobile broadband to fill the connectivity void (ITU, 2012). Following the promising takeoff of mobile broadband in developing nations, it is expected to transform governance and support growth in the economy more than fixed broadband has done For instance, according to ITU (2012), mobile broadband has been driving financial inclusion through mobile banking and mobile money in Africa, and it supports new ways of delivering healthcare in many developing nations.

3. The Mobile Opportunity in Kenya

The fast rate of penetration of mobile phones in developing nations has presented these countries with a grand opportunity to leapfrog in adoption of mobile technologies in their governance structure. This is demonstrated by the fact that governments of developing nations are implementing mobile technology solutions to better deliver government services to the public. Mobile phone penetration rate is a term generally used to describe the number of active mobile beyond 100% due the fact that one person can have more than one SIM-card. This can be noted from countries like Qatar which has 170% and most of Europe with 128% (Langat et al., 2015). According to a study by Mulas (2012), it is estimated that broadband are growing faster in the developing world with a compound average growth rate of over 200% since 2009. However, fixed broadband penetration remains very low in Africa with an estimated penetration of only 0.2% by the end of 2011 (ITU, 2012). According to Lee et al. (2011), initially, mobile broadband complemented fixed broadband but technological progress in mobile broadband has gradually resulted to substitution of fixed broadband by mobile broadband.

Kenya is one of the countries experiencing the highest smart phone growth rate as well as Internet penetration rate in Sub- Saharan Africa. Data from a broadband sector report by ITU show that while the number of fixed telephone lines in Kenya has been decreasing, the number of Mobile cellular subscriptions have been increasing between the years 2002 and 2013 as shown in Table 1 and Figure 1 (ITU, 2015). The proportion of households with fixed broad band decreased between the year 2007 and 2012 but the number of households accessing internet via mobile phones increased

Table 1. number of fixed lines vs. number of mobile subscriptions in Kenya (Source: ITU, 2015)

Year	no of mobile subscriptions	no of fixed telephone lines
2002	1,187,122	321,482
2003	1,590,785	328,358
2004	2,546,157	299,255
2005	4,611,970	286,729
2006	7,340,317	293,364
2007	11,349,412	463,766
2008	16,303,573	646,356
2009	19,364,559	664,099
2010	24,968,891	380,748
2011	28,080,771	283,546
2012	30,731,754	251,567
2013	31,830,003	204,354

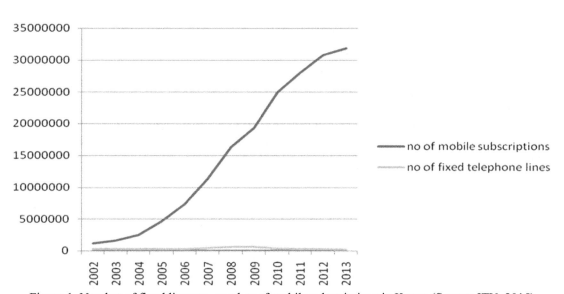

Figure 1. Number of fixed lines vs. number of mobile subscriptions in Kenya (Source: ITU, 2015)

By the year 2015 there were more than 7 billion mobile cellular subscriptions worldwide, up from less than 1 billion in 2000. Globally 3.2 billion people were using the Internet of which 2 billion were from developing countries (ITU, 2015). According to CCK, at the end of June 2011, Kenya had 25.27 million mobile subscribers (CCK, 2011). Kenya's high mobile subscription number indicated that mobile technology was a promising business opportunity, and an indispensible tool for empowering the country's citizens. Mobile penetration in Kenya between May 2009 and March 2010 as recorded by the Communications Commission of Kenya is shown in Figure 2 (CCK, 2010).

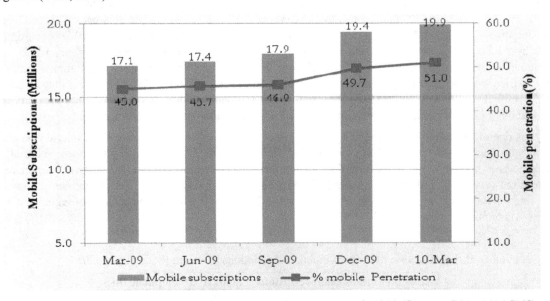

Figure 2. Mobile Penetration in Kenya between May 2009 and March 2010 (Source: CCK, 2010 [18])

The statistics presented above provides a splendid opportunity for the Civil Society and Government agencies to explore the utilization of the mobile / wireless applications to improve access to public services, including electronic government services, to those who can afford to use a personal or shared mobile phone.

4. Justification for Adoption of m-Governance to Complement e-Governance

e-Governance entails application of ICTs in delivery of government services. Advancement of computer networks from intranets to the Internet has played a major role in revolutionizing how governments operate worldwide by creating a wealth of new digital connections within and without government. These connections facilitate governance in the following three main domains of e-governance, illustrated in Figure 1

- Improving government processes: e-Administration
- Connecting citizens: e-Citizens and e-Services
- Building interactions with and within civil society: e-Society

As illustrated in Figure 3, below for e-Governance to succeed an efficient network is a necessity. This implies that broadband connectivity is an essential ingredient of e-Governance. However as observed by ITU (2012) , fixed broadband penetration remains very low in Africa with an estimated penetration of only 0.2% by the end of 2011. For developing nations, rural connectivity challenges has for a long time hindered the progression and adoption of e-Governance.

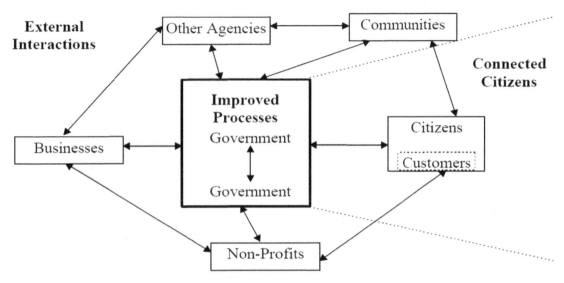

Figure 3. Focal domains of e-Governance initiatives

According to the ITU (2011), the total number of mobile users worldwide as of late 2006 was about 2.7 billion and the number of internet users was just above 1.1 billion. This means that there is at least 23.6% of world population (and at least 22.2% of developing countries population but in reality more) who already have mobile phones but are not yet using the Internet. This situation is illustrated in Figure 4. The situation as presented provide a strong case for leveraging the mobile channel to dramatically improve access to public services, including electronic government services, to those who can afford to use a personal or shared mobile phone (e.g., Village Phone). This creates an opportunity to connect in the near future the next two billion people to some of the benefits of e-government, e-health, e-education, e-banking, e-commerce etc.

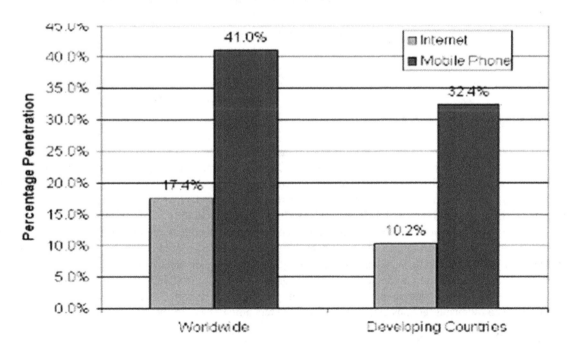

Figure 4. Internet connectivity vs. Mobile connectivity (ITU)

The implication of this scenario is that adoption of mobile phones in provision of government services can transform the lives of common people in developing countries significantly. The next section shows how the

Kenya government has leveraged mobile technology to extend the reach of e-Governance to its citizens.

5. Mobile Governance in Kenya

The Kenya government has made considerable effort to extend the reach of its e-governance services to its citizens by taking advantage of the high rate of penetration of mobile broadband. Several government services are available via mobile phones using short message service (SMS) and Unstructured Supplementary Service Data (USSD) codes. Some of these services are summarized in Table 2:

Table 2. M-services in government departments

Govt. body / parastatal	M-Services provided	USSD, SMS or paybill
Ministry of immigration	Check passport Status	Send tracking no. to 2030
	Check ID card Status	Send 1st 6 digits of waiting card to 2031
The Ministry of Education Science and Technology	Check kcse results via sms	Send index no to 22252
	Check school to Join	Send index no to 20042
Ministry of higher education (KUCCPS)	Degree or diploma course review	Paybill business no. 820201
	Informing successful applicants	sms sent to successful applicants
Kenya Power	e-bill via sms	Check bill by sending account to 95551
	pay bill via mpesa	Pay bill via business no. 888888
Teachers service commission	Inquiry services	Send querry to 5556
Credit reference beaural	Check credit status	SMS name to 21272 or 21CRB
Kenya Revenue Authority (KRA)	Domestic, custom, traffic revenue services	USSD: *572#, sms 22572
eCitizen	Access government services	Pay for government services via mpesa
National Hospital Insurance Fund (NHIF)	Check accounts contribution status	Accounts contribution status via sms
	Remitting NHIF contribution	Remitting NHIF contribution via M-pesa
Independent Elections and Boundaries Commission (IEBC)	Check registration details	sending their national ID card or passport number to 15872
	Transmitting Voting Station Results	Transmit results via sms

As can be observed in Table 2 above, the Kenyan government has adopted the use of mobile phones in provision of a variety of services ranging from enquiry services, online submission of tax returns, verification of credit status of persons etc. This reduces the amount of manpower wasted while travelling to government offices to seek for certain government services and may translate to more productive work. According to Bertot et al., (2010), mobile phone allow access to social site, thus, mobile and fixed line web-based social media in developing countries empower individuals and groups by supporting applications such as crowd sourcing, citizen reporting and education. Social media may also contribute to poverty eradication by facilitating sharing of information such as job opportunities and benefits advice; sharing of resources such as expertise, time and support and sharing of opportunities for capacity-building. Use of mobile technology can also reduce corruption and increase institutional transparency enabling the improvement in the effectiveness of state poverty reduction initiatives. The following sections discusses how mobile technology have impacted various sectors

5.1 Mobile Agriculture

A survey conducted by CountrySTAT indicated that majority of Kenyans (78.4 %) lived in rural areas (CountrySTAT Kenya, 2009). Mobile technology offer potential for rural communities to communicate and exchange information and has brought about revolutionization in the way of living among people, conducting of businesses and the social activities (Litondo et al., 2013). The authors further state that mobile phones have the potential to create wealth for the poor. This can only be made possible by the availability of the mobile phones together with the capability to use and adapt them which facilitates the generation and access of power, wealth and knowledge.

Initially, a major problem in many rural areas was that small entrepreneurs and farmers had no way of knowing prices before they travel to the market because of poor communication facilities (Rashid & Elder 2009). They had to rely on middlemen who took advantage of their ignorance. This is because small-scale farmers had poor market infrastructure, inadequate agricultural inputs and marketing experience (Munyua, 2007).

The adoption of mobile phones in agriculture positively impacted lives of farmers. This is due to the provision of timely information. According to Rashid and Elder (2009), accurate and timely market information, and that of perishable items in particular, significantly reduces travel, communication and transaction costs making agricultural extension activities more effective, which leads to extra efficient markets that can benefit both consumers and producers. A mechanism through which mobile phones lead to improved market efficiency is a change in the middlemen marketing behavior. The middlemen operating in mobile phone markets search in a greater number of markets sell in more markets and have more market contacts as compared to their non-mobile phone counterparts (Aker, 2011). By reducing communication costs, mobile phones may assist farmers in identifying potential buyers or facilitating the purchase of inputs in rural areas (Aker & Mbiti, 2011).

A study on fish prices by Jensen (2007) provides a strong evidence of the micro-economic impact of mobile phones where he states that the adoption of mobiles brought noteworthy and immediate reductions in the prices variability and the waste amount in the fishing system. Studies by Souter et al., (2005) and Donner, (2004) show greater use of mobile phone for social purposes and emergencies such as calling customers or suppliers which increased the response time. Mobile phones facilitate greater export orientation in agricultural practice and marketing, which potentially brings higher income for farmers (de Silva, 2008) .

A study of animal health workers and farmers in two districts in Kenya in 2007 acknowledged the mobile phone use for the identification and management of diseases in livestock and for coordinating better attendance and participation in organization meetings [29]. From the study, farmers indicated that mobile phones enabled the reduction of their transportation costs by helping them to gain remote access to group support and agricultural information. Also, the adoption of mobile phones by dairy farmers in rural areas highlighted mobile phones' ability to provide advantageous information and encourage greater efficiency. According to Brandie and Abbott (2011), mobile phones are used in agriculture for coordinating access to agricultural inputs, accessing market information, seeking agriculture emergency assistance, monitoring financial transactions and consulting with expert advice.

Muto and Yamano (2009), estimated the impact of mobile phones on agricultural markets in Uganda, focusing on farmers' market participation. Using a panel dataset on farm households between 2003 and 2005, they found out that mobile phone coverage was associated with a 10% increase in farmers' probability of market participation.

Mobile phones may also help with agricultural extension outreach (Crandall, 2011). Short Message Service (SMS) is a widely used application of mobile technology in agriculture (Gichamb etal., 2012) . The farmers can interact with experts and systems via SMS examples being to receive weather updates and information on best practices on various sectors of agriculture.

Also, the Sygenta Foundation established Kilimo Salama, a program that is aimed to support small scale farmers to deal with weather risks by developing and piloting agricultural micro insurance products (Webb, 2010). Murray (2010) presented a report on the impact of mobile technology on farmers through the Kenya Farmers Helpline. It is from the call center that agricultural experts talk to farmers from across the country where they address various issues regarding agriculture.

5.2 Health

Mobile devices facilitate the delivery of important health services in developing countries (Rashid & Elder, 2009). In fact, the mobile phones looked at as a more helpful technology for e-health because of their pervasiveness and relative affordability. Idowu et al. (2003) states that doctors use mobiles to communicate among themselves across different parts of a large hospital, and to take action to emergencies when offsite. Also, Lester et al. (2006) presents the mobile phones are used in facilitating flow of information for HIV AIDS intervention programs. Diverse efforts have been in place to exploit mobile technologies in health communication, including the collection of health data and provision of health information (Muheebwa, 2009). This has especially been applied in malaria and Human Immunodeficiency Virus/Acquired Immunodeficiency Syndrome (HIV/AIDS).

5.3 Disaster Management/Environmental Protection

Many developing countries experience natural disasters such as floods. Mobile technologies play an important role in disaster intervention as they can save critical time. LIRNEasia (2008), states that ICT tools can be used as a warning technology. Also, communication is vital in the ability of the strategy of the community in coping with disasters. Inadequate support during and after disaster events can significantly affect survival and livelihoods.

According to Aker and Mbiti (2010), Sub-Saharan Africa is an inherently risky environment since natural disasters, epidemics and conflicts routinely affect households. Kenya being in Sub-Saharan Africa, kinship ties play both important economic and social functions by creating informal insurance networks and increasing access to credit and savings while reducing the risk. Mobile phones allow households to obtain information about potential shocks, enabling them to use the information to make decisions concerning planting and harvesting, which can have important effects on yields (Aker & Mbiti 2010).

Mobile phones have been used in disaster management and rescue missions through the implementation of Ushahidi, a crowdsourcing system developed in Kenya (Gichamba et al., 2012). The platform is used in activities which include rescue missions and monitoring election violence worldwide. The information is then translated into a graphical map that may be viewed from anywhere over the Internet.

6. Conclusion

This paper set out to find out how mobile technology contributes to governance in Kenya. Findings indicate that the mobile phones are not only being adopted for social reasons, but is viewed as a tool to improve governance in various areas which include agriculture, health and many more. Generally, a mobile phone is viewed as a tool that allow for more efficient response to economic opportunities. This can only be achieved if basic knowledge on how to use the mobile device exist among the individuals in Kenya.

References

Afridi, A., (2011). Social networks: their role in addressing poverty. Report. Joseph Rowntree Foundation Programme Paper on Poverty and Ethnicity. York: Joseph Rowntree Foundation.

Aker, J. (2011). Dial A For Agriculture: a review of information and communication technologies for agricultural extension in developing countries. *Agricultural Economics,* 42(6), 631-647.

Aker, J. C., & Mbiti, I. M. (2010). Mobile Phones and Economic Development in Africa. *Journal of Economic Perspectives, 24*(3).

Bertot, J. C., Jaeger, P. T., & Grimes, J. M., (2010). Using ICTs to create a culture of transparency: E-government and social media as openness and anti-corruption tools for societies

Brandie, L. M., & Abbott, E. (2011). Mobile Phones and Rural Livelihoods: Diffusion, Uses, and Perceived Impacts Among Farmers in Rural Uganda. Research Article

Budhiraja, R. (2003). Electronic Governance – A Key Issue in the 21st Century. Additional Director, Electronic Governance Division, Ministry of Information Technology, Government of India.

CCK (2008). Communications statistics report 2008. Nairobi, Kenya.

CCK (2010). *Quarterly Sector Statistics Report 3 Quarter Jan-Mar 2009/2010.* Retrieved January 5, 2011 from http://www.cck.go.ke

Communications Commission of Kenya (CCK). (2011). Quarterly Sector Statistics Report April-June 2010/2011. Retrieved November 2011 from http://www.cck.go.ke/resc/downloads/SECTOR_STATISTICS_REPORT_Q4_2010-11.pdf

Country STAT Kenya (2009). Key Indicators. Retrieved November 2011 from http://www.countrystat.org/KEN/cont/pages/page/indicators/en

Crandall, A. (2011). Kenyan Farmers' Use of Cell Phones: Calling preferred over SMS. *Fulbright Research Program.*

de Silva, H. (2008) *Using ICTs to Create Efficiencies in Agricultural Markets: Some Findings from Sri Lanka.* Paper presented to IDRC 23 May 2008. Ottawa

Donner, J. (2004). Microentrepreneurs and Mobiles: An Exploration of the Uses of Mobile Phones by Small Business Owners in Rwanda. *Information Technologies and International Development, 2*(1), 1-21.

Gichamba, A., & Lukandu, I. A. (2012). A Model for designing M-Agriculture Applications for Dairy Farming," *The African Journal of Information Systems,* 4(4), 1. Retrieved from http://digitalcommons.kennesaw.edu/ajis/vol4/iss4/1

Harris, R. (2004). The Internet Could Help Reduce Poverty. WSI: Internet Business.

Heeks, R. (2001). Building e-Governance for Development: A Framework for National and Donor Action. i-Government Working Paper Series, No. 12. Manchester: Institute for Development Policy and Management, University of Manchester.

Idowu, B., Ogunbodede, E., & Idowu, B. (2003) Information and Communication Technology in Nigeria: The Health Sector Experience, *Journal of Information Technology Impact, 3*(2), 69–76.

International Telecommunication Union (ITU). (2012). ICT Statistics Database. Retrieved July, 2016, from http://www.itu.int/ict/statistics

ITU, OECD. (2011). Report on *M-Government: Mobile Technologies for Responsive Governments and Connected Societies,* International Telecommunication Union (ITU) and the Organisation for Economic Co-operation and Development (OECD), in collaboration with the United Nations Department of Economic and Social Affairs (DESA).

ITU. (2012b). Key statistical highlights: ITU data release June 2012. Retrieved May 10, 2016, from http://www.itu.int/ITUD/ ict/statistics/material/pdf/2011%20Statistical%20highlights_June_2012.pdf

ITU. (2015). International Telecommunication Union Key Global Telecom Indicators.Retrieved May 15, 2016 from https://knoema.com/atlas/Kenya/topics/Telecommunication/Telecomm-Services/Fixed-telephone-lines

ITU. (2015). *The world in 2015, ICT facts and figures.* Retrieved May 15, 2016 from https://www.itu.int/en/ITU-D/Statistics/Documents/facts/ICTFactsFigures2015.pdf

Jensen, R. (2007). The Digital Provide: Information (Technology), Market Performance and Welfare in the South Indian Fisheries Sector, *Quarterly Journal of Economics, 122*(3), 879-924.

Langat P. K., Omae M. O., Ndungu E. N. (2015). Mobile Subscription, Penetration and Coverage Trends in Kenya's Telecommunication Sector. *International Journal of Advanced Research in Artificial Intelligence, 4*(1).

Lee, S., Marcu, M., & Lee, S. (2011). An empirical analysis of fixed and mobile broadband diffusion. *Information Economics and Policy, 23*(3), 227-233.

Lester, R. T., Gelmon, L., & Plummer, F. A. (2006). Cell Phones: Tightening the Communication Gap in Resource-Limited Antiretroviral Programmes? *AIDS,* 20, 2242–2244.

LIRNEasia (2008) *Evaluating Last-Mile Hazard Information Dissemination.* IDRC. Retrieved from http://www.lirneasia.net/wp-content/uploads/2008/05/hazinfo-technical-report.pdf

Litondo, K. O., & Ntale, F. J. (2013). Determinants of Mobile Phone Usage for E-Commerce among Micro and Small Enterprises in the Informal Sector of Kenya. *International Journal of Applied Science and Technology, 3*(6).

Masuki, K. F. G., Kamugisha, R., Mowo, J. G., Tanui, J., Tukahirwa, J.. Mogoi, J., & Adera E. O. (2010). Role of mobile phones in improving communication and information delivery for agricultural development: Lessons from South Western Uganda. *Workshop at Makerere University, Uganda. 22-23 March 2010.*

Muheebwa, H. (2009). M-Health launched in Uganda. Digital Activism Survey. Retrieved from http://www.digiactive.org/2009/07/02/mhealth-launched-in-uganda/. Reviewed 23/12/2010

Mulas, V. (2012). *Policies for Mobile Broadband. In IC4D2012: Maximizing Mobile (pp. 103 - 112).* World Bank

Munyua, H. (2007). *ICTs and Small-scale Agriculture in Africa: A Scoping Study.* Ottawa: IDRC.

Murray, S. (2010). Mobile technology and the Kenya farmers helpline. *The Financial Times.* Retrieved January 14, 2010 from http://www.ft.com

Muto, M., & Yamano, T. (2009). The impact of mobile phone coverage expansion on market participation: panel data evidence from Uganda. World Development.

Rashid, A., T., & Elder, L. (2009). MOBILE PHONES AND DEVELOPMENT: AN ANALYSIS OF IDRC-SUPPORTED PROJECTS. *Electronic Journal on Information Systems in Developing Countries, 36*(2).

Souter, D., Garforth, C., Jain, R., Mascarenhas, O., McKerney, K., & Scott, N. (2005) *The Economic Impact of*

Telecommunications on Rural Livelihoods and Poverty Reduction: A Study of Rural Communities in India (Gujarat), Mozambique, and Tanzania. Commonwealth Telecommunications Organisation for UK Department for International Development.

Webb, T. (2010). Three Reasons why mobile technology is helping farmers in Kenya. Retrieved January 14, 2011 from http://webdigital.com.

10

Invarianceness for Character Recognition Using Geo-Discretization Features

Aree Ali[1] & Bayan Omer[2]

[1] School of Science, University of Sulaimani, Sulaimani, KRG, Iraq

[2] College of Science and Technology, University of Human Development, Sulaimani, KRG, Iraq

Correspondence: Aree Ali, School of Science, University of Sulaimani, Sulaimani, KRG, Iraq. E-mail: aree.ali@univsul.edu.iq

Abstract

Recognition rate of characters in the handwritten is still a big challenge for the research because of a shape variation, scale and format in a given handwritten character. A more complicated handwritten character recognition system needs a better feature extraction technique that deal with such variation of hand writing. In other hand, to obtain efficient and accurate recognition rely on off-line English handwriting character, the similarity in the character traits is an important issue to be differentiated in an off-line English handwriting to. In recognizing a character, character handwriting format could be implicitly analyzed to make the representation of the unique hidden features of the individual's character is allowable. Unique features can be used in recognizing characters which can be considerable when the similarity between two characters is high. However, the problem of the similarity in off-line English character handwritten was not taken into account thus, leaving a high possibility of degrading the similarity error for intra-class [same character] with the decrease of the similarity error for inter-class [different character]. Therefore, in order to achieve better performance, this paper proposes a discretization feature algorithm to reduce the similarity error for intra-class [same character]. The mean absolute error is used as a parameter to calculate the similarity between inter and/or intra class characters. Test results show that the identification rate give a better result with the proposed hybrid Geo-Discretization method.

Keywords: document analysis, unique representation, off-line English handwriting, recognition, discretization

1. Introduction

Pattern recognition provides services for various engineering and scientific fields such as computer vision, biology and artificial intelligence. Pattern recognition in handwriting considered as a wide-ranging term which covers all kinds of application field together with identification based on handwriting (Guo, Christian, & Alex, 2010), verification based on handwriting (Srihari, & Ball, 2009), authentication (Muzaffar, & Jurgen, 2009; Behzad, & Mohsen, 2010) and character recognition (Tonghua, Zhang, Guan, & Huang, 2009; Bayan, 2013).

Recently, the field of pattern recognition is considerably improved and revealed due to the emerging applications which are not only challenging but also attracted many researchers' attention. New applications include (data mining, web searching, retrieval of multimedia data, face recognition, handwritten recognition).These techniques require robust and intelligent pattern recognition techniques. Pattern recognition described by (Anil, Robert, & Jianchang, 2000) as a most critical role in human decision making task, even though we as a human can easily refuse to understand how actually human could recognize patterns.

The character recognition based off-line English handwriting is an open research area in pattern recognition and computer vision fields (Bayan, 2013; Binod, & Goutam, 2012). The shape or style in off-line English character is complex and has similarity among some characters (Binod, & Goutam, 2012; Nisha, Hem, & Singh, 2012). However, there are still unique features for each character. These unique features can be generalized as the individual's character handwriting even though there can be complex and high similarity in off-line English language characters. Figure 1 shows an example of off-line English characters and the similarity among them. An improvement step is added to provide a better representation for the input samples from the same or different characters. Extracted features in the feature extraction process show that the character in an off-line English language has similar style or format which affects the accuracy of the performance.

2. Off-Line English Character Individuality

Off-line English Handwriting character has long been considered individualistic and character individuality rests on the hypothesis that each individual character has consistent handwriting (Binod, & Goutam, 2012; Azmi, Kabir, & Badi, 2003; Bayan, 2012; Nisha, Hem, & Singh, 2012). Figure 1 shows the handwriting of the same character and Figure 2 of different character by four writers. Characters are shown as taking a specific texture (Binod, & Goutam, 2012) and can be seen in below figures. The character structure is faintly different for the identical character and completely different for non-identical character, this is known as individuality of English character. Intra-class measurement is showed for features of the same character, and inter-class for different character. Well-being single features must acquire the minimum error of similarity for intra-class and the maximum similarity error for inter-class.

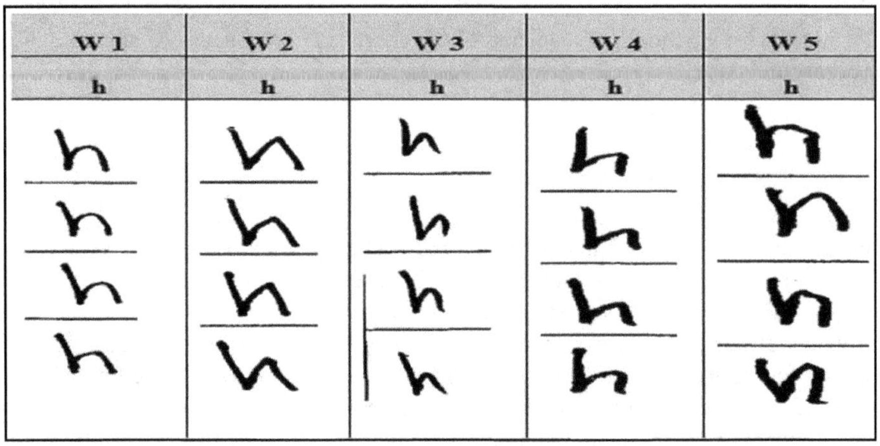

Figure 1. Same Character by Different Writers

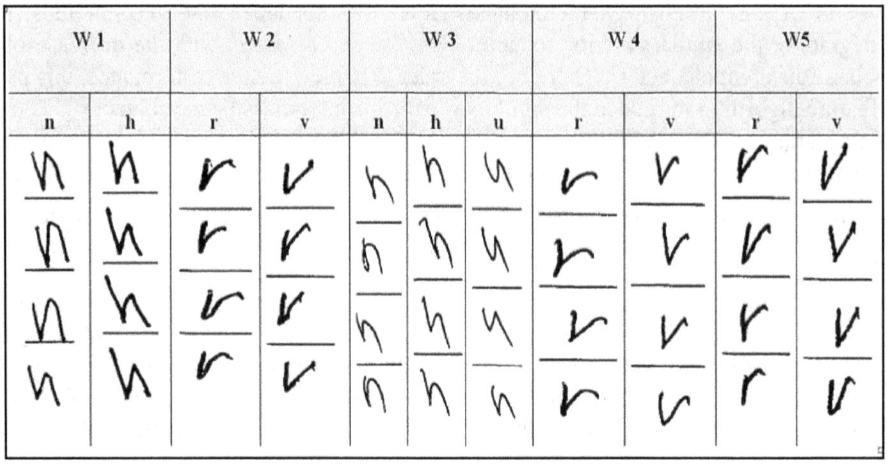

Figure 2. Different Character by Different Writers

3. Uniqueness in Off-line English Character Representation

Selecting most predominant features acting as an input to a classifier are very interesting to get better performance in the process of recognition. These kinds of feature do not represent individual features of the character because of representing the character by different features. The proposed method is based on an invariant discretization algorithm which is studying by (Muda, Shamsuddin, & Ajith, 2010; Azmi, Kabir, & Badi, 2003; Bayan, 2012;]. It acts by reducing the dissimilarity between features for intra-class and increasing the dissimilarity between features for inter-class. The traditional and the proposed framework are shown in Figure 3 and 4 respectively.

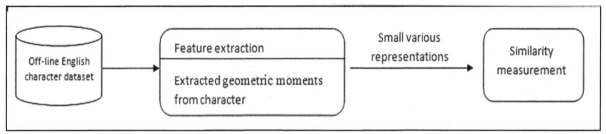

Figure 3. Traditional Framework

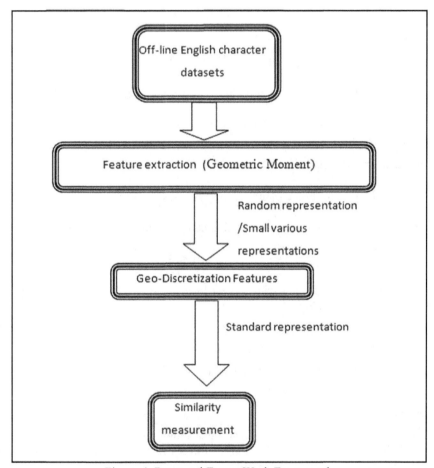

Figure 4. Proposed Frame Work Framework

3.1 Discretization Process

Discretization is considered as a divider that performs two essential operations the first task is to convert the value of the continuous characteristics into discrete. The second one is to divide the value and categorized them into appropriate intervals. The main objective of the discretization of the continuous characteristics is to represent the min a better way (Fabrice, & Ricco, 2005). There are some well-known techniques for discretization including Equal Information Gain, Maximum Entropy, and Equal Interval Width. Another method proposed in (Muda, Shamsuddin, & Ajith, Fabrice, & Ricco, 2005)), the Invariants Discretization method, is proved to be better in efficiency by having higher accuracy and better rates of identification. The method is supervised type and starts by choosing the suitable intervals to represent the writer's information (Muda, Shamsuddin, & Ajith, 2010; Fabrice, & Ricco, 2005; Bayan, & Shamsuddin, 2012; Bayan, & Siti, 2011). The upper and lower boundaries are then set for each interval. The number of intervals for an image must be the same as the number of the feature vectors.

3.2 Feature Extraction Phase

Techniques that transform the input sample data into the set of features are called feature extraction method. The characteristic of feature extraction is to reduce the dimension of the given data. Selection of the feature extraction method types is crucial and affects the performance evaluation of any pattern recognition system (Bayan, 2013; Trier, & Jain, 1996). Different extractors are proposed to recognize handwritten digits and characters such as (FT, IM, GM and Characteristic Loci) (Takahashi, 1991; Azmi, Kabir, & Badi, 2003). In this paper, geometric moment method is used to recognize handwritten off-line English characters. Geometric Moment is used in object recognition and pattern recognition applications. A set of distinctive features computed for an object must be capable of identifying the same object with another possible different size and orientation (Muralidharan, & Chandrasekar, 2011; Bayan, 2015; Bayan, 2012).

The computation steps of geometric moments are described as below:

1) Read an input image data from left to right and from top to bottom.

2) Threshold the image data to extract the target process area.

3) Compute the image moment value, m_{pq} until third order with formula:

$$m'_{pq} = \int\int_{\delta} (x')^p (y')^q f'(x', y') dx' dy' \quad ; \quad p, q = 0,1,2, \dots \tag{1}$$

4) Compute the intensity moment, (x_0, y_0) of image with formula:

$x_0 = m_{10}/m_{00} ; \quad y_0 = m_{01}/m_{00}$ (2)

5) Compute the central moments, μ_{pq} with formula:

$$\mu_{pq} = \iint_{\delta} (x - x_0)^p (y - y_0)^q f(x, y) dx dy \quad ; \quad p, q = 0,1,2 \dots \tag{3}$$

6) Compute normalized central moment, η_{pq} to be used in image scaling until third order with formula:

$$\gamma = \frac{(p+q+2)}{2}, \quad \eta_{pq} = \frac{\mu_{pq}}{\mu_{00}^{\frac{\gamma}{2}}}, \quad p+q \le 3 \tag{4}$$

7) Compute geometric moments, ϕ_1 to ϕ_4 with respect to translation, scale and rotation (geometric moment invariants) invariants with formula below:

$$\phi_1 = \eta_{20} + \eta_{02} \tag{5}$$
$$\phi_2 = (\eta_{20} - \eta_{02})^2 + 4\eta_{11}^2 \tag{6}$$
$$\phi_3 = (\eta_{30} - 3\eta_{12})^2 + (3\eta_{21} - \eta_{03})^2 \tag{7}$$
$$\phi_4 = (\eta_{30} + \eta_{12})^2 + (\eta_{21} + \eta_{03})^2 \tag{8}$$

3.3 Discretization Phase

The process of discretization determines a set of interval that shows the representation of features to be extracted. To obtain an interval, the lowest and highest data range of every writer is distributed along number of intervals (cuts) with equally size. Interval numbers are described according to the number of feature vector in the feature extraction process. An interval value representation is estimated based on the character class. If two characters have an identical invariant value, they take identical interval for these two classes. The Discretization method does not affect or change the properties of character; it is only representing the basic feature vector which is extracted invariantly in a standard representation with global features. Figure 5 depicts the discretization process method.

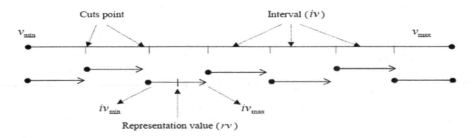

Figure 5. Invariant Discretization Line (Muda, Shamsuddin, & Ajith, 2010)

Invariant discretization line uses minimum (v_{min}) and the maximum (v_{max}) feature vectors to determine the invariant intervals range. The width of an interval can be found as:

$$Width= (V_{max}- V_{min})/f \quad , \tag{9}$$

Where:

v_{min}: represent lowest value for a character.

v_{max}: represent highest value for a character.

f: represent invariant feature vector number.

The width in equation (9) is performed to find out the number of cut points of in the discretization line process. Figure 6 and 7 illustrate the process of transformation from invariant feature vector to the discretized feature vector respectively.

-5.1929	34.8813	14.6934	1.1676	h
-5.6195	42.6242	23.2186	0.1510	h
-5.0995	32.8712	66.0584	0.2161	h
-5.4027	37.5240	59.8230	0.0183	h
-5.0719	33.1140	17.0302	1.3501	h
-5.5533	40.0610	133.0801	4.4533	h
-5.2357	34.4782	33.3672	0.2034	h
-4.9348	29.7254	12.5396	9.2442	h
-5.3091	36.2166	78.0286	0.0018	h
-4.7482	26.3275	11.2760	8.0895	h
-5.3089	35.0716	15.1506	0.0015	n
-5.3591	35.9965	5.8633	0.1437	n
-5.0140	30.3710	7.0963	0.5946	n
-5.0444	32.4682	5.0991	4.8752	n
-4.9365	30.4682	28.1710	1.6511	n
-5.3528	35.8507	9.6482	0.0398	n
-5.0780	31.4367	39.0458	0.1924	n
-4.8918	28.8666	11.6713	5.5281	n
-4.7232	25.6728	11.3610	3.8595	n
-5.3625	35.9186	1.1150	1.2288	n

Figure 6. Invariant Feature Vector Data for Character (h) and (n)

The discretized data yielded from the discretization scheme clearly shows the unique feature of every character in English handwriting.

11.7179	46.3928	11.7179	11.7179	h
11.7179	46.3928	11.7179	11.7179	h
11.7179	46.3928	81.0677	11.7179	h
11.7179	46.3928	46.3928	11.7179	h
11.7179	46.3928	11.7179	11.7179	h
11.7179	46.3928	0	11.7179	h
11.7179	46.3928	46.3928	11.7179	h
11.7179	46.3928	11.7179	11.7179	h
11.7179	46.3928	81.0677	11.7179	h
11.7179	11.7179	11.7179	11.7179	h
0.1885	33.4948	11.2906	0.1885	n
0.1885	33.4948	11.2906	0.1885	n
0.1885	33.4948	11.2906	0.1885	n
0.1885	33.4948	0.1885	0.1885	n
0.1885	33.4948	33.4948	0.1885	n
0.1885	33.4948	11.2906	0.1885	n
0.1885	33.4948	33.4948	0.1885	n
0.1885	33.4948	11.2906	0.1885	n
0.1885	22.3927	11.2906	0.1885	n
0.1885	33.4948	0.1885	0.1885	n

Figure 7. Example of Discretized Feature Data for Character (h)and(n)

4. Uniqueness Test Results

Mean Absolute Error (MAE) function is used to measure the uniqueness of the character. Table. 1 and 2 present the test result values of the MAE when the number of samples is 10 for every character. Feature (1 to 4) is an extracted feature that represents a character. The invarianceness of character and reference image (first image) is given by the MAE value. The small errors mean that the image is close to the reference image. An average of MAE is taken from the value of whole results.

$$MAE = \frac{1}{n}\sum_{i=1}^{f}|(x_i - r_i)| \qquad\qquad (10)$$

Where,

n : is the number of images.

x_i : is the current image.

r_i: is the reference image or location measure.

f : is the number of features.

i : is the feature column of image.

Table 1. MAE Results using Geometric Moments

Image	Feature 1	Feature 2	Feature 3	Feature4	MAE
V	-5.8208	43.3300	145.7606	10.6865	-
V	-5.2686	34.0231	32.6906	0.0387	13.3577
U	-4.8517	29.3801	51.8342	4.1312	11.5401
V	-5.5301	37.6985	83.2967	6.1862	7.2886
V	-5.6034	39.7011	139.7753	10.0286	1.0490
Vᴧ	-5.0146	29.7276	5.0744	0.3166	16.5465
V	-5.2040	34.7365	31.9852	0.6482	13.3024
V	-5.3170	35.3809	38.1249	0.0696	12.6706
Y	-5.2492	36.7666	150.5069	7.6241	1.4944
V	-5.1119	31.3749	5.8567	0.3519	16.2903
Average MAE					9.353

Table 2. MAE Results using Geo-Discretization

Image	Feature 1	Feature 2	Feature 3	Feature4	MAE
V	13.7202	52.8021	130.9659	13.7202	--
V	13.7202	52.8021	13.7202	13.7202	11.7246

$\cup$	13.7202	13.7202	52.8021	13.7202	11.7246
V	13.7202	52.8021	91.8840	13.7202	3.9082
ψ	13.7202	52.8021	130.9659	13.7202	0
$v\wedge$	13.7202	13.7202	13.7202	13.7202	15.6328
V	13.7202	52.8021	13.7202	13.7202	11.7246
$\cup$	13.7202	52.8021	52.8021	13.7202	7.8164
γ	13.7202	52.8021	130.9659	13.7202	0
$\cup$	13.7202	13.7202	13.7202	13.7202	15.6328
Average MAE					7.8164

The profession of writing invarianceness for the geometric (moment and Geo-discretized) data value is determined by applying the intra-class and inter-class analysis of MAE value. The test result demonstrates that the dissimilarity between feature for intra-class (identical character) and inter-class (non-identical character) using the Geo-Discretization scheme gives a better result compared to geometric moments data. It has improved the recognition process where the MAE value for intra-class using Geo-discretized data is smaller than geometric moment's data, and MAE value for inter-class using Geo-discretized data is higher than geometric moment's data. The minimum MAE value in intra-class indicates that features are highly identical to each other for the identical character whilst the maximum MAE value for inter-class indicates that they are widely differ to each other for non-idnetical characters. These results have proved the hypothesis that the discretization process can improve the recognition process with a standard representation of individual features for the individuality representation in off-line English handwriting character. Figure 8 and 9 show the MAE results comparison of recognition process for the Geometric feature technique with Geo-discretized data and geometric moment's data.

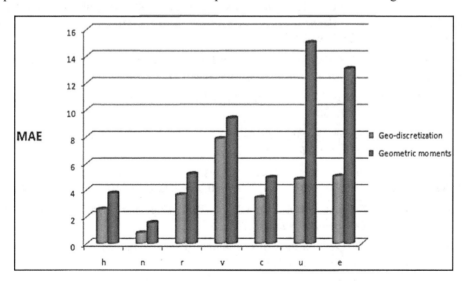

Figure 8. MAE Comparison for Intra-Class

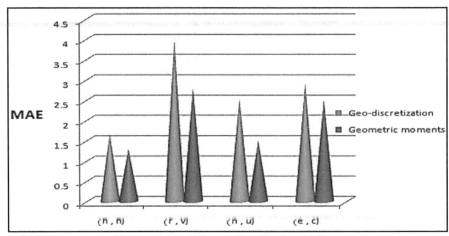

Figure 9. MAE Comparison for Inter-Class

5. Discussion

In this research work, a new framework for off-line English Handwritten Character Recognition is proposed. The effect of discretization process is shown during successful experimental tests. Individual features in the handwritten character can be systematically represented with the use of the invariants discretization algorithm. The results reveal that with the use of the invariant discretization technique, the accuracy of the off-line English handwritten character recognition is significantly improved with the general arrangement to get improved accuracy paralleled to geometric moment's information. For the future work, the similar experiment could be done over some other characters to improve more the accuracy of the proposed method.

References

Anil, K. J., Robert, P. W., & Jianchang, D. M. (2000). *Statistical pattern recognition: A review*. In Proc. 4th IEEE Trans on Pattern analysis and Machine intelligence, 22, 4-37.

Azmi, K., Kabir, R., & Badi, E. (2003). Recognition printed letters witZonong features. *Iran Computer Group*, (1), 29-37.

Bayan, O. M. (2015). Individuality Representation in Character Recognition. *Journal of University of Human Development, 1*(2), 300-305.

Bayan, O. M., & Shamsuddin, S. M. (2012). Improvement in twins handwriting identification with invariants discretization. *EURASIP Journal on Advances in Signal Processing, 48*, 3-12. http://dx.doi.org/10.1186/1687-6180-2012-48

Bayan, O. M., & Siti, M. S. (2011). Feature discretization for individuality representation in twins handwritten identification. *Journal of Computer Science, 7*(7), 1080-1087.

Bayan, O. M. (2012). Uniqueness in Kurdish handwriting. *International Journal of Engineering & Computer Science IJECS-IJENS, 12*(6), 42-50.

Bayan, O. M. (2013). Handwritten Kurdish character recognition using geometric discretization feature. *International Journal of Computer Science, 4*(1), 51-55.

Behzad, H., & Mohsen, M. (2010). A text-independent Persian writer identification based on feature relation graph (FRG). *Pattern Recognition*, (43), 2199–2209. http://dx.doi.org/10.1016/j.patcog.2009.11.026

Binod, K. P., & Goutam, S. (2012). A model approach to off-line English character recognition. *International Journal of Scientific and Research Publications, 2*(6), 1-6.

Fabrice, M., & Ricco, R. (2005). Discretization of continuous attributes. In John Wang (Ed.), *Encyclopedia of Data Warehousing and Mining* (pp. 397-402).

Guo, X. T., Christian, V. G., & Alex, C. K. (2010). Individuality of alphabet knowledge in online writer identification. IJDAR Springer Berlin. *Heidelberg, 13*(2), 145-147. http://dx.doi.org/10.1007/s10032-009-0110-z

Muda, A. K., Shamsuddin, S. M., & Ajith, A. (2010). Improvement of authorship invarianceness for individuality representation in writer identification. *Neural Network World, 3*(10), 371–387.

Muralidharan, R., & Chandrasekar, C. (2011). Object Recognition using SVM-KNN based on geometric moment invariant. *International Journal of Computer Trends and Technology, 1*(3), 215-219.

Muzaffar, B., & Jurgen, K. (2009). *Person authentication with RDTW based on handwritten PIN and signature with a novel biometric smart Pen device*, IEEE Workshop, 63-68.

Nisha V., Hem J. P., & Singh V. (2012). Offline character recognition system using artificial neural network. *International Journal of Machine Learning and Computing, 2*(4), 449-452.

Srihari, N. S., & Ball, R. G. (2009). *Semi-supervised learning for handwriting recognition.* ICDAR, 26-30.

Takahashi H. (1991). *A neural Net OCR using geometrical and zonal pattern features.* In Proc. 1th. Conf. Document Analysis and Recognition, 821-828.

Tonghua, S., Zhang, T. W., Guan, D. J., & Huang, H. J. (2009). Off-line recognition of realistic chinese handwriting using segmentation-free strategy. *Pattern Recognition, 42*(1), 167-182. http://dx.doi.org/10.1016/j.patcog.2008.05.012

Trier, I. D., & Jain, A. K. (1996). Feature extraction methods for character recognition: A survey. *Pattern Recognition, 29*(4), 641- 662. http://dx.doi.org/10.1016/0031-3203(95)00118-2

11

Accessible and Navigable Representation of Mathematical Function Graphs to the Vision-Impaired

Azadeh Nazemi[1], Chandrika Fernando[1], Iain Murray[1] & David A. McMeekin[2]

[1] Department of Electrical and Computer Engineering, Curtin University Perth, Western Australia

[2] Department of Spatial Sciences, Curtin University Perth, Western Australia

Correspondence: Azadeh Nazemi, Department of Electrical and Computer Engineering, Curtin University Perth, Western Australia. E-muil: uzudeh.nazemi@curtin.cdu.au

Abstract

Vision-impaired students have several issues accessing mathematical documents, which are associated with the representation of mathematical expressions and graphs of mathematical functions. Graphs of mathematical functions are visual presentations of mathematical information and useful to illustrate numerical or qualitative information, which are sometimes difficult or even impossible to describe. A graph is a picture that shows how sets of data are related to each other. Graphs of mathematical functions generally convey the intended message of a mathematical document. Therefore, access to graphs is essential in learning mathematics. Finding a solution to represent graphs of mathematical functions in an accessible format is necessary for the vision-impaired. This paper describes an approach to develop an application to address this issue by detecting, extracting and categorising important information from graphs of mathematical functions using three open source packages, namely, ImageMagick, GNUPLOT and Octave.

Keywords: vision-impaired, graphs of mathematical functions, navigation ability, text to speech (TTS), digitisation, assistive technology

1. Introduction

Results from the National Assessment of Educational Progress show that there is a great disparity between the mathematical skills of students with disabilities and students without disabilities (Noble, 2008). Accessibility of graphs of mathematical functions is one of the areas, which needs to be facilitated. Currently, Haptic feedback is used for guidance and assistance in graph navigation (Ramloll & Brewster, 2001). However, it is not efficient to present exact data values to the user. In addition, it is expensive and may take users some time to familiarize themselves with the new interface. The limitations of Haptic feedback devices hinder users' ability to explore graphs (University of South Australia, 2004). Traditionally, there are two other methods to represent visual components such as graphs to vision-impaired, namely, tactile and audio method.

In the tactile method, graphs and diagrams are presented in Braille or raised dots and lines on swell-paper, which has raised surfaces for a vision-impaired person to feel (Yu, & Brewster, 2002). They are used to convey non-textual information such as maps, paintings, graphs and diagrams. Picture in a Flash (PIAF) is a tactile graph method, and the general shape of the graph can be understood by touching it carefully. Some drawbacks of using tactile graphs are the costs of translating into an accessible graphic format, the use of expensive tactile graphics and peripheral devices (Goncu & Marriot, 2008), and lack of congruence with the original visual graphic (Diagram 2012, 2012). Tactile diagrams are not durable and easy to edit. They provide only a rough idea about the content. Furthermore, only a small proportion of blind people can use Braille, as reading it requires sufficient tactile sensitivity, which not all vision-impaired people have (Murray, 2008).

Presenting mathematical graph audibly is more complicated. Passively hearing the graphed mathematical formulae alone is not sufficient to transfer and describe complex mathematical constructs. Sonification is conveying data via sound pitch and 2-dimensional acoustics (Brown & Brewster, 2003). It is difficult to convey data accurately with the acoustic method (non-speech sound), and moreover, since acoustics are volatile, information can easily be misheard.

2. Method

The proposed method in this research provides an opportunity for vision-impaired, to listen passively to extracted classified data from graphs using Text-to-Speech (TTS), and actively interact with it by navigating through classified information and digitized data tables without requiring another device or peripheral.

The framework of a graph of mathematical functions contains two crossed axes, which meet at the origin. The axes divide the plane into four quadrants. Scaled values are increased from left to right on the horizontal axis and from down to up on the vertical axis. In addition, a data table is a table with two columns to show dependent variable values for each independent variable value. Generally, data tables are converted to graphs for better understanding of the relationship between the vertical and horizontal values (visualisation). Since vision-impaired students are not able to use visual components such as graphs, the graph must be converted into a data table using digitization.

A mathematical function of a graph has several properties which support the extraction of essential information. Regardless of parameter values, the shape of the graph depends on the form of the function. Hence, in most cases, a form of a mathematical function can guess shape of a graph.

The developed Linux command Bash Script application (MathGraphReader) by this research reads the function of the graph as input, performs digitization and extracts all prominent information from the graph using mathematical function properties and concepts of the function followed by plotting the function with GNUPLOT (Williams & Kelly, 2004) and image processing it with ImageMagick (Still, 2005)

This application classifies extracted information, saves them using Mark-up format and represents it by navigation ability. It provides a complete textual description for linear, quadratic, power, polynomial, exponential, logarithmic, and sinusoidal graphs to be replaced with the graph.

2.1 General Concepts

The following are reminders of some common concepts in different graph types:

- If for a specific interval, $x_2 > x_1$ and $y_2 < y_1$, then in this interval graph is decreasing.
- If for a specific interval, $x_2 > x_1$ and $y_2 > y_1$, then in this interval graph is increasing.
- If for a specific interval, $y_2 = y_1$, then in this interval the graph is constant.
- If $f(x) = -f(-x)$, then the graph is symmetric with respect to y axis.
- If $f(x) = f(-x)$, then the graph is symmetric with respect to the origin.
- If at $x = p$, first derivative of a function is positive then function is increasing at this point.
- If at $= p$, first derivative of a function is negative then function is decreasing at this point.
- If the first derivative of a function is equal to 0 at the point $x = p$ then this point is critical point of the function and behavior of the function is not predictable at this point. The first derivatives determine that the function is increasing or decreasing, consequently the second derivative shows first derivative is increasing or decreasing. If the second derivative is positive, then the first derivative is increasing, so that the slope of the tangent line to the function is increasing as x increases and graph of the function is concave up
- If the second derivative is negative, then the first derivative is decreasing, so that the slope of the tangent line to the function is decreasing as x increases.
- If the second derivative is zero, the graph may be concave up or concave down, it may change from concave up to concave down or from concave down to concave up. This point is an inflection point if third derivative is not zero at this point.
- Maxima and minima points are obtained by finding the roots of second derivative
- y-intercepts are calculated by finding function value when $x = 0$
- x-intercepts are calculated by finding the root(s) of function $y = 0$

2.2 Mathematical Function properties

1. Linear: $y = ax + b$

a) Graphs of these functions are straight lines.
b) 'a' is the slope and 'b' is the y- intercept.
c) If $a > 0$ then the line rises.
d) If $a < 0$then the line falls.

2. Quadratic: $y = a x^2 + bx + c$
   a) The graph is called parabola.
   b) Graph crosses y-axis at c. The y-intercept point is c.
   c) If $a > 0$ then the parabola opens upward, the graph will be 'U' shaped
   d) If $a < 0$ the parabola opens downward, the graph will be 'n' shaped
3. Power: $y = ax^b$
   a) If $b > 0$ then:
      When $x = 0$ graph meets origin point
      When x is large and positive they are all large and positive.
      When x is large and negative and b is, even: y is large and positive.
      When x is large and negative and b is odd: y is large and negative.
   b) If $b < 0$ then:
      When $x = 0$ these functions suffer a division by zero and therefore are all infinite.
      When x is large and positive they are small and positive.
      When x is large and negative and b is even: y is small and positive.
      When x is large and negative and b is odd: y is small and negative
   c) If b is a fraction between 0 and 1 then:
      When x = zero these functions are all zero.
      The curves are vertical at the origin and as x increases they increase but curve toward the x-axis.
4. Polynomial:$y = a_n x^n + a_{n-1} x^{n-1} + a_2x^2 + a_1x^1 + a_0x^0$
   a) The highest power of x is the degree of the polynomial.
   b) Polynomials of degree greater than 2 can have more than one maximum or minimum value.
   c) The largest possible number of minima or maxima points is 'n-1'
5. Exponential: $y = ab^x$
   a) If the base $b > 1$ then the result is exponential growth.
   b) If the base $b < 1$ then the result is exponential decay.
6. Logarithmic: $y = alog(x) + b$
   a) For small x, y is negative.
   b) For large x, y is positive but stay small.
7. Sinusoidal: $y = asin(bx + c)$
   a) Graph of Sinusoidal functions has a wave shape with respect to position or time.
   b) Parameter 'a' is the amplitude, which affects the height of the wave.
   c) Parameter 'b' is the angular velocity, which affects the width of the wave.
   d) Parameter 'c' is the phase angle that shifts the wave left or right.

2.3 Data Extraction

To provide an accurate textual description from graph the following points must be found:

- Intercept values (meeting points of the graph with axes)
- Inflection point (graph behaviour is changed)
- Starting/Ending points
- Minima/Maxima points(critical points)

   Finding these points in most cases is a complicated process, which involves a large amount of mathematical problem solving. The method to extract these points is plotting the graph using GNUPLOT (open source package) and associated graph function with predefined dimensions and specified range of axes. GNUPLOT plots a graph using the configuration file (graph.gnu). The snippet to create a configuration file is available in Appendix A (Create configuration file)

Assuming plotted graph is saved in output.png using graph.gnu(configuration file) and plotting information is saved in range.txt. According to graph.gnu, the plotted graph by GNUPLOT is in green colour so that graph-only can be extracted from output.png pixels.

Gnuplot graph.gnu>&range.txt

Graph –only pixels, dimensions of output.png, Xmax, Xmin , Ymax ,Ymin, X-axis range ,Y-axis range, X-ratio and Y-ratio are obtained using the snippet given in Appendix A (Essential parameters)

Graph-only pixels are saved in file called green-graph-pixels.

X-ratio and Y-ratio are used to convert pixel coordinate points to real values.

The following command removes all pixels except green ones, which indicate graph-only pixels.

Origin point is located at (Width/2, Height/2) which is intersection point of two axes.

To find graph locations in plane, Table 1 is used. First column of the table indicates that mathematical graph function area is divided into four quadrants. The second column shows coordinate value conditions in each quadrants.

Table 1. Graph location in plane

Location	Real value	Gnuplot Graph	Command
Quadrant 1	x>0 y>0	x>Width/2 y>Height /2	cat pixel.txt|awk '$1>'$xOrogin' && $2>'$yOrigin |wc -l
Quadrant 2	x<0 y>0	x<Width/2 y>Height /2	cat pixel.txt|awk '$1<'$xOrogin' && $2>'$yOrigin |wc -l
Quadrant 3	x<0 y<0	x<Width/2 y<Height /2	cat pixel.txt|awk '$1<'$xOrogin' && $2<'$yOrigin |wc -l
Quadrant 4	x>0 y<0	x>Width/2 y<Height /2	cat pixel.txt|awk '$1>'$xOrogin' && $2<'$yOrigin |wc -l

x-intercept where the graph crosses x-axis is extracted by finding root(s) which is usually complicated, this point is extracted by finding green pixel(s) in graph image of GNUPLOT with y=Height/2.

Similarly, y-intercept where the graph crosses the y-axis is extracted by assigning zero to x in graph equation and obtaining y. This point is extracted by finding green pixel(s) in GNUPLOT graph image with x=Width/2.

Also, absolute minima is obtained by finding $(X_{Ymin}, Ymin\_of\_Green\_Pixels)$, and absolute maxima is obtained by finding$(X_{Ymax}, Ymax\_of\_Green\_Pixels)$.

In order to convert all obtained pixel scaling coordinate values to real scale values:

X-Real=X-Ratio*X-in-GNUPLOT-graph

Y-Real=Y-Ratio*Y-in-GNUPLOT-graph

For finding critical and inflection points first and second derivatives are obtained using Octave. Then using GNUPLOT graph of derivatives are plotted and roots of them calculated. Root(s) of first derivative represent critical points and root(s) of second derivative nominate inflection points.

digitizer and derivative are two bash scripts utilizing Octave Package to help vision-impaired students to digitize and find derivatives of function. Appendix A (digitizer) and Appendix A (derivative) provide codes for these two functions.

2.4 Testing

Figure. 1 illustrates the mathematical graph of function y= $x^4 + 3x^3 + 4$ (left) and generated graph by GNUPLOT for y=x**4+3*x**3+4 (right).

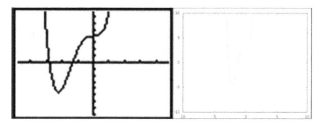

Figure 1. Mathematical graph and its similar product by GNUPLOT for **y= $x^4 + 3x^3 + 4$**

Figure 1 (left) indicates that: the minimum is located at x = -2.25 and the minimum value is approximately -4.54.

Figure 1 (right) is plotted by GNUPOLT using y=x**4+3*x**3+4.

The following is all data extracted by the developed application from Figure 1 (right):

- The degree of this graph is 4
- It is a polynomial.
- There are 3 possible maxima and minima.
- The y-intercept is (0, 4).
- The x-intercept are (-3, 0),(-1,0).
- The graph is located at quadrants 1, 2 and 3.
- Absolute minima is located at: (-2.14815 ,-4.40191), it is a critical point
- First derivative is $4x^3 + 9x^2$
- Second derivative is $12x^2 + 18x$

2.5 Tagging Classified Information and Mark-up Format Generation to Implement Navigation Ability

MathGraphReader uses MathML to represent original function and its derivatives, classifies extracted information and saves them as Mark-up format. Mark-up format is a collection of information with meaningful tags. Figure 2 illustrates graph of function ($2x^4 + x^3 - 3x^2$) in blue, first derivative in red and second derivative in green.

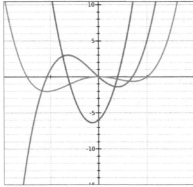

Figure 2 Graph of function ($2x^4 + x^3 - 3x^2$) in blue, first derivative in red and second derivative in green

Table 2 indicates Markup format such as MathML for representing function, its derivatives and the results of digitization. MathML representation for function and its derivatives and data table.

Table 2. Represent digitization results for a mathematical function in Mark-up format

Original function	First Derivative	Second Derivative	Digitization result
<math $2x^4 + x^3 - 3x^2$>	<math $8x^3 + 3x^2 - 6x$>	<math $24x^2 + 6x - 6$>	<data table>
<mrow>	<mrow>	<mrow>	<mi>x,y,y'</mi> <mo>=</mo>
<mrow>	<mrow>	<mrow>	<mn>-3,108,-171</mn>
<mn>2</mn>	<mn>8</mn>	<mn>24</mn>	<mm>-2,12,-40 </mn>
<msup>	<msup>	<msup>	<mn>-1,-2,1</mn>
<mi>x</mi>	<mi>x</mi>	<mi>x</mi>	<mn>0,0,0</mn>
<mn>4</mn>	<mn>3</mn>	<mn>2</mn>	<mn>1,0,5</mn>
</msup>	</msup>	</msup>	<mn>2,28,64</mn>
</mrow>	</mrow>	</mrow>	<mn>3,162,225</mn>
<mo>+</mo>	<mo>+</mo>	<mo>+</mo>	</data table>
<msup>	<mrow>	<mrow>	
<mi>x</mi>	<mn>3</mn>	<mn>6</mn>	
<mn>3</mn>	<msup>	<mi>x</mi>	
</msup>	<mi>x</mi>	</mrow>	
	<mn>2</mn>	<mo>-</mo>	

<mo>-</mo>	</msup>	<mn>6</mn>
<mrow>	</mrow>	</mrow>
<mn>3</mn>	<mo>-</mo>	</math>
<msup>	<mrow>	
<mi>x</mi>	<mn>6</mn>	
<mn>2</mn>	<mi>x</mi>	
</msup>	</mrow>	
</mrow>	</mrow>	
</mrow>	</math>	
</math>		

This research considers several tags to classify extracted information from graph. Table 3 indicates these tags and their utilization.

Table 3. Markup-Tags to classify extracted data by MathGreaph Reader

Classified information	Tag
<functionType><polynomial</functionType>	<functionType></functionType>
<degree><4></degree>	<degree></degree>
<yIntercept>0</yIntercep	<yIntercept></yIntercept>
<xIntercept>0</xIntercept>	<xIntercept></xIntercept>
<xIntercept>1/xIntercept>	
<xxIntercept>-1.5</xIntercept>	
<y_axisSymmetry>No</y_axisSymmetry>	<y_axisSymmetry></y_axisSymmetry>
<originSymmetry>No</originSymmetry>	<originSymmetry></originSymmetry>
<derivativeRoot><0></derivativeRoot>	<derivativeRoot></derivativeRoot>
<derivativeRoot><0.6></derivativeRoot>	
<derivativeRoot>-1.07></derivativeRoot>	
<relativeMnima>0</relativeMinina>	<relativeMnima></relativeMinina> or Maxima
<location><Q1<location>	<location></location>
<location><Q2<location>	
<location><Q3<location>	
<location><Q4<location>	
<decreasing><-3,-1.07</decreasing>	<decreasing></decreasing>
<increasing><-1.07,0</increasing>	<increasing></increasing>
<decreasing><0,0.6</decreasing>	
<increasing><0,6,3</increasing>	

3. Evaluation

To estimate how MathGraphReader can be practical and useful before developing this application, in order to extract information from mathematical graphs, a survey was conducted using a questionnaire among 28 vision-impaired students. They were asked the following question:

"The following is an alternative description for a mathematical function graph. Please rate how you understand the graph by listening to this description once?"

Horizontal axis is labeled x and its range is between -3 to 3. Vertical axis is labeled y and its range is between -3 to 3. Shape of graph is parabola. Horizontal and vertical step value is 1.This graph is plotted from the equation: y is equal x power 2 minus 2 times x. The graph is started from point (-1, 3) until (3,3). The graph is located at (1,2) and 4 quadrants. x-intercept occurs at points (0,0) and (2,0). y-intercept occurs at point (0,0). The graph has absolute minimum at point (1,-1).

Figure 3 illustrates the participants' responses and how they communicated with this alternative text description while students listened to text only once and did not use navigation ability to explore data table.

Figure 4 shows Participants responses about .understanding mathematical graph by listening to text description

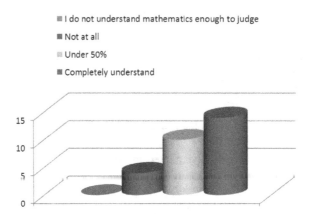

Figure 3. illustrates how important navigation ability is for participants when accessing graph information

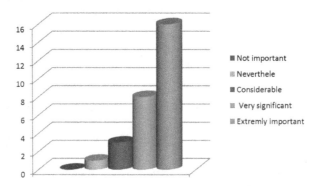

Figure 4. Participants' responses about navigation ability importance to access to graph information

4. Conclusion

The research undertaken achieved graph data extraction or graph digitization to create alternative textual descriptions by developing MathGraphReader.

MathGraphReader utilizes text processing, image processing, plotting and mathematical concepts to extract information from visual graphs and represent it in a non-visual /textual environment.

This application provides the opportunity for vision impaired students to access interactively graph information utilising navigation ability.

After developing this application, another questionnaire was embedded in an interactive application to evaluate the usability of this method in representing graph information to vision-impaired students,

The evaluation questionnaire application helps vision impaired students to receive graph information, navigate and rehear missing parts, and then ask a question to determine their understanding level. The evaluation questionnaire is still in progress and has not been finalised yet, it is available in Appendix B

References

American Psychological Association. (1972). *Ethical standards of psychologists*. Washington, DC: American Psychological Association.

Anderson, C. A., Gentile, D. A., & Buckley, K. E. (2007). *Violent video game effects on children and adolescents: Theory, research and public policy*. http://dx.doi.org/10.1093/acprof:oso/9780195309836.001.0001

Beck, C. A. J., & Sales, B. D. (2001). *Family mediation: Facts, myths, and future prospects* (pp. 100-102). Washington, DC: American Psychological Association. http://dx.doi.org/10.1037/10401-000

Brown, L. M., & Brewster, S. A. Drawing by Ear: Interpreting Sonified Line Graphs. Proc. 9th International

Conference   on   Auditory   Display   -ICAD   2003,   152-156.   Retrieved   from
http://icad.org/Proceedings/2003/BrownBrewster2003a.pdf

Goncu, C., & Marriott, K. (2012). Accessible Graphics: Graphics for Vision Impaired People. Proc. 7th
International   Conference   on   the   Theory   and   Application   of   Diagrams,   2012,   6.
http://dx.doi.org/10.1007/978-3-642-31223-6_5

Goncu, C., & Marriott, K. (2008). Tactile Chart Generation Tool. Proc. 10th International ACM SIGACCESS
Conference   on   Computers   and   Accessibility   2008,   ACM   Press   (2008),   255-256.
http://dx.doi.org/10.1145/1414471.1414525

Murray, I. (2008). Instructional eLearning Technologies for the Vision Impaired. PhD Thesis, Curtin University,
2008.

Nazemi, A., Murray, I., & Mohammad, N. (2012). Mathspeak: An audio method for presenting mathematical
formulae to blind students: Proceeding of the 5th International Conference on Human System Interactions
(HSI). (p. 48-58). http://dx.doi.org/10.1109/HSI.2012.17

Noble, S. (2007). Universal Design for Math Learning: Bridging the Technology and Policy Divide. 1st
International Conference on Technology-based Learning with Disability–LWD07, 2007, 7-12. Retrieved
from https://www.dessci.com/en/reference/articllwd07es/-noble.htm

Still, M. (2006). The Definitive Guide to ImageMagick. Springer 2006. Retrieved from
http://dl.acm.org/citation.cfm?id=1121616

University of South Australia. (2004). Online Accessibility Action Plan. Retrieved from
http://w3.unisa.edu.au/footer/accessibility/ actionplan.pdf

Williams, T., & Kelly. C. (2004). Gnuplot 4.6 An Interactive plotting Program. Retrieved from
http://www.gnuplot.info/docs_4.6/gnuplot.pdf

Yu, W., & Brewster, S. (2002). Multimodal Virtual Reality Versus Printed Medium in Visualization for Blind
People. Proc. 5th International ACM Conference on Assistive Technologies ACM Press (2002), 57-64.
Retrieved from http://dl.acm.org/citation.cfm?id=638261

Yu, W., Ramloll, R., & Brewster, S. A. (2001). Haptic Graphs for Blind Computer Users. Proc. 1st International
Workshop   on   Haptic   Human-Computer   Interaction,   2001,   41-51.   Retrieved   from
http://www.dcs.gla.ac.uk/~stephen/papers/HHCI-ray.pdf

Appendix A

Create configuration file:

function=$1

echo "set term png" >graph.gnu

echo 'set output "output.png"'>>graph.gnu

echo 'set xrang restore'>>graph.gnu

echo 'set yrange restore'>>graph.gn

echo 'show xrange'>>graph.gnu

echo 'show yrange'>>graph.gnu

echo plot $function in with lines lc rgb '"green"' notitle>>graph.gnu

Gnuplot graph.gnu>&range.txt

Essential parameters

Gnuplot graph.gnu>&range.txt

convert output .png txt :-| grep green |sed 's /:.*#/ /g;1d;s/,/ /g '| awk '{ print $1,$2}' > green-graph-pixels.txt
Height=$(identify -format %h output.png)

Width=$(identify -format %w output.png)

Xmin=$(cat range.txt|grep xrange|sed 's/:.*//g'|sed 's/.*\[//g')

Xmax=$(cat range.txt|grep xrange|grep -o -P '(?<=:).*(?=])')

Ymin=$(cat range.txt|grep yrange|sed 's/:.*//g'|sed 's/.*\[//g')

Ymax=$(cat range.txt|grep yrange|grep -o -P '(?<=:).*(?=])')

X-Axis-Range=(echo $Xmax-$Xmin|bc)

Y-Aaxis-Range=$(echo $Ymax-$Ymin|bc)

X-Ratio=X-Axis-Range/Width
Y-Ratio=Y-Axis-Range/Height

digitizer

Formula=$1

initial=$2

Star="*";power="^"

OctaveForm1=$(echo $Formula|sed "s/$Star/star/g"|sed "s/starstar/$power/g"|sed $

OctaveForm2=$(echo $OctaveForm1|sed 's/x/x(1)/g')

echo "function F=NewFunc(x)">>NewFunc.m

echo "F=["$OctaveForm2"]">>NewFunc.m

echo "end" >> NewFunc.m

initial="x0=["$initial"]"

echo $initial>>initialize.m

new="'NewFunc'"

expression="[x,fval]=fsolve("$new",x0)"

echo $expression>>initialize.m

octave --silent --eval "initialize"

derivative

echo "syms x ">>differ.m
echo "differentiate ("$OctaveForm1",x)">>differ.m

octave --silent --eval "differ"

Appendix B

Evaluation Questionnaire

Welcome to the mathematical function graph questionnaire system .This system first presents some information about a graph , helps you to extract prominent points of the graph then, ask some question about graph such as shape and location. The purpose of this questionnaire is to evaluate mathematical function graph understanding by listening to the audio text description using navigating ability. It is not for assessing your knowledge so if you are not familiar with scope of any question feel free to press B(for Bypass) to ignore this question . You do not have time limitation . You do not need to provide your identification details.

- By clicking N(for No), you do not want to participate to this research questionnaire and exit
- By clicking Y(for Yes), you consent that you are willing to answer the questions in this questionnaire and continue
- After listening each question if you are ready to answer Press: Y for yes and Submit and go to the next question pressing: S(for Submit)
- Rehear this talking guide press **I(for Info)**
- Ignore the question pressing: B (for Bypass)
- Rehear whole description pressing: A(for All).
- Navigate through description and rehear missing part pressing: F (for forward) and R(for rewind)

Description :the graph is plotted from the function :

y is equal 2 times x power 4 plus x power three minus three times x power 2

Assuming domain for x is between -3 to 3

Results of digitization are

X equal -3, y equal   108, first derivative equal -171

X equal -2, y equal   12, first derivative equal -40

X equal -1, y equal -2, first derivative equal 1

X equal 0, y equal 0, first derivative equal 0

X equal 1, y equal 0, first derivative equal 5

X equal 2, y equal 28, first derivative equal 64

X equal 3, y equal 162, first derivative equal 225

First derivative= $(3.0)*x^{(2.0)}+(8.0)*x^{(3.0)}-(6.0)*x$

Second derivative $=-6.0+(24.0)*x^{(2.0)}+(6.0)*x$

Question 1

What is the degree of function?

Question 2

What is y- intercept ?

Question 3

How many possible Maxima/Minima points it has **?**

Question 4

Does this graph meet the origin point type yes or no?

Question 5

What is(are) x- intercept?

Question 6

Does the graph have symmetry with respect to y axis ?

Question 7

Does the graph have symmetry with respect to the origin.?

Question 8

In which quadrants this graph function locates ?

Question 9

What are the roots value of the first derivative?

Question 10

What is second derivative value at x=0?

Question 11

Origin point is relative maxim or minima?

Thank you for participating in this research

12

Design and Simulation Analysis of Multi-Agent Online Dissemination Model on the Basis of "The Spiral of Silence" Theory

Qiuyun Miao[1] & Yang Shen[1]

[1] School of Economics and Management, Nanjing University of Aeronautics and Astronautic, China

Correspondence: Yang Shen, School of Economics and Management, Nanjing University of Aeronautics and Astronautic, Nanjing, China. E-mail: shen.y@nuaa.edu.cn

Abstract

This article studies the classical theory of communications—the Spiral of Silence. The key factors are extracted for multi-agent modeling and simulation with Netlogo. It turns out that opinion climate is the external formation of the Spiral of Silence. Besides, the size of opinion climate has no direct effects on the Spiral of Silence.

Keywords: the Spiral of Silence, multi-agent modeling, simulation, Netlogo

1. Introduction

The innovation of "The Spiral of Silence" theory has attracted many researchers under today's network communication environment, some scholars believe that the the Spiral of Silence in cyberspace is weakening which plays a new role in network media. GAO Xianchun et al. think that: "Mass media and specific individual communities make a difference in the new media environment constructed by Internet, mobile phones and others which are in the construction of specific event. And they both trigger the double helix of silence. In other words, mass media and individual communities form spirals respectively, meanwhile, both games lead to opinion cassette which is the factor affecting individual perception. As a result, the double helix of silence influences individual expressions of opinion. "(GAO Xianchun et al,2014) Yang Zhibiao supports the thory despite of its assumptions and limitations. In his opinion, it is still available in network environment. What is more, "the spiral of silence" is alive with "Against the Spiral of Silence".

However, other scholars believe that the Spiral of Silence is still spinning in the new era. To explore the views of "Gay Bullying", Sherice Gearhart et al. investigate 760 participants. It was found that the the Spiral of Silence still exists in social networks, besides, personal ideology will also have an impact on the willingness of expression (Sherice Gearhart et al, pp. 18-36, 2014.). Li Chuansheng points out that the Spiral of Silence still works because of the fear of isolation and group pressure in the network. What is more, the Internet has a character of anonymity, but net users' behavior is not unrestricted and complete freedom does not exist which due to group norm and social norm in the network community. That is the reason why the Spiral of Silence is still in the spin (Li Chuansheng, pp. 4-12, 2014). Na Yeon Lee et al. carry out a series of studies on controversial topics among journalists who work for nine national newspapers and two networks broadcasting corporation through the empirical research. It turns out that the Spiral of Silence still exists, especially in the social networking site—Twitter (YL Na, pp. 443-458, 2015). Cheng Yao also points out that because of unconverted habits of netizens, squelch on the Internet and attention which the country begins paying to supervising public opinion online, the Spiral of Silence will coexist with public opinion on the network for a long time in a more subtle way. Moreover, according to a report released by the Pew Research Center and the Rutgers University, social media such as Twitter and Facebook will contain the diversification of views, hinder public affairs debates and limit people to state their views. Especially when they find that their opinions are different the fear of isolation; climate of opinion, and quasi-statistical sensewith friends'. The report also said that very few people who use social media regularly express different points of view offline.

In order to study the impacts mechanisms of the Spiral of Silence, Scholars adopt empirical research through questionnaire to explore the impact of " the climate of opinion " – one factor of the Spiral of Silence. In Chang Ning's research, it is found that post-90 college students adhere to the "expression"of the highest degree in real life. Unexpectedly, under the anonymous network, post-90 college students tend be more silence. The study also shows that the anonymity of the network is not the main factor to promote the expression. Zhou Baohua investigates the willingness of college students and its factors by sampling survey. Based on the test results and analysis, different climate of opinion has different effects on college students which is suggested. The degree of consensus with the majority in society and those online has no obvious effects on the expression of college students on the Internet. However, opinions of college students are not the same as those of main medium or those of parents', the network has a significant positive effect on college students to express their opinions.

Above all, the Spiral of Silence may not be fully consistent with the characteristics of dissemination of public opinion in the new era, but it still works. At the same time, there are few papers exploring the propagation mechanism of the Spiral of Silence by multi-agent modeling. The paper attempts to describe communicating characteristics of the Spiral of Silence from relatively objective perspectives. At first, this paper will construct propagation model of the Spiral of Silence by using multi-agent modeling. Then, the paper adopts Netlogo to simulate the model. Finally, the model will be validated.

2. Framework of the Digest Format

The Spiral of Silence theory put forward by German communication scholar Elisabeth Noelle-Neumann explains how people decide whether or not to express their own true feelings. According to the theory, the will of expression is associated with external pressure, such as the media and the views of people around. The spiral of silence is widely used in media and communication research to describe the silence of controversial events.

In 1980, Elisabeth Noelle-Neumann published *The Spiral of Silence: Public Opinion-Our Social Skin*, she thought the spiral of silence comes from the nature of the society, at the same time, it comes from entrenched fear of human beings. When people found himself/herself is a member of the minority, he/she would tend to be silence because of fear of isolation. On the contrary, when a person is a member of the majority, he/she would be more willing to express himself/herself. In this book, she thought that the theory was made up of five basic hypotheses in summary.

(1)Individual fear of isolation;

(2)The individual evaluates the climate of opinion constantly because of fear of isolation.

(3)The fear of isolation is used to deal with individuals who deviate from the mainstream by the society.

(4)The results of evaluation affect individual behavior and opinion in public, especially by revealing or hiding their views.

(5)This hypothesis relates to four hypotheses above and they combine to explain the formation and change of public opinion and so on. (Noelle-Neumann, pp. 143-158, 1977)

Due to the fear of isolation, the agents will change their opinions according to majority opinion. To avoid isolation, people will try to seek the mainstream views and observe the rally of all kinds of views. Repeat the cycle, one voice is growing, while the other tends to be silence which is called the Spiral of Silence.

3. Modeling and Simulation based on the Theory

3.1Modeling based on the Spiral of Silence

According to Neumann's theory, there are three main factors of the theory: the fear of isolation; climate of opinion and quasi-statistical sense. The paper summarizes model as shown in Figure1.

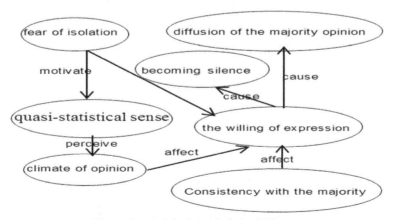

Figure 1. Model of the Spiral of Silence.

According to the model, the ultimate source of the Spiral of Silence is fear of isolation, but "climate of opinion" and "consistency with the majority" can affect the willing of expression directly. In order to facilitate research, this paper raises some brief and necessary assumptions:

Hypothesis 1: There are only two sides in the dissemination of public opinion. That is to say there are only positive opinion and negative opinion. At the same time, climate of opinion can be simulated by adjusting the ratio of positive and negative comments.

Hypothesis 2: There is only one kind of the majority opinion online. On the basis of the theory, there is always an overwhelming view in the dissemination of public opinion. Thus, adjusting the proportion of two sides of the opinion by which the majority opinion can be randomly decided in the Internet can simulate the propagation mechanism of the Spiral of Silence well.

Hypothesis 3: In given conditions, Individual views may change along with the spread of public opinion.

There are two main agents in the construction of simulation model, as shown in Figure 2.

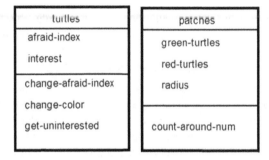

Figure 2. Class Diagram

The agent "turtle" is made up of two attributes: afraid-index and interest. When external climate of opinion changes, individual afraid-index will change accordingly and agents may change their opinions. Setting methods includes the followings: "change-afraid-index"、 "change-color" (Color changes indicate the changing of opinion in the program) and "get-interest". Properties of the agent "patch" consist of "green-turtles"、 "red-turtles" and "radius". Properties are used to count the number of green and red turtles within a radius of "radius" around a certain "patch" in order to simulate the climate of opinion around a certain "turtle" and the method "count-around-num" is needed to achieve the goal.

3.2 Simulation based on the Spiral of Silence

(1) Properties Settings

The fear of isolation and external climate of opinion affect the circumstances of information dissemination system in the theory which prompts the views of some events, evaluations and opinions in society. The evolution of Spiral of silence online exists in complex social network. The "Agent" can be seen as main element of view changes in this network. Attitude changes of netizens can be reflected by the change of the "Agent". The "Agent" influences each other through interactions which causes individual to change opinions. The study designs agent's properties in Table I:

Table 1. Introduction of Property Settings

Agent	variable name	explanation
Turtles	Initial-people	value scope [0,1000] representing the number of people in the initial state
	Initial-chance	value scope [0,1] representing the probability distribution of initial state
	r-afraid-index g-afraid-index	representing red or green turtles' fear index and it will change as the climate changes.
Patches	red-turtles green-turtles	representing the number of green and red turtles within a radius of "radius" around a certain "patch"
	radius	value scope [1,10] representing the radius of the climate of opinion in which the turtle can be affected

Most Internet users will try to avoid isolation caused by separate attitudes and views. When agents find their own views are different from those of most Internet users or those of the mainstream media, they will not tend to express their opinions. Instead, they may choose to change views to correspond to the mainstream views online.

(2) Settings of initial state

The slider--initial-chance is set to represent the distribution of initial state. The proportion of positive and negative opinions will vary when setting different ratios. Besides, The "initial-people" stands for the number of people who know the event and express their views. The "radius" is on behalf of the size of the climate of opinion in which the agent can be affected. According to the spiral of silence, the fear of isolation is inherent nature of the people, thus the initial values of "r-afraid-index" and "g-afraid-index" are set to 50 each.

(3) Settings of interaction rules

a. Collecting Statistics of climate of opinion around some individual: through Netlogo program, the climate of opinion can be collected automatically. (Here's the code.)

```
to count-around-num
    ask turtles [set red-turtles(sum[count turtles with [color = red] ]of turtles in-radius radius)
      set green-turtles( sum[count turtles with [color = green] ]of turtles in-radius radius)]
end
```

b. Changing Attitudes: when the value of the fear of isolation reaches a certain critical value, Internet users may change their views. What is more, when corresponding to the majority, agents will be willing to express their opinions and try to influence other agents. That's why there is a process called "hatch", here's the code.

```
to change-color
        if red-turtles > green-turtles [
            if color = green and   random r-afraid-index < 35
          [set color red fd random 10
            hatch 1 [set color red fd random 10 set r-afraid-index 50 ]]
end
```

c. The ultimate source--"fear of isolation": the fear index will change accordingly when the individual is affected by the surroundings. In addition, different agents have different degrees of changes on the fear index.   This part of the code is as follows:

```
to change-afraid-index
        if red-turtles > green-turtles
[set r-afraid-index(r-afraid-index - random 10)
set g-afraid-index(g-afraid-index + random 10)]
        if red-turtles < green-turtles
[set g-afraid-index(g-afraid-index - random 10)
  set r-afraid-index(r-afraid-index + random 10)]
    end
```

3.3 Analysis of Experimental Results

The initial value of " initial-people" is set to 880 which represents the number of people knowing the event at the first time. The initial value of " radius" is set to 1. The percentage of two sides is randomly decided and different percentages have direct impacts on future climate trends. In this paper, the values of initial-chance are 0.1, 0.3, 0.5, 0.7 and 0.9 respectively. Parameters are shown in Table II..

Table 2. Parameter 1

No.	initial-people	initial-chance	radius	r-afraid-index	g-afraid-index
1	880	0.1	1	50	50
2	880	0.3	1	50	50
3	880	0.5	1	50	50
4	880	0.7	1	50	50
5	880	0.9	1	50	50

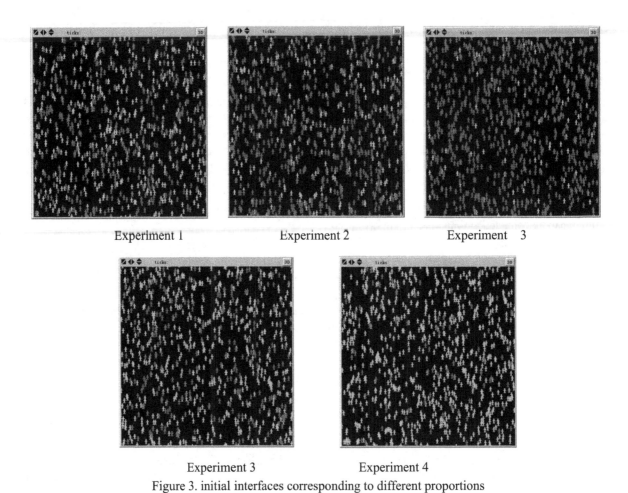

Experiment 1   Experiment 2   Experiment   3

Experiment 3   Experiment 4

Figure 3. initial interfaces corresponding to different proportions

Then, Press the "go" button to start running the program. Agents with different views in the interface will begin to change, and the corresponding graphs also began to be painted to show the change of different opinions as follows.

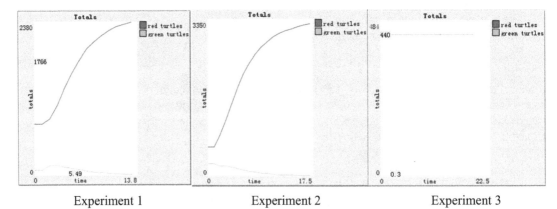

Experiment 1   Experiment 2   Experiment 3

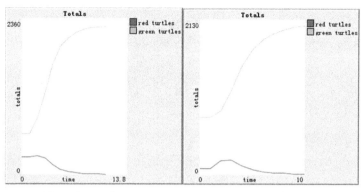

Experiment 4   Experiment 5

Figure 4. change curve chart

As can be seen in Figure 4., characteristics of spiral of silence are reflected clearly regardless of different opinion ratios in the initial state (0.1, 0.3, 0.7 or 0.9): The "majority" opinion keeps increasing, while the "minority" opinion represents significantly fluctuate declining. When the value of "initial-chance" is 0.5, the spiral of silence does not work. It can be concluded that uneven distribution of opinions is necessary for the theory, and that is to say, the distribution of views affects the formation of spiral of silence. Besides, it can be seen from the picture above that the climate of opinion is able to make the majority opinion strengthen, while it can make the minority opinion weaken.

In order to study the relationship between the theory and the parameter—radius which stands for the radius of the climate of opinion in which the turtle can be affected, five groups of experimental parameters are set up for the study, as shown below.

Table 3. Parameter 2

No.	initial-people	initial-chance	radius	r-afraid-index	g-afraid-index
1	880	0.1	1	50	50
2	880	0.1	4	50	50
3	880	0.1	7	50	50
4	880	0.1	10	50	50

Through these experiments, corresponding changes of curves are shown as below:

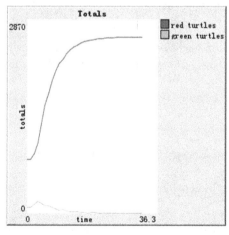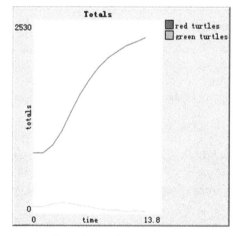

Experiment 1   Experiment 2

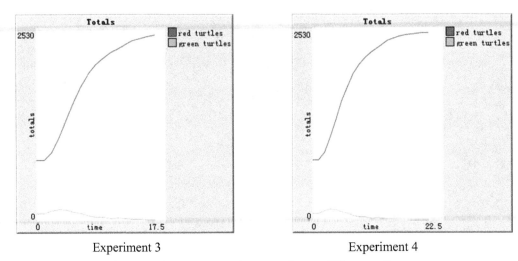

Experiment 3	Experiment 4

Figure 5. change curves corresponding to different radius

It is easy to find that the size of climate of opinion does not affect the formation of spiral of silence. To explore the inner mechanism and the relationship between the size of climate of opinion and the rate of opinion changes, a few comparative tests were conducted. Apart from the value of "radius" other parameters are invariant. The results are summarized in Table IV :

Table 4. Research between radius and opinions change rate

radius	$R^{(1)}$	$R^{(2)}$	$G^{(1)}$	$G^{(1)}$	$R^{(AVG)}$	$G^{(AVG)}$
1	792	2014	88	69	174.57	2.71
4	792	1998	88	70	172.28	2.57
7	792	1975	88	75	169	1.86
10	792	1987	88	71	170.71	2.42

$R^{(1)}$ represents the number of red-turtles at first; $R^{(2)}$ represents the number of red-turtles after 7 seconds; $G^{(1)}$ represents the number of green-turtles at first; $G^{(2)}$ represents the number of green-turtles after 7 seconds; $R^{(AVG)}$ represents red-turtles' average rate of rise; $G^{(AVG)}$ represents green-turtles' average rate of rise.

There is no direct link between the radius and the change rate of opinion. Thus, it can be concluded that the size of climate of opinion has no direct impact on the formation of spiral of silence.

4. Conclusion

The paper is based on the framework of the spiral of silence. At the same time, the study simulates the theory and analyses it. We can draw the following conclusions experiments: (1) The spiral of silence can make the majority opinion grow in strength while the minority opinion tend to die out finally; (2) The climate of opinion is the external factor of the spiral of silence; (3) The size of climate of opinion has no direct effects on the formation of spiral of silence.

References

Chang, N. (2015). Complex Performance of the Spiral of silence theory in the new media environment", *Journal of Communication University of China, 6,* 109-113.

Cheng, Y. (2013). Studying the 'spiral of silence' status seen from BBS network environment. *Jin Tian, 316,* 403-405.

Gao, X. C. et al. (2014). From "passive silence" to "active interaction": "double spiral of silence" effect in new media environment. *Press, 9,* 43-54.

Li, C. S. (2014). The applicability of spiral of silence in the network era. *Spread and Copyright, 8,* 4-12.

Na, Y. L. (2015). Tweeting the public: journalists' Twitter use, attitudes toward the public's tweets, and the relationship with the public. *Information Communication & Society, 18*(4), 443-458.

Noelle-Neumann. (1977). Turbulences in the Climate of Opinion: Methodological Applications of the spiral of silence theory. *Public Opinion Quarterly, 41*(2), 143-158.

Sherice, G. et al. (2014). Gay Bullying and Online Opinion Expression: Testing Spiral of Silence in the Social Media Environment. *Social Science Computer Review, 32*(1), 18-36.

Yang, Z. B. (2014). New 'Silence Spiral' Theory in the Environment of Internet Communication. *Journal of Harbin University, 35*(7), 95-98.

Zhou, B. H. (2014). Empirical study of college students ' network expression and factors—the 'Spiral of silence' and the 'climate of opinion' as the core. *Contemporary Communication, 5*, 34-37.

13

Survey on Pressure Situation of Professional Women and Causes Analysis

Xu Tingting[1], Zuo Yuxiu[1] & Ma Cunhong[2]

[1] College of Information Engineering, Taishan Medical University, Tai'an, China

[2] Enrollment and Employment Office, Taian Technician College, Tai'an, China

Correspondence: Xu Tingting, College of Information Engineering, Taishan Medical University, Chang Cheng Road, Tai'an, China. E-mail: xutingtinghot@163.com

The research is financed by the research project of Taian Philosophy and Social Science (project number: 15skx029,15skx039), research project of Taian Technology Bureau (project number: 201430774-13), Shandong Provincial Arts and Sciences (project number ZX2015002), and the research project of Shandong Provincial Department of Education (project number: J14LN22).

Abstract

With the development of society and the rise of women's status, professional women become non-ignorable in the workplace. The development of professional women also results in all kinds of pressure. Through the survey of the status of professional women's occupational pressure, this paper aims to analyze the differences of the total pressure in age, disposition, education, marital status, type of work and demographics, so as to explore the main factors; besides, this paper will also study the coping situation and discuss the relationship between the way of release and occupational pressure. Hope to conduct a more in-depth study of professional women's stress from wider angles in all around, providing a scientific basis for most professional women to adjust the physical and mental state, relieve stress, avoid the negative effects of burnout and improve work efficiency. This research has adopted cluster sampling method, surveyed by way of questionnaire, and discussed the status and influencing factors of women's occupational stress. The investigation on the influencing factors and countermeasures of female occupational stress could provide a more effective way of pressure relief for the majority of women, improve their work efficiency and better serve society! Therefore, it becomes an important topic to study the stress of professional women.

Keywords: profession women, stress, influencing factors, way of coping

1. Introduction

In recent years, due to the progress of modernization and rapid changes of social systems, in urban society, women's role has changed significantly, accounting for a significant proportion of the total labor forces in society, who, like men, are under the same evaluation criteria as well as the same pressure, becoming the backbone of the social development. Women are no longer as in the past, but gradually play an increasingly important role in society, and also bear various conflicts and pressures.

The study of professional women started relatively later and less in China. The research is targeted at the relationship between occupational burnout, stress and job satisfaction, and focuses on quantitative research, less qualitative one. Based on the data from the World Bank, about 64% of Chinese women are in the workplace, ranking second to none in the top 10 largest economies in the world. Last year, about 52% of 7 million college graduates in China are women. There is no doubt that pressure on women is also growing, so research on occupational stress is in desperate demand. As women's role in society will affect family stability, thereby affecting social stability, the study of women's pressure has very important value of society and times.

The investigation on the influencing factors and countermeasures of female occupational stresses could provide a more effective way of pressure relief for the majority of women, improve their work efficiency and better serve society.

2. Methods

This survey focused on female insurance employees, female teachers, female nurses, and ordinary female staff, to understand the source of stress from their age, marital status, education, work experience, position, self-perception, ability etc.

Questionnaires were designed based on the factors affecting women's stresses to survey from their age, education, work experience, position and facing pressures. The method of questionnaire was used to understand women's basic condition and their facing pressures. Investigators was responsible to issue the questionnaire and explain the content while the respondent filled in according to actual situation.

3. Analysis of Survey Result

3.1 Analysis of Respondent Demographics

Among the respondents, 33.3% were ordinary workers, 26% teachers, 20% nurse and 20% insurance employees, from ago from 20 to 35, accounting for 80%, and age of above of 35 account for 20%. Marital status: single women accounted for 33.3%, while married for 53.3%. Education: junior college and below accounted for 53.3%, bachelor for 26.7% and master for 20%. Disposition: introverted women accounted for 46.7%, the extroverted for 53.3%; release method included sports, talk, sleep and reading, accounted for 20%,40%,20% and13.3% respectively.

Table 1. Survey on pressure situation of professional women

Occupation	number of people	percentage
nurse	21	20%
Teacher	28	26.70%
insurance	21	20%
worker	35	33.30%
Age	**number of people**	**percentage**
20-25	20	19%
25-30	29	27.60%
30-35	35	33.30%
35-50	21	20%
Marital status	**number of people**	**percentage**
single	35	33.30%
married	56	53.30%
divorced	14	13.30%
education background	**number of people**	**percentage**
low education level	21	20%
College degree	35	33.30%
Bachelor's degree	28	26.70%
Master's degree	21	20%
Personality tendency	**number of people**	**percentage**
Introverted	49	46.70%
extroverted	56	53.30%
Way of release stress	**number of people**	**percentage**
sports	21	20%
shopping	42	40%
sleep	21	20%
read	21	20%

3.2 Relationship between Age and Stress

The age was concentrated between 20 and 50. As Figure 1:

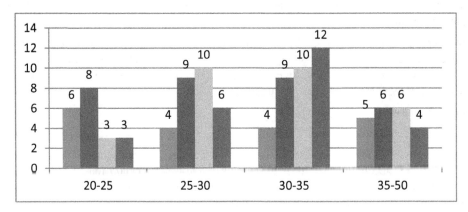

Figure 1. Relationship between Age and Stress value

It showed that the age between 20 and 25 suffered minimum stress, possibly because women at this age basically were just graduated from college, so they were full of curiosity to work and life, and assigned with easy work; women from 25 to 35 suffered the greatest stress, because most of them have married, and facing multiple pressure from marriage, family and career, they need stabilize their marriage and their family within this period and lay solid foundation for their career, thus their pressure were largest from various aspects; women over 35 years were comparatively in peace, because they have a relatively stable career and family.

3.3 Relationship between Marital Status and Stress

The marital status of study object includes the single, the married and the divorced. Analysis of occupational stress in different marital status groups showed as the following Figure 2:

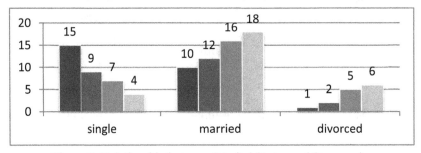

Figure 2. Relationship between Marital Status and Stress value

As shown in Figure 2, marital status affected women's stress to a large extent. A stable and united family would definitely reduce the stress on women, more conducive for them to fully play their talents at work! Married women faced pressure from children, caught in the family and work, they had to inevitably confront various conflicts and stresses; single women still held the hope to balance life and work, so it is uncertain whether the condition will be reversed.

3.4 Relationship between Occupational Group and Stress

This survey mainly focused on nurses, teachers, insurance employees and company workers and respectively made analysis of their stress from life and career, it was concluded as following in Figure 3:

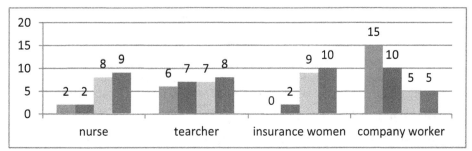

Figure 3. Relationship between Career and Stresses

According to the result, there are different stress in different industry. By the four industries in the survey, as Figure 3, the pressure higher to low: insurance employees > nurses > teachers > company workers, determined by the nature of industry, to be specific, insurance industry belongs to emerging services, with great risk, and their performance assessment will directly affect their salary and further influence their life. The second is nurse. Nurse belongs to professional technicians with big intensity of work, big career risk and low social status, so they have to work in high-concentrated attention and high-tensed, while their income fails to be in proportion to their workload. Additionally, this profession determines that nurses have narrowed range of career. Furthermore, it is very common for them to work overtime, which further increase their pressure. The profession of teachers is relatively stable. As teachers deal with students, there is rare intrigue; besides, this profession makes teachers have summer vacation, which is conducive for them teachers to better organize their work and life, and relax themselves. For ordinary workers, they are from the grass-roots level, whose work is single and share simple interpersonal relationship, so they have small stress.

3.5 Relationship between Deposition and Stress

Disposition in this study includes introverts and extroverts, the stress value of different disposition as showed in Figure 4:

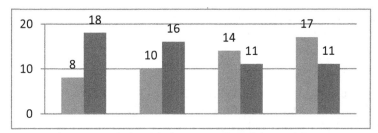

Figure 4. Relationship between Disposition and Stress

As we can see from Figure 4, there were 46% introverted women and 54% extrovert women in this survey, disposition has an influence on stress relieving, the introverted prefer to complain or swallow hard, which is not good to release stress and health; while the extroverted are outgoing, energetic, confident and sociable, tend to look at things with a positive attitude, and can rationally analyze and make response to stress.

3.6 Relationship between Education and Stress

Educational level would affect the stress and way of coping. In this survey, the surveyed groups had the education background of below junior college, junior college, undergraduate and master, as shown in Figure 5:

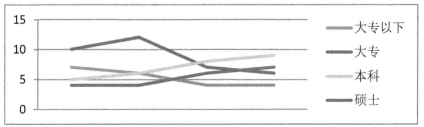

Figure 5. Relationship between Education and Stress

Through above comparison, it could be concluded that education determines the level of knowledge and conflicts in the work. The survey results showed that workers with and below junior college took relatively common simple work, whose ability was well matched with their work, so they had less stress. Most undergraduates suffered huge pressures because their abilities failed to meet their demand in the pursuit of their career, so the current work was not their ideal one. Graduate worked in middle or high management level in a company, but they were critical to their work and it was hard for them to cope with interpersonal relationship.

3.7 Relationship between Way of Release and Pressure

On the whole, the way of coping stress for occupational women shows mixing features, and most of them choose active way. Talk is the most common way for female workers to cope with stress. When feeling stressful, they will turn to friends, not only helpful in timely solving their problems but also conductive to reduce the negative effects from stress. The second is sleep and sports, which facilitates emotional persuasion and pressure release. The third is reading, which is an effective way to release stress.

4. Suggestions and Countermeasures

At present, stress has become shortcoming for women in the workplace, if you fail to release, your life and work will be disordered by enormous stress, possibly resulting in worse impact. So to learn to release stress will improve work efficiency and enhance work excellence.

1. Have a positive attitude to reality

What women need to do is get yourself a precise position, have a positive attitude to reality, and learn to know themselves, because no one has no shortcomings but virtue, and otherwise is the same. So you should learn to accept yourself, and also rightly evaluate, understand and know others.

2. Find a suitable way of release

Swimming, walking, jogging, yoga and other aerobic exercises are good to release pressure, release negative emotions and keep a positive attitude! Appropriate exercise will help to eliminate fatigue and can also improve brain function. In order to relax yourself, you can select your favorite sports which can generate joy of motion, let yourself enjoy catharsis in sports, and make yourself sweat. Such a person will be a lot more comfortable.

3. Try to communicate and exchange idea with others

It is benefit to learn to balance your work and life, try to communicate and exchange idea with others, and get the support from your family. After all, it is the key to maintain the balance between family and career in order to get happy family and successful career!

4. Strengthen yourself cultural accomplishment

Finally, we should improve our knowledge and skills in the workplace, and recharge ourselves in our spare time. In addition, we should also strengthen our own cultivation and foster a broad mind. Moreover, we should establish the concept of fair competition and mutual assistance. Last but not least, we should give yourself the confidence to meet new challenges!

In short, women's stress comes from a wide aspects, affected by many factors, such as age, occupation, marital status, education, work experience and disposition. Women should improve their pressure under their own circumstances and enhance their physical and mental health so as to improve work efficiency; meanwhile, family and society should give women more love and understanding. Only in this way can they be more relaxed and enjoy exciting life.

References

Cheng, C. P. (2008). Occupational Stress and Social Support of Young Female White-collar Worker [D]. Suzhou: Suzhou University.

Guo, X. P. (2009). Women's Work Stress Survey and Stress Management Research in Shanghai [D]. Shanghai: Tongji University.

Jin, P. (2008). Discussion on Pressure Management of Female Employees. *Managers, 2008*(11). 23.

Liu, F., & Tu, X. J. (2007). Investigation and Analysis of Female Workers' Working Pressure in State-owned Enterprise. *Career Era, 4.*

Wang, L. J. (2008). Study on the Relationship between Work Stress and Performance of Occupational Women [D]. Zhejiang: Zhejiang Industrial and Commercial.

Wang, R., & Shi, M. (2011). Investigation on Factors of Part of Occupational Women's Work Stress. *M. China Market,* (39).

Yu, H. (2007). View on Pressure Management of Female Employees. *M. Market Weekly,* (4), 22-23.

14

Technological Aspects of E-Learning Readiness in Higher Education

Asma Ali Mosa[1], Mohd. Naz'ri bin Mahrin[1] & Roslina Ibrrahim[1]

[1] Advanced Informatics School, Universiti Teknologi Malaysia (UTM), Malaysia

Correspondence: Asma Ali Mosa, Advanced Informatics School, Universiti Teknologi Malaysia (UTM), Kuala Lumpur, Malaysia. E-mail: asma4_ali@yahoo.com

Abstract

E-learning has become one of the most important technologies of the modern era. E-learning is a learning process which aims to create an interactive learning environment based on the use of computers and the internet. Through e-learning, learners can access resources and information from anywhere and at anytime. Many higher education institutions have expressed an interest in implementing e-learning, and e-learning readiness is a critical aspect in achieving successful implementation. Higher education institutions should therefore assess their readiness before initiating an e-learning project. E-learning readiness involves many components of e-learning, including students, lecturers, technology and the environment, which must be ready in order to formulate a coherent and achievable strategy. One of the aspects of e-learning readiness is technological readiness, which plays an important role in implementing an effective and efficient e-learning project. This paper explores the gaps in the knowledge about the technological aspects of e-learning readiness through the conduct of a literature review. In particular, the review focuses on the models that have been developed to assess e-learning readiness.

Keywords: E-learning readiness, technological aspects of readiness, assessment, higher education

1. Introduction

Information and communication technology has created new opportunities to improve the existing education systems and learning styles, and has helped to develop and innovate new and effective teaching and learning methods (Salem, 2006). It has also helped to develop many modern concepts and tools in the field of education, such as e-learning. E-learning is the use of electronic media, educational technology and information and communication technologies (ICT) in education (Contreras & Shadi, 2015). E-learning involves the application of new technologies, such as the internet, intranet, email and satellite broadcasts, to the learning process (Puteh (2008). E-learning helps to increase the flexibility of the educational process and facilitate communications and interactions between teachers and students. The provision of this service on the internet makes it available and easy to use by most students anytime and anywhere through the use of their personal computers. E-learning plays a prominent role in the field of education but faces a number of challenges that hinder the achievement of its objectives (Najib & Rebhi, 2006).

E-learning has become an increasingly significant element of the pedagogy adopted in higher education institutions (HEIs) (Kituyi & Tusubira, 2013). According to Tarus, Gichoya, & Muumbo (2015), e-learning is an increasingly popular approach to teaching and learning in most institutions of higher learning worldwide. A review of the literature shows that, in order to adopt a successful e-learning system, the HEI should assess its readiness before initiating an e-learning project. A primary reason for the failure to adopt an e-learning system in higher education is the lack of assessment of readiness for e-learning (Hanafizadeh & Ravasan, 2011; Odunaike, Olugbara, & Ojo, 2013).

E-learning readiness can be defined as the assessment of how ready an institution is to adopt and implement e-learning (Bowles, 2004). According to Borotis and Poulymenakou (2004), e-learning readiness is "the mental or physical preparedness of an individual for some e-learning experience or action". E-learning readiness is also defined as "those factors that must be accomplished before e-learning implementation can be regarded as being successful" (Odunaike et al., 2013).

According to Nyoni (2014), e-learning readiness provides the key information that organisations require in order to develop strategies which can cater for the specific needs of each learning group. (Borotis & Poulymenakou, 2004) pointed out that e-learning readiness helps an instructional designer to design e-learning strategies and experiences comprehensively and helps a lecturer to effectively deliver learning experiences to students. All aspects of e-learning must be "ready" in order to develop a coherent and achievable strategy. Thus, all aspects of e-learning including students, lecturers, technology and the environment must be ready. The readiness of technological aspects also plays an important role in implementing successful e-learning. AbuSneineh and Zairi (2010) stated that access and ease of technology are the most important factors that contribute to the overall effectiveness of an e-learning system. Bridges et al. (Bridges, Juceviciene, Jucevicius, Mclaughlin, & Stankeviciute, 2014) pointed out that the adoption of new technologies in the field of education has enabled access to education to become easy and universal.

Bhuasiri et al. (2012) highlighted technological aspects as an important factor in a successful e-learning system; hence, the readiness of the technological aspects needs to be thoroughly explored in order to analyze the overall e-learning readiness. Holsapple and Lee-Post (2006) explained that, in an e-learning context, online users must use the technology to complete their online tasks in the online learning environment. Some technological factors such as proper software and hardware or bandwidth can play a crucial role in e-learning outcomes (Keramati, Afshari, & Kamrani, 2011). Low speed internet and problems while using the system may result in student dissatisfaction and lead to students dropping out from the course. Therefore, it is necessary to assess the technological readiness for e-learning before the implementation of an e-learning system in order to realize the benefits of e-learning and reduce the challenges during e-learning implementation (Alshaher, 2013). For this reason, the measurement of e-learning readiness is essential to support successful e-learning implementation in higher education (Rohayani, Kurniabudi, & Sharipuddin, 2015).

Having introduced the concept of e-learning, the remainder of this paper is structured as follows: Section 2 presents a review of e-learning readiness models and frameworks. Section 3 discusses the reviewed e-learning models and frameworks. Section 4 presents the conclusion and the future directions for our work.

2. E-Learning Readiness Models and Frameworks: A Review

Different factors affect the implementation and effectiveness of e-learning in the education environment, but readiness is the critical success factor in the successful adoption of the e-learning mode of acquiring knowledge (Albarrak, 2010). This section presents a review of the various models on e-learning readiness in the literature. These models have been developed to identify the factors that affect e-learning readiness in various work settings.

Darab and Montazer (2011) proposed a model for assessing e-learning readiness in higher education in Iran (Figure 1). In this model, the technological aspects can be determined in the form of readiness related to the equipment, security and communication network. The factors identified by the model include policy, networks, equipment, management, standards, content regulations, financial and human resource sources, culture and security. Policies and standards are necessary to make any system or operation work effectively and in a uniform manner. Management of the e-learning mode includes the formulation of the required rules and the design of an effective management system. In addition, the network element should be clearly assessed in order for e-learning to be successfully accomplished because the deliberate architecture of an appropriate network will assist the teacher to better catalyze and motivate the students in the learning process as a vital and life-long behavioral trait (Almada de Aseencio, 1996). Culture is identified as a factor that significantly contributes to the e-learning environment: the culture must be such that the teachers, students and employees understand the important advantages of e-learning and accept the use of the system. Equipment is essential to make the system work as it is based on technology and technological equipment. According to Bridges et al. (2014), a centralized system is adopted in almost all e-learning modes as highly efficient management is required to make the e-learning mode function easily and to benefit the institute and the students in acquiring their goals through e-learning.

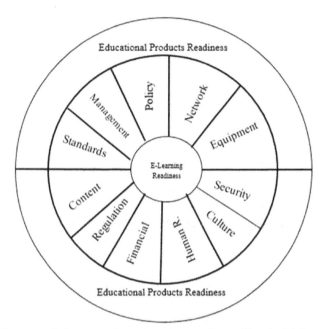

Figure 1. Framework for assessing e-learning readiness (Darab & Montazer, 2011)

Akaslan and Law (2011) investigated the extent to which HEIs in Turkey were prepared to include e-learning as part of their learning business. They identified various factors that affect the readiness for e-learning in a developing country where education is given significance and, due to changing living patterns, the educational institutions are moving from traditional learning modes to e-learning modes. These e-learning factors are based on two beliefs: that e-learning will reduce the efforts required from teachers and at the same time increase the educational level, and that some training is needed for students as well as for teachers in order to move from traditional learning to the e-learning mode. These beliefs affect the perceptions of the related entities. According to Ford, Ford, and D'Amelio (2008), when a change is implemented, it initially faces some issues and resistance but later on will be accepted. This process is reflected in Akaslan and Law's e-learning model (Figure 2). In the first phase of readiness, it is essential to consider four aspects, namely, the people, technology, content and institution. Resistance is to be expected from people who are concerned about the implementation of e-learning along with the institution as it inculcates e-learning in its activities.

The technological aspects in Akaslan and Law's (2011) model are the hardware, software and stability of the internet. Hardware refers to the physical components, and software refers to the information aspect of technology. This requires having access to the internet with a PC or laptop as the hardware along with a web browser such as Internet Explorer or Firefox as the software. In the second phase, when the users identify the benefits of e-learning, they accept the e-learning mode and consider it to be useful. In the third phase, training is given in order to completely adapt to the e-learning mode. Learners, teachers, facility managers (i.e. the managers of the university facilities that are relevant to e-learning) and other personnel (i.e. the employees whose roles are relevant to e-learning) are included in this training.

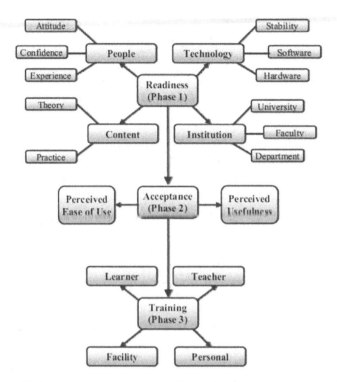

Figure 2. Model for measuring students' readiness for e-learning (Akaslan & Law, 2011)

Keramati et al. (2011) designed a model to determine the effect of factors affecting the outcomes of the e-learning process in high schools (Figure 3). The factors that affected the e-learning most included the perceptions of students and teachers along with IT and support. Moreover, readiness factors were found to include technology, organizational factors and social factors. The interaction of e-learning factors and readiness factors creates an effect on the outcomes of e-learning. If the interaction is positive, then the benefits will also be positive; if the interaction is negative, it leads to no or pessimistic results for the teacher, student and the institution. The positive interaction is appreciable and leads to teachers' progress in terms of reaching more students within a limited time along with higher flexibility, and leads to students' progress in terms of gaining higher knowledge through a variety of resources and books available online. Flexibility and convenience are positive points for both students and teachers as they can learn or make others learn from any location. The benefits to the HEI include an increase in the education level and an increase in the number of students graduating each year, resulting in an increased literacy rate. The technical readiness factors in this study included the hardware, software, content, internet access and bandwidth.

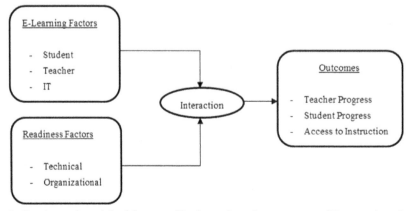

Figure 3. Conceptual model of factors affecting e-learning outcomes (Keramati et al., 2011)

(Omoda & Lubega, 2011) conducted a study to identify the factors that affect the e-learning readiness process implemented by HEIs in Uganda. They proposed ways to encourage the use of e-learning systems in order to increase access to education and improve the educational level in Uganda. They collected and analyzed data from eight institutions. The analysis revealed that the factors that affect the implementation of e-learning systems and that are therefore important to consider include awareness, culture and technology along with pedagogy and content. Regardless of the particular country in which the e-learning is to be implemented, these factors are significant and need to be considered and managed well in order to reduce the resistance level and to increase the outcomes that are to be attained. The model developed by (Omoda & Lubega, 2011) (Figure 4) depicts a hierarchy of factors, with awareness and culture having the most effect on implementation and readiness, followed by technology, pedagogy and content.

The study by (Omoda & Lubega, 2011) further found that level of awareness about technology and learning methods can help in facilitating the implementation of e-learning systems. Culture is another aspect that can affect the implementation, as culture is a combination of values, beliefs, norms and behaviors that are followed by the teachers and learners and by the institution. An e-learning project may face resistance due to culture; therefore, organizations wanting to embrace a successful e-learning strategy must ensure that they are fully prepared culturally. Technology is an essential consideration as the latest technology facilitates effective implementation. Moreover, pedagogy is a vital consideration as the way of teaching and learning in e-learning differs from the traditional teaching system and teachers need to be trained in order to teach well through e-learning. The technological aspects in the study were about the availability of resources for e-learning: for example, a sufficient number of computers in the computer laboratories and the provision of reasonably fast and stable internet services in the institute.

Figure 4. Model for e-learning institutional readiness assessment (Omoda & Lubega, 2010)

Alshaher (2013) proposed an e-learning system readiness assessment (ELSRA) model based on McKinsey's 7S model utilizing fuzzy logic analysis (Figure 5). The 7S model comprises strategy, structure, systems, style/culture, staff, skills and shared values. If properly followed, consideration of these elements can assist the implementation of a new system or project. Alshaher collected data through interviews and questionnaires and identified 23 7S-related factors that affect ELSRA in HEIs in Iraq. These factors can affect the implementation and result in strengths or weaknesses in the e-learning system. A proper strategy is to be formulated in the first place in order to determine the organization's goals and objectives that are to be achieved by all its functions. It includes the vision and the mission that is divided into goals and objectives through strategic plans that help the organization respond to changes in the external environment and remain competitive. The structure to be followed in the implementation of an e-learning system includes centralization to take decisions on a single basis as e-learning is similar for everyone and is not customized. Moreover, the size of the organization and the role of the chief information officer can also facilitate the implementation of an e-learning system.

In this model, the system includes: technology, content, platform support, documentation and style. In order to get higher benefits, easy access to technology and the internet is to be made available for the learners and teachers. Content is to be designed to be effective and highly beneficial along with regular amendments in order to inculcate the latest knowledge and utilize the latest resources. Documentation is essential to reduce the technology gap between the learner and the teacher. Style includes culture, leadership, communication and top management support. Higher levels of top management support will lead to higher levels of e-learning readiness among the teachers and learners. According to Goi and Ng (2009), top management support consists of three parts, namely, technological support, funding support, and experiencing support. The culture should be developed in a way that encourages the use of e-learning and the leadership style to be followed should be transformational in order to include various innovative means and methods to acquire knowledge. Decision making and problem solving are also important leadership skills required to deal with the issues faced in the initial stages of e-learning implementation. Communication should affect not only the direct stakeholders but should include all of those who are part of e-learning including technicians, lecturers and management.

In Alshaher's (2013) model, the staff component includes sufficient manpower, project team, trust and training and learning. Without the support of the staff, effective implementation of an e-learning system is not possible. Skills are the competencies of the organization and that of management, IT staff and students. The shared values include the beliefs of the people that can help in accepting or creating resistance to the e-learning system. The technology aspects in this model include: computers (that should be available to learners), the hosting network (capable of providing the content at speed), the security level, and IT support to help learners and solve technological problems such as speed and reliability issues with the internet.

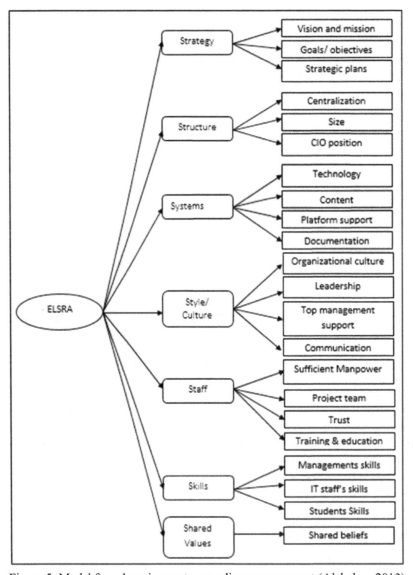

Figure 5. Model for e-learning system readiness assessment (Alshaher, 2013)

Engholm and McLean (2001) proposed a model (Figure 6) that identifies an organization's need for e-learning and the factors in e-learning readiness. The need for e-learning is identified by external sources and need analysis; e-learning emerges as a solution when there is a need to cater to diverse learning needs accompanied by convenience and quality but less cost in order to provide learners with a competitive edge. The factors affecting e-learning readiness include organizational culture, individual learners and the technology at large. These three factors are considered as organizational and industry factors. Handling these factors well results in e-learning readiness. This model guides managers and personnel in the field of training and development in their respective organization's e-learning readiness assessment.

Engholm and McLean (2001) stated that, in order to ensure a successful e-learning experience, organizational culture is to be supportive of learning, self-directed learning is to be followed, training and development is to be highly observed, e-learning is to be aligned well with the organization's goals, and the organization is to be managed as a learning organization to support and encourage learning. Individual learners are directed in such a way that they take responsibility and manage their time well, are provided with enough flexibility but encouragement to learn, possess basic technical and learning skills, are computer literate and are willing to share information and knowledge along with the ability to gain knowledge from a variety of sources. Content is to be adequately provided to learners from a variety of sources. The content should be user friendly and accommodate different learning styles. Technological factors are to be catered for well by giving learners access to technology and user-friendly technology. Learners are to have adequate hardware and software with proper internet connection and bandwidth, along with supported versions of the latest software.

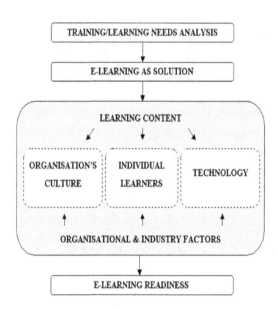

Figure 6. Model for e-learning readiness (Engholm & McLean, 2001)

Lopes (2007) proposed a model to evaluate the e-learning readiness of a HEI (Figure 7) and reported the results of its application. The model shows that the business, technology, content, culture, human resources and financial resources affect the e-learning readiness. E-learning can only be accepted if it is aligned with business aims and objectives and leads to the effective accomplishment of the business aims. Technology infrastructure is to be aligned in order to support the e-learning; a centralized system is effective. The content to be delivered through e-learning should be of high quality and standards, as well as easily understandable. The technical language is to be at the level of learners. In addition, the content is to be from a variety of sources. The institution is to be financially strong, as e-learning in the initial stages requires a high amount of capital. This spending should be seen as an investment rather than as a cost as it leads to higher benefits in the long term. The culture should encourage e-learning readiness and innovative learning. Moreover, the human resource of sound knowledge is to be maintained to ensure successful transition from traditional learning to the e-learning mode. The e-learning system must have enough support along with teachers who will be able to make the system a success. The technology aspects in this model focus on the HEI's technological infrastructure and on the degree of access to computers and the internet.

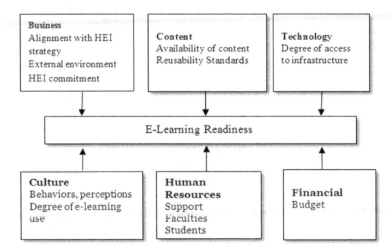

Figure 7. E-learning readiness dimensions (Lopes, 2007)

Chapnick (2000) proposed a framework to assess organizational readiness for e-learning whereby, in order to measure the readiness to adopt e-learning, it is necessary that the factors associated with psychological readiness, sociological readiness, environmental readiness, human resource and other factors are analyzed (Figure 8). Analysis of the eight categories as facilitated by the framework leads to the assessment of e-learning readiness and identifies the factors that are necessary for the successful implementation of e-learning. Furthermore, it is necessary that the identified factors are evaluated collectively in order to determine the overall readiness to adopt e-learning.

The eight categories in Chapnick (2000) framework are used to analyze the overall e-learning readiness and the factors associated with it. It is observed that this model also considers the factors related to financial and sociological readiness. The model identifies that, for the successful assessment of readiness to adopt and implement e-learning, it is extremely important that the financial capability should be considered in addition to the sociological factors that determine the overall readiness to adopt e-learning. These sociological factors include the overall culture and the perceptions of individuals regarding the implementation of the new and innovative technology of e-learning and the overall process of acquiring education. The technological aspects related to readiness in this model are equipment and technological skills.

E-Learning Readiness Factors	Explanation of Factors
Psychological readiness	The effect of an individual's state of mind on the outcome of the e-learning initiative. Considered a particularly important factor, because it can sabotage the implementation process
Sociological readiness	The interpersonal aspects of the environment within which the e-learning program will be implemented
Environmental readiness	The major forces operating on stakeholders, both inside and outside the organization
Human resource readiness	The availability and design of the human support system
Financial	The budget size and allocation process for the e-learning program
Technological skill (aptitude) readiness	The observable and measurable technical competencies of the organization and individuals involved
Equipment readiness	Possession of the proper equipment
Content readiness	The subject matter and goals of construction

Figure 8. E-learning readiness framework (Chapnick, 2000)

Psycharis (2005) proposed a model for the assessment of e-learning readiness in an educational system at a country level (Figure 9). In the model, several factors need to be considered under the categories of resources, education and environment. The factors in the resources category determine the technological readiness, economic readiness and human resource readiness. The education category refers to the readiness related to content and the overall educational readiness. The environment category includes leadership, culture and entrepreneurial readiness. The three categories comprise eight factors that are used to assess the overall readiness to adopt and implement e-learning. These factors are extremely important for the success of an e-learning system; hence, it is necessary that they should be considered and evaluated to ascertain the level of readiness among the general public to adopt the new concept of e-learning.

The three categories of assessing e-learning readiness in Psycharis (2005) model take the factors associated with e-learning in a holistic view in order to analyze the ability and willingness of the users for whom the e-learning is being implemented. The environment and resources categories are extremely important in this case as they analyze the exact capacity related to the technology, human resource and economic readiness. At the same time, the environment category analyzes the support from the leadership and the overall environment regarding the adoption of e-learning. The technological aspects related to readiness in this model include hardware, software and access to the internet.

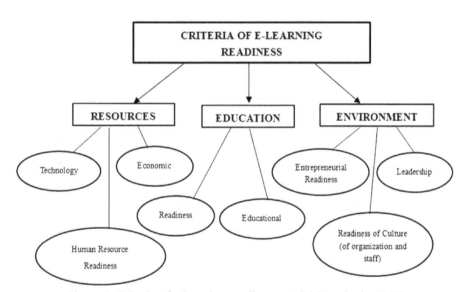

Figure 9. Criteria of e-learning readiness model (Psycharis, 2005)

Aydin and Tasci (2005) proposed a model that identifies four areas that determine the overall readiness to adopt e-learning in an organization, namely, technology, innovation, people and self-development (Figure 10). The factors identified in the model collectively determine the ability and willingness of an organization to adopt e-learning. The area of technology includes the access to computers and the internet and the ability of individuals to use such facilities. The model includes the attitudes of users towards the adoption of e-learning as an important aspect of assessing e-learning readiness. The model further includes the education level of employees as another factor that influences the overall readiness to adopt e-learning. The budget of an organization and the self-belief among the employees are other factors that determine the overall readiness to adopt and implement e-learning.

The categories of resources, skills and attitude are also well considered in this model to determine the overall readiness to adopt e-learning. Aydin and Tasci (2005) identified that these factors facilitate the successful implementation of an e-learning system in an organization as they determine the necessary requirements for the new technology of e-learning and the factors associated with it.

	Restores	Skills	Attitudes
Technology	Access to computers and the internet	Ability to use computers and the internet	Positive attitude toward use of technology
Innovation	Barriers	Ability to adopt innovations	Openness to innovations
People	• Educated level of employees • Experienced HR specialist • An e-learning champion • Vendors and external parties	Ability to learn via/with technology	
Self-Development	Budget	Ability to manage time	Belief in self-development

Figure 10. E-learning readiness model (Aydin & Tasci, 2005)

3. Discussion

The review of e-learning readiness models in the previous section identified that there are various factors that can be used to measure readiness for e-learning implementation in HEIs. Table 1 presents a comparison of the e-learning readiness factors in the literature.

Table 1. Comparison of factors related to e-learning readiness

Author(s) / Components /Factors	Darab and Montazer (2011)	Akaslan and Law (2011)	Keramati et al. (2011)	Omoda-Onyait and Lubega	Alshaher (2013)	Engholm and McLean (2001)	Lopes (2007)	Chapnick (2000)	Psycharis (2005)	Aydin and Tasci (2005)	Total	Frequency
Technology	√	√	√	√	√	√	√	√	√	√	10	1
Learners	√	√	√		√	√	√		√	√	8	2
Content	√	√		√			√	√	√		6	3
Resources	√	√					√	√	√	√	6	3
Social and cultural	√		√	√		√	√				5	4
Awareness			√	√				√	√	√	5	4
Equipment	√							√	√	√	4	5
Management	√				√				√		3	6
Standards	√			√						√	3	6
Institution			√	√					√		3	6
Acceptance of e-learning		√								√	2	7
Pedagogy				√			√				2	7
Human resources								√	√		2	7
Financial								√	√		2	7
Security	√										1	8
Laws and Regulations	√										1	8
Training procedure										√	1	8

The comparison in Table 1 shows that, among the factors that are identified in the literature as the important factors to be considered in e-learning readiness assessment, the factor with the highest frequency is technology, followed by learners (at the second highest frequency), and then content and resources (both at the third highest frequency). Social and cultural factors and awareness are not far behind on the list of the most important factors to be considered in assessing e-learning readiness (both at the fourth highest frequency). The comparison shows that equipment is another factor that determines the e-learning readiness (at the fifth highest frequency), as well as management, standards and institution (at the sixth highest frequency. The factors of pedagogy, human resources, acceptance of e-learning, financial, security, laws and regulations and training procedure are recognized in the literature as important factors that influence e-learning readiness, but with low frequency.

As shown in the comparison of various models in Table 1 above, technology appears with the highest frequency in the literature and is therefore identified as the most important factor among all factors in e-learning readiness. This result attracted our attention and motivated us to learn more about the technological aspects that influence e-learning readiness. We therefore compared the factors related to the technological aspects of e-learning readiness in the ten models and frameworks that were reviewed above in Section 2. Table 2 presents a summary of the comparison.

Table 2. Comparison of factors related to technological aspects of e-learning readiness

Factors of Technology	Darab and Montazer (2011)	Akaslan and Law (2011)	Keramati et al. (2011)	Omoda-Onya it and Lubega (2011)	Alshaher (2013)	Engholm and McLean	Lopes (2007)	Chapnick (2000)	Psycharis (2005)	Aydin and Tasci (2005)	Total
Internet access		√	√	√	√	√	√		√	√	8
Hardware	√	√	√					√	√		5
Availability of computers				√	√	√				√	4
Software		√	√						√		3
IT support					√	√					2
Technical skills								√		√	2
Security	√				√						2
Communication network	√					√					2
Infrastructure							√				1

On the basis of the summary in Table 2, it is observed that there are several technological factors that influence the overall readiness to adopt and implement e-learning. The comparison of these technological factors indicate that internet access, hardware and availability of computers are commonly emphasized in all of the models. On the other hand, a few studies emphasized software, IT support, technical skills, security, communication and infrastructure. Thus, the analysis of these models leads to the conclusion that these technological factors are not considered in every model and there is no single model that encompasses each of the identified factors. There are factors that are missing from some models but are reported in other models. For example, the IT support factor is not mentioned in seven of the ten reviewed models but is mentioned in three of the reviewed models which recommend that IT support should exist to help learners if something goes wrong and to solve problems such as network issues (Engholm, 2002). IT support is important in the successful implementation of e-learning as, without this factor, the general consumers of this new technology would not be able to adopt it (Ghavamifar, Beig, & Montazer, 2008). From our point of view, the IT support factor is extremely important in the successful implementation of e-learning. The lack of appropriate IT support in the higher education sector results in subsequent challenges and barriers for students. This lack of IT support can complicate the entire process of attaining education and would influence the overall readiness of individuals to accept this new and innovative technology. The network and internet settings in addition to the hardware requirements that are necessary for successful implementation of e-learning system are difficult for most students to manage; hence, students require appropriate IT support and expertise to acquire their education electronically.

The security factor is included in two of the ten reviewed models and is missing from the remaining eight models. According to Alshaher (2013), the aim of security is to adopt various approaches for securing both individual and organizational information, ensuring the authenticity of the transmitted information, preventing the intrusion of hackers into the educational environment, and maintaining a safe environment for all users (whether they are students, professors, administrators or managers). Aydin and Tasci (2005) claimed that, among the various factors, the security factor is one of the most important factors that influences the readiness to adopt e-learning in higher education. It is observed that the lack of security prevents individuals from accepting this new technology and benefiting from it. Similarly, Omoda-Onyait and Lubega (2011) argued that the lack of security should be considered in assessing the readiness of individuals to accept e-learning. A lack of security results in fear among the typical education-seeking individual, because of which they resist the new concept. From our point of view, security is one of the most important factors that influences the readiness to adopt e-learning in the higher education sector especially because an e-learning system is prone to several security threats such as hacking and malware viruses. These intentional security breaches not only harm the hardware that individuals are using but also hamper the overall process of acquiring education and knowledge through e-learning.

The technical skills factor is included in three of the reviewed models while it is missing from the remaining seven models. This factor refers to the ability of individuals to use computers and the internet (Oketch, Njihia, & Wausi, 2014). If the participants in e-learning do not have the skills to use the technology and learn the content, e-learning will not succeed (Berge, Collins, & Dougherty, 2000). Thus, we conclude that the technical skills factor is important for the successful adoption of an e-learning project, as the lack of technical skills will result in individuals' resistance to e-learning technology.

The infrastructure factor is included in one of the reviewed models. The infrastructure related to e-learning includes hardware, networks, computers, software and the internet (Guruvadoo (2003); Mohammad and Job (2012). Accordingly, we note that some of the factors related to infrastructure are included in some models, such as internet access, hardware, software, availability of computers and communication network. According to Lopes (2007), the implementation of an e-learning system is also dependent on the available infrastructure. The non-availability of the required infrastructure influences the readiness to accept e-learning as it becomes extremely challenging and difficult for the users (e.g. students) to access the new technology (Laohajaratsang, 2009). Moreover, the lack of appropriate infrastructure increases the costs of adopting e-learning which is a significant factor in assessing e-learning readiness. Hence, it is concluded that the implementation of a new and innovative e-learning system should be accompanied by the enhancement and modernization of the available infrastructure. This would include the following components:

Internet access – Most of the reviewed models identify access to the internet as one of the most important technological factors that determine the readiness to adopt e-learning. For e-learning to succeed, access to the internet should be easy. In addition, Omoda-Onyait and Lubega (2011) pointed out that access is not the only issue related to the internet: the speed and availability of the service are other factors related to the internet. Borotis and Poulymenakou (2004) argued that, in order for an e-learning system to be successfully adopted, it is necessary that a reliable internet service with the required speed is available. The lack of appropriate internet infrastructure, speed and reliability affects the readiness of a country to adopt e-learning in its higher education system and ensure that students are able to benefit from the various advantages of e-learning. The adoption of e-learning requires a bandwidth which is sufficient for transferring the video and audio forms of communication that are essential elements of e-learning (Schreurs, Ehlers, & Sammour, 2008). The assessment of the importance and significance of the internet in the evaluation of e-learning readiness indicates that the availability, reliability and speed of the internet are the main factors that determine the overall readiness of individuals to accept e-learning. We therefore note that the most important factor among the technological aspects of e-learning readiness is the internet. The internet factor is further subdivided into the components of access, bandwidth, broadband and speed and reliability. The assessment of the importance and significance of the internet in the evaluation of e-learning readiness indicates that the affordability, availability, reliability and speed of the internet are the main factors that determine the overall readiness of individuals to accept e-learning.

Hardware – Hardware refers to the physical components of technology (Aydin, & Tasci, 2005). The hardware part of e-learning includes the physical equipment that must be available and able to supply e-learning (e.g., computers, servers and networks) along with equipment for end-users to be able to access the services. Without appropriate equipment and easy access, it is difficult, if not impossible, to implement any e-learning (Oliver & Towers, 2000). According to Akaslan and Law (2011), any assessment instrument should include identification of the available hardware such as computers and network connection. We note that all of the reviewed models include hardware as an important factor among the technological aspects of e-learning readiness. Some of the models mention the hardware factor and other models mention the availability of computers as a factor which is related to hardware. Thus, the access and availability of the hardware required to successfully implement the e-learning concept are important factors that determine the overall readiness of individuals to adopt e-learning in higher education.

Software – Software refers to the information management tools that help the user perform certain tasks (Aydin & Tasci, 2005). In the e-learning environment, software includes operating systems, learning management systems and application systems such as browsers among other relevant applications. The successful adoption of e-learning requires at least the minimum hardware requirements and the software required to use that hardware.

This factor is included in three of the reviewed models and is missing from the remaining seven models. From our point of view, the software factor is required for the successful implementation and adoption of e-learning; therefore, it is highlighted as one of the most important factors that determine e-learning readiness in higher education.

To sum up, a number of e-learning readiness models are proposed in the literature but there is a lack of agreement on the necessary factors related to the technological aspects of e-learning readiness. Some of the technological factors are included in some models but are missing from other models. Hence, a clear gap is identified in the literature regarding the technological aspects of e-learning readiness.

4. Conclusion

The use of e-learning is an attractive teaching and learning strategy for many HEIs around the world. Therefore, it is important to assess e-learning readiness, including the technological aspects of readiness, in order for the implementation and adoption of e-learning to be successful. The goal of this paper is to explore the gaps in knowledge regarding the technological aspects of e-learning readiness. This paper presented a review of the models and frameworks for assessing e-learning readiness. The review showed that there is a lack of investigation and agreement about the factors that shape the technological aspects of e-learning readiness; hence, a clear gap is identified in the knowledge on the technological aspects of e-learning readiness. This work indicates a useful direction in future research to investigate the factors related to the technological aspects of e-learning readiness. Hence, future research will be conducted to generate a list of the factors shaping the technological aspects of e-learning readiness. This list will help HEIs to identify and understand the technological aspects that must be considered when assessing the readiness to adopt e-learning. In addition, the list of technological readiness factors can be used by designers and developers as a guideline for identifying the necessary technological requirements for e-learning implementation.

References

AbuSneineh, W., & Zairi, M. (2010). An evaluation Framework for E-learning Effectiveness in The Arab World. *International Encyclopedia of Education*, 521-535.

Akaslan, D., & Law, E. (2011). *Measuring Teachers' Readiness for E-learning in Higher Education Institutions Associated With The Subject of Electricity in Turkey.* Paper presented at the Global Engineering Education Conference (EDUCON), 2011 IEEE.

Albarrak, A. (2010). Designing E-Learning Systems in Medical Education: A Case Study. *International Journal of Excellence in Healthcare Management, 3*(1), 1-8.

Almada de Aseencio, M. (1996). *Information and Communication Technologies and Basic Education.* Paper presented at the The proceeding of FID, 48Th conference and congress.

Alshaher, A. (2013). The Mckinsey 7s Model Framework For E-learning System Readiness Assessment. *International Journal of Advances in Engineering & Technology, 6*(5).

Aydin, C., & Tasci, D. (2005). Measuring Readiness For E-Learning: Reflections From An emerging Country. *Educational Technology & Society, 8*(4), 244-257.

Berge, Z., Collins, M., & Dougherty, K. (2000). Design Guidelines for Web-based Courses. *Instructional and Cognitive Impacts of web-based Education*, 32-40.

Bhuasiri, W., Xaymoungkhoun, O., Zo, H., Rho, J., & Ciganek, A. (2012). Critical Success Factors For E-learning in Developing Countries: A comparative Analysis Between ICT Experts and Faculty. *Computers & Education, 58*(2), 843-855.

Borotis, S., & Poulymenakou, A. (2004). *E-Learning Readiness Components: Key Issues to Consider Before Adopting e-Learning Interventions.* Paper presented at the World Conference on E-Learning in Corporate, Government, Healthcare, and Higher Education 2004, Washington, DC, USA. Retrieved from http://www.editlib.org/p/11555

Bowles, M. (2004). What is Electronic Learning? In M. Bowles (Ed.), *Relearning to E-learn: Strategies for Electronic Learning and Knowledge*, 3-19. Carlton, Vic: Melbourne Unversity Press.

Bridges, D., Juceviciene, P., Jucevicius, R., Mclaughlin, T., & Stankeviciute, J. (2014). *Higher Education and National Development: Universities and Societies in Transition.* U.S: Routledge.

Chapnick, S. (2000). Are you ready for e learning. *ASTD's Online Magazine All About Learning, 9.*

Contreras, J., & Shadi, M. (2015). Assessment in E-Learning Environment Readiness of Teaching Staff, Administrators, and Students of Faculty of Nursing-Benghazi University. *International Journal of the*

Computer, the Internet and Management, 23(1), 53-58.

Darab, B., & Montazer, G. (2011). An eclectic Model For Assessing E-learning Readiness in The Iranian Universities. *Computers & Education, 56*(3), 900-910.

Engholm, P. (2002). *What Determines an organisation's Readiness for E-learning.* (Bachelor), Monash University, Australia.

Engholm, P., & McLean, J. (2001). What Determines An organisation's Readiness For elearning? Retrieved from http://www.x-konsult.se/academia/Thesis%20FINAL.htm

Ford, J., Ford, L., & D'Amelio, A. (2008). Resistance to Change: The Rest of The Story. *Academy of Management Review, 33*(2), 362-377.

Ghavamifar, A., Beig, L., & Montazer, G. (2008). *The Comparison of Different E-Readiness Assessment Tools.* Paper presented at the 3rd International Conference on Information and Communication Technologies: From Theory to Applications, 2008. ICTTA 2008,

Goi, C., & Ng, P. (2009). E-learning in Malaysia: Success Factors in Implementing E-learning Program. *International Journal of Teaching and Learning in Higher Education, 20*(2), 237-246.

Guruvadoo, P. (2003). *A conceptual Framework for Effective Strategies for Information and Communication Technologies in Education: A case Study of Mauritius.* (Doctor of Education), University of Massachusetts Amherst.

Hanafizadeh, P., & Ravasan, A. (2011). A McKinsey 7S Model-based Framework For ERP Readiness Assessment. *International Journal of Enterprise Information Systems (IJEIS), 7*(4), 23-63.

Keramati, A., Afshari Mofrad, M., & Kamrani, A. (2011). The Role of Readiness Factors in E-learning Outcomes: An empirical Study. *Computers & Education, 57*(3), 1919-1929.

Kituyi, G., & Tusubira, I. (2013). A framework For The Integration of E-learning in Higher Education Institutions in Developing Countries. *International Journal of Education and Development using Information and Communication Technology, 9*(2), 19.

Laohajaratsang, T. (2009). E-Learning Readiness in the Academic Sector of Thailand. *International Journal on E-Learning, 8*(4), 539-547.

Lopes, C. (2007). *Evaluating E-learning Readiness in A health Sciences Higher Education Institution.* Paper presented at the Proceedings of IADIS International Conference of E-learning, Porto.

Mohammad, S., & Job, M. (2012). Evaluation of Infrastructure for E-Learning System in AOU-Bahrain Branch. *International Journal of Information, 2*(4).

Najib, N. A., & Rebhi, H. M. (2006). *Computer Technology in Education.* Gaza: Aafaq for Printing and Publishing. Arabic.

Nyoni, J. (2014). E-readiness of Open and Distance Learning (ODL) Facilitators: Implications for Effective Mediation. *Perspectives in Education, 32*(3), 78-91.

Odunaike, S., Olugbara, O., & Ojo, S. (2013). E-learning Implementation Critical Success Factors. *Innovation, 3*, 4.

Oketch, H., Njihia, J., & Wausi, A. (2014). E-learning Readiness Assessment Model In Kenyas' Higher Education Institutions: A Case Study Of University Of Nairobi. *International Journal of Scientific Knowledge, 5*(6).

Oliver, R., & Towers, S. (2000). *Up time: Information Communication Technology: Literacy and Access for Tertiary Students in Australia.* Canberra: Department of Education, Training and Youth Affairs.

Omoda, G., & Lubega, J. (2011). E-learning Readiness Assessment Model: A case Study of Higher Institutions of Learning in Uganda *Hybrid Learning*, 200-211. Springer.

Psycharis, S. (2005). Presumptions and Action Affecting An e-learning Adoption by The Educational System. Implementation Using Virtual Private Networks. *European Journal of Open and Distance Learning, 2*, 2005.

Puteh, M. (2008). E-Learning Concepts and Literature Review. In Salleh (Ed.), *E-Learning Issues in Malaysian Higher Education*: Universiti Teknologi Malaysia

Rohayani, A., & Kurniabudi, Sh. (2015). A Literature Review: Readiness Factors to Measuring e-Learning Readiness in Higher Education. *Procedia Computer Science, 59*, 230-234.

http://dx.doi.org/10.1016/j.procs.2015.07.564

Salem, W. (2006). *Educational Technology Innovations in The Information Age.* Amman: Alfekr House for Publishing and Distribution. Arabic.

Schreurs, J., Ehlers, U., & Sammour, G. (2008). ERA - E-Learning Readiness Analysis: A eHealth Case Study of E-Learning Readiness. *International Journal of Knowledge and Learning, 4*(5), 496-508. http://dx.doi.org/10.1007/978-3-540-87783-7_34

Tarus, J., Gichoya, D., & Muumbo, A. (2015). Challenges of Implementing E-learning in Kenya: A case of Kenyan Public Universities. *The International Review of Research in Open and Distributed Learning, 16*(1).

15

Securing Healthcare Records in the Cloud Using Attribute-Based Encryption

Huda Elmogazy[1] & Omaimah Bamasag[1]

[1] Department of Computer Science, Faculty of Computing and Information Technology, King AbdulAziz University, Saudi Arabia

Correspondence: Omaimah Bamasag, Department of Computer Science, Faculty of Computing and Information Technology, King AbdulAziz University, P.O.Box 42808, Jeddah 21551, Saudi Arabia. E-mail: obamasek@kau.edu.sa

Abstract

Cloud Computing has attracted interest as an efficient system for storing and access of data. Sharing of personal electronic health record is an arising concept of exchanging health information for research and other purposes. Cconfidentiality except for authorized users, and access auditability are strong security requirements for health record. This study will examine these requirements and propose a framework for healthcare cloud providers that will assist in securely storing and sharing of patient' data they host. It should also allow only legitimate users to access portion of the records' data they are permitted to. The focus will be on these precise security issues of cloud computing healthcare and how attribute-based encryption can assist in addressing healthcare regulatory requirements. The proposed attribute-based encryption guarantees authentication, data confidentiality, availability, and integrity in a multi-level hierarchical order. This will allow the healthcare provider to easily add/delete any access rule in any order, which is considered beneficial particularly in medical research field.

Keywords: cloud computing, cryptography, threats, attribute-based encryption

1. Introduction

Cloud Computing is an arising technology which revolutionize the use of computing resources. Cloud Computing technology provides users with flexibility, scalability of infrastructure, reliability, sustainability and cost effectiveness. The cloud is defined by google as "the collective power of thousands of computers that serve information to you from far-away rooms distributed around the world."

In current healthcare systems, there is a high demand on establishing a framework that minimizes time-consuming work and expensive procedures to retrieve a patient's medical record and integrating this varying set of medical data consistently to deliver it to the healthcare industry. Electronic health records (EHRs) (DesRoches et al., 2008) (Eichelberg et al., 2005) have been widely accepted to allow patients, insurance companies, and healthcare providers to initiate, control and process patients' healthcare information from any place, and at any time.

Thus, healthcare providers accept moving their data and operations to the clouds that can perform their operations more efficiently and eliminate the physical distance concern between patients and providers. Cloud service enables different doctors to obtain an access to a patient's health record even if they are kilometres apart. There is no need for the doctors to make a phone call to ask for a move of the health records; they will just access them in the clouds.

Despite all the benefits cloud computing provides for healthcare systems, data privacy and security are among the major concerns, which make healthcare move slowly towards the acceptance of these new technologies. Cloud computing benefits come at a price of the emergence of different risks related to information security that must be cautiously addressed. Risks differ according to the criticality of the data to be processed or stored, and how the specific cloud provider has developed their specific cloud services.

In order to be appealing to healthcare community, cloud computing should maintain required guarding to address HIPAA (Health Information Portability and Accountability Act) of U.S. Department of Health and Human Services (2013) and other security and privacy requirements. Although Electronic Health Records (EHRs) has been regulated in standards, such as HIPAA, several cloud providers are still not compliant with them.

In order to secure healthcare data, the first step to be taken is to categorize the data in the Electronic Health Records (EHRs) in correspondence to its level of security sensitivity. The first category is Personally Identifiable Information (PII), such as patient records, normally saved in a relational database as structured data. The second category is Healthcare data, which is typically consists of large media files such as radiology, CT scan, x-ray, and other types of video and images that conceal patient's identity. Such files are often stored in distributed storage.

A medical record has some components that are classified by both individuals and organizations, such as HIPAA of U.S. Department of Health and Human Services (2005) and HITECH (Health Information Technology, 2009), as highly critical and should be disclosed only to the entities that have an explicit access right to them. This is because revealing such data can lead to unjustly show bias against an individual or refuse them chances that they otherwise entitled to. For example, knowing that a person is diabetic might negatively influence their professional growth, personal relationships, insurance cost, and employment opportunities.

Outsourcing the storage of unencrypted information in the cloud, is of a high danger. For a highly sensitive data, such as Electronic Health Records (EHRs), locating them unencrypted, out of site, is considered against the law. However, to access data stored on a distance server, the Cloud providers need to access the primitive, i.e. un-encrypted, data. Most people do not have full confident on the Cloud providers for their sensitive healthcare data because there is no law regulating how they use this data and whether the patients have control over them. On the other hand, data encryption might counteract the advantages of cloud computing, unless the cloud service providers get the secret decryption key. Traditional cryptography is not a solution in this situation (Alomgazi & Bamasak, 2013).

Patients may only want portions of their record made available to all doctors and specific portions to be available to specific users, i.e. insurance company. Patients can be given maximum control over their data by encrypting each portion of a patient's record under a different policy. Access control policies should be active to ensure that accessing sensitive information is restricted only to parties that have a valid privilege. This feature can be provided by Attribute-Based encryption.

The rest of this paper is organized as follows: in Section 2, we introduce the concept of cloud computing. Section 3 discusses background technologies on using cryptography to secure cloud computing. In section 4, we outline the security issues surrounding healthcare application in the cloud. Section 5 proposes secure healthcare cloud computing framework. Finally, Section 6 concludes this paper and discusses our future direction.

2. Background

The National Institute of Standards and Technology (NIST) (Mell & Grance, 2009) has defined Cloud Computing as "a model for enabling ubiquitous, convenient, on-demand network access to a shared pool of configurable computing resources (e.g. networks, servers, storage, applications, and services) that can be rapidly provisioned and released with minimal management effort or service provider interaction". The cloud framework consists of five important components, four deployment models and three service models (Alomgazi & Bamasak, 2013).

2.1 Cloud Computing Characteristics

Cloud Computing has many essential characteristics and features. Cloud service users benefit from many features: cost-effectiveness, variability of resources, seamless self-service, flexibility and elasticity, reliability, location independence, and broad network access (Peng et al., 2009). Cloud providers also gain the advantages of scalability of infrastructure, cost-effectiveness, and sustainability (Zissis & Lekkas, 2012).

• *Cost-effectiveness*: One of the major benefits that are offered to both the clients and providers of cloud computing is cost-effectiveness. For clients, it allows the allocation of as much or as little resources necessary for accomplishing the tasks at hand. It also spares the client from the cost of actually allocating the resources on-site when they are not highly utilized (Peng et al., 2009). Furthermore, it saves the maintenance cost of resources. For service providers, it allows for locating resources in an inexpensive real-estate and/or close to cheap power source (Zissis & Lekkas, 2012).

• *Resource utilization*: Cloud Computing service paradigm is centred around better resource utilization leading to long-term sustainability for the resource owner (Zissis & Lekkas, 2012). With different modes of delivery, Cloud Computing allows the client to access varying types of services. Clients can easily demand basic infrastructure services such as power or network, or deployment platform to run their application such as Java or Python, or rented application.

- *Self*-service: Seamless self-service is yet another remarkable feature of Cloud Computing. Clients of cloud services are able to allocate the necessary resources automatically without requiring manual interaction with the cloud service providers via simple user interfaces.

- *Flexibility and elasticity*: Cloud Computing also offers clients great flexibility and elasticity of service according to demand. Clients of cloud services can swiftly benefit from allocated resources. Services can be scaled up by allowing clients to acquire more resources as they progress in their task without additional effort. Scaling down of service is also accomplished seamlessly by releasing unnecessary resources automatically. Hence, resources seem unlimited to clients of cloud services.

- *Reliability*: Reliability is an important feature to the cloud service client which is usually accomplished through the use of multiple redundant service sites providing business continuity and easier recovery in case of disaster (Zissis & Lekkas, 2012).

- *Location independence*: Another feature of Cloud Computing is location independence. Clients need not be aware of the exact location of resources, nor do they need to control it. Still, they are able to specify an abstract location such as a country or city if it is needed (Zissis & Lekkas, 2012).

- *Broad network access*: Cloud services offer broad network access to its clients. Service clients benefit from the standard mechanisms employed by the providers, allowing for diverse access platforms such as, PDA's, laptops or mobile phones (Zissis & Lekkas, 2012). Cloud service providers benefit from scalability of infrastructure. It allows the network to grow or shrink by adding or dropping nodes or servers to the network with minimal modifications at the infrastructure level as well as at the software level (Zissis & Lekkas, 2012). These key features are what make Cloud Computing a promising technology for providing computing resources.

2.2 Deployment Models

There are different ways to deploy and manage service deliveries to Cloud clients. The different ways (also referred to as deployment models) dictate the disposition of resources and the relationships between cloud providers and clients. There are four deployment models: public, private, community and hybrid clouds.

- *Public Cloud*: In the public cloud, Infrastructure and computational resources are owned and operated by a cloud provider, offering to render services to the public over the Internet. Presumably, the provider is an external entity from all the clients.

- *Private cloud*: a private cloud is owned and operated by the organization itself for exclusive resource provision. The organization may also hand cloud management to a third party. In this case, the cloud may be hosted either within the organization's data center or outside of it (Jansen & Grance, 2011). For private clouds, the organization has more control over the infrastructure, the clients, and the services provided.

- *Community cloud*: In the middle between public and private clouds is the community cloud. For this model, the cloud infrastructure and services are customized to a community of clients. The community of clients belong to organizations who share the same policy and security requirements among other considerations (Jansen & Grance, 2011). Cloud infrastructure may be owned and operated by a third party, or one or more of the organizations within the community.

- *Hybrid cloud*: The more complex cloud deployment model is the hybrid model. Hybrid clouds are composed of more than one type, perceived as separate entities while being combined via a set of standards and rules, allowing them to share data and applications among them (Peng et al., 2009).

Different cloud deployment models have different implications on the provision of security and client privacy in the cloud. For private clouds, security provision stays within the organization since it owns the cloud facility or rents it exclusively. However, for public clouds, security provision is managed by service providers leading to challenging circumstances. As for community and hybrid clouds, security provision has the same circumstances as public clouds only for data and processes handled by public facilities.

2.3 Service Models

While deployment models define resource disposition and cloud management, service models define control and level of service abstraction. Most literature identifies three service models: Infrastructure-as-a-Service (IaaS), Platform-as-a-Service (PaaS), Software-as-a-Service (SaaS) (Peng et al., 2009).

IaaS refers to hard-core infrastructure capabilities rendered to the client such as storage space, network bandwidth, power for processing, or any basic computing resource. These resources are obtained by clients as virtualized objects controlled via a service interface, giving clients the freedom to choose the operating system and development environment hosted on these resources (Zissis & Lekkas, 2012). PaaS model allows clients to develop and deploy their applications on programming platforms rented by the provider such as Python or Java. This model can help the client reduce resource allocation cost and simplify the development and deployment process. It will also allow the client to control applications and application environment settings of the platform (Zissis & Lekkas, 2012). The cloud provider will spare the client the expense and hassle of purchasing, hosting, and controlling underlying hardware and software components, as well as program and database development tools. In the SaaS model, services rendered are applications running on the cloud infrastructure and platform of the service provider via a browser interface or any other thin client. It decreases the cost of software and hardware development, maintenance, and operations for the client. In this case, the client does not have any control over the underlying cloud infrastructure or individual applications, except for selecting usage preference and some administrative settings (Zissis & Lekkas, 2012).

3. Literature Review

For access control of patients' EHR outsourced to cloud providers, we assume that they are partially trusted. The goal of cryptographic techniques is to administer who has 'read' access to which portion of a patient's EHR in a detailed way. Three types of cryptography are commonly used to secure EHR records: symmetric key cryptography, public key cryptography, and attribute-based encryption, explained in the following (Madnani & Sreedevi, 2013).

3.1 Symmetric Key Cryptography- Based Solutions

Symmetric-key algorithms belong to a category of cryptography algorithms that use the same cryptographic keys for both encryption of plaintext and decryption of ciphertext. The encryption and decryption keys are equal. A solution for protecting off-site data on semi-trusted clouds was proposed by Vimercati et.al.(di Vimercati, Foresti, Jajodia, Paraboschi & Samarati 2007). Using symmetric-key algorithms, it was able to achieve fine-grained access control. However, the challenges in file creation and the operations of user grant/revocation are in-line with the number of authorized users, which is not scalable.

3.2 Public key cryptography (PKC) based solutions

Public-key based solutions were proposed as it is able to set apart read and write privileges. J. Benaloh, M. Chase, E. Horvitz, and K. Lauter (Benaloh et al., 2009) proposed a public-key based encryption scheme that solved the issue of implementing fine-grained access control. However, this work suffers from high overhead of key management.

A hybrid encryption scheme that integrates RSA, 3- DES and Random Number generator algorithm, is proposed in (Kaur & Bhardwaj, 2012) to improve the security of cloud data storage. This scheme offers the adaptability in sequence and range to the user's selection. This is due to a user may choose to perform all of the three encryption methods or cancel any in any order. The default is applying the random number generator algorithm despite the user not selecting any encryption method, hence, ensuring at least a single layer of security. The selected sequence will also be saved in the database for decryption purpose. The downside of this system is that it heavy on the query performance due to the layered nature of encryption and decryption. In addition, the computation time goes up linearly with the size of data.

3.3 Attribute-Based Encryption solutions

The authors in (Kaur, 2012) described Attribute-Based Encryption ABE as it links both the attributes and policies with the encrypted message. The user then decides which entity, according to the defined attributes, can decrypt the ciphertext. Secret keys for the users are created by a central authority based on attributes/policies specified for each user. Each user in the system is linked with attributes; he receives a key ("or group of keys") from a trusted authority corresponding to his set of attributes. Ciphertext embeds a policy in the form of Boolean predicate over the attribute space. A user can use his group of keys to decrypt the ciphertext only if his attribute set comply with the policy.

Authors in (Akinyele et al., 2010) described ABE in two formulations: ciphertext policy ABE and key policy ABE, explained in the following.

- *Ciphertext policy ABE*: a ciphertext is coupled with a policy specifying which entity is authorized to decrypt it. These policies are generally described as boolean formulae showing a list of attributes that are enclosed into the secret key of the encryptor. As an example, given the attributes: Doctor, Nurse, Massachusetts General Hospital (MGH), InsureCo, the following example policy represents a record that can be read by an MGH doctor or nurse or an insurance agent:

   ((Doctor _ Nurse) ^ MGH) _ ((InsureCo ^ Agent)

- *Key policy ABE*: reverses the relationship between ciphertext and key so that each record is labeled with its corresponding attributes, e.g. Lab Result (record), Cardio (attribute). In order to get access to portion of a record, the record owner, i.e. patient, generates unique key comprising the policy formulae that decides on which entity can access which records.

Collusion resistance is a basic feature of ABE systems (Akinyele et al., 2010). This feature is about individuals who are not able to integrate attributes with their secret keys to fulfill a given policy. For instance, the following policy might denote that only the insurance agent, associated with either the billing company or MGH, can read the patient's prescriptions:

(Billing _ MGH) ^ (InsureCo ^ Agent)

The insurance agent's key associated with the attribute InsureCo cannot be integrated with the billing company's key (i.e., Billing attributes) or with the Doctor's key (i.e, MGH attribute) to fulfill the policy. In this example, a trust relationship has to be established between the insurance agent and the hospital so as to obtain the MGH or Billing attributes. Each symmetric key is generated with a different random initial value, therefore, integrating keys cannot generate a new relevant one (Akinyele et al., 2010).

The depiction of the policy access formulae is considered the strong point of ABE. Access policies can be articulated with AND, OR, and other boolean operators such as <, _, >, and _. Binary numbers typically represents numerical values used in boolean operators so that each bit in the number relates to a non-numerical attribute. A mixture of OR and AND gates are employed to construct a binary tree that depicts contrasting over the non-numerical attributes similar to the ciphertext policy employment of Bethencourt, Sahai and Waters (Goyal, Pandey, Sahai & Waters, 2006). Therefore, ABE enables indicative access control that is cumbersome to achieve with classical access control parameters.

4. Security Challenges

With the many promises of better resource utilization and client-empowerment in healthcare systems, Cloud Computing also presents many challenges, and one of these challenges lies in the issue of security assurance. Xiaoping claims that security issues in the cloud paradigm present the biggest challenge for service providers (Jansen & Grance, 2011). Zissis and Lekkas identify two main security issues in Cloud Computing, which are placement of trust and identification of security threats (Zissis & Lekkas, 2012). In Cloud Computing, the boundaries separating an organization from outsiders become fuzzy making it more difficult to identify trusted parties and to locate security measures (Zissis & Lekkas, 2012). Identification of security threats is also necessary to implement a security system with the appropriate countermeasures.

The security system of a cloud platform should ensure confidentiality and privacy, service availability, data and application integrity and recovery.

- *Confidentiality* assures that information is not disclosed to unauthorized parties while privacy extends further to assure that individuals control who can collect or store information related to them.

- *Availability* assures that services are not denied to authorized clients.

- *Integrity* ensures that data and software can be modified only by authorized parties and in a specified manner.

Our proposed solution will aim to address the above mentioned security requirements using ABE.

5. ABE-Based EHR Security in the Cloud

We propose a secure centralized data sharing framework for healthcare cloud-based EHR, addressing the security requirements specified in Section 4. We shall assume that we have three basic organizations A, B and C in our healthcare industry, as shown in Figure 1.In this section, an overview of the framework is presented. This is followed by the assumptions considered in the design of the proposed ABE-based solution, then the proposed solution is presented.

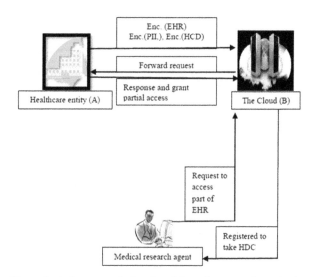

Figure1. A framework for cloud-based secure data sharing

5.1 General Framework

Healthcare entity (A), representing different fields, i.e. primary care, clinical lab, primary, emergency care and pharmacy, host their patients' EHRs in cloud (B). This is to minimize cost of operation and maximize compatibility and seamless delivery of services. Healthcare data can be requested by the research institute (C) for its medical research. EHRs ownership belongs to the healthcare entity (A), which sets policies for access control to enforce which entity/organization can access which fields of its EHRs, with different roles. To address HIPAA and related security and privacy requirements, the medical research institute (C) must not have the right to access Personally Identifiable Information (PII). Administrators carry out management operations, e.g. turning users on or off, and enrolling or de-enrolling medical research institute.

The PII consists of record owner's (patient) type-identifier, e.g. doctor, patient, pharmacy, and attributes that define the identity and specifications of the record owner, e.g. ID, name, specialization, location, etc. In our EHR suggested framework, the patient specifies the entities that can access the data in his medical record and, therefore, decides on the attribute set under which the record is encrypted

The access policies for our proposed solution comprise boolean formulas that employs logical AND and logical OR, on the attributes. For example, the policy ' ID999 $\wedge$ doctor' indicates that only an entity who owns the attributes 'ID999' and 'doctor' is allowed access. Our scheme assumes that there is a trusted authority for key generation, which validates the entity's attributes prior to issuing the secret key. The patient can trust that his record can be accessed by user 999 only if he is a doctor by specifying the above access policy (Narayan, Gagne & Naini, 2010).

A patient grants a subject X access to his medical data by adding the subject ID and type-identifier, and other subject specific features, depending on the access policy specified by the patient. An index set is associated with the ciphertext that consists of the unique subject ID. The access requestor cannot decrypt the data if his subject ID is not in the index set.

5.2 Assumptions

Our proposed solution is built on the following assumptions.

- There exists a trusted authority (TA) who is honoured by all parties in the framework to generate keys for system's users. TA also publishes, in a public directory, the system's public parameters, i.e. public keys, and other data required for cryptographic functions.

- A subject X is coupled with an exclusive identifier (ID), and a set of attributes (ω). Each subject is linked with a public key and a corresponding private key. Both keys are created and released by the TA after authenticating the subject's attributes.

- The EHR database is located in and stored by a cloud service provider. This provider is trusted by the system's entities to perform the required operations but should not have the ability to perform any operation beyond what was specified.

5.3 Proposed Solution

The attribute-based ciphertext policy encryption scheme, which we will use, inspired by (Narayan, Gagne & Naini, 2010), comprises five algorithms namely: Initialize, Key-Gen, Encrypt, Decrypt, and Revoke.

- *Initialize(y):* having a security parameter y, the algorithm generates the public key *pub-key* and master secret key *Master-sk*. The system public key *pub-key* is a collection of public information.

- *Key-Gen(pub-key, Master-sk, ω, ID):* having as input an attribute set ω, user-ID *ID*, public key *pub-key*, and the master secret key *Master-sk*, the algorithm generates the private key $pk_{ID,\omega}$ related to ω.

- *Encrypt(pub-key, M, IS, AS):* Given a message M (EHR), *pub-key*, user-id set *IS* and an access structure *AS*, the encryption algorithm outputs the ciphertext *CT* holding the encrypted message.

- *Decrypt(pub-key,CT, $pk_{ID,\omega}$):* This algorithm's inputs are the ciphertext *CT* and the private key $pk_{ID,\omega}$ for the attribute set ω. It decrypts the ciphertext *CT* if $\omega \in AS$ and $ID \in IS$. If it decrypted successfully, it outputs the plaintext *M,* else outputs 0.

- *Revoke(HP$_i$, CT):* A user, i.e. a patient, can remove the access of a client *HP$_i$,* i.e. healthcare provider, to the encrypted record *CT*.

Here, we will explain the steps of the ABE algorithms in our proposed framework, as shown in Figure 1. The setup step consists of the generation of system's parameters using Initialize(y) algorithm. This is followed by generating the private key $pk_{ID,\omega}$ using Key-Gen(*pub-key, Master-sk, ω, ID*) algorithm. Both steps are performed by the trusted authority TA. The healthcare entity (A) then encrypt EHRs using Encrypt(*pub-key, M, IS, AS*) algorithm. The patient uploads the encrypted record *CT* together with the access policy and search index to the cloud (B). Only approved entities (C) can be granted access to the corresponding parts of the encrypted EHR data by the decryption algorithm Decrypt(*pub-key, CT, $pk_{ID,\omega}$*), hence satisfying the confidentiality, availability and integrity requirements mentioned in Section 4. The user will sign in into the system via a web application. The identity of the user will be verified against sign in database, which will perform the check based on attribute authentication system. The medical research agent (C) will ask to access parts of EHRs to conduct their research. This request is forwarded to healthcare entity to get authorization to access specific healthcare data for specific time. After that this access will be invalidated using *Revoke(HP$_i$, CT)* algorithm.

5.4 Security Analysis

Our proposed solution provides confidentiality of EHR through the use of strong attribute-based encryption. The encrypted EHR can be decrypted by an entity with private key pk$_{ID,\omega}$ only if its attribute set ω is in the EHR access structure AS and its ID is in the user-id set IS. Therefore, if the EHR database is attacked, the attacker will not learn anything about the EHR stored in the cloud without the corresponding private keys.

Consequently, only legitimate entities, with the appropriate private keys and access privileges can read, change, or delete EHR from the database in the cloud, hence, ensuring integrity of the EHR.

Both the cloud service provider and the underlying ABE encryption are assumed to work properly and meet the demand of all system's entities, i.e. A, B, C. Hence, addressing the availability requirement.

6. Conclusion

In this paper, we have explored the use of Attribute-Based encryption to secure EHRs. For future work, we plan to further investigate and implement the proposed system in a suitable simulation platform. We will also evaluate the security and performance of the proposed system after being implemented and compare them with the most related work in the area.

References

Akinyele, J., Lehmann, C., Green, M., Pagno, M., Peterson, Z., & Rubin, A. (2010). Self-Protecting Electronic Medical Records Using Attribute-Based Encryption. *Technical Report 2010/565*, Cryptology e-Print Archive.

Alomgazi, H., & Bamasak, O. (2013). Towards Healthcare Data Security in Cloud Computing, *Proceedings of the International Conference for Internet Technology and Secured Transactions*, IEEE Society, 363-368, http://dx.doi.org/10.1109/ICITST.2013.6750223

Benaloh, J., Chase, M., Horvitz, E., & Lauter, K. (2009). Patient controlled encryption: ensuring privacy of electronic medical records. *Proceedings of the 2009 ACM Workshop on Cloud Computing Security CCSW'09*, 103–114. http://dx.doi.org/10.1145/1655008.1655024

DesRoches, C., Campbell, Rao, E, S., Donelan, K., Ferris, T., Jha, A., Kaushal, R., Levy, D., Rosenbaum, S., &

Shields, A., (2008). Electronic health records in ambulatory care - a national survey of physicians. *New England Journal of Medicine, 359*(1), 50-60. http://dx.doi.org/10.1056%2FNEJMsa0802005

Vimercati, S. D. C., Foresti, S., Jajodia, S., Paraboschi, S., & Samarati, P. (2007). Over-encryption: management of access control evolution on outsourced data. *Proceedings of the 33rd International Conference on Very Large Databases VLDB '07*, 123–134.

Eichelberg, M., Aden, T., Riesmeier, J., Dogac, A., & Laleci, G., (2005). A survey and analysis of electronic healthcare record standards. *ACM Computing Surveys (CSUR), 37*(4), 277-315. http://dx.doi.org/10.1145/1118890.1118891

Goyal, V., Pandey, O., Sahai, A., & Waters, B. (2006). Attribute-based encryption for fine-grained access control of encrypted data. *Proceedings of the 13th ACM Conference on Computer and Communication Security CCS '06*, 89–98. http://dx.doi.org/10.1145/1180405.1180418

Health Information Technology. (2009). *The Health Information Technology for Economic and Clinical Health (HITECH) Act,* Retrieved from https://www.healthit.gov/sites/default/files/hitech_act_excerpt_from_arra_with_index.pdf

Jansen, W., & Grance, T. (2011). Guidelines on security and privacy in public cloud computing, *NIST special publication, 800*, p. 144.

Kaur, A., & Bhardwaj, M., (2012). *Hybrid Encryption for Cloud Database Security*, IJESAT, 2(3), 737 – 741, Retrieved from http://www.ijesat.org

Kaur, S., (2012). Cryptography and Encryption In Cloud Computing. *VSRD International Journal of CS & IT, 2*(3), 242-249.

Madnani, B., & Sreedevi, N. (2013). Attribute Based Encryption for Scalable and Secure Sharing of Medical Records in Cloud Computing Design and Implementation. *International Journal of Innovative Research in Computer and Communication Engineering*, 1(3).

Mell, P., & Grance, T., (2009). *The NIST Definition of Cloud Computing*, version 15, National Institute of Standards and Technology (NIST). Retrieved from http://www.csrc.nist.gov

Narayan, S., Gagne, M., & Naini, R. (2010). Privacy Preserving HER System Using Attribute-based Infrastructure. *Proceedings of 2010 ACM Workshop on Cloud Computing Security Workshop CCSW' 10*, 47-52. http://dx.doi.org/10.1145/1866835.1866845

Peng, J., Zhang, X., Lei, Z., Zhang, B., Zhang, W., & Li., Q. (2009). Comparison of several cloud computing platforms. *Proceedings of The Second International Symposium on Information Science and Engineering (ISISE)*, 23-27. http://dx.doi.org/10.1109/ISISE.2009.94

U.S. Department of Health and Human Services. (2013). *The health insurance portability and accountability act.* Retrieved from http://www.hhs.gov/ocr/privacy/hipaa/understanding/index.html

Zissis, D., & Lekkas, D. (2012). Addressing cloud computing security issues. *Future Generation Computer Systems, 28*(3), 583-592. http://dx.doi.org/10.1016/j.future.2010.12.006

16

A Multistep Approach for Managing the Risks of Software Requirements Volatility

Nedhal A. Al-Saiyd[1]

[1] Applied Science Private University, Jordan

Correspondence: Dr. Nedhal A. Al-Saiyd, Faculty of Information Technology, Applied Science Private University, Amman, Jordan. E-mail: nedhal_alsaiyd@asu.edu.jo

The research is financed by (Applied Science Private University).

Abstract

Software is changed continuously in order to respond to different users and business needs. Requirements are changed dynamically to improve software usability and increase its value, but requirement volatility sometimes cause failures for many projects because of inadequate understanding of the changing causes and the consequences of these changes. This research highlights the importance of managing requirement changes, classify them, and control the impact risks of requirement volatility on software project. The proposed model is designed based on software requirements risks factors and how to reduce their impacts. Generally, requirements changing is considered as a difficult, costly and time-consumed task, and consequently it is too important to study the inter-relationships between the changes and their impacts on the other phases of software system. The good understanding of the changing causes and their consequences can improve and support requirements management process and also lead successfully to the predicted goals of changes. The high quality of the requirements influences the success of a software project during software development and maintenance processes.

Keywords: change control, impact analysis, requirements changes types, requirement management, software maintenance, volatile requirements

1. Introduction

Software is dynamic and is evolved continuously over time in order to respond to different customers, end users and business needs. Adding new requirements, deleting or modifying existing requirements may be required through software development process phases or at software maintenance, where demands for changes cannot be avoided (McGee & Greer, 2012). Requirements that are changed during the software development life cycle may occur at the design phase, coding, testing until the software product is produced (Nurmuliani, Zowghi & Powell, 2004). One fourth of requirements changes occur during maintenance phase, which is more costly than changes occur during development phase; because the software adapted to the new environment, business and end users requests (McGee & Greer, 2012), (Sudhakar, 2005). These changes have an influence on the design, code, test, deployment and their related artifacts that may require further work on them to keep the software work effectively and efficiently. Approximately 70 percent of software projects have failed to deliver the qualified and business-valued services, and caused user's dissatisfactions. Consequently, the cost estimation of requirement changes will be increased significantly at the latter phases of the software development (NIST, 2002).

Changing requirements may exist at the requirement engineering, analysis modeling, system design, design modeling, implementation phase, or at maintenance phase. Requirements volatility is a measure of how much requirements change through the software development life cycles and operational phase after software delivery. The traditional measure of requirement volatility is done by counting the modification, deletion, and addition of requirements, through certain period of time. Requirements volatility has relatively great impact on software project cost, schedule, resources and the quality of final product release (Sudhakar, 2005), (Thakurta & Ahlemann, 2010), (Dev & Awasthi, 2012). The software requirements changes can be classified as (Singh & Vyas, 2012):

1. **Pre-Release Requirements Changes:** it is referred to the requirement changes at the software development process. It can be implicitly classified into two sub-classes:

    i. **Pre-Functional Specification:** it involves the changing requirements during requirement elicitation, analysis activities of requirement engineering and before completing the functional specification.

    ii. **Post-Functional Specification:** it involves changing requirements during software design, coding, and testing, after completing the functional specification, and they are done by the customers and software developers.

2. **Post-Release Requirements Changes:** The changes occur in the maintenance phase, after the software product is deployed. It includes adaptive, preventive, corrective and perfective maintenance types.

Requirement volatility can be risky at software development and costly particularly at the late stages, since it may require re-engineering. The problem is with insufficient changing management data and systematic approach; not with requirements volatility. Identifying the problems help to minimize the risks, cost and poor communication between stakeholders and developer. In software development life cycle, a lot of work was spend on requirement changing, and changing management but not that much work has been done on minimizing the impact of requirement volatility (NIST, 2002), (Thakurta, 2010).

The misunderstanding of problem domain, lack of well-specified requirements, missing requirements, unavailability of practical structured methods to trace requirements, lack of requirements traceability templates, unavailability of conceptual models to find the interrelationships and dependencies among requirements, may negatively impact the quality of software design and consequently the quality of software systems. Most software system stakeholders found it almost impossible to understand how changes to a requirement will impact the overall system, since tracking the requirements changes need understanding their textual-based artifacts that consists of detailed requirements documents that are difficult to understand.

To compromise the difficulties and related problems, a comprehensive methodology and a management approach is needed to early identify changing requirements risks, follow changing on requirements particularly in the late stages of software development process, check requirements completeness and consistency, and enhance software quality processes to make them more responsive and more efficient. We need first to understand the factors that make changing difficult and costly.

The paper structure is organized as follows: Section 2 provides the related work on the subject matter. Section 3 briefly explains the reasons and causes of change requirements. Section 4 presents and elaborates the proposed comprehensive model and methodology. Discussion and key findings are discussed in section 5. Finally, section 6 concludes the paper with a summary that outlines the main findings.

2. Related Work

Research by (Bhatti, Hayat, Ehsan, Ahmed, Ishaque, & Z.Sarwar, 2010) statistically analyzed the changing requirements in each development phases. They found that the effects of changed requirements in earlier phases have significant potential impact on the following phases. The more changing requirements in RE, the fewer amount of changes are requested in design phase. The total effort of changing requirements at post-release phases of SDLC (i.e. maintenance) is higher than effort of changing requirements at pre-release of SDLC phases; as in designing, coding and testing. Requirements volatility usually occurred after proving them by customers at RE and it affect the estimations of cost, time, effort, the product quality and the success of the resulting product. It may cause negative effects on the later phases of software development (Thakurta & Ahlemann, 2010).

A careful choosing of software development model could lead to some control over the predicted volatility risks, where the characteristic of software process models influence the complexity, requirement management and the ultimate software objectives (Thakurta & Ahlemann, 2010).

(Nurmuliani and Zowghi, (Nurmuliani, Zowghi & Fowell, 2004) indicated that the major reasons of requirement volatility were the customer needs. Developers increasingly understand the software products, market demand and changes in the organization politics. There is a multifaceted relationship between requirement volatility and software project performance, which can be measured by developing and delivering the software product in time and within estimated budget assigned to the project.

However, the findings of (Zhao, Yang, Xiang & Xu 2002) in their paper confirmed the usefulness of the changing impact analysis in software maintenance and evolution, regression testing, and debugging. They studied the impact analysis of changes on the system design level; as a collection of interacting components, rather than the implementation details. To evaluate the effect of the changes on software design, they suggested architectural slicing technique to analyze the formal architectural specification. The analysis consists of three basic design entity types: components, connectors and the configuration topology. The cost-precision tradeoffs for program behavior are examined based on "Coverage Impact" and "Path Impact" dynamic impact analysis techniques. They compared several source codes concerning their execution time, space and costs, and found that "Path Impact" is more precise and more expensive than "Coverage Impact" (Orso, Apiwattanapong, Law, Rothermel & Harrold, 2004).

To control the change process, (O'Neal, 2001), (O'Neal, 2003) presented a traceability-based impact analysis methodology that determines the impact of changed requirements on SDLC. The changing requirements are classified according to their similarities and impact on software development work. The empirical studies showed that improving the requirement changing management increased the software productivity of the developers and improved the project planning and cost estimation (Damian, Chisan, & Thamsamy, 2005).

Researchers proposed a mathematical model to identify the requirements volatility; they found that the maximum changing rates depend on source code size and duration of requirements volatility, where the volatility is calculated from the function points and lines of source code in the software product (Kulk & Verhoef, 2008). A linear regression analysis models are proposed to help project managers in predicting the volatility of requirements of a medium-size software project and to minimize the risks caused by volatile requirements, like schedule and cost overruns. The correlation-based estimation model is presented to derive the size of changed requirements. Four dependent variables, number of actors, use cases, words, and lines; are extracted from requirements documents and applied into the prediction system. It can be used for all use case documents that are written in textual form (Loconsole, 2008). (Ferreira, Collofello, Shunk & Mackulak, 2009) showed that dynamic simulation model assist in well-understanding of the cost, schedule, and quality impacts of requirements volatility on the development of software project. The model is based on 50 parameters and used as an effective tool.

3. Reasons and Causes of Change Requirements

Software requirements are dynamically evolved and changed due to numerous and diverse reasons (McGee & Greer, 2012), (Sudhakar, 2005), (Dev & Awasthi, 2012), (Tripathy & Naik, 2015). They require further study to extract and propose others to enhance the new software release and the management decision making. In this work, we gathered, and studied 32 critical factors, and classified them into four main categories. They represent the potential risk areas that may lead to software success or failure and to estimate how much it might cost to implement the change. Also, they help us to explore the proposed approach to control and manage requirements changing risks in IT software projects. The main categories and the corresponding factors are defined as:

A. Organizational Factors:

- Government regulations and politics.
- Business policy that is related to organization strategy and vision is changed.
- Business value of the system is decreased.
- Changing in organization structure.
- Changing in leadership and shifting business focus.
- Market competitors changed or increased.
- Decision-making procedures.

B. Project Factors:

- Software project domain, scope and role are unclear.
- Project size is large-scaled and requirements are overload.
- Project price/developing time are changed because of under or over-estimation.

C. Development Process Factors:

- Software product quality factors are changed or enhanced.
- Requirements priorities are not well-handled.
- Software product constraints are changed and have conflicts.
- Requirements priorities are changed.
- Complexity of development technology.

- Design weakness and the inter-relationships and interfaces among system components are complex.
- Changing the data structure.
- Large-volume of data is transformed into new technology.
- Redundant and irrationalized data objects.
- Misunderstanding of the system.
- Lack of using software tools.
- Limited usage of good programming styles.
- The associated documentations are not available or inadequate.
- Unclear feedback from design reviewers and /or requirement specification reviews.
- Uncertainty of upgrading the system platform.

D. Project Stakeholder Factors:

- Potential changes of users/customers/business managers demands.
- Developers experience and skills are limited and inadequate.
- Customers are not well-collaborated or may miss some requirements.
- Customers/users changed their minds and scope.
- Leadership characteristics and team member characteristics.
- Communication skills among development team members, project and organizational managers, customers and users.
- Strong appearance of market competitors.

At pre-processing stage, the studying of all the above factors and examining the interrelationships among them will reduce risks of system failure and help to make a decision on which changes to implement. To measure requirements volatility, the requirements functionalities, properties, dependencies, interrelationships, the main causes and issues are identified before suggesting the methodology. Changes management and risks control will help to enhance design, implementation, maintenance and the overall software quality. Fig. 1 depicts the main causes and the issues of controlling and managing the risks.

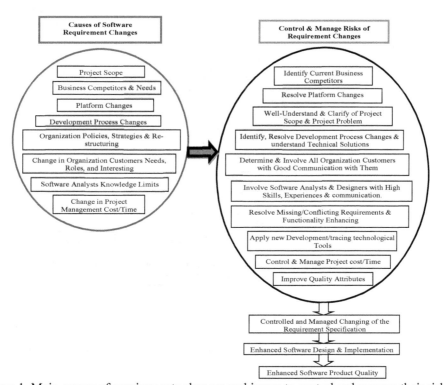

Figure 1. Main causes of requirements changes and issues to control and manage their risks

4. Methodology of Controlling Changing Risks and Managing Requirement Volatility

Dealing with reliable, complete, consistent and high-quality requirements is not easy task, it demands much effort from developers and maintainers, better involvement of interested stakeholders and a solid knowledge in quality management techniques. The suggested comprehensive methodology focuses on the formal tasks that are needed to be followed to change requirements particularly in the late stages of software development, and after completing requirement specification in requirement engineering phase. The objectives of using this model are to better understand the change causes and their underlying failure risks; during the later stages of software development process, understand the requirement volatility process, enhance decision-making process, improve the productivity of implementing change requirements, reduce failure risks and enhance the software product release quality.

The proposed model is based on descriptive and qualitative methods. Descriptive analysis provides rich information to understand the corresponding problems of requirements volatility as well as related aspects; such as organizational policy, customer needs and product changes, whereas qualitative methods are employed to analyze the collected data and to evaluate the change process. The ad-hoc maturity approach has a set of interrelated actions and activities to manage requirement volatility, and to control and reduce risks impacts. The work information model is represented in Figure 2.

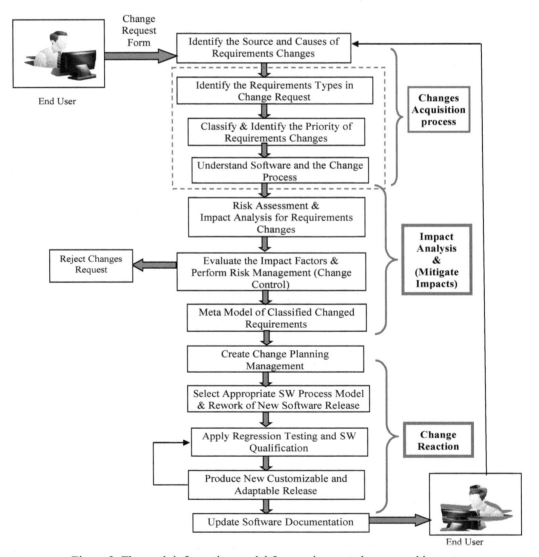

Figure 2. The work information model for requirement changes and impacts

4.1 Identify the Source and Causes of Requirements Changes

Change request is issued by customers, end users, business manager or according governmental regulation. The causes are explained previously in section 3. The formal request is written using a dedicated change request form. The form is checked and confirmed, then it is used through impact analysis. 4.2 Identify the Requirements Types in Change Request; whether the changes are in functional, data requirements, system platform, or in software project constraints. The customers, managers, technical staffs and end users are cooperated to identify the desired requirements and constraints that they really want.

4.2 Identify the Requirements Types in Change Request

Whether the changes are in functional, data requirements, system platform, or in software project constraints. The customers, managers, technical staffs and end users are cooperated to identify the desired requirements and constraints that they really want.

4.3 Classify and Identify the Subjective Priority of Requirements Changes

The priority is concerned to its relative importance in business or as suggested by business top managers or customers with high-position. The requirements have different importance and the customer may have different views about their importance. It is impossible to implement all requirement changes within limited time and budget during the current release. Priorities are identified according to user/customer preferences, the changes and business goals. These facts make requirements prioritization a critical task, especially when there are a large number of changes and have incompatible priorities. Therefore, the collaboration of the business managers, customers and users is needed to resolve this issue.   It can be performed by:

- Prioritization of changes importance; where some changes are more critical than others, and
- Prioritization of development order; where some changes have great values to business and software capabilities.

Subjective prioritization is done iteratively and incrementally using Business Case Analysis technique, and using Technical Weighting Scale of range 1 to 5 that represents (low, low-moderate, moderate, high-moderate, high) correspondingly. It depends on weighting the importance to customers and business. Subjective prioritization is important to eliminate the impact of the requirement volatility, improve business value, and improve customers' satisfaction.

4.4 Understand Software and the Change Process

The developers need to well-understand the software development process model, software design, software functionalities, data and product documentation before proceeding with the changing procedures. Product documentations incorporate requirement specification, design documentation, source code of its programs and test oracle, if this documentations are not up-to-date it will make software maintenance difficult, but practically they were not updated after maintenance and are outdated.

4.5 Risk Assessment and Impact Analysis for Requirements Changes

It identifies the risk factors that are involved in implementing requirements change and examines during impact analysis of requirements changes how these factors are related to each other. Sometimes, the changing of one requirement may have impact on other dependent requirements and the changes may expand to affect organizational goals. Hence, it is used to assess which parts will change and which dependent parts are influenced with the changes. The changing propagation beyond the intended parts and examining methodically the existing environment to predict the potential effects make the evaluation of impact ambiguous and complicated task. The results of impact analysis need to be accurate to positively direct the changes control and management (Rahman, Razali R. & Singh, 2014) and to avoid failures in such projects. Therefore, the following issues are taken into our consideration in this study:

- The volume of incompleteness and inconsistent of requirements in changing request form.
- Requirement changing types; Requirement addition, modification, deletion.
- Requirement changes state (urgent or not).
- Changing priority and business values.
- Suitable selection of elicitation technique.
- Requirement dependencies; requirements functionalities and their interrelationships
- The complexity of changes.

- Software application domain, type and objectives.
- Software project size and age.
- Availability of up-to-date documentation (i.e. requirement specification, design specification, test suites).
- Software architecture style (i.e. data-centered, data-flow, object-oriented, or layered architecture), architectural patterns, factoring levels, and design models.
- Availability of source code of the programming language and the clarity degree of programming styles.
- Software development process model and implementation of design methodology.
- The degree of desired quality attributes.
- Organization polices and regulations
- Development platform (i.e. memory, CPU, communication and operating systems); for the post release requirements changes.
- Software engineers motivations, experiences and skills levels.
- Software engineering productivity rate.
- Customers and users' involvement and cooperation with software development team and relationship level between software developers and customers and frequent communication between them in requirement engineering phase and the following phases.
- Organization size and policies.
- Availability and usability of software tools.
- Underestimating or overestimating of Cost/Time/Effort in planning may negatively influence planning process.

The success of software development / maintenance projects depends on the investigation of risks, level of awareness concerning requirement volatility, the software project attributes, the management approaches used and the accuracy and correctness of impact analysis.

4.6 Evaluate the Impact Factors and Do Risk Management (Change Control Board)

The qualitative and quantitative methods are used to evaluate different impacts of changing requirements to determine the feasibility of implementing the requested changes. The evaluation that deals with assessing risks is performed by analysts, who eliminate the risks and their impacts.

The requirement volatility measures are used to determine the adequacy of software engineering process, resources, and developers' number and productivity. Requirement volatility measurement is important to find whether our project is moving on track or not, to know which changes have more impact on project than other one. It is also helpful to predict the future product and. Requirements volatility is measured using mathematical formula (Stark, Oman, Skillicorn & Ameele, 1999), (Roedler & Rhodes, 2010):

$$R_V \approx C / Q \qquad (1)$$

Where:

R_V: Requirement volatility,

C: Cost, and

Q: Release Quality.

$$R_V = \frac{R_a + R_c + R_d}{VCN} \times 100 \qquad (2)$$

Where:

R_v: Requirement volatility,

R_a: Added Requirements,

R_c: Modified Requirements,

R_d: Deleted Requirements, and

VCN: Version Content Notice = set of requirements agreed by both the developer and customer.

Requirements volatility can be measured depending on the size of change in use case model and is measured by counting the number of minor change, and major changes. It is defined as:

$$R_V = \frac{\sum_{i=1}^{m} changed\ requirements}{\sum_{j=1}^{n} Requirements} \qquad (3)$$

Where:

R_v: Requirement volatility,

m: Total number of change requirements change (i.e. requirements addition, requirements deletion, and requirements modification), and

n: Total number of requirements for a certain development phase.

But Eq.1, Eq.2 and Eq.3; did not consider the increasing effect of requirement addition, changing or deletion in the late phases of software development when it is evolved and grown. Therefore, to find the influence of changing requirements at the late stages of software development on the requirement volatility, requirements volatility is defined as:

$$R_v = \frac{R_a + R_c + R_d}{VCN} \times (10^{p/2} - 1) \qquad (4)$$

Where:

R_v: Requirement volatility,

R_a: Added Requirements,

R_c: Modified Requirements,

R_d: Deleted Requirements,

VCN: Set of requirements agreed by the developer and customer,

p: Number of software development passed phases, and

$(10^{p/2}-1)$: The volatility impact factor.

During the requirements engineering phase, p=0; thus $(10)^{0/2} = 1$, and $(10^{p/2}-1) = 1-1= 0$. It means that the requirement engineering phase has no considerable effect on volatility impact factor.

Requirement inspection and validation are also needed to discover requirement defects to enhance the requirements quality and succeed software projects. The square matrix is used as an evaluation process model to measure the quality of requirements changes, which will influence later the quality of new software release. Evaluation consists of five tasks:

    a. Establishing requirements evaluation. This is performed through identifying the software type, preferred quality characteristics, and identifying the evaluation purpose and model?

    b. Specifying requirements evaluation. It is done through identifying the internal and external quality issues and rating the each quality issues ranking. Correctness weight must be not less than 0.9 Completeness must be no less than 0.8 and consistency must be not less than 0.75.

    c. Designing requirements evaluation.

    d. Executing requirements evaluation.

    e. Assess the results of measuring and comparing the criteria that are verified by experts.

4.7 Comprehensive Meta Model of Classified Changed Requirements

Semi-formal definitions of requirements that are classified into clusters related to requirement types (i.e. functional, data, and non-functional requirements); which in turn can be subdivided into subclasses and so on, the levels of details, implementation complexity, source of the requirements, requirement values, description of change, date of elicitation, and risk level (i.e. high or low risks), where:

Domain of Changed Requirement ⊆ Domain Changed Requirement Meta-Data.

Changed Requirement ⊆ Requirement Types x Composition x Levels of Details x Implementation Complexity x Source of the Requirements x Requirement Values x Description of Change x Date of Elicitation x Risk Level.

4.8 Create Change Planning Management

It is very important for project manager to have adequate information and knowledge about requirements changes introduced during software development to make the appropriate decisions. Since unstable requirements influence and exceed the planned software development time schedule and budget, the new planning estimation is needed; for the time schedule, cost and number skilled developers, according to new long-term requirements. After analyzing the possible consequences of changes on other software development phases and parts of the project, the plans are put to determine the assumed actions with respect to the predefined changes. Re-planning will assist to make reasonable decisions during the next development phases.

4.9 Select Appropriate SW Process Model & Rework of New Software Release

Selecting the software development model and selecting the appropriate requirement elicitation technique have an influence on the level of requirement specification details and product success rate (Rehman, Khan & Riaz, 2013). Implementation of requirement changes should match with the current software architecture and design, data design, and code. The modification of the internal structure of the software may be done without changing the functionality of the programming using software refactoring technique. Architectural refactoring is mainly needed to detect and remove design defects, which in turn will reduce the complexity, ensure the improvement of software quality and minimize the long-term maintenance. Verification is done after refactoring to ensure that the modules are functionally conformed to requirement specification and interact as designed. The test cases are redesigned to overcome the new and modified requirements. Integration testing is also applied to ensure that the modules are well-integrated to form the complete software product. The effort in implementing requirements changes implementation is high in the requirement specification, impact analysis, and testing phases.

4.10 Apply Software Qualification and Regression Testing for the Pre and Post-Release of System

Concerning requirement changes, with adequate test cases that cover the portions of software that are affected by changes. It is considered as an objective evaluation process that is used to determine the scope of the changing impact, monitor and detect the defects as a consequence of changes, and to verify software specifications to achieve its goals. To achieve the model objectives, test cases are then written to check on the functional validation and effectiveness. The model evaluation process is based on cost-benefit evaluation model.

4.11 Produce New Customizable and Adaptable Software Release

A new low-risk software release is issued after applying the customer's required changes and a matching between the expected software outcomes and the actual implementation outcomes.

4.12 Update the Related Software Documentation to fit the Applied Changes, Since Documentation Engineering is a Sub-Domain of the Software Engineering

It is needed to update the descriptive information that specifies the applied changes to be more consistent, well-understandable and up-to-date. Documentation is the basis for communication among development team members and a system information repository for maintainers. Documentation consists of many different kinds of documents produced at different points after changing requirements are performed.

5. Discussion and Key Findings

The study includes 10 different projects, and the changes are classified into added, modified and deleted requirements. The table 1 shows the acquired data, total changed requirements, total project requirements, requirements volatility rate and volatility impact factor. Figure 3 and shows the requirement volatility impact factor in design phase and figure 4 shows the requirement volatility impact factor in maintenance phase for the same 10 projects. During the study, sensitive data is collected to avoid as much as possible the negative effects of changing requirements and to perform risk management. .But in actual software applications, it is not an easy task, due to:

- The application end-users are not well-specified the change request forms (CRF). They did not explain the underlying reasons for the proposed change. Sometimes, CRF requires an experienced user.
- The requirements impact analysis (i.e. dependency analysis) of requirements change is not adequately performed and the maintainer is unable to predict the potential risks with requirements evolving.
- The complex relationships among requirements cause the ripple effects of requirement changes and management.
- Classifying requirement dependencies into different classes and identifying requirement dependencies and their relationship types are difficult tasks.

- The traceability between the changing requirements and other requirements and artifacts are not identified.
- Increasing in requirement volatility and their business values will raise the developer and maintainer job size, due to the additional work, and consequently increase the estimated project's cost, resources costs and time schedule.
- The application complexity
- Reconfiguration of reused set of requirements and software components.
- The collaboration among the developer, managers and the users will reduce cost overruns.
- The large number of participants and roles may influence negatively on the project development/maintenance work progress and quality, when adding new functionalities or classifying defects in requirements specification.

Table 1. Changed requirements and their impacts

Type of Changed Requirements	Project 1	Project 2	Project 3	Project 4	Project 5	Project 6	Project 7	Project 8	Project 9	Project 10
Added Requirements	3	2	3	2	3	1	3	2	4	3
Delete Requirements	2	2	3	0	1	2	2	2	1	2
Modify Requirements	2	5	5	5	6	2	6	5	3	6
Total Number of changed Requirements	7	9	11	7	10	5	11	9	8	11
Total Number of Requirements	65	74	60	83	67	58	79	63	59	71
Change Percentage %	10.77	12.16	18.33	8.43	14.93	8.62	13.92	14.29	13.56	15.49
Requirements Volatility Rate	0.11	0.12	0.18	0.08	0.15	0.09	0.14	0.14	0.14	0.15
Volatility Impact Factor	0.97	1.09	1.65	0.76	1.34	0.78	1.25	1.29	1.22	1.39

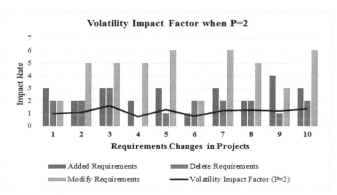

Figure 3. Volatility Impact Factor when P=2 (Design)

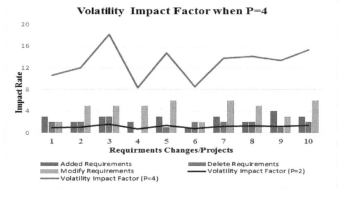

Figure 4. Volatility Impact Factor when P=4 (Maintenance)

6. Conclusion

Software developers need high-level of expertise and knowledge to deliver high quality software products, which increase the requirement engineers' efforts to elicit and analyze the requirements, represent them into comprehensive models and process in systematic and qualitative technique. Requirements volatility has an influence on different phases of SDLC and software maintenance; hence it has a great impact on the estimated project cost, schedule and the quality of final product release.   In this paper, we have studied different aspects of requirements volatility, and analyzed the reasons for requirements changes, their risks, and the impact analysis on software development process.

Requirements volatility cannot be fully avoided but its impact can be reduced and its causes can be minimized. A requirement volatility model is presented, which included the information required for the change acquisition process, impact analysis by measuring the size of changed requirements in use case models and classifying them into major and minor changes, to find the influence of changing requirements at the late stages of software development. The planning management is measured accordingly to produce new customizable and adaptable release. The model will help to reduce the influence of changing requirements on the design or implementation of the software. If the model is not adopted in a right way then the developers may face more problems; depending on the software application type and size. The impact of requirement change is used to evaluate their risks and to understand the degree of risk. If the requirement volatility rate is high, after completing requirement specification; then the scheduled time, costs and efforts increase and may lower release quality.

Acknowledgment

The authors are grateful to the applied science private university, Amman-Jordan, for the full financial support granted to cover the publication fee of this research article.

References

Bhatti, M. W., Hayat, F., Ehsan N., Ahmed, S., Ishaque, A., & Z.Sarwar, S. (2010, Oct. 8-10). An investigation of changing requirements with respect to development phases of a software project. *International Conference on Computer Information Systems and Industrial Management Applications (CISIM)*, 323-3327, Oct. 8-1, 2010, Krakow, Poland.

Damian, D., Chisan, J., & Thamsamy, L. V. (2005). Requirements Engineering and Downstream Software Development: Finding from a Case Study. *Empirical Software Engineering, 10*(3), 255-283. http://dx.doi.org/10.1007/s10664-005-1288-4

Dev, H., & Awasthi, R. (2012). A Systematic Study of Requirement Volatility during Software Development Process. *International Journal of Computer Science Issues (IJCSI), 9*(2), 1, March.

Ferreira, S., Collofello, J., Shunk, D., & Mackulak, G. (2009, Oct.). Understanding the Effects of Requirements Volatility in Software Engineering by Using Analytical Modeling and Software Process Simulation. *Journal of Systems and Software, 82*(10), 1568–1577. http://dx.doi.org/10.1016/j.jss.2009.03.014

Kulk, G. P., & Verhoef, C. (2008). Quantifying requirements volatility effects. *Science of Computer Programming, 72*(3), 136–175. Elsevier. http://dx.doi.org/10.1016/j.scico.2008.04.003

Loconsole, A. (2008, June 26-27). A Correlational Study on Four Measures of Requirements Volatility. *12th International Conference on Evaluation and Assessment in Software Engineering (EASE)*, University of Bari, Italy. Retrieved from http://www.bcs.org/upload/pdf/ewic_ea08_paper18_1.pdf

McGee, S., & Greer, D. (2012). Towards an Understanding of the Causes and Effects of Software Requirements Change: Two Case Studies. *Requirement Engineering*, Springer-Verlag, London, *17*(2), 133-155. http://dx.doi.org/10.1007/s00766-012-0149-0

NIST (National Institute of Standards and Technology). (2002). *The Economic Impacts of Inadequate Infrastructure for Software Testing*. Gaithersburg, Maryland, RTI Project No. 7007.011, U.S Department of Commerce Technology Administration. Retrieved from http://www.nist.gov/director/planning/upload/report02-3.pdf

Nurmuliani, N., Zowghi, D., & Powell, S. (2004). *Analysis of Requirements Volatility during Software Development Life Cycle*. In Proceedings Australian software engineering conference, ASWEC'04, Australia, 28–37. http://dx.doi.org/10.1109/ASWEC.2004.1290455

O'Neal, J. S. (2001, November). *Analyzing the Impact of Changing Requirements*. 17th IEEE International Conference on Software Maintenance (ICSM'01), 190-195. http://dx.doi.org/10.1109/ICSM.2001.972729

O'Neal, J. S. (2003). *Analyzing the Impact of Changing Software Requirements: A Traceability-Based Methodology*. Department of Computer Science, Faculty of the Louisiana State University and Agricultural and Mechanical College (Doctoral dissertation). Retrieved from http://etd.lsu.edu/docs/available/etd-0929103-120652/unrestricted/O'Neal_dis.pdf

Orso, A., Apiwattanapong, T., Law, J., Rothermel, G., & Harrold, M. J. (2004, 23-28 May). *An empirical comparison of dynamic impact analysis algorithms*. Proceedings of the 26th International Conference on Software Engineering (ICSE'04), Edinburgh, Scotland, 491–500. http://dx.doi.org/10.1109/ICSE.2004.1317471

Rahman, M. A., Razali, R., & Singh, D. (2014, Jan.). A Risk Model of Requirements Change Impact Analysis. *Journal of Software, 9*(1), 76-81. http://dx.doi.org/ 10.4304/jsw.9.1.76-81

Rehman, T., Khan, M. N. A., & Riaz, N. (2013 February). Analysis of Requirement Engineering Processes, Tools/Techniques and Methodologies, *International Journal of Information Technology and Computer Science, 5*(3), 40-48. http://dx.doi.org/10.5815/ijitcs.2013.03.05

Roedler, G., & Rhodes, D. (2010, Jan. 29). *Systems Engineering Leading Indicators Guide: Version 2*. Massachusetts, Institute of Technology, INCOSE, and PSM. Retrieved from http://seari.mit.edu/documents/SELI-Guide-Rev2.pdf

Singh, M. P., & Vyas, R. (2012, Sep.). Requirements Volatility in Software Development Process. *International Journal of Soft Computing and Engineering (IJSCE), 2*(4), 259-264. Retrieved from http://www.ijsce.org/attachments/File/v2i4/D0960082412.pdf

Stark, G., Oman, P., Skillicorn, A., & Ameele, R. (1999). An Examination of the Effects of Requirements Changes on Software Maintenance Releases. *Journal of Software Maintenance: Research and Practice, 11*(5), September/October. 1999, 293-309. http://dx.doi.org/ 10.1002/(SICI)1096-908X

Sudhakar, M. (2005, Apr.). *Managing the Impact of Requirements Volatility*, Department of Computing Science, Umeå University, Sweden, 29th April (Master MSc. Thesis). Retrieved from http://www8.cs.umu.se/education/examina/Rapporter/MundlamuriSudhakar.pdf

Thakurta, R. (2010). Management of Requirement Volatility - A Study of Organizational Competency and How It Is Influenced by The Project Environment. *Journal of Information Technology Management, XXI* (2), 24-34. Retrieved from http://jitm.ubalt.edu/XXI-2/article3.pdf

Thakurta, R., & Ahlemann, F. (2010). *Understanding Requirements Volatility in Software Projects: An Empirical Investigation of Volatility Awareness, Management Approaches and Their Applicability.* Proceedings of the 43rd Hawaii International Conference on System Sciences. http://dx.doi.org/ 10.1109/HICSS.2010.420

Tripathy, P. I., & Naik, K. (2015). *Software Evolution and Maintenance: A Practitioner's Approach*. John Wiley & Sons, Jan 2015.

Zhao, J., Yang, H., Xiang, L., & Xu, B. (2002). Change Impact Analysis to Support Architectural Evolution. *Journal of Software Maintenance and Evolution: Research and Practice*, 317-333. http://dx.doi.org/10.1002/smr.258

17

The Impact of the Pattern-Growth Ordering on the Performances of Pattern Growth-Based Sequential Pattern Mining Algorithms

Kenmogne Edith Belise[1]

[1] Faculty of Science, Department of Mathematics and Computer Science, Cameroon

Correspondence: Kenmogne Edith Belise, Faculty of Science, Department of Mathematics and Computer Science, LIFA, Po. Box. 67 Dschang, Cameroon. E-mail: ebkenmogne@gmail.com

Abstract

Sequential Pattern Mining is an efficient technique for discovering recurring structures or patterns from very large dataset widely addressed by the data mining community, with a very large field of applications, such as cross-marketing, DNA analysis, web log analysis, user behavior, sensor data, etc. The sequence pattern mining aims at extracting a set of attributes, shared across time among a large number of objects in a given database. Previous studies have developed two major classes of sequential pattern mining methods, namely, the candidate generation-and-test approach based on either vertical or horizontal data formats represented respectively by GSP and SPADE, and the pattern-growth approach represented by FreeSpan and PrefixSpan. In this paper, we are interested in the study of the impact of the pattern-growth ordering on the performances of pattern growth-based sequential pattern mining algorithms. To this end, we introduce a class of pattern-growth orderings, called linear orderings, for which patterns are grown by making grow either the current pattern prefix or the current pattern suffix from the same position at each growth-step. We study the problem of pruning and partitioning the search space following linear orderings. Experimentations show that the order in which patterns grow has a significant influence on the performances.

Keywords: sequence mining, sequential pattern, pattern-growth direction, pattern-growth ordering, search space, pruning, partitioning

1. Introduction

A sequence database consists of sequences of ordered elements or events, recorded with or without a concrete notion of time. Sequences are common, occurring in any metric space that facilitates either partial or total ordering. Customer transactions, codons or nucleotides in an amino acid, website traversal, computer networks, DNA sequences and characters in a text string are examples of where the existence of sequences may be significant and where the detection of frequent (totally or partially ordered) subsequences might be useful. Sequential pattern mining has arisen as a technology to discover such subsequences. A subsequence, such as buying first a PC, then a digital camera, and then a memory card, if it occurs frequently in a customer transaction database, is a (frequent) sequential pattern.

Sequential pattern mining (Dam et al., 2016; Mabroukeh & Ezeife, 2010; Lin et al., 2016a; Linet al., 2016b; Lin et al., 2016c; Lin et al., 2016d) is an important data mining problem widely addressed by the data mining community, with a very large field of applications such as finding network alarm patterns, mining customer purchase patterns, identifying outer membrane proteins, automatically detecting erroneous sentences, discovering block correlations in storage systems, identifying plan failures, identifying copy-paste and related bugs in large-scale software code, API specification mining and API usage mining from open source repositories, and Web log data mining. Sequential pattern mining aims at extracting a set of attributes, shared across time among a large number of objects in a given database.

The sequential pattern mining problem was first introduced by Agrawal & Srikant (1995) based on their study of customer purchase sequences, as follows: *Given a set of sequences, where each sequence consists of a list of events (or elements) and each event consists of a set of items, and given a user-specified minimum support threshold min_sup, sequential pattern mining finds all frequent subsequences, that is, the subsequences whose occurrence frequency in the set of sequences is no less than min_sup.*

In this paper, we are interested in the study of the impact of the pattern-growth ordering on the performances of pattern growth-based sequential pattern mining algorithms. It aims at enhancing understanding of the pattern-growth approach. To this end, the important key concepts upon which that approach relies, namely pattern-growth direction, pattern-growth ordering, search space pruning and search space partitioning, are revisited. We introduce a class of pattern-growth orderings, called linear orderings, for which patterns are grown by making grow either the current pattern prefix or the current pattern suffix from the same position at each growth-step. This class contains PrefixSpan (Pei et al., 2001; Pei et al., 2004) and involves both unidirectional and bidirectional growth. Thus, it is a generalization of PrefixSpan (Pei et al., 2001; Pei et al., 2004). However, it does not contain FreeSpan (Han et al., 2000) as it makes grow patterns from any position. We study the problem of pruning and partitioning the search space following linear orderings. Experimentations show that the order in which patterns grow has a significant influence on the performances.

The rest of the paper is organized as follows. Section 2 presents the formal definition of the problem of sequential pattern mining. Section 3 presents previous results. Section 4 presents the theoretical contribution of the paper. Section 5 presents experimental results. Concluding remarks are given in section 6.

2. Problem statement and Notation

The problem of mining sequential patterns, and its associated notation, can be given as follows: Let $I=\{i_1, i_2, \ldots, i_n\}$ be a set of literals, termed **items**, which comprise the alphabet. An **itemset** is a subset of items. A **sequence** is an ordered list of itemsets. Sequence s is denoted by $\langle s_1, s_2, \ldots s_n \rangle$, where s_j is an itemset. s_j is also called an **element** of the sequence, and denoted as $(x_1, x_2,\ldots,x_m)$, where x_k is an item. For brevity, the brackets are omitted if an element has only one item, i.e. element (x) is written as x. An item can occur at most once in an element of a sequence, but can occur multiple times in different elements of a sequence. The number of instances of items in a sequence is called the length of the sequence. A Sequence with length 1 is called an **l-sequence**. The length of a sequence α is denoted $|\alpha|$. A sequence $\alpha=\langle a_1 a_2 \ldots a_n \rangle$, is called **subsequence** of another sequence $\beta=\langle b_1 b_2 \ldots b_m \rangle$ and β a **supersequence** of α, denoted as $\alpha \subseteq \beta$, if there exist integers $1 \leq j_1 < j_2 < \ldots < j_n \leq j_m$ such that $a_1 \subseteq b_{j1}$, $a_2 \subseteq b_{j2}, \ldots a_n \subseteq b_{jn}$. Symbol ε denotes the **empty sequence**.

We are given a database S of input-sequences. A **sequence database** is a set of tuples of the form $\langle sid, s \rangle$ where sid is a **sequence_id** and s a sequence. A tuple $\langle sid, s \rangle$ is said to contain a sequence α if α is a subsequence of s. The **support** of a sequence α in a sequence database S is the number of tuples in the database containing α, i.e.

$$support(S, \alpha) = |\{\langle sid, s \rangle \mid \langle sid, s \rangle \in S \text{ and } \alpha \subseteq s\}|.$$

It can be denoted as support(α) if the sequence database is clear from the context. Given a user-specified positive integer denoted min_support, termed the **minimum support** or the **support threshold**, sequence α is called a **sequential pattern** in the sequence database S if support(S,α)$\geq$ min_support. A sequential pattern with length 1 is called an **l-pattern**. Given a sequence database and the min_support threshold, **sequential pattern mining** is to find the complete set of sequential patterns in the database.

3. Related work

Sequential pattern mining is an important data mining problem. Since the first proposal of this data mining task and its associated efficient mining algorithms, there has been a growing number of researchers in the field and tremendous progress (Mabroukeh & Ezeife, 2010) has been made, evidenced by hundreds of follow-up research publications, on various kinds of extensions and applications, ranging from scalable data mining methodologies, to handling a wide diversity of data types, various extended mining tasks, and a variety of new applications.

Improvements in sequential pattern mining algorithms have followed similar trend in the related area of association rule mining and have been motivated by the need to process more data at a faster speed with lower cost. Previous studies have developed two major classes of sequential pattern mining methods : Apriori-based approaches (Agrawal & Srikant, 1995; Ayres et al., 2002; Garofalakis et al., 1999; Gouda et al., 2007; Gouda et al., 2010; Masseglia et al., 1998; Savary & Zeitouni, 2005; Yang & Kitsuregawa, 2005; Zaki, 2000; Zaki, 2001) and pattern growth algorithms (Han et al., 2000; Pei et al., 2000; Pei et al., 2001; Pei et al., 2004; Hsieh et al., 2008; Seno & Karypis, 2008).

The Apriori-based approach form the vast majority of algorithms proposed in the literature for sequential pattern mining. Apriori-like algorithms depend mainly on the Apriori anti-monotony property, which states the fact that any super-pattern of an infrequent pattern cannot be frequent, and are based on a candidate generation-and-test paradigm proposed in association rule mining (Agrawal et al., 1993; Agrawal & Srikant, 1994). This candidate generation-and-test paradigm is carried out by GSP (Agrawal & Srikant, 1995), SPADE (Zaki, 2001), and SPAM (Ayres et al., 2002). Mining algorithms derived from this approach are based on either vertical or horizontal data formats. Algorithms based on the vertical data format involve AprioriAll, AprioriSome and DynamicSome (Agrawal & Srikant, 1995), GSP (Agrawal & Srikant, 1995), PSP (Masseglia et al., 1998) and SPIRIT (Garofalakis et al., 1999), while those based on the horizontal data format involve SPADE (Zaki, 2001), cSPADE (Zaki, 2000), SPAM (Ayres et al., 2002), LAPIN-SPAM (Yang & Kitsuregawa, 2005), IBM (Savary & Zeitouni, 2005) and PRISM (Gouda et al., 2007; Gouda et al., 2010) . The generation-and-test paradigm has the disadvantage of repeatedly generating an explosive number of candidate sequences and scanning the database to maintain the support count information for these sequences during each iteration of the algorithm, which makes them computationally expensive. To increase the performance of these algorithms constraint driven discovery can be carried out. With constraint driven approaches systems should concentrate only on user specific or user interested patterns or user specified constraints such as minimum support, minimum gap or time interval etc. With regular expressions these constraints are studied in SPIRIT (Garofalakis et al., 1999).

To alleviate these problems, the pattern-growth approach, represented by FreeSpan (Han et al., 2000), PrefixSpan (Pei et al., 2001; Pei et al., 2004) and their further extensions, namely FS-Miner (El-Sayed et al , 2004), LAPIN (Hsieh et al., 2008 ; Yang et al., 2007), SLPMiner (Seno & Karypis, 2002) and WAP-mine (Pei et al., 2000), for efficient sequential pattern mining adopts a divide-and-conquer pattern growth paradigm as follows. Sequence databases are recursively projected into a set of smaller projected databases based on the current sequential patterns, and sequential patterns are grown in each projected database by exploring only locally frequent fragments (Han et al., 2000; Pei et al., 2004). The frequent pattern growth paradigm removes the need for the candidate generation and prune steps that occur in the Apriori-based algorithms and repeatedly narrows the search space by dividing a sequence database into a set of smaller projected databases, which are mined separately. The major advantage of projection-based sequential pattern-growth algorithms is that they avoid the candidate generation and prune steps that occur in the Apriori-based algorithms. Unlike Apriori-based algorithms, they grow longer sequential patterns from the shorter frequent ones. The major cost of these algorithms is the cost of forming projected databases recursively. To alleviate this problem, a pseudo-projection method is exploited to reduce this cost. Instead of performing physical projection, one can register the index (or identifier) of the corresponding sequence and the starting position of the projected suffix in the sequence. Then, a physical projection of a sequence is replaced by registering a sequence identifier and the projected position index point. Pseudo-projection reduces the cost of projection substantially when the projected database can fit in main memory.

PrefixSpan (Pei et al., 2001; Pei et al., 2004) and FreeSpan (Han et al., 2000) differ at the criteria of partitioning projected databases and at the criteria of growing patterns. FreeSpan (Han et al., 2000) creates projected databases based on the current set of frequent patterns without a particular ordering (i.e., pattern-growth direction), whereas PrefixSpan projects databases by growing frequent prefixes. Thus, PrefixSpan follows the unidirectional growth whereas FreeSpan follows the bidirectional growth. Another difference between FreeSpan and PrefixSpan is that the pseudo-projection works efficiently for PrefixSpan but not so for FreeSpan. This is because for PrefixSpan, an offset position clearly identifies the suffix and thus the projected subsequence. However, for FreeSpan, since the next step pattern-growth can be in both forward and backward directions from any position, one needs to register more information on the possible extension positions in order to identify the remainder of the projected subsequences.

4. Proposed Work

4.1. Pattern-Growth Directions and Orderings

Definition 1 (*Pattern-growth direction*). A pattern-growth direction is a direction along which patterns could grow. There are two pattern-growth directions, namely *left-to-right* and *right-to-left* directions. Do grow a pattern along *left-to-right* (resp. *right-to-left*) direction is to add one or more item to its right (resp. left) hand side.

Definition 2 (*Pattern-growth ordering*). A pattern-growth ordering is a specification of the order in which patterns should grow. A pattern-growth ordering is said to be unidirectional iff all the patterns should grow along a unique direction. Otherwise it is said to be bidirectional. A pattern-growth ordering is said to be static (resp. dynamic) iff it is fully specified before the beginning of the mining process (resp. iff it is constructed during the mining process).

Definition 3 (*Basic-static pattern-growth ordering*). A basic-static pattern-growth ordering, also called basic pattern-growth ordering for sake of simplicity, is an ordering which is based on a unique pattern-growth direction, and grow a pattern at the rate of one item per growth-step.

There are two basic-static pattern-growth orderings, namely *left-to-right ordering* (also called *prefix-growth ordering*), which consists in growing a prefix of a pattern at the rate of one item per growth-step at its right hand side, and *right-to-left ordering* (also called *suffix-growth ordering*), which consists in growing a suffix of a pattern at the rate of one item per growth-step at its left hand side.

Definition 4 (*Basic-dynamic pattern-growth ordering*). A basic-dynamic pattern-growth ordering is an ordering which grow a pattern at the rate of one item per growth-step, and whose pattern-growth direction is determined at the beginning of each growth-step during the mining process. It is denoted *-growth.

Definition 5 (*Basic-bidirectional pattern-growth ordering*). A basic-bidirectional pattern-growth ordering is an ordering which is based on the two distinct pattern-growth directions, and grow a pattern in each direction at the rate of one item per couple of growth-steps.

There are two basic-bidirectional pattern-growth orderings, namely *prefix-suffix-growth ordering* (i.e. *left-to-right direction* followed by *right-to-left direction*), which consists in growing a pattern at the rate of one item per growth-step during a couple of steps by first growing a prefix (i.e. adding of one item at the right-hand side) of that pattern followed by the growing of the corresponding suffix (i.e. adding of one item at the left-hand side), and *suffix-prefix-growth ordering* (i.e. *right-to-left direction* followed by *left-to-right direction*), which consists in growing a pattern at the rate of one item per growth-step during a couple of steps by first growing a suffix of that pattern followed by the growing of the corresponding prefix.

Definition 6 (*Linear pattern-growth ordering*). A linear pattern-growth ordering is a series of compositions of *-growth*, *prefix-growth* and *suffix-growth* orderings, and denoted o_0-o_1-o_2 ... o_{n-1}-growth for some n, where $o_i \in$ {prefix, suffix, *} $(0 \leq i \leq n-1)$. It is said to be static iff $o_i \in$ {prefix, suffix} for all $i \in$ {0, 1, 2, ..., n-1}. Otherwise, it is said to be dynamic.

The o_0-o_1-o_2 ... o_{n-1}-growth linear ordering consists in growing a pattern at the rate of one item per growth-step during a series of n growth-steps by growing at step i $(0 \leq i \leq n-1)$ a prefix (resp. suffix) of that pattern if o_i denotes prefix (resp. suffix). If $o_i \in$ {*}, a pattern-growth direction is determined and an item is added to the pattern following that direction. For instance, stemming from the *prefix-suffix-suffix-prefix-growth* static linear ordering, one should grow a pattern in the following order:

- *Growth-step 0*: Add an item to the right hand side of a prefix of that pattern.
- *Growth-step 1*: Add one item to the left hand side of the corresponding suffix of the previous prefix.
- *Growth-step 2*: Repeat step 1.
- *Growth-step 3*: Repeat step 0.
- *Growth-step k (k ≥4)*: Repeat step k mod 4.

The *prefix-suffix-*-prefix-growth* dynamic linear ordering grows patterns as *prefix-suffix-suffix-prefix-growth* ordering except for steps k that satisfy (k mod 4) = 3. During such a particular step, a pattern-growth direction is determined and an item is added to the pattern following that direction.

FreeSpan and PrefixSpan differ at the criteria of growing patterns. FreeSpan creates projected databases based on the current set of frequent patterns without a particular ordering (i.e., pattern-growth direction). Since a length-k pattern may grow at any position, the search for length-(k+1) patterns will need to check every possible combination, which is costly. Because of this, FreeSpan do not follow the linear ordering. However PrefixSpan follows the prefix-growth static ordering as it projects databases by growing frequent prefixes.

Given a database of sequences, an open problem is to find a linear ordering that leads to the best mining performances over all possible linear orderings.

4.2 Search Space Pruning and Partitioning

Definition 7 (*Prefix of an itemset*). Suppose all the items within an itemset are listed alphabetically. Given an itemset $x = (x_1x_2 ... x_n)$, another itemset $x' = (x'_1x'_2 ... x'_m)$ $(m \leq n)$ is called a prefix of x if and only if $x'_1 = x_i$ for all $i \leq m$. If $m < n$, the prefix is also denoted as $x = (x_1x_2... x_{m\_})$.

Definition 8 (*The corresponding suffix of a prefix of an itemset*). Let $x = (x_1x_2 ... x_n)$ be a itemset. Let $x' = (x_1x_2 ... x_m)$ $(m \leq n)$ be a prefix of x. Itemset $x'' = (x_{m+1}x_{m+2}... x_n)$ is called the suffix of x with regards to prefix x', denoted as $x'' = x/x'$. We also denote $x = x'.x''$. Note, if $x = x'$, the suffix of x with regards to x' is empty. If $1 \leq m < n$, the suffix is also denoted as $(\_x_{m+1}x_{m+2} ... x_n)$.

For example, for the itemset iset=(abcdefgh),(_efgh) is the suffix with regards to the prefix (abcd_), iset=(abcd_).(_efgh), (abcdef_) is the prefix with regards to suffix (_gh) and iset=(abcdef_).(_gh).

The following definition introduces the dot operator. It permits itemset concatenations and sequence concatenations.

Definition 9 (*"." operator*). Let e and e′ be two itemsets that do not contain the underscore symbol (_). Assume that all the items in e′ are alphabetically sorted after those in e. Let $\gamma=\langle e_1 \dots e_{n-1}a\rangle$ and $\mu=\langle be'_2 \dots e'_m\rangle$ be two sequences, where e_i and e'_i are itemsets that do not contain the underscore symbol, a ∈ {e, (_items in e), (items in e_), (_items in e_)} and b ∈ {e′, (_items in e′), (items in e′_), (_items in e′_)}. The dot operator is defined as follows.

1. e . e′ = ee′

2. e . (_items in e′) = (items in e ∪ e′)

3. e . (items in e′_) = e (items in e′_)

4. e . (_items in e′_)= (items in e ∪ e′_)

5. (items in e_) . e′ = (items in e ∪ e′)

6. (items in e_) . (_items in e′) = (items in e ∪ e′)

7. (items in e_) . (_items in e′_)= (items in e ∪ e′_)

8. (items in e_) . (items in e′_)= (items in e ∪ e′_)

9. (_items in e) . e′ = (_items in e)e′

10. (_items in e) . (items in e′_) = (_items in e)(items in e′_)

11. (_items in e) . (_items in e′_)= (_items in e ∪ e′_)

12. (_items in e) . (_items in e′)= (_items in e ∪ e′)

13. (_items in e_) . e′ = (_items in e ∪ e′)

14. (_items in e_) . (_items in e′_) = (_items in e ∪ e′_)

15. (_items in e_) . (items in e′_)=(_items in e ∪ e′_)

16. (_items in e_) . (_items in e′)= (_ items in e ∪ e′)

17. $\gamma.\mu = \langle e_1 \dots e_{n-1}a.be'_2 \dots e'_m\rangle$

For example, s=⟨a(abc)(ac)(efgh)⟩=⟨(a).(a_).(_b_).(_c).(a_).(_c).(e).(_f_).(_g_).(_h)⟩ and s=⟨(a)⟩.⟨(a_)⟩.⟨(_b_)⟩.⟨(_c)⟩.⟨(a_)⟩.⟨(_c)⟩.⟨(e)⟩.⟨(_f_)⟩.⟨(_g_)⟩.⟨(_h)⟩.

Definition 10 (*Prefix of a sequence*) (Pei et al., 2004). Suppose all the items within an element are listed alphabetically. Given a sequence $\alpha=\langle e_1e_2 \dots e_n\rangle$, a sequence $\beta= \langle e'_1e'_2 \dots e'_m\rangle$ (m ≤ n) is called a prefix of α if and only if 1) $e'_1=e_i$ for all i ≤ m-1; 2) $e'_m \subseteq e_m$; and 3) all the frequent items in $e_m - e'_m$ are alphabetically sorted after those in e'_m. If $e'_m\neq\varnothing$ and $e'_m \subseteq e_m$ the prefix is also denoted as $\langle e'_1e'_2 \dots e'_{m-1}(\text{items in } e'_m\_)\rangle$.

Definition 11 (*The corresponding suffix of a prefix of a sequence*) (Pei et al., 2004). Given a sequence $\alpha=\langle e_1e_2 \dots e_n\rangle$. Let $\beta=\langle e_1e_2 \dots e_{m-1}e'_m\rangle$ (m ≤ n) be a prefix of α. Sequence $\gamma=\langle e''_me_{m+1} \dots e_n\rangle$ is called the suffix of α with regards to prefix β, denoted as $\gamma= \alpha/\beta$, where $e''_m = e_m - e'_m$. We also denote $\alpha=\beta.\gamma$. Note, if β=α, the suffix of α with regards to β is empty. If e''_m is not empty, the suffix is also denoted as $\langle (\text{_items in } e''_m) e_{m+1} \dots e_n\rangle$.

For example, for the sequence s=⟨a(abc)(ac)(efgh)⟩, ⟨(ac)(efgh)⟩ is the suffix with regards to the prefix ⟨a(abc)⟩, ⟨(_bc)(ac)(efgh)⟩ is the suffix with regards to the prefix ⟨aa⟩, ⟨(_c)(ac)(efgh)⟩ is the suffix with regards to the prefix ⟨a(ab)⟩, and ⟨a(abc)(a_)⟩ is the prefix with regards to the suffix ⟨(_c)(efgh)⟩.

Given three sequences, y, α and α′, we denote spc(y,α) (resp. ssc(y,α′)) the shortest prefix (resp. suffix) of y containing α (resp. α′). If no prefix (resp. suffix) of y contains α (resp. α′) spc(y,α) (resp. ssc(y,α′)) does not exist. If the two sequences spc(y,α) and ssc(y,α′) exist and do not overlap in sequence y, there exists a sequence $y_{\alpha,\alpha'}$ such that y=spc(y,α).$y_{\alpha,\alpha'}$.ssc(y,α′). Hence, we have the following definition.

Definition 12 (*Canonical sequence decomposition*). Given three sequences, y, α and α′ such that spc(y,α) and ssc(y,α′) exist and do not overlap in y. Equation y=spc(y,α).$y_{\alpha,\alpha'}$.ssc(y,α′) is the canonical decomposition of y following prefix α and suffix α′. The left, middle and right parts of the decomposition are respectively spc(y,α), $y_{\alpha,\alpha'}$ and ssc(y,α′).

For example, consider sequence s=⟨a(abc)(ac)(efgh)⟩, we have spc(s,⟨a⟩)=⟨a⟩, spc(s,⟨(ab)⟩)=⟨a(ab)⟩, spc(s,⟨(ac)⟩)= ⟨a(abc)⟩, ssc(s,⟨(c)(e)⟩)=⟨(c)(efgh)⟩, ssc(s, ⟨a⟩)=⟨(ac)(efgh)⟩,ssc(s,⟨(bc)⟩)=⟨(_bc)(ac)(efgh)⟩, s=spc(s,⟨(ab)⟩).⟨(_c)(a_) ⟩.ssc(s,⟨(c)(e)⟩) and s=spc(s,⟨(ac)⟩).ε.ssc(s,⟨a⟩). The two sequences spc(s,⟨(ab)⟩) and spc(s,⟨(ab)⟩) overlap in sequence s as two sets of the index positions of their items in s are not disjoint.

Stemming from the canonical decompositions of sequences following prefix α and suffix α', we define two sets of the sequence database S as follows. We denote $S_{\alpha,\alpha}$ the set of subsequences of S prefixed with α and suffixed with α' which are obtained by replacing the left and right parts of canonical decompositions respectively with α and α'. We have $S_{\alpha,\alpha'}=\{\langle \text{sid}, \alpha.y_{\alpha,\alpha'}.\alpha'\rangle \mid \langle \text{sid}, y\rangle \in S$ and $y=\text{spc}(y,\alpha).y_{\alpha,\alpha'}.\text{ssc}(y,\alpha')\}$. We denote $S^{\alpha,\alpha'}$ the set of subsequences which are obtained by removing the left and right parts of canonical decompositions. We have $S^{\alpha,\alpha'}=\{\langle \text{sid}, y_{\alpha,\alpha'}\rangle \mid \langle \text{sid}, y\rangle \in S$ and $y=\text{spc}(y,\alpha).y_{\alpha,\alpha'}.\text{ssc}(y,\alpha')\}$. We also have $S=S_{\varepsilon,\varepsilon}$ and $S=S^{\varepsilon,\varepsilon}$ as ε denotes the empty sequence.

Definition 13 (*Extension of the "." operator*). Let S be a sequence database and let α be a sequence that may contain the underscore symbol (_). The dot operator is extended as follows. We have $\alpha.S=\{\langle \text{sid},\alpha.s\rangle \mid \langle \text{sid},s\rangle \in S\}$ and $S.\alpha =\{\langle \text{sid},s.\alpha\rangle \mid \langle \text{sid},s\rangle \in S\}$.

Corollary 1 (*Associatively of the "." operator*). The dot operator is associative, i.e. given a sequence database S and three sequences α, α' and α'' that may contain the underscore symbol (_), we have:

1. $(\alpha.\alpha').\alpha'' = \alpha.(\alpha'.\alpha'')$
2. $\alpha.(\alpha'.S)=(\alpha.\alpha').$
3. $(S.\alpha).\alpha'=S.(\alpha.\alpha')$
4. $(\alpha.S).\alpha' = \alpha.(S.\alpha')$

Proof. It is straightforward from the dot operation definition.

We have the following lemmas.

Lemma 1 (*The support of z in $S^{\alpha\alpha'}$ is that of its counterpart in S*). Given a sequence database S and two sequences α and α', for any sequence y prefixed with α and suffixed with α', i.e. $y=\alpha.z.\alpha'$ for some sequence z, we have $\text{support}(S,y)=\text{support}(S^{\alpha,\alpha'},z)$.

Proof. Consider the function f from dataset $S_{\alpha,\alpha'}$ to dataset $S^{\alpha,\alpha'}$ which assigns tuple $\langle \text{sid}, y_{\alpha,\alpha'}\rangle \in S^{\alpha,\alpha'}$ to tuple $\langle \text{sid}, \text{spc}(y,\alpha).y_{\alpha,\alpha'}.\text{ssc}(y,\alpha')\rangle \in S_{\alpha,\alpha'}$ where tuple $\langle \text{sid},y\rangle \in S$ and sequence y admits a canonical decomposition following prefix α and suffix α'.

Let's prove that function f is injective. Consider two tuples of S, $\langle \text{sid}, y\rangle$ and $\langle \text{sid}',y'\rangle$, each having a canonical decomposition following prefix α and suffix α'.

Assume that $f(\langle \text{sid}, \text{spc}(y,\alpha).y_{\alpha,\alpha'}.\text{ssc}(y,\alpha')\rangle)=f(\langle \text{sid}', \text{spc}(y',\alpha).y'_{\alpha,\alpha'}.\text{ssc}(y',\alpha')\rangle)$. This implies that $\langle \text{sid},y_{\alpha,\alpha'}\rangle=\langle \text{sid}',y'_{\alpha,\alpha'}\rangle$, which in turn implies that sid=sid'. This implies that tuple $\langle \text{sid},y\rangle$ is equal to $\langle \text{sid}',y'\rangle$ as the identifier of any tuple is unique. It comes that y=y'. Thus $\langle \text{sid}, \text{spc}(y,\alpha).y_{\alpha,\alpha'}.\text{ssc}(y,\alpha')\rangle=\langle \text{sid}', \text{spc}(y',\alpha).y'_{\alpha,\alpha'}.\text{ssc}(y',\alpha')\rangle$. Therefore function f is injective.

Let's prove that function f is surjective. Consider $\langle \text{sid}, z_{\alpha,\alpha'}\rangle \in S^{\alpha,\alpha'}$, where $\langle \text{sid},z\rangle$ belongs to S and admits a canonical decomposition following prefix α and suffix α'. From the definition of function f, $f(\langle \text{sid}, \text{spc}(z,\alpha).z_{\alpha,\alpha'}.\text{ssc}(z,\alpha')\rangle)=\langle \text{sid},z_{\alpha,\alpha'}\rangle$. This means that $\langle \text{sid},z_{\alpha,\alpha'}\rangle \in S^{\alpha,\alpha'}$ admits a pre-image in $S_{\alpha,\alpha'}$. Thus function f is surjective.

Function f is bijective because it is injective and surjective. Let consider a sequence y prefixed with α and suffixed with α', i.e. $y=\alpha.z.\alpha'$ for some sequence z. Denote $S(y)=\{\langle \text{sid},s\rangle \mid \langle \text{sid},s\rangle \in S$ and $y \subseteq s\}$. Recall that $\text{support}(S,y)=|S(y)|$. The definition of S(y) means that it is the set of sequences of S having a canonical decomposition following prefix α and suffix α' and containing sequence z in their middle part. It comes that $S(y)=\{\langle \text{sid},s\rangle \mid \langle \text{sid},s\rangle \in S_{\alpha,\alpha'}$ and $z \subseteq s_{\alpha,\alpha'}\}$. This implies that $f(S(y))=\{\langle \text{sid},s_{\alpha,\alpha'}\rangle \mid \langle \text{sid},s\rangle \in S_{\alpha,\alpha'}$ and $z \subseteq s_{\alpha,\alpha'}\}$. We have $|S(y)|=|f(S(y))|$, as function f is bijective. Therefore $\text{support}(S,y)=|S(y)|=|f(S(y))|=\text{support}(S^{\alpha,\alpha'},z)$. Hence the lemma.

Lemma 2 (*What does set $\alpha.\text{patterns}(S^{\alpha\,\alpha'}).\alpha'$ denote for patterns(S) ?*). The complete set of sequential patterns of S which are prefixed with α and suffixed with α' is equal to $\alpha.\text{patterns}(S^{\alpha,\alpha'}).\alpha'$, where function patterns denotes the complete set of sequential patterns of its unique argument.

Proof. Let x be a sequence. Assume that $x \in \alpha.\text{patterns}(S^{\alpha,\alpha'}).\alpha'$. This means that $x=\alpha.z.\alpha'$ for some $z \in \text{patterns}(S^{\alpha,\alpha'})$. From lemma 1, we have $\text{support}(S^{\alpha,\alpha'},z) = \text{support}(S,\alpha.z.\alpha')$. It comes that, x is also a sequential pattern in S as z is a sequential pattern in $S^{\alpha,\alpha'}$. Thus, $\alpha.\text{patterns}(S^{\alpha,\alpha'}).\alpha'$ is included in the set of sequential patterns of S which are prefixed with α and suffixed with α'.

Now, assume that x is a sequential pattern of S which is prefixed with α and suffixed with α'. We have $x=\alpha.z.\alpha'$ for some sequence z. From lemma 1, we have $\text{support}(S^{\alpha,\alpha'},z)=\text{support}(S, \alpha.z.\alpha')$. It comes that, z is also a sequential pattern in $S^{\alpha,\alpha'}$ as x is a sequential pattern in S. This means that $z \in \text{patterns}(S^{\alpha,\alpha'})$. Thus, the complete set of sequential patterns of S which are prefixed with α and suffixed with α' is included in $\alpha.\text{patterns}(S^{\alpha,\alpha'}). \alpha'$.

Hence the lemma.

Lemma 3 (*Sequence decomposition lemma*). Let $\beta=\langle e'_1 e'_2 \ldots e'_m\rangle$ be a sequence such that $\beta=\gamma.\mu$ for some non-empty prefix γ and some non-empty suffix μ. Either $\gamma=\langle e'_1 \ldots e'_k\rangle$ and $\mu=\langle e'_{k+1} \ldots e'_m\rangle$ for some integer k or $\gamma=\langle e'_1 \ldots e'_{k-1}\gamma_{k\_}\rangle$, $\mu=\langle\_\mu_k e'_{k+1} \ldots e'_m\rangle$, $e'_k=\gamma_{k\_} \cup \_\mu_k$, all the items in $\gamma_{k\_}$ are alphabetically before those in $\_\mu_k$ (this implies that $\gamma_{k\_} \cap \_\mu_k=\varnothing$), $\gamma_{k\_} \neq\varnothing$ and $\mu_{k\_} \neq\varnothing$ for some integer k such that $1\leq k \leq m$.

Proof. Let $\beta=\langle e'_1 e'_2 \ldots e'_m\rangle = \gamma.\mu$, where $\gamma\neq\varepsilon$ and $\mu\neq\varepsilon$. According to definitions 10 and 11, $\gamma=\langle e'_1 \ldots e'_{k-1}\gamma_{k\_}\rangle$, $\mu=\langle\_\mu_k e'_{k+1} \ldots e'_m\rangle$, $e'_k = \gamma_{k\_} \cup \_\mu_k$ and all the items in $\gamma_{k\_}$ are alphabetically before those in $\_\mu_k$ for some integer k ($1\leq k \leq m$). We have the following cases:

Case 1: k = 1. This means that $\gamma=\langle\gamma_{1\_}\rangle$ and $\mu=\langle\_\mu_1 e'_2 \ldots e'_m\rangle$. We have $\gamma_{1\_} \neq\varnothing$ as $\gamma\neq\varepsilon$. We also have $\_\mu_1\neq e'_1$ as the contrary, i.e. $\_\mu_1 = e'_1$, implies that $\gamma=\varepsilon$. If $\_\mu_1 = \varnothing$, $\gamma_{1\_}=e'_1$ and it comes that $\gamma=\langle e'_1\rangle$ and $\mu=\langle e'_2 \ldots e'_m\rangle$, which corresponds to the first half of the claim of the lemma. Otherwise, we have $\gamma_{1\_} \neq\varnothing$ and $\mu_{1\_} \neq\varnothing$, which leads to the second half of the claim of the lemma.

Case 2: k=m. This means that $\gamma=\langle e'_1 \ldots e'_{m-1}\gamma_{m\_}\rangle$ and $\mu=\langle\_\mu_m\rangle$. We have $\_\mu_m\neq\varnothing$ as $\mu\neq\varepsilon$. We also have $\gamma_{m\_} \neq e'_m$ as the contrary, i.e. $\gamma_{m\_} = e'_m$, implies that $\mu=\varepsilon$. If $\gamma_{m\_} = \varnothing$, $\_\mu_m=e'_m$ and it comes that $\gamma=\langle e'_1 \ldots e'_{m-1}\rangle$ and $\mu=\langle e'_m\rangle$, which corresponds to the first half of the claim of the lemma. Otherwise, we have $\gamma_{m\_} \neq\varnothing$ and $\mu_m\neq\varnothing$, which leads to the second half of the claim of the lemma.

Case 3: k≠1, k≠m and $\gamma_{k\_}=\varnothing$. This implies that $\mu_{k\_}=e'_k$. It comes that $\gamma=\langle e'_1 \ldots e'_{k-1}\rangle$ and $\mu=\langle e'_k \ldots e'_m\rangle$, which corresponds to the first half of the claim of the lemma.

Case 4: k≠1, k≠m and $\_\mu_k=\varnothing$. This case is similar to case 3. We have $\gamma_{k\_}=e'_k$. This implies that $\gamma=\langle e'_1 \ldots e'_k\rangle$ and $\mu=\langle e'_{k+1} \ldots e'_m\rangle$, which corresponds to the first half of the claim of the lemma.

Case 5: k≠1, k ≠ m, $\gamma_{k\_} \neq\varnothing$ and $\_\mu_k\neq\varnothing$. This leads to the second half of the claim of the lemma. $\square$

Definition 14 (*Static and dynamic search-space partitioning*). A search space partition is said to be static iff it is fully specified before the beginning of the mining process. It is said to be dynamic iff it is constructed during the mining process.

Lemma 4 (*Search-space partitioning based on prefix and/or suffix*). We have the following.

1. Let $\{x_1, x_2, \ldots , x_n\}$ be the complete set of length-1 sequential patterns in a sequence database S. The complete set of sequential patterns in S can be divided into n disjoint subsets in two different ways:

   a. *Prefix-item-based search-space partitioning* (Pei et al., 2004): The i-th subset ($1\leq i \leq n$) is the set of sequential patterns with prefix x_i.

   b. *Suffix-item-based search-space partitioning* (Pei et al., 2004): The i-th subset ($1\leq i \leq n$) is the set of sequential patterns with suffix x_i.

2. Let α be a length-l sequential pattern and $\{\beta_1, \beta_2, \ldots ,\beta_p\}$ be the set of all length-(l+1) sequential patterns with prefix α. Let α' be a length-l' sequential pattern and $\{\gamma_1, \gamma_2, \ldots ,\gamma_q\}$ be the set of all length-(l'+1) sequential patterns with suffix α'. We have:

   a. *Prefix-based search-space partitioning* (Pei et al., 2004): The complete set of sequential patterns with prefix α, except for α itself, can be divided into p disjoint subsets. The i-th subset ($1\leq i\leq p$) is the set of sequential patterns prefixed with β_i.

   b. *Suffix-based search-space partitioning* (Pei et al., 2004): The complete set of sequential patterns with suffix α', except for α' itself, can be divided into q disjoint subsets. The j-th subset ($1\leq j\leq q$) is the set of sequential patterns suffixed with γ_j.

   c. *Prefix-suffix-based search-space partitioning*: The complete set of sequential patterns with prefix α and suffix α', and of length greater or equal to l+l'+1, can be divided into p or q disjoint subsets. In the first partition, the i-th subset ($1\leq i \leq p$) is the set of sequential patterns prefixed with β_i and suffixed with α'. In the second partition, the j-th subset ($1\leq j\leq q$) is the set of sequential patterns prefixed with α and suffixed with γ_j.

Proof. Parts (1.a) and (2.a) of the lemma are proven in (Pei et al., 2004). The proof of parts (1.b) and (2.b) of the lemma is similar to the proof of parts (1.a) and (2.a). Thus, we only show the correctness of part (2.c).

Let μ be a sequential pattern of length greater or equal to l+l'+1, with prefix α and with suffix α', where α is of length l and α' of length l'. The length-(l+1) prefix of μ is a sequential pattern according to an Apriori principle which states that a subsequence of a sequential pattern is also a sequential pattern. Furthermore, α is a prefix of the length-(l+1) prefix of μ, according to the definition of prefix. This implies that there exists some i ($1\leq i\leq p$)

such that β_i is the length-$(1+1)$ prefix of μ. Thus μ is in the i-th subset of the first partition. On the other hand, since the length-k prefix of a sequence is unique, the subsets are disjoint and this implies that μ belongs to only one determined subset. Thus, we have (2.c) for the first partition. The proof of (2.c) for the second partition is similar. Therefore we have the lemma. $\square$

Corollary 2 (*Partitioning S with sets x_i.patterns($S^{xi,\varepsilon}$) and patterns($S^{\varepsilon,xi}$).x_i*). Let $\{x_1, x_2, \dots, x_n\}$ be the complete set of length-1 sequential patterns in a sequence database S. The complete set of sequential patterns in S can be divided into n disjoint subsets in two different ways:

1. *Prefix-item-based search-space partitioning*: The i-th subset ($1 \le i \le n$) is x_i.patterns($S^{xi,\varepsilon}$), where function patterns denotes the set of sequential patterns of its unique argument.

2. *Suffix-item-based search-space partitioning*: The i-th subset ($1 \le i \le n$) is patterns($S^{\varepsilon,xi}$).x_i.

Proof. According to part 1.(a) of lemma 4, the i-th subset is the set of sequential patterns which are prefixed with x_i. From lemma 2, this subset is x_i.patterns($S^{xi,\varepsilon}$). Similarly, according to part 1.(b) of lemma 4, the i-th subset is the set of sequential patterns suffixed with x_i. From lemma 2, this subset is patterns($S^{\varepsilon,xi}$).x_i. $\square$

Lemma 5 (*A linear ordering induces a recursive pruning and partitioning*). A linear ordering induces a recursive pruning and partitioning of the search space. The recursive partitioning is static if the linear ordering is static and dynamic otherwise.

Proof. Let us consider the initial sequence database S, two integer numbers l and l', a length-l sequential pattern α, a length-l' sequential pattern α', and a linear ordering $L_0 = o_0 \text{-} o_1 \text{-} o_2 \dots o_{n-1}$-growth. Note that $\varepsilon.S^{\varepsilon,\varepsilon}.\varepsilon = S$ is the starting database of the recursive pruning and partitioning of the search space. In the following, we show how L_0 induces a recursive pruning and partitioning of $\alpha.S^{\alpha,\alpha'}.\alpha'$.

Case 1: $o_0 \in \{\text{prefix}\}$. Let $\{\beta_1.\alpha', \beta_2.\alpha', \dots, \beta_p.\alpha'\}$ be the set of all length-$(l+l'+1)$ sequential patterns with respect to database $\alpha.S^{\alpha,\alpha'}.\alpha'$, prefixed with α and suffixed with α'. From lemma 3, either $\beta_I = \alpha.\langle(x_i)\rangle$ or $\beta_I = \alpha.\langle(\_x_i)\rangle$, where x_i is an item and $1 \le i \le p$. This implies that $X = \{\langle x_1 \rangle, \langle x_2 \rangle, \dots, \langle x_p \rangle\}$ is the complete set of length-1 sequential patterns with respect to database $S^{\alpha,\alpha'}$. It comes that any item that does not belong to X is not frequent with respect to $S^{\alpha,\alpha'}$. Thus, any sequence that contains an item that does not belong to X is not frequent with respect to $S^{\alpha,\alpha'}$ according to an Apriori principle which states that any supersequence of an infrequent sequence is also infrequent. Because of this, all the infrequent items with respect to $S^{\alpha,\alpha'}$ are removed from the z part (also called the middle part) of all sequence $\alpha.z.\alpha' \in \alpha.S^{\alpha,\alpha'}.\alpha'$. This pruning step leads to a new sequence database $\alpha.S'^{\alpha,\alpha'}.\alpha'$ whose middle parts of sequences do not contain infrequent items with respect to $S^{\alpha,\alpha'}$. Then, $\alpha.S'^{\alpha,\alpha'}.\alpha'$ is partitioned according to part (2.c) of lemma 4. The i-th sub-database ($1 \le i \le p$) of $\alpha.S'^{\alpha,\alpha'}.\alpha'$, denoted $\alpha.x_i.S'^{\alpha,xi,\alpha'}.\alpha'$, is the set of subsequences of $\alpha.S'^{\alpha,\alpha'}.\alpha'$ with prefix $\beta_i = \alpha.x_i$ and with suffix α'. Each sub-database is in turn recursively pruned and partitioned according to $L_1 = o_1 \text{-} o_2 \dots o_{n-1}$-growth linear ordering.

Case 2: $o_0 \in \{\text{suffix}\}$. Let $\{\alpha.\gamma_1, \alpha.\gamma_2, \dots, \alpha.\gamma_p\}$ be the set of all length-$(l+l'+1)$ sequential patterns with respect to database $\alpha.S^{\alpha,\alpha'}.\alpha'$, prefixed with α and suffixed with α'. From lemma 3, either $\gamma_I = \langle(x_i)\rangle.\alpha'$ or $\gamma_I = \langle(x_i\_)\rangle.\alpha'$ ($1 \le i \le p$). As in case 1, $\alpha.S'^{\alpha,\alpha'}.\alpha'$ is partitioned according to part (2.c) of lemma 4. The i-th sub-database ($1 \le i \le p$) of $\alpha.S'^{\alpha,\alpha'}.\alpha'$, denoted $\alpha.S'^{\alpha,xi.\alpha'}.x_i.\alpha'$, is the set of subsequences of $\alpha.S'^{\alpha,\alpha'}.\alpha'$ with prefix α and with suffix $\gamma_I = x_i.\alpha'$. As in case 1, each sub-database is in turn recursively pruned and partitioned according to $L_1 = o_1 \text{-} o_2 \dots o_{n-1}$-growth linear ordering.

Case 3: $o_0 \in \{*\}$. A pattern-growth direction is determined during the mining process. Then, $\alpha.S^{\alpha,\alpha'}.\alpha'$ is recursively pruned and partitioned as in case 1 if the determined direction is left-to-right and as in case 2 otherwise. From definitions 6 and 14 it is easy to see that the recursive partitioning is static if the linear ordering is static and dynamic otherwise. $\square$

5. Experimental results

The data set used here is collected from the webpage of SPMF software (Fournier-Viger et al., 2014). This webpage (http://www.philippe-fournier-viger.com/spmf/index.php) provides large data sets in SPMF format that are often used in the data mining literature for evaluating and comparing algorithm performance.

Experiments were performed on real-life data sets. The first data set is *LEVIATHAN*. It contains 5834 sequences and 9025 distinct items. The second data set is *Kosarak*. It is a very large data set containing 990000 sequences of click-stream data from an hungarian news portal. The third data set is *BIBLE*. It is a conversion of the Bible into a sequence database (each word is an item). It contains 36 369 sequences and 13905 distinct items. The fourth data set is *BMSWebView2 (Gazelle)*. It is called here *BMS2*. It contains 59601 sequences of clickstream data from e-commerce and 3340 distinct items.

All experiments were done on a 4-cores of 2.16GHz Intel(R) Pentium(R) CPU N3530 with 4 gigabytes main memory, running Ubuntu 14.04 LTS. The algorithms are implemented in Java and grounded on SPMF software (Fournier-Viger et al., 2014). The experiments consisted of running the pattern-growth algorithms related to the left-to-right and the right-to-left orderings on each data set while decreasing the support threshold until algorithms became too long to execute or ran out of memory. The performances are presented in figures 1, 2, 3 and 4. These figures show that the order in which patterns grow has a significant influence on the performances.

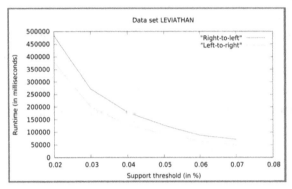 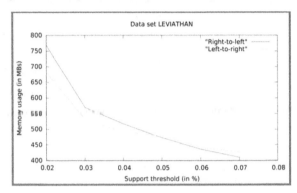

Figure 1. Performances of left-to-right and right-to-left pattern-growth orderings on the real-life data set LEVIATHAN. The left-to-right pattern-growth ordering is 1.27-1.4 times faster, and requires less memory if the support threshold is less than 0.05 and a little more memory otherwise

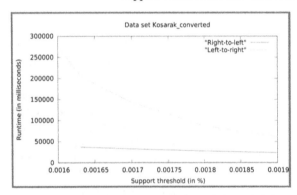 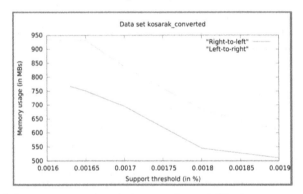

Figure 2. Performances of left-to-right and right-to-left pattern-growth orderings on the real-life data set kosarak_converted. The right-to-left pattern-growth ordering is 2.6-5.6 times faster and requires almost 1.2 times less memory than the other direction

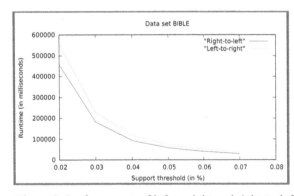 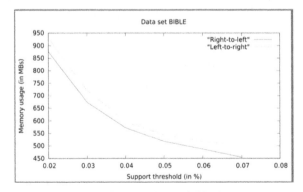

Figure 3. Performances of left-to-right and right-to-left pattern-growth orderings on the real-life data set BIBLE. The right-to-left pattern-growth ordering is 1.21-1.25 times faster and requires almost 1.04-1.10 times less memory than the other ordering

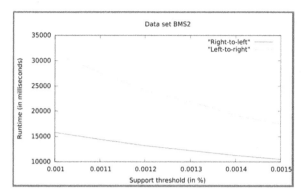 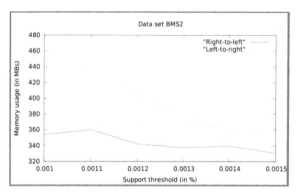

Figure 4. Performances of left-to-right and right-to-left pattern-growth orderings on the real-life data set BMS2. The right-to-left pattern-growth ordering is 1.5-2 times faster and requires almost 1.07-1.3 times less memory than the other ordering

6. Conclusion

In this article, we have study the theoretical foundations of pattern growth-based sequential pattern mining algorithms. The important key concepts of the pattern-growth approach are revisited, formally defined and extended. A new class of pattern-growth algorithms inspired from a new class of pattern-growth orderings, called linear orderings, is introduced. Issues of this new class of pattern-growth algorithms related to search space pruning and partitioning are investigated. Experimentations show that the order in which patterns grow has a significant influence on the performances.

References

Agrawal, R., Imielinski, T., & Swami, A. N. (1993). Mining association rules between sets of items in large databases, 207–216.

Agrawal, R., & Srikant, R. (1994). Fast algorithms for mining association rules in large databases. In VLDB'94, Proceedings of 20th International Conference on Very Large Data Bases, September 12-15, 1994, Santiago de Chile, Chile, 487–499.

Agrawal, R., & Srikant, R. (1995). Mining sequential patterns. In Proceedings of the Eleventh International Conference on Data Engineering, March 6-10, 1995, Taipei, Taiwan, 3–14.

Ayres, J., Flannick, J., Gehrke, J., & Yiu, T. (2002). Sequential pattern mining using a bitmap representation. In Proceedings of the Eighth ACM SIGKDD International Conference on Knowledge Discovery and Data Mining, July 23-26, 2002, Edmonton, Alberta, Canada, 429–435.

Dam, T., Li, K., Fournier-Viger, P., & Duong, Q. (2016). An efficient algorithm for mining top-rank-k frequent patterns. *Appl. Intell., 45*(1), 96–111.

El-Sayed, M., Ruiz, C., & Rundensteiner, E. A. (2004). Fs-miner: efficient and incremental mining of frequent sequence patterns in web logs. In Sixth ACM CIKM International Workshop on Web Information and Data Management (WIDM 2004), Washington, DC, USA, 12-13, 128–135.

Fournier-Viger, P., Gomariz, A., Gueniche, T., Soltani, A., Wu, C., & Tseng, V. S. (2014). SPMF: a java open-source pattern mining library. *Journal of Machine Learning Research, 15*(1), 3389–3393.

Garofalakis, M. N., Rastogi, R., & Shim, K. (1999). SPIRIT: sequential pattern mining with regular expression constraints. In VLDB'99, Proceedings of 25th International Conference on Very Large Data Bases, September 7-10, 1999, Edinburgh, Scotland, UK, 223–234.

Gouda, K., Hassaan, M., & Zaki, M. J. (2007). Prism: A primal-encoding approach for frequent sequence mining. In Proceedings of the 7th IEEE International Conference on Data Mining (ICDM 2007), October 28-31, 2007, Omaha, Nebraska, USA, 487–492.

Gouda, K., Hassaan, M., & Zaki, M. J. (2010). Prism: An effective approach for frequent sequence mining via prime-block encoding. J. Comput. Syst. Sci., 76(1):88–102.

Han, J., Pei, J., Mortazavi-Asl, B., Chen, Q., Dayal, U., & Hsu, M. (2000). Freespan: frequent pattern-projected sequentialpattern mining. In Proceedings of the sixth ACM SIGKDD international conference on Knowledge discovery and data mining, Boston, MA, USA, August 20-23, 355–359.

Hsieh, C., Yang, D., & Wu, J. (2008). An efficient sequential pattern mining algorithm based on the 2-sequence matrix. In Workshops Proceedings of the 8th IEEE International Conference on Data Mining (ICDM 2008), December 15-19, 2008, Pisa, Italy, 583–591.

Lin, J. C., Gan, W., Fournier-Viger, P., Hong, T., &Tseng, V. S. (2016). Efficient algorithms for mining high-utility itemsets in uncertain databases. *Knowl. Based Syst., 96*, 171–187.

Lin, J. C., Gan, W., Fournier-Viger, P., Hong, T., & Tseng, V. S. (2016). Fast algorithms for mining high-utility itemsets with various discount strategies. *Advanced Engineering Informatics, 30*(2), 109–126.

Lin, J. C., Gan, W., Fournier-Viger, P., Hong, T., & Zhan, J. (2016). Efficient mining of high-utility itemsets using multiple minimum utility thresholds. Knowl.-Based Syst., 113, 100–115.

Lin, J. C., Li, T., Fournier-Viger, P., Hong, T., Zhan, J., & Voznak, M. (2016). An efficient algorithm to mine high average-utility itemsets. *Advanced Engineering Informatics, 30*(2), 233–243.

Mabroukeh, N. R., &Ezeife, C. I. (2010). A taxonomy of sequential pattern mining algorithms. *ACM Comput. Surv., 43*(1), 3.

Masseglia, F., Cathala, F., & Poncelet, P. (1998). *The PSP approach for mining sequential patterns.* In Principles of Data Mining and Knowledge Discovery, Second European Symposium, PKDD '98, Nantes, France, September 23-26, Proceedings, 176–184.

Pei, J., Han, J., Mortazavi-Asl, B., Pinto, H., Chen, Q., Dayal, U., & Hsu, M. (2001). *Prefixspan: Mining sequential patterns by prefix-projected growth.* In Proceedings of the 17th International Conference on Data Engineering, April 2-6, 2001, Heidelberg, Germany, 215–224.

Pei, J., Han, J., Mortazavi-Asl, B., Wang, J., Pinto, H., Chen, Q., Dayal, U., & Hsum, M. (2004). Mining sequential patterns by pattern-growth: The prefixspan approach. IEEE Trans. *Knowl. Data Eng., 16*(11), 1424–1440.

Pei, J., Han, J., Mortazavi-Asl, B., & Zhu, H. (2000). *Mining access patterns efficiently from web logs.* In Knowledge Discovery and Data Mining, Current Issues and New Applications, 4th Pacific-Asia Conference, PADKK 2000, Kyoto, Japan, April 18-20, Proceedings, 396–407.

Savary, L., & Zeitouni, K. (2005). *Indexed bit map (IBM) for mining frequent sequences.* In Knowledge Discovery in Databases: PKDD 2005, 9th European Conference on Principles and Practice of Knowledge Discovery in Databases, Porto, Portugal, October 3-7, 2005, Proceedings, 659–666.

Seno, M., & Karypis, G.. (2002). *Slpminer: An algorithm for finding frequent sequential patterns using length-decreasing support constraint.* In Proceedings of the 2002 IEEE International Conference on Data Mining (ICDM 2002), 9-12 December 2002, Maebashi City, Japan, 418–425.

Yang, Z., & Kitsuregawa, M. (2005). LAPIN-SPAM: an improved algorithm for mining sequential pattern. In Proceedings of the 21st International Conference on Data Engineering Workshops, ICDE 2005, 5-8 April 2005, Tokyo, Japan, 1222.

Yang, Z., Wang, Y., & Kitsuregawa, M. (2007). LAPIN: Effective sequential pattern mining algorithms by last position induction for dense databases. In Advances in Databases: Concepts, Systems and Applications, 12th International Conference on Database Systems for Advanced Applications, DASFAA 2007, Bangkok, Thailand, April 9-12, 2007, Proceedings, 1020–1023.

Zaki, M. J. (2000). Sequence mining in categorical domains: Incorporating constraints. In Proceedings of the 2000 ACM CIKM International Conference on Information and Knowledge Management, McLean, VA, USA, November 6-11, 2000, 422–429.

Zaki, M. J. (2001). SPADE: an efficient algorithm for mining frequent sequences. *Machine Learning, 42*(1/2), 31–60.

18

Exploiting Data-Parallelism on Multicore and SMT Systems for Implementing the Fractal Image Compressing Problem

Rodrigo da Rosa Righi[1], Vinicius F. Rodrigues[1], Cristiano A. Costa[1] & Roberto Q. Gomes[1]

[1] Applied Computing Graduate Program, Universidade do Vale do Rio dos Sinos, Brazil

Correspondence: Rodrigo R. Righi, Applied Computing Graduate Program, Universidade do Vale do Rio dos Sinos, Unisinos Av. 950, São Leopoldo, Rio Grande do Sul, Brazil. E-mail: rrrighi@unisinos.br

Correspondence: Rodrigo da Rosa Righi, Applied Computing Graduate Program, Universidade do Vale do Rio dos Sinos, Brazil. E-mail: rrrighi@unisinos.br

Abstract

This paper presents a parallel modeling of a lossy image compression method based on the fractal theory and its evaluation over two versions of dual-core processors: with and without simultaneous multithreading (SMT) support. The idea is to observe the speedup on both configurations when changing application parameters and the number of threads at operating system level. Our target application is particularly relevant in the Big Data era. Huge amounts of data often need to be sent over low/medium bandwidth networks, and/or to be saved on devices with limited store capacity, motivating efficient image compression. Especially, the fractal compression presents a CPU-bound coding method known for offering higher indexes of file reduction through highly time-consuming calculus. The structure of the problem allowed us to explore data-parallelism by implementing an embarrassingly parallel version of the algorithm. Despite its simplicity, our modeling is useful for fully exploiting and evaluating the considered architectures. When comparing performance in both processors, the results demonstrated that the SMT-based one presented gains up to 29%. Moreover, they emphasized that a large number of threads does not always represent a reduction in application time. In average, the results showed a curve in which a strong time reduction is achieved when working with 4 and 8 threads when evaluating pure and SMT dual-core processors, respectively. The trend concerns a slow growing of the execution time when enlarging the number of threads due to both task granularity and threads management.

Keywords: image compression, fractal compression, simultaneous multithreading, big data.

1. Introduction

Considering the era of Big Data, the thematic of image compression becomes more and more relevant (Chen et al., 2012; Revathy & Jayamohan, 2012; Sundaresan & Devika, 2012). The main objective consists in reducing the irrelevance and redundancy of the image data to store or transmit data in an efficient way. For instance, images obtained by experiments in the fields of astronomy, medicine and geology may present several gigabytes in memory, emphasizing the use of image compression properly (Pinto & Gawande, 2012). In this context, a technique called Fractal Image Compression (FIC) appears as one of most efficient solutions for reducing the size of files (Jeng et al., 2009; Khan & Akhtar, 2013). An expensive encoding phase characterizes the FIC method, since the search used in the algorithm to find self-similarities is time-consuming. A square image with 1024 pixels as dimension may take more than an hour to be compressed in a single processing system. This elucidates why this technique is not so widespread among the traditional operating systems. However, at high compression ratios, fractal compression may offer superior quality than JPEG and Discrete-cosine- transform (DCT)-based algorithms (George & Al-Hilo, 2009). Unlike the coding phase, the decoding one occurs quickly, for instance, enabling users to download compressed images or videos from Web servers and visualize them in their hosts in a reasonable time interval.

Considering a lower encoding phase of FIC method, some alternatives are considered to minimize this process. Basically, the most alternatives try to reduce the coding time by reducing the search for the best-match block in a large domain pool (Fu & Zhu, 2009; Jeng et al., 2009; Mitra et al., 1998; Qin et al., 2009; Revathy & Jayamohan, 2012; Rowshanbin et al., 2006; Sun & Wun, 2009; Vahdati et al., 2010). Other possibilities consist in exploring the power of parallel architectures like nCUBE (Jackson & Blom, 1995), SIMD (Single Instruction Multiple

Data) (Khan & Akhtar, 2013; Wakatani, 2012) processors and clusters (Righi, 2012; Qureshi & Hussain, 2008). The use of multitasking on recent computing systems is a possibility not deeply explored for solving the FIC problem (Cao & Gu, 2010; Cao & Gu, 2011). The authors of these last initiatives presented an OpenMP solution that was tested over a quad-core processor. Besides multicore, we are focusing our attention on SMT (Simultaneous Multithreading) (Raasch & Reinhardt, 2003) capability, since both technologies are common on off-the-shelf computers. Some researchers affirm that we will have tens or hundreds of cores, each one with multiple execution threads (Note 1), inside a processor in the next years (Diamond et al., 2011; Rai et al., 2010). This emphasizes the significance of modeling applications for such architectures.

The improvement in performance obtained by using multicore and SMT technologies depends on the software algorithms and their implementations. Task granularity, threads synchronization and scheduling, memory allocation, conditional variables and mutual exclusion are parameters under user control that must be carefully analyzed for extracting the power of these technologies in a better way. In this context, the present paper describes the FIC technique and its threads-based implementation. The FIC problem allows a program organization without data dependencies among the threads, which is special useful for observing key performance factors on parallel machines. Therefore, we modeled an embarrassingly parallel application by exploiting data-parallelism on the aforemesaid problem. Contrary to (Cao & Gu, 2010; Cao & Gu, 2011), we obtained the results by varying the input image, the application parameters as well as the target machine. Particularly, we used two dual-core machines, one with and another without SMT capacity. In this case, SMT doubles the number of execution threads from 1 per core to 2, increasing processor throughput by multiplexing the execution threads onto a common set of pipeline resources. Our evaluation confirmed gains up to 29% when enabling SMT. Besides computer architecture information, this paper also discusses the impact of the number of threads and task granularity on the obtained results.

This paper is organized as follows. Section 2 describes the two traditional approaches for image compression. The FIC method is presented in Section 3 in details. Section 4 shows the parallel modeling proposed for the FIC problem, while Section 5 describes its implementation. The tests and the discussion of the results are presented in Section 6. Section 7 presents some related works. Finally, Section 8 points out the concluding remarks, future works and emphasizes the main contribution of the work.

2. Image Compression

A Pixel is the minimum unit to define an image. A digital image is a bi-dimensional matrix composed by a set of pixels whose spatial resolution is $I \times J$, where both I and $J \in$ N and corresponding matrix element value identifies a set of discretized attributes (ex. gray level, color, transparency, and so on). Consequently, the larger the size of the image, greater will be the number of its pixels and attribute discretization, where each pixel is represented by a collection of bits, normally 16, 24 or 32 bits. In case, 16 Mbytes of memory are required to store a single image of 2048 × 2048, with 32 bits/pixel. In addition, some square images obtained by researchers can present dimensions up to 106, which turns clear the importance of the image compression field. We could classify the compression process in two subprocesses: (i) lossless compression and; (ii) lossy compression.

2.1 Lossless Compression

Situations in which the information needs to be kept intact after uncompressing usually employ Lossless compression. Medical images, technical drawings or texts are examples of using the lossless approach (Chen & Chuang, 2010). First, this process consists in transforming an input image $f(x)$ in $f'(x)$. According to Fu and Zhu (2009), this transformation can include differential and predictive mapping, unitary transforms, sub-band decomposing and color spacing conversion. After that, the data-to-mapping stage converts the $f'(x)$ in symbols, using the partitioning or run-length coding (RLC).

Lossless symbol coding stage generates a bit-stream by assigning binary codewords to symbols that were already mapped. Lossless compression is usually achieved by using variable-length codewords. This variable-length codeword assignment is known as variable-length coding (VLC) and also as entropy coding. Figure 1 depicts the process for obtaining a compressed image through the lossless method. Such method is used on algorithms for producing BMP, TGA, TIFF and PNG-typed images.

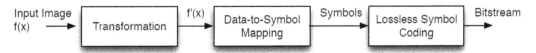

Figure 1. Common steps for compressing an image when using a lossless encoder

2.2 Lossy Compression

Lossy compression is an irreversible method, but yields better compact ratio results. After the uncompressing process, the resultant image will be almost identical to the original one, however never will be the same again (Jeng et al., 2009; Khan & Akhtar, 2013). Analogous to lossless compression, there are three stages on any lossy compression: (i) transform, (ii) quantization and; (iii) coding. The transformation stage reduces the correlation among pixels that results in a matrix of values. The quantizer stage is used to reduce quantity of bits per pixel, for example to transform color images into gray-scale ones. This process is irreversible and defines the loss level of the image quality. The stage coding process utilizes some methods that avoid more losses in the entire coding. Figure 2 depicts the functioning of the lossy compression methods. Among lossy techniques often used are Predictive coding, JPEG coding, and Fractal coding.

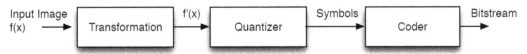

Figure 2. Common steps for image compression for a lossy-based encoder

3. Fractal Image Compression

Mandelbrot and Fisher described the concept of fractal, which are infinitely self- similar, iterated and described by mathematical formalisms (Chaurasia & Somkuwar, 2009; Wakatani, 2012). To better understand the feature of "self-similarity", for instance, we could make an analogy to zooming in with a lens or other device, which uncovers finer, previously invisible, new structure in digital images. Therefore, fractals are structures that have irregularities and fragmentations in a large range such as clouds, smokes, mountains and other nature elements. Fractal image compression is an example of asymmetrical methods. They take more time/effort compressing an image than decompressing it. The idea is to do most of the work during the compression, thus creating an output file that can be decompressed very quickly.

Coding phase of the Fractal Image Compression (FIC) method uses the self-similarity concept to represent image blocks through the transformation of coefficients (Jeng et al., 2009; George & Al-Hilo, 2009). This technique does not store or send blocks of pixels, but rather only functions that represent their transformations. This is because a fractal represents a shape that contains parts that are replicas among them- selves under some transformation aspect, as shown Figure 3 (a). The fractal compression is a technique based in the iterated function system (IFS) theory. To understand, consider the following formalism. Let F a gray-scale image with size $m \times m$, then F is divided in squares non-overlapped of size $r \times r$ called *Range Blocks*. The set of range blocks is R. Also, F is partitioned in squares $d \times d$ called *Domain Blocks*. The set of domain blocks is D. Usually $d = 2 \times r$ as shown in Figure 3 (b). In dark blue it is a subset of D and in light blue a subset of R. Then $R = \{R_0, R_1, ..., R_M\}$, with $M = (m \div r)^2 - 1$, and $D = \{D_0, D_1, ..., D_N\}$ with $N = (m \div d)^2 - 1$.

Contractive Mapping Fixed-Point theorem is the main idea behind a fractal encoding (Chaurasia & Somkuwar, 2009; Sharabayko & Markov, 2012). The theorem affirms "if a transformation is contractive then when applied repeatedly starting with any initial point, we converge to a unique fixed point". Let X a complete metric space and f a function. If $f : X \to X$ is contractive, then f has a unique fixed point $|f|$. The Eq. (1) defines a contractive function, where s is a contractive factor with $0 < s < 1$ and o the offset value (in this case o represents brightness level).

$$f(x) = s(x) + o \tag{1}$$

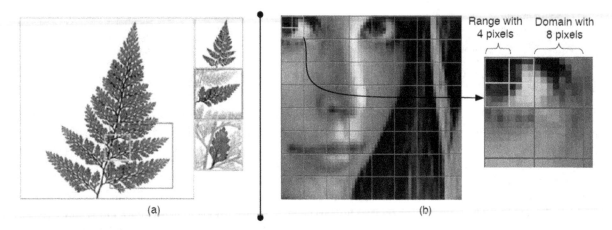

Figure 3. (a) Observing the recurrent pattern of fractals in the leaves of a plant; (b) Analyzing the relation of a subset R with $r = 4$ and a subset D with $d = 8$ in a sample image

Besides the fixed-point theorem, Affine Transformations (Sharabayko & Markov, 2012) are useful to adapt D_j to match to R_i. These transformations are performed in the following characteristics of the block D_j: (i) isometric (usually eight); (ii) scale and; (iii) contrast. An Affine Transformation is given by Eq. (2), where T() is an isometric transformation, s is a contractive scale and o means a specific brightness level. $S(D_j)$ represents a scale factor that contracts D_j size to R_i size. The values of s and o are defined in Eq. (3) and (4), respectively. The following works (Cao & Gu, 2011; Sharabayko & Markov, 2012; Wakatani, 2012) provide detailed discussion regarding these equations.

$$f(x) = s_i T_i \left(S(D_j) \right) + o \tag{2}$$

$$s_i = \frac{\sum S(D_j) \sum R_i - N^2 \sum S(D_j) R_i}{(\sum S(D_j))^2 - N^2 \sum S(D_j)^2} \tag{3}$$

$$o_i = \frac{\sum S(D_j) \sum R_i - \sum S(D_j)}{(\sum S(D_j))^2 - N^2 \sum S(D_j)^2} \tag{4}$$

$$MSE(R_i, R'_i) = \frac{1}{r^2} \sum_{k=0,l=0}^{r-1} (R_i(k,l) - R'_i(k,l))^2 \tag{5}$$

Considering the aforementioned context, IFS represents the operations performed over Affine Transformations. For any initial value of $D_j(x, y)$, there is a finite value n that will be the amount of iterative operations needed to get the fixed-point near to the original value $D_j(x, y)$. The main goal is to find a $D_j \in D$ which presents a high similarity to $R_i \in R$. In this context, the metric used to discover a best matching is a mean square error (MSE). Eq. (5) shows how the MSE is found. In this equation, $R_i(x, y)$ is an original pixel from F. R'_i is D_j modified by Affine transformations. Before evaluating MSE, each D_j is contracted in factor $r \div d$. This contraction can be used as the average among a group of nearest pixels as the absolute value of defined position in D_j. $S(D_j)$ will suffer all the eight standard isometric transformations: (i) rotation 0°; (ii) rotation 90°; (iii) rotation 180°; (iv) rotation 270°; (v) flip H; (vi) flip V; (vii) flip HV and; (viii) flip HV inverted. The next step is to define which D_j yields the minor MSE value. Finally, for each R_i will be found a D_j , an isometry, a scale and a brightness. According to Fu and Zhu (Fu & Zhu, 2009), this matching operation has complexity of $O[N^4]$.

4. Parallel Program Modelling

Commonly, we need to rewrite sequential programs to take the advantages of parallel architectures. Basically, a parallel program can follow one or a combination of the following paradigms: (i) message-passing in a multicomputer environment; (ii) multithreading programming by exploring multiprocessors (or multicore) systems; (iii) GPU (Graphical Processing Unit) programming on vectorial-based machines. This article presents a modeling approach in accordance with the second paradigm. In this context, the threads may communicate among themselves through a common shared-memory space in which they can both read from and write to. A multithreaded program can either define the launching of threads by using function calls explicitly or use library-assisted mechanisms for creating them implicitly. In the same way, the operating system is in charge of scheduling each created thread to a specific processor (or core) without user intervention or he/she can aid the operating system with scheduling instructions.

In particular, gains are limited by the fraction of the software that can be run in parallel simultaneously on multiple cores. This effect is described by Amdahl's law. In the best case, so-called embarrassingly parallel problems may realize speedup factors near the number of cores, or even more if the problem is split up enough to fit within each core's cache(s), avoiding use of much slower main system memory. As already presented by Kim and Choi (Kim & Choi, 2011), FIC has a natural parallelism. Each comparison between ranges and domains is independent. Therefore, we modeled an application for exploiting data-parallelism upon this feature. The main idea is to start more than one FIC threads at the same time by not defining data dependencies among them. Each one will be responsible for a subset of the original image. Following Garcia and Gao (2013), embarrassingly parallel applications are ideal for parallel computers. Their basic argument concerns that it is possible to achieve higher speedups if the interprocess communication is either lower or non-existent. These authors affirm that this performance level is hardly matched by another application model. Thus, Figure 4 illustrates the proposed model when employing 4 threads.

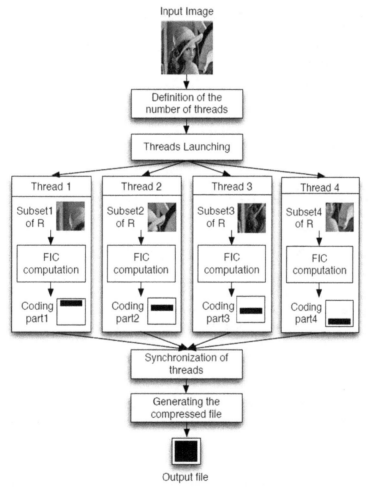

Figure 4. Example of the Parallel Model for the FIC problem with 4 threads

The first step of the model consists in splitting the original image in y equal subsets of R (see Section 3 for details). The value of y indicates the number of threads employed on compression coding. Each thread works with a whole set of D and must test all elements of this set against each range element received previously. Thus, each thread computes the FIC algorithm for its own block, generating both s and o sets. The final step concerns the appending of all blocks for generating the final compressed image. This task only occur after a synchronization point, which waits for the ending of all threads. Naturally, the performance depends on the number of cores or processors on a multiprocessing machine, as well as the granularity of the work. Commonly, the execution curve presents a performance peak when the number of threads is close to the processing elements in the system. A modeling without data dependencies is useful to concentrate the discussion in the following issues: (i) what is the performance in terms of application time when employing different number of cores; (ii) which is the impact of r (dimension of the range) and m (dimension of the image) on multicore and SMT systems.

5. Application Development and Evaluation Methodology

Concerning the model explained earlier, we developed an application written in C programming language that uses the routines from Pthreads for enabling the threads facilities. Our implementation uses the following directive groups from this library: (i) thread management for creating, detaching, and joining threads; (ii) mutexes management for creating, destroying, locking, and unlocking mutexes; (iii) synchronization barriers. Figure 5 delineates the steps executed in the main program. Concerning the input image, the most references found in the computing graphics literature (Chen & Chuang, 2010; Garg, 2011; George & Al-Hilo, 2009; Jeng et al., 2009; Sundaresan & Devika, 2012) employed square-shaped gray-scale images. We have decided to keep this configuration and used two 24bpp BMP-typed input files. We are testing the application with different range of dimensions ($r \times r$): 2x2, 4x4, 8x8, 16x16 and 32x32. Basically, the shorter the dimension of the ranges, the larger the computational time to solve the FIC problem. This parameter has an impact on application execution, since the threads management overhead is the same when maintaining the number of them. Our application creates one, two, four, eight, sixteen, or thirty two threads. Each thread has the task of operating on a quadrant of the image. We evaluated each range belonging to the quadrant against all domains. In addition, tests are multiplied by 8 since each domain has 8 isometries.

```
Input: The number of threads "y" and a target image.
Output: Compressed Image.
1. Open the image and collects its dimensions.
2. Clones the image in order to compute the PSNR index after compressing.
3. Allocates a memory array to be send for each thread (range subset, domain set D)
4. Initialize a timer t1.
5. Launching of "y" threads for coding subparts of the image.
6. Synchronization procedure for receiving data from all threads.
7. Initialize a timer t2 and take the elapsed time between t2 and t1.
8. Collecting the results for generating the compressed image.
9. Decompress the resultant image in order to compare it with the original one.
```

Figure 5. The algorithm executed by the main program.

The peak signal-to-noise ratio (PSNR) (Sharabayko & Markov, 2012) measures the error or distortion between original image f and a decoded one f'. At the end of the decompress algorithm, the gerated image is compared to the original one, pixel-by-pixel, in order to compute the PSNR value. The Eq. (6) defines PSNR. MSE indicates the mean error and was defined in Eq. (5) previously. Several works use PSNR metric to qualify the reconstruction of a lossy compression method (Sharabayko & Markov, 2012; Kim & Choi, 2011; Sun & Wun, 2009; Qin et al., 2009). The parallel environment, in its turn, has two nodes, each one with a dual- core processor. Although they present the same number of cores, they present different compositions: (i) Intel E7500, 2.93 GHz, with 3 Mbytes of Cache L2; (ii) Intel i5-460M, SMT capacity with 4 execution threads, 2.53 GHz, 512 Kbytes Cache L2, 3 Mbytes Cache L3. The first configuration presents two execution threads, one per each processing core.

$$PSNR = 10 \times log_{10}\left(\frac{255^2}{MSE(f,f')}\right) \tag{6}$$

Simultaneous Multithreading is a way to virtualize one or more cores on a single one. At operating system level, a SMT-assisted dual-core processor will be reported as four logical processors. The main strength of SMT is that it allows for flexible scheduling of all available execution slots, which increases efficiency by keeping the execution core as busy as possible. For accomplishing this, the main function of SMT technology is to decrease the number of dependent instructions on the pipeline by taking advantage of a superscalar architecture (multiple instructions operating on separate data in parallel) (Diamond et al., 2011). Thus, SMT enables each core to handle multiple tasks by allowing one task to work while the other is waiting for a result, or allowing both instructions to be completed simultaneously because they use non-conflicting resources (Rai et al., 2010). Especially applications like FIC with data-parallelism, where multiple execution threads execute the same code on different sets of data, SMT can improve their performance in approximately 30% when compared with non-SMT solutions (Raasch & Reinhardt, 2003).

6. Experimental Results and Discussion

We have used two input images for performing our evaluation. The first refers to the Lenna (Note 2) picture and presents 256x256 pixels, while the second is a Coliseum photo with 512x512 pixels. Each experiment was run 30 times and we got the mean value and the standard deviation. Considering all the tests, the highest standard deviation for the 256x256 image as 2.78% from the average, while 1.51% was the index obtained for the 512x512 input. We started the time counter before launching the first thread and stopped it after finalizing the execution of all threads. This method discarded sequential code in the measures. Table 1 presents the obtained PSNR when varying the number of ranges. The number of threads does not matter for evaluating this index since the output image is always the same. The 2x2-sized range achieved the best results resulting from its better entropy when compared to larger ranges. Visually, images with PSNR greater than 21 have a good visualization capacity for human beings (Türkan et al., 2012). We achieved a compression rate of 2:1 in both images when employing a range with dimensions 2x2. However, 234:1 and 250:1 compression ratios were observed for 32x32-sized ranges when manipulating Lenna and Coliseum images, respectively.

Table 1. Analyzing the obtained PSNR (measured in decibels) for both evaluated images.

Input Image	Dimension of ranges				
	2x2	4x4	8x8	16x16	32x32
Lenna	35	31	26	22	19
Coliseum	38	27	22	19	18

Tables 2 and 3 present the evaluation of both input images when using a dual-core machine without SMT facility. As expected, the best results appear when testing 2 or 4 threads. For example, when testing only one thread with a range dimension equal to 4 the result was 6.57 seconds. This configuration does not take profit of the parallel machine. However, the execution with 32 threads presented the highest execution time when comparing executions of multiple threads. This behavior is explained by the overhead of mutex, synchronization and thread management primitives. The larger the number of threads, the higher this overhead. This elucidates a common behavior on evaluating threads on dual-core processors, where the application time decreases abruptly with 2 and 4 threads and grows up slowly when enlarging the number of threads. Figure 6 illustrates the speedup (*sequential_time ÷ parallel_time*) and the parallel efficiency (*Speedup ÷ processors*) for the tests with 2x2 range. Our application presents a poor speedup because the number of threads is greater than the number of execution cores. This statement becomes clear in the efficiency graph. Considering that we have only 2 physical cores, the execution with two threads presented the highest efficiency (92%). The execution with 4 up to 32 threads expresses the dilemma of concurrence, since each pair of threads competes for a single processor.

Figure 7 depicts the speedup evaluation results of the Coliseum image over a dual-core machine. This image presents a larger computation grain if compared with the Lenna one. In other words, the overhead associated with threads are better amortized when testing the Coliseum image since each thread has more work to compute in comparison with the other image. In this way, the execution with 2 threads reaches indexes up to 1.97 of speedup which is considered a good measure since the ideal speedup for this configuration is 2. Besides this analysis, it is possible to observe other two behaviors in the graph of Figure 7. Firstly, the larger the dimension of the ranges, the lower the captured speedup. For example, the execution with a range of 32x32 presents a lowest computation grain per each thread. Secondly, we can observe an execution pattern among the threads. Independent of the number of threads, the speedup curve presents the same aspect.

Table 2. Evaluating a dual-core processor without SMT support with a 256x256-sized image (Lenna) - Time in seconds.

Range	Sequential	Threads				
		2	4	8	16	32
2x2	45.379	24.899	25.352	25.583	25.490	25.548
4x4	6.576	3.523	3.459	3.520	3.540	3.562
8x8	1.249	0.834	0.779	0.790	0.796	0.825
16x16	0.268	0.219	0.213	0.219	0.226	0.245
32x32	0.058	0.059	0.062	0.069	0.081	0.117

Table 3. Evaluating a dual-core processor without SMT support with a 512x512-sized image (Coliseum) - Time in seconds.

Range	Sequential	Threads				
		2	4	8	16	32
2x2	682.097	346.828	343.326	344.427	347.849	350.961
4x4	114.911	59.910	58.306	58.450	59.042	59.792
8x8	21.523	10.948	11.028	11.076	11.234	11.309
16x16	4.563	2.476	2.442	2.492	2.525	2.593
32x32	1.023	0.661	0.623	0.637	0.665	0.725

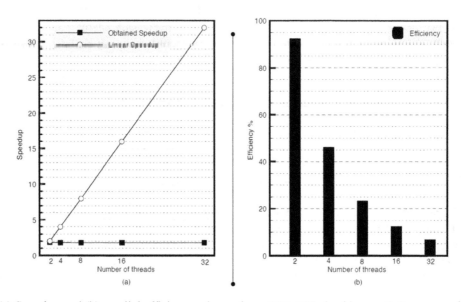

Figure 6. (a) Speedup and (b) parallel efficiency when using a 256x256-sized image, 2x2 range and a dual-core machine without SMT support

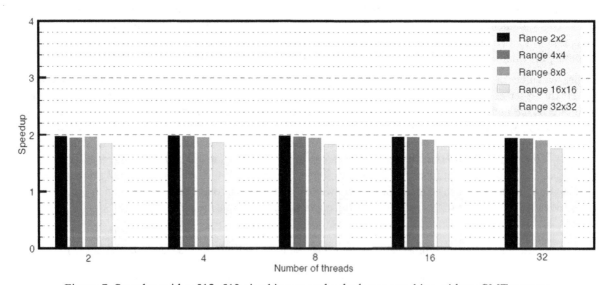

Figure 7. Speedup with a 512x512-sized image and a dual-core machine without SMT support

Both Tables 4 and 5 present the results when changing the infrastructure to the processor with SMT support. Different from the evaluation on Tables 2 and 3, the employment of 4 execution threads favors the execution time when using 4 threads significantly. Figure 8 shows the gain measured by *sequential_time ÷ parallel_time* when analyzing the coliseum picture with SMT-assisted dual-core processor. The performance of two threads obtained gains up to 1.98, which are considered a good measure for this number of threads. However, we can observe that the use of 2 threads does not take profit from the entire power of the parallel architecture, since an execution thread remains allocated per core. The execution with 4 up to 32 cores took profit from the SMT solution. Particularly, we obtained a gain of 3.05 when testing 4 threads and ranges with dimension 16x16, which represents more than 75% of usage considering the execution threads inside the cores. The most relevant verifications concern the execution with 2x2 ranges. As we can see in Figure 8, the performance of this configuration does not scale well when treating for 4 or more threads. The calculus with this dimension of ranges is more computationally intensive than others. Furthermore, interactions require more memory since the subset of ranges belonging to each thread is larger than other range configurations. Clearly, any of the following observations causes a system bottleneck (Diamond et al., 2011): (i) memory contention; (ii) cache miss; (iii) concurrent access to components in the superscalar pipeline of the SMT core.

Table 4. Evaluating a SMT dual-core processor with a 256x256-sized image (Lenna) - Time in seconds.

Range	Sequential	Threads				
		2	4	8	16	32
2x2	39.872	23.804	20.735	20.493	20.518	20.717
4x4	6.241	3.190	2.700	2.704	2.726	2.763
8x8	1.476	0.768	0.612	0.557	0.562	0.597
16x16	0.345	0.191	0.159	0.157	0.163	0.213
32x32	0.077	0.046	0.045	0.050	0.068	0.112

Figure 9 illustrates a comparison graph considering both configuration of dual-core processors and the Lenna image. Although the SMT processor operates with 4 execution threads, our evaluation showed that the best results were obtained with 8 user threads. This combination was the best one for enlarging the efficiency regarding the cores utilization. Despite a large number of threads rises the operating system time for both managing and scheduling them efficiently, the threads are useful for exploiting superscalar and preemption facilities found on SMT processors. Logically, the number of threads must be analyzed with the thread granularity. In out case, 8 threads and 8x8 ranges compose the set with better performance. Finally, Figure 10 depicts the tests in which a range of 32x32 pixels and the Coliseum image were employed. This configuration points out the traditional curve when working with threads. We have a perceptible reduction in time when enabling threads and the time grows up when enlarging the number of threads as well. This is explained by computational work grain. The larger the number of threads, the lower the grain to be calculated by each thread (each thread receives a subset of ranges uniformly). In addition, more threads implies in a higher cost on synchronization and mutex primitives.

Table 5. Evaluating a SMT dual-core processor with a 512x512-sized image (Coliseum) - Time in seconds.

Range	Sequential	Threads				
		2	4	8	16	32
2x2	627.877	329.060	281.961	273.816	271.517	272.759
4x4	126.557	64.227	43.187	43.158	43.340	43.657
8x8	24.872	13.404	8.513	8.527	8.604	8.751
16x16	5.869	2.977	1.946	1.967	1.993	2.103
32x32	1.381	0.711	0.523	0.512	0.536	0.613

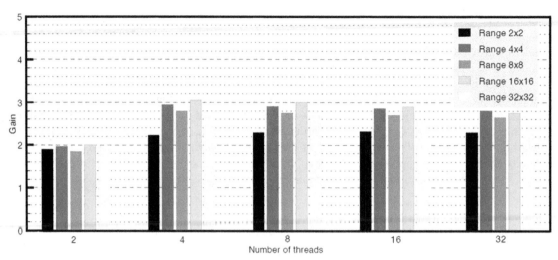

Figure 8. Evaluating the Coliseum figure with the SMT-assisted dual-core. The gain in *y* axis is equal to *sequential time ÷ parallel time*

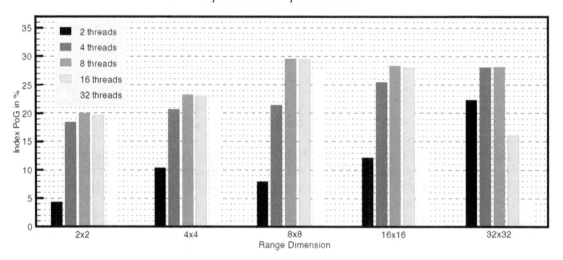

Figure 9. Evaluating both dual-core configuration with the Lenna image. Percentage of Gain (PoG) is computed as (1 - *SMT_dual-core ÷ Non_SMT_dual-core*).100

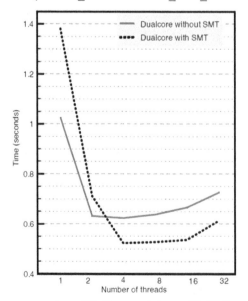

Figure 10. Evaluating the compression of Coliseum picture with 32 threads on both non-SMT and SMT-assisted dual-core systems.

7. Related Work

FIC technique has grabbed much attention in recent years because of manifold advantages, very high compression ratio, high decompression speed, high bit-rate and resolution independence. There have been many techniques, and improvements published in this field since 1990. Most of them are focused on some algorithm improvements for a smart search, which both reduce the size of search pool for range-domain matching and yield a significant speedup in execution time (Fu & Zhu, 2009; Jeng et al., 2009; Mitra et al., 1998; Qin et al., 2009; Revathy & Jayamohan, 2012; Rowshanbin et al., 2006; Sun & Wun, 2009; Vahdati et al., 2010). In particular, Revathy and Jayamohan (2012) proposed a dynamic preparation of a domain pool for each range block, instead of working with a set of static domains from the beginning of the execution (Revathy & Jayamohan, 2012). Vahdati et al. (2010) presented a Chaotic particle swarm optimization (CPSO) based on the characteristics of fractal and partitioned iterated function system. In addition, Ant Colony (Li et al., 2008), Neural Networks (Sun et al., 2001) and Genetic Algorithm (Mitra et al., 2000; Mitra et al., 1998; Wu & Lin, 2010) techniques were proposed to greatly decreases the search space for finding the self similarities in the given image. Contrary of exploring a reduction in the application time, Selim et al. focused on procuring a high compression index by maintaining a peak signal to noise ratio (PSNR) larger than 30 (Selim et al., 2008).

Regarding the exploration of parallel architectures, for the best of our knowledge there are the following initiatives for solving the FIC problem. Jackson and Blom (1995), based in a nCUBE multiprocessor, showed a parallel solution implementing a "host and nodes" solution, where a single processor was dedicated for distributing the workload to nodes and gathering results. Another message-passing solution were proposed by Qureshi and Hussein (2008), who implemented a three static master-worker MPI (Message Passing Interface) strategies for enabling load balancing on a Beowulf cluster of workstations. The authors measured both the speedup and the worker idle time of each implementation. Other features used in the context of FIC, considering a multicomputer environment, were Web Services (Fang et al., 2011) and process migration (Righi, 2012). Particular, this second work applies process rescheduling in grid environments for dealing with architecture heterogeneity and application dynamicity. Some works explore SIMD (Single Instruction Multiple Data) architectures, and more especially GPU (Graphical Processing Unit) (Wakatani, 2012; Khan & Akhtar, 2013). Kim and Choi (2011) combined both GPU and multithreading in their 2D DCT (discrete cosine transform) solution for the FIC problem (Kim & Choi, 2011). The article focused on the OpenCL parallel modeling. The authors just used an Intel core 2 Duo for the tests. Cao and Gu (Cao & Gu, 2010; Cao & Gu, 2011) presented a multithreading-based FIC implementation with OpenMP library by putting pragma codeword on iterative constructions simply. Albeit they pointed out a multicore implementation, the authors just presented tests with a quad-core system. Analyzing the contemplated related works, we observed a lack of studies on comparing the power of the recent multicore and SMT architectures for calculating the FIC problem. Hence, this opportunity of work was explored in this article.

8. Conclusion

With the help of recent development on semiconductor design, modern processors can provide a great opportunity to increase the performance on processing multimedia data by exploiting data-parallelism in multicore and SMT systems. Aiming to verify this statement, we employed in this article a parallel modeling of the so-called Fractal Image Compression (FIC) problem. Over the recent decades, FIC is a field of intensive research, applied not only in image processing but also in database indexing, texture mapping and pattern recognition problems. We designed a fork-join modeling to explore the fully potential of the parallel architecture, where each thread has a copy of the entire D (Domain) set and receives from the main program its own subset of ranges, which represents a subpart of the input image. The threads run without dependencies among themselves and are synchronized once for collecting the compressed image.

We confirmed the Garcia and Gao's (2013) affirmation, that says applications with data-parallelism, where multiple threads execute the same code on different sets of data, can improve their performance dramatically when taking profit from SMT and multicore technologies. The results showed gains up to 68% (with SMT) and 48% (without SMT) when comparing multiple and single-thread scenarios in both configurations of dual-core processors. We can explain this rate by: (i) our modeling strategy and; (ii) fact that FIC is a CPU-bound problem. The benefits of data parallelism exploration were more evident in the SMT configuration. The use of 4 execution threads in SMT-assisted dual-core provided a performance gain up to 29% if compared to a non-SMT configuration. Particularly, we obtained this index with 8 user threads, which occupy each execution thread in a better way. In the best of our knowledge, this article is the first that presents a parallel FIC application focused on multicore and SMT systems, showing a detailed evaluation on them. Besides this, we can extend our contribution to operating systems. They can include the parallel FIC implementation proposed here as an optional for compressing images, since multicore systems have become state-of-the-art in processor architecture field.

Finally, the tests allow us to conclude that the performance of a multithreading system depends on the computational grain on each thread, the number of processors in the target machine and the mutex/synchronization directives in the code. Future work comprises the execution of the FIC problem by modeling a message-passing application to execute over AMPI (Adaptive MPI) (Rodrigues et al., 2010). In this way, we intent to evaluate the problem with threads, with MPI solely and by combining both threads and MPI approaches.

Acknowledgments

The authors would like to thank to the following Brazilian agencies: CNPq, CAPES and FAPERGS.

References

Cao, H., & Gu, X. J. (2010). Openmp parallelization of jacquin fractal image encoding. In *E-Product E-Service and E- Entertainment (ICEEE), 2010 International Conference on*, pages 1-4. http://dx.doi.org/10.1109/ICEEE.2010.5661366

Cao, H., & Gu, X. Q. (2011). Implement research of fractal image encoding based on openmp parallelization model. In *Electric Information and Control Engineering (ICEICE), 2011 International Conference on*, 62–465. http://dx.doi.org/10.1109/ICEICE.2011.5777994

Chaurasia, V., & Somkuwar, A. (2009). Speed up technique for fractal image compression. In *Digital Image Processing, 2009 International Conference on*, pages 319–323. http://dx.doi.org/10.1109/ICDIP.2009.66

Chen, S., Cheng, X., & Xu, J. (2012). Research on image compression algorithm based on rectangle segmentation and storage with sparse matrix. In *Fuzzy Systems and Knowledge Discovery (FSKD), 2012 9th International Conference on*, pages 1904 –1908. http://dx.doi.org/10.1109/FSKD.2012.6233969

Chen, T. J., & Chuang, K.-S. (2010). A pseudo lossless image compression method. In *Image and Signal Processing (CISP), 2010 3rd International Congress on*, volume 2, pages 610 –615. http://dx.doi.org/10.1109/CISP.2010.5647247

Diamond, J., Burtscher, M., McCalpin, J. D., Kim, B. D., Keckler, S. W., & Browne, J. C. (2011). Evaluation and optimization of multicore performance bottlenecks in supercomputing applications. In *Proceedings of the IEEE International Symposium on Performance Analysis of Systems and Software*, ISPASS '11, pages 32–43, Washington, DC, USA. IEEE Computer Society. http://dx.doi.org/10.1109/ISPASS.2011.5762713

Fang, Y., Cheng, H., & Wang, M. (2011). Parallel implementation of fractal image compression in web service environment. In *Distributed Computing and Applications to Business, Engineering and Science (DCABES), 2011 Tenth International Symposium on*, pages 59–63. http://dx.doi.org/10.1109/DCABES.2011.66

Fu, C., & Zhu, Z. L. (2009). A dct-based fractal image compression method. In *Chaos-Fractals Theories and Applications, 2009. IWCFTA '09. International Workshop on*, pages 439–443. http://dx.doi.org/10.1109/IWCFTA.2009.99

Garcia, E., & Gao, G. (2013). Strategies for improving performance and energy efficiency on a many-core. In *Proceedings of the ACM International Conference on Computing Frontiers*, CF '13, pages 9:1–9:4, New York, NY, USA. ACM. https://doi.org/10.1145/2482767.2482779

Garg, A. (2011). Article: An improved algorithm of fractal image compression. *International Journal of Computer Applications*, 34(2):17–21. Published by Foundation of Computer Science, New York, USA.

George, L., & Al-Hilo, E. (2009). Fractal color image compression by adaptive zero-mean method. In *Computer Technology and Development, 2009. ICCTD '09. International Conference on*, volume 1, pages 525 –529. http://dx.doi.org/10.1109/ICCTD.2009.150

Jackson, D. J., & Blom, T. (1995). A parallel fractal image compression algorithm for hypercube multiprocessors. In *Proceedings of the 27th Southeastern Symposium on System Theory (SSST'95)*, SSST '95, pages 274–, Washington, DC, USA. IEEE Computer Society. http://dx.doi.org/10.1109/SSST.1995.390570

Jeng, J. H., Tseng, C. C., & Hsieh, J. G. (2009). Study on huber fractal image compression. *Image Processing, IEEE Transactions on*, 18(5):995 –1003. http://dx.doi.org/10.1109/TIP.2009.2013080

Khan, S., & Akhtar, N. (2013). Parallelization of fractal image compression over cuda. In Das, V. V., editor, *Proceedings of the Third International Conference on Trends in Information, Telecommunication and*

Computing, volume 150 of Lecture Notes in Electrical Engineering, pages 375–382. Springer New York. http://dx.doi.org/10.1007/978-1-4614-3363-7_42

Kim, C. G., & Choi, Y. S. (2011). Exploiting multi- and many-core parallelism for accelerating image compression. In *Multimedia and Ubiquitous Engineering (MUE), 2011 5th FTRA International Conference on*, pages 12–17. http://dx.doi.org/10.1109/MUE.2011.13

Li, J., Yuan, D., Xie, Q., & Zhang, C. (2008). Fractal image compression by ant colony algorithm. In *Young Computer Scientists, 2008. ICYCS 2008. The 9th International Conference for*, pages 1890–1894. http://dx.doi.org/10.1109/ICYCS.2008.222

Mitra, S., Murthy, C., & Kundu, M. (1998). Technique for fractal image compression using genetic algorithm. *Image Processing, IEEE Transactions on*, 7(4):586–593. http://dx.doi.org/10.1109/83.663505

Mitra, S., Murthy, C., & Kundu, M. (2000). Image compression and edge extraction using fractal technique and genetic algorithm. In Pal, S., Ghosh, A., and Kundu, M., editors, *Soft Computing for Image Processing*, volume 42 of *Studies in Fuzziness and Soft Computing*, pages 79–100. Physica-Verlag HD. https://doi.org/10.1007/978-3-7908-1858-1_4

Pinto, S., & Gawande, J. (2012). Performance analysis of medical image compression techniques. In *Internet (AH-ICI), 2012 Third Asian Himalayas International Conference on*, 1-4. http://dx.doi.org/10.1109/AHICI.2012.6408455

Qin, F. Q., Min, J., Guo, H. R., & Yin, D. H. (2009). A fractal image compression method based on block classification and quadtree partition. In *Computer Science and Information Engineering, 2009 WRI World Congress on, 1*, 716–719. http://dx.doi.org/10.1109/CSIE.2009.230

Qureshi, K., & Hussain, S. S. (2008). A comparative study of parallelization strategies for fractal image compression on a cluster of workstations. *International Journal of Computational Methods, 5*(3), 463–482. http://dx.doi.org/10.1142/S0219876208001534

Raasch, S. E., & Reinhardt, S. K. (2003). The impact of resource partitioning on smt processors. In *Proceedings of the 12th International Conference on Parallel Architectures and Compilation Techniques*, PACT '03, 15, Washington, DC, USA. IEEE Computer Society. http://dx.doi.org/10.1109/PACT.2003.1237998

Rai, J. K., Negi, A., Wankar, R., & Nayak, K. D. (2010). Performance prediction on multi-core processors. In *Proceedings of the 2010 International Conference on Computational Intelligence and Communication Networks*, CICN '10, pages 633–637, Washington, DC, USA. IEEE Computer Society. http://dx.doi.org/10.1109/CICN.2010.125

Revathy, K., & Jayamohan, M. (2012). Dynamic domain classification for fractal image compression. CoRR, abs/1206.4880. http://doi.org/10.5121/ijcsit.2012.4208

Righi, R. R. (2012). *Process Migration in Grid Computing: Combining Multiple Metrics to Control Process Rescheduling in Response to Resource and Application Dynamics*. Lambert Academic Publishing.

Rodrigues, E. R., Navaux, P. O. A., Panetta, J., Fazenda, A., Mendes, C. L., & Kale, L. V. (2010). A Comparative Analysis of Load Balancing Algorithms Applied to a Weather Forecast Model. In *Proceedings of 22nd International Symposium on Computer Architecture and High Performance Computing (SBAC-PAD)*, Itaipava, Brazil. http://dx.doi.org/10.1109/SBAC-PAD.2010.18

Rowshanbin, N., Samavi, S., & Shirani, S. (2006). Acceleration of fractal image compression using characteristic vector classification. In *Electrical and Computer Engineering, 2006. CCECE '06. Canadian Conference on*, pages 2057–2060. http://dx.doi.org/10.1109/CCECE.2006.277529

Selim, A., Hadhoud, M., Dessouky, M., & El-Samie, F. (2008). A simplified fractal image compression algorithm. In *Computer Engineering Systems, 2008. ICCES 2008. International Conference on*, 53–58. http://dx.doi.org/10.1109/ICCES.2008.4772965

Sharabayko, M. P., & Markov, N. G. (2012). Fractal compression of grayscale and color images: Tools and results. In *Strategic Technology (IFOST), 2012 7th International Forum on*, 1–5. http://dx.doi.org/10.1109/IFOST.2012.6357622

Sun, K., Lee, S., & Wu, P. (2001). Neural network approaches to fractal image compression and decompression. *Neurocomputing, 41*(14), 91-107. http://dx.doi.org/10.1016/S0925-2312(00)00349-0

Sun, Z., & Wun, Y. (2009). Multispectral image compression based on fractal and k-means clustering. In *Proceedings of the 2009 First IEEE International Conference on Information Science and Engineering,*

ICISE '09, pages 1341–1344, Washington, DC, USA. IEEE Computer Society. http://dx.doi.org/10.1109/ICISE.2009.772

Sundaresan, M., & Devika, E. (2012). Image compression using h.264 and deflate algorithm. In *Pattern Recognition, Informatics and Medical Engineering (PRIME), 2012 International Conference on*, 242-245. http://dx.doi.org/10.1109/ICPRIME.2012.6208351

Türkan, M., Thoreau, D., & Guillotel, P. (2012). Self-content super-resolution for ultra-hd up-sampling. In *Proceedings of the 9th European Conference on Visual Media Production*, CVMP '12, 49-58, New York, NY, USA. ACM. https://doi.org/10.1145/2414688.2414695

Vahdati, G., Yaghoobi, M., & Akbarzadeh-T, M. (2010). Fractal image compression based on particle swarm optimization and chaos searching. In *Computational Intelligence and Communication Networks (CICN), 2010 International Conference on*, 62-67. http://dx.doi.org/10.1109/CICN.2010.23

Wakatani, A. (2012). Implementation of fractal image coding for gpu systems and its power-aware evaluation. In *Systems Conference (SysCon), 2012 IEEE International*, 1-5. http://dx.doi.org/10.1109/SysCon.2012.6189434

Wu, M. S., & Lin, Y. L. (2010). Genetic algorithm with a hybrid select mechanism for fractal image compression. *Digit. Signal Process., 20*(4), 1150–1161. http://dx.doi.org/10.1016/j.dsp.2009.12.009

Notes

Note 1. We used the term "execution threads" in the remaining of this document for treating SMT technology, while we employed just "threads" for denoting multiple execution entities created by a parallel application.

Note 2. Standard test image which has been in use since 1973 in the computer graphics area. http://www.cs.cmu.edu/~chuck/lennapg/editor.html

19

Complex Network Analysis of the Contiguous United States Graph

Natarajan Meghanathan[1]

[1] Department of Computer Science, Jackson State University, USA

Correspondence: Natarajan Meghanathan, Department of Computer Science, Mailbox 18839, Jackson State University, Jackson, MS 39217, USA. E-mail: natarajan.meghanathan@jsums.edu

The research is financed by the NASA EPSCoR sub award (#: NNX14AN38A) from University of Mississippi.

Abstract

We model the contiguous states (48 states and the District of Columbia) of the United States (US) as an undirected network graph with each state represented as a node and there is an edge between two nodes if the corresponding two states share a common border. We determine a ranking of the states in the US with respect to a suite of node-level metrics: the centrality metrics (degree, eigenvector, betweenness and closeness), eccentricity, maximal clique size, and local clustering coefficient. We propose a normalization-based approach to obtain a comprehensive centrality ranking of the vertices (that is most likely to be tie-free) encompassing the normalized values of the four centrality metrics. We have applied the proposed normalization-based approach on the US States graph to obtain a tie-free ranking of the vertices based on a comprehensive centrality score. We observe the state of Missouri to be the most central state with respect to all the four centrality metrics. We have also analyzed the US States graph with respect to a suite of network-level metrics: bipartivity index, assortativity index, modularity, size of the minimum connected dominating set, algebraic connectivity and degree metrics. The approach taken in this paper could be useful for several application domains: transportation networks (to identify central hubs), politics (to identify campaign venues with larger geographic coverage), cultural and electoral studies (to identify communities of states that are relatively proximal to each other) and etc.

Keywords: Network Analysis, Centrality, Clique, Bipartivity, Modularity

1. Introduction

Network Science is one of the emerging fields of Data Science to analyze real-world networks from a graph theory point of view. Several real-world networks have been successfully modeled as undirected and directed graphs to study the intrinsic structural properties of the networks as well as the topological importance of nodes in these networks. The real-world networks that have been subjected to complex network analysis typically fall under one of these categories: social networks (Ghali et al., 2012), transportation networks (Cheung & Gunes, 2012), biological networks (Ma & Gao, 2012), citation networks (Zhao & Strotmann, 2015), co-authorship networks (Ding, 2011) and etc. One category of real-world networks for which sufficient attention has not yet been given are the regional networks featuring the states within a country.

In this paper, we present a comprehensive analysis of a network graph of the states within a country with respect to various node-level and network-level metrics typically considered in the field of Network Science and demonstrate the utility of information that can be obtained from the analysis. We also propose a normalization-based approach to obtain comprehensive centrality scores for the vertices encompassing the normalized individual centrality scores and illustrate the use of these comprehensive scores to obtain a ranking of the vertices (that is most likely to be tie-free). We also illustrate the procedure to identify the centrality metric whose scores and ranking are relatively the closest to the normalized comprehensive centrality scores and ranking.

We opine the paper to serve as a model for anyone interested in analyzing a connected graph of the states within a country from a Network Science perspective. The approaches presented in this paper could be useful to determine the states (and their cities) that are the most central and/or influential within a country. For example, the ranking of the vertices based on the shortest path centrality metrics (closeness and betweenness) could be useful to choose the states (and their cities) that could serve as hubs for transportation networks (like road and airline networks). We could identify the states that are most the central states as well as identify the states that could form a connected backbone and geographically well-connected to the rest of the states within a country and use this information to design the road/rail transportation networks. The degree centrality and eigenvector centrality metrics as well as the network-level metrics like minimum connected dominating set and maximal clique size could be useful to identify fewer number of venues (with several adjacent states to draw people) for political campaigns/meetings that would cover the entire country. Node-level metrics like local clustering coefficient could be useful to identify the states that are critical to facilitate communication between the neighbor states. One could develop an optimal regional classification of states for cultural studies (language accent, eating habits, etc) and electoral studies (like scheduling of elections) by identifying communities of states (that are relatively more proximal with each other) with high modularity scores.

Table 1. List of Contiguous States (including DC) of the US in Alphabetical Order

ID	State/District	Code	ID	State/District	Code
1	Alabama	AL	26	Nebraska	NE
2	Arizona	AZ	27	Nevada	NV
3	Arkansas	AR	28	New Hampshire	NH
4	California	CA	29	New Jersey	NJ
5	Colorado	CO	30	New Mexico	NM
6	Connecticut	CT	31	New York	NY
7	Delaware	DE	32	North Carolina	NC
8	District of Columbia	DC	33	North Dakota	ND
9	Florida	FL	34	Ohio	OH
10	Georgia	GA	35	Oklahoma	OK
11	Idaho	ID	36	Oregon	OR
12	Illinois	IL	37	Pennsylvania	PA
13	Indiana	IN	38	Rhode Island	RI
14	Iowa	IA	39	South Carolina	SC
15	Kansas	KS	40	South Dakota	SD
16	Kentucky	KY	41	Tennessee	TN
17	Louisiana	LA	42	Texas	TX
18	Maine	ME	43	Utah	UT
19	Maryland	MD	44	Vermont	VT
20	Massachusetts	MA	45	Virginia	VA
21	Michigan	MI	46	Washington	WA
22	Minnesota	MN	47	West Virginia	WV
23	Mississippi	MS	48	Wisconsin	WI
24	Missouri	MO	49	Wyoming	WY
25	Montana	MT			

We choose the United States (US) as the country for analysis and build a connected network graph of the contiguous states (48 states and the District of Columbia, DC) of the US: each state and DC is a node (vertex) and there exists a link (edge) between two vertices if the two corresponding states/DC share a common border. Though some prior studies have been conducted on transportation networks (Cheung & Gunes, 2012) and food flow networks (Lin et al., 2014) in the United States, to the best of our knowledge, there has been no prior study of network analysis on the graph of the contiguous US states solely based on their geographical locations. In this paper, we have implemented the algorithms to compute several node-level metrics (such as the degree centrality, eigenvector centrality (Newman, 2010), betweenness centrality (Brandes, 2001), closeness centrality (Newman, 2010), maximal clique size (Meghanathan, 2015b), eccentricity (Cormen et al., 2009) and local clustering coefficient) as well as several network-level metrics (such as bipartivity index (Estrada & Rodriguez-Velazquez, 2005), modularity (Newman, 2006), minimum connected dominating set (Meghanathan, 2014b), algebraic connectivity (Ficdler, 1973), average path length (Cormen et al., 2009), diameter (Cormen et al., 2009), assortativity index (Newman, 2010) and spectral radius (Meghanathan, 2014a)) and analyze the US States network graph with respect to these metrics. We also analyze random network instances (generated with the same degree sequence using the Configuration model (Meghanathan, 2016c)) of the US States graph to study the correlation of the node-level metrics and proximity of values for the network-level metrics. Finally, we illustrate the application of the proposed normalized comprehensive centrality (NCC) scores-based ranking of the vertices on the US States network graph and observe that the NCC-based ranking of the vertices is indeed tie-free for the graph. We also identify the eigenvector centrality metric to be the centrality metric whose normalized scores and ranking of the vertices have relatively the lowest RMSD (root mean square difference) value to that of the NCC scores and the NCC-based ranking of the vertices.

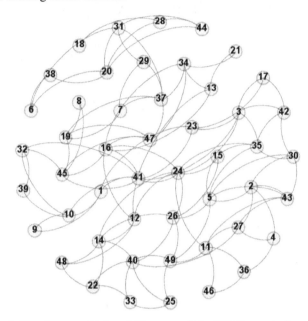

Figure 1. Fruchterman Reingold Layout of the US Network States Graph

Table 1 lists the contiguous states and DC in alphabetical order, their two character codes and the IDs used to refer to them in the paper. The rest of the paper is organized as follows: Section 2 introduces the node-level metrics and presents the results of the analysis on the states graph for each of them. Section 3 introduces the network-level metrics and presents the results of analysis on the states graph for each of them. Section 4 presents the normalization-based approach to obtain a comprehensive centrality ranking of the vertices and its application on the US States graph. Section 5 analyzes the random network instances (generated with the same degree sequence using the Configuration model) of the US States graph and compares the correlation of the node-level metrics and proximity of the network-level metrics. Section 6 discusses related work. Section 7 concludes the paper by summarizing the results of Sections 2-5. For the rest of the paper, the terms 'network' and 'graph', 'node' and 'vertex', 'link' and 'edge' are used interchangeably. They mean the same. The layout for the US States Network graph presented in Figure 1 is drawn using the Fructherman Reingold layout algorithm (Fruchterman & Reingold, 1991), available in Gephi (Cherven, 2015).

2. Node-Level Metrics

In this section, we introduce the node-level metrics for which we will run their respective algorithms on the US States Network graph and present the results (including their distribution and ranking of the vertices). The node-level metrics discussed include the four centrality metrics (degree centrality, eigenvector centrality, closeness centrality and betweenness centrality), maximal clique size, local clustering coefficient and the distance metrics: path length, eccentricity and radius. Since the US States graph is an undirected graph, the adjacency matrix of the graph is symmetric and there is only one value per vertex for each node-level metric.

2.1 Degree Centrality

The degree centrality (DegC) of a vertex is the number of edges incident on it. Table 2 presents the degree centrality of the vertices and the corresponding rank (in the decreasing order of their values) in the US States Network graph; vertices with identical values for DegC have the same rank. The state of Missouri has the largest degree centrality value of 9, followed by the state of Tennessee with the second largest degree centrality value of 8. The state of Maine has the smallest degree centrality value of 1 (as New Hampshire is its only adjacent state). There are no ties among vertices for the largest and second largest values of degree centrality as well as for the vertex with the smallest degree centrality. However, as we can notice (from Table 2): for other values of degree centrality, there are several instances of ties among vertices (we assign the same rank for all such vertices with identical values for degree centrality).

Table 2. Ranking of the Vertices in the US States Network Graph based on Degree Centrality (DegC)

Rank	ID	DegC	Rank	ID	DegC	Rank	ID	DegC	Rank	ID	DegC
1	24	9	5	2	5	6	23	4	7	48	3
2	41	8	5	30	5	6	42	4	7	28	3
3	5	7	5	27	5	6	15	4	7	44	3
3	16	7	5	43	5	6	32	4	7	33	3
3	40	7	5	49	5	6	13	4	7	25	3
4	3	6	5	20	5	6	22	4	8	9	2
4	35	6	5	31	5	7	4	3	8	38	2
4	26	6	5	19	5	7	17	3	8	8	2
4	37	6	5	12	5	7	36	3	8	39	2
4	45	6	5	34	5	7	6	3	8	46	2
4	11	6	5	47	5	7	7	3	8	21	2
4	14	6	6	1	4	7	29	3	9	18	1
5	10	5									

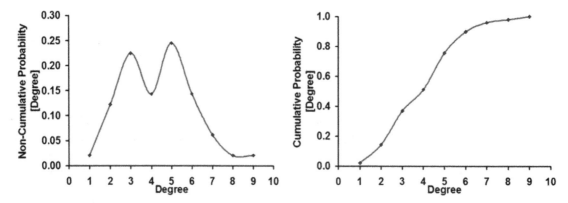

Figure 2. Bi-Modal Poisson Distribution (Non-Cumulative and Cumulative) for the Degree Centrality Metric of the US States Graph

Figure 2 illustrates that the non-cumulative and cumulative degree distributions of the vertices in the states graph. The non-cumulative distribution curve illustrates that the degree distribution is bi-modal with a Poisson pattern (Balakrishnan & Nevzorov, 2003) with the peaks observed at degree values of 3 and 5; the cumulative distribution curve indicates that more than 85% of the vertices have degree of 6 or lower (the degree values are mostly $\pm$ 1 away from either of the two peaks), even though the largest degree observed is 9.

2.2 Eigenvector Centrality

The eigenvector centrality (EVC) of a vertex is a measure of the degree of the vertex as well as the degree of its neighbors. A vertex is likely to have a higher EVC if it has a larger degree and its neighbor(s) also have a larger degree. The EVC for a vertex corresponds to the entry for the vertex in the principal eigenvector of the adjacency matrix of the graph (Chung, 2006). The EVC of the vertices is computed by implementing the power-iteration algorithm (Lay et al., 2015). Table 3 lists the EVC values (rounded to four decimal places) of the vertices in the US States graph. We observe a tie between the states of Vermont and Connecticut (values of 0.0050 each). The rest of the 47 vertices have a unique ranking. The US States graph is another example to illustrate that (unlike the degree centrality metric) the eigenvector centrality metric is more likely to return unique values for the vertices in real-world network graphs (Meghanathan, 2015a). The state of Missouri has the largest EVC value (0.3697), distantly followed by the states of Nebraska (0.2605) and Tennessee (0.2546); the state of Maine has the lowest EVC value (0.0004), far away from the immediately larger value of 0.0020 for the state of Rhode Island. The largest values for the state of Missouri with respect to both the degree centrality and eigenvector centrality metrics indicate that the state of Missouri not only has the largest degree, its neighboring states also have a relatively larger degree.

Table 3. Ranking of the Vertices in the US States Network Graph based on Eigenvector Centrality (EVC)

Rank	ID	EVC	Rank	ID	EVC	Rank	ID	EVC	Rank	ID	EVC
1	24	0.3697	14	11	0.1703	26	48	0.0951	38	21	0.0380
2	26	0.2605	15	43	0.1595	27	10	0.0946	39	39	0.0354
3	41	0.2546	16	45	0.1506	28	1	0.0927	40	9	0.0344
4	5	0.2509	17	2	0.1423	29	17	0.0880	41	7	0.0298
5	35	0.2494	18	42	0.1346	30	25	0.0803	42	29	0.0212
6	16	0.2362	19	27	0.1330	31	19	0.0742	43	31	0.0191
7	3	0.2235	20	23	0.1210	32	33	0.0696	44	20	0.0061
8	14	0.2227	21	47	0.1158	33	37	0.0666	45	44	0.0050
9	15	0.2076	22	22	0.1065	34	4	0.0597	45	6	0.0050
10	40	0.1924	23	13	0.1039	35	36	0.0496	46	28	0.0021
11	12	0.1887	24	34	0.1029	36	8	0.0413	47	38	0.0020
12	49	0.1752	25	32	0.0983	37	46	0.0404	48	18	0.0004
13	30	0.1720									

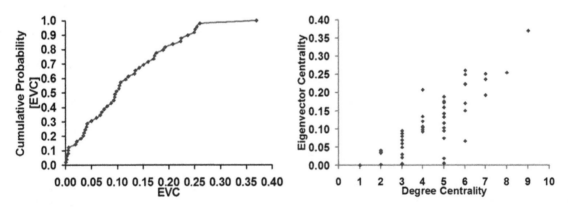

(a) Cumulative Probability Distribution of EVC (b) Degree Centrality vs. Eigenvector Centrality

Figure 3. Eigenvector Centrality of the Vertices in the US States Graph

Figure 3-a illustrates the cumulative probability distribution of the EVC values of the vertices in the US States graph. Except the state of Missouri (that has an EVC value much larger than the rest of the vertices), each of the other states have an EVC value that is closer to one or two other states. Thus, the distribution of the EVC values of the vertices follows a Poisson distribution. Figure 3-b presents a comparison of the degree centrality and eigenvector centrality values of the vertices and the Spearman's rank-based correlation coefficient (Daniel, 2000) between the two degree-based centrality metrics is 0.80. We observe that vertices with the same degree centrality have a wide range of values for the eigenvector centrality. Though vertices with larger degree centrality appear to be more likely to have a larger eigenvector centrality, there are several vertices for which the eigenvector centrality is relatively lower (compared to the EVC of vertices that have a relatively lower degree centrality) even if they have a higher degree centrality. For example, the state of Massachusetts (degree centrality - 5) has a much lower EVC (0.0061) than the state of Georgia (degree centrality - 3; EVC - 0.0946): primarily, attributed to the relatively higher degree of the neighbors for the state of Georgia.

2.3 Betweenness Centrality

The Betweenness Centrality (BWC) of a vertex is a measure of its presence among the shortest paths between any two vertices in the graph. The BWC of a vertex v_i is the sum of the fractions of the shortest paths between any two vertices (v_j and v_k; $i \neq j \neq k$) that go through v_i. Quantitatively,

$$BWC(i) = \sum_{j \neq k \neq i} \frac{sp_{jk}(i)}{sp_{jk}},$$

where sp_{jk} is the total number of shortest paths between vertices v_j and v_k; $sp_{jk}(i)$ is the number of such shortest paths between v_j and v_k that go through vertex v_i. We determine the BWC of the vertices in the US States graph by implementing the Brandes' algorithm (Brandes, 2001). Table 4 ranks the vertices in the US States graph based on BWC; the state of Missouri has the largest BWC value (821.4), followed by the states of Kentucky (602.4) and Pennsylvania (554.4). Seven vertices (DC, Florida, Maine, Michigan, Rhode Island, South Carolina and Washington) have a BWC value of 0.0 - indicating that these vertices do not lie on the shortest path between any two vertices in the graph. In addition to the above tie, when rounded to the first decimal value for the non-zero values of BWC, we notice that there are ties between Delaware and New Jersey (with a lower BWC of 7.0 each). A total of 42 distinct rank values could be assigned for the vertices.

Table 4. Ranking of the Vertices in the US States Network Graph based on Betweenness Centrality (BWC)

Rank	ID	BWC	Rank	ID	BWC	Rank	ID	BWC	Rank	ID	BWC
1	24	821.4	14	20	140.0	26	1	47.0	38	7	7.0
2	16	602.4	15	19	131.0	27	30	45.5	38	29	7.0
3	37	554.4	16	26	127.2	28	6	43.0	39	17	4.7
4	41	472.7	17	35	121.4	29	22	36.7	40	25	4.5
5	31	403.0	18	28	94.0	30	23	31.3	41	33	1.7
6	11	368.9	19	44	86.0	31	36	30.4	42	8	0.0
7	34	305.6	20	27	81.8	32	42	28.1	42	9	0.0
8	47	294.1	21	5	80.4	33	2	25.4	42	18	0.0
9	45	264.4	22	10	79.3	34	43	25.2	42	21	0.0
10	14	179.8	23	13	78.9	35	15	25.1	42	38	0.0
11	12	163.2	24	32	76.9	36	48	21.9	42	39	0.0
12	3	152.6	25	49	61.7	37	4	7.5	42	46	0.0
13	40	144.3									

Figure 4-a illustrates the cumulative probability distribution of the BWC of the vertices. We notice that about 81% of the vertices have BWC values less than 180; while the largest BWC value observed is 821.4. Thus, the BWC metric exhibits a Power-law style distribution (Balakrishnan & Nevzorov, 2003) for the vertices in the US States graph. From Figure 4-b, we also notice that though vertices with a higher degree are more likely to have a higher BWC and the Spearman's rank-based correlation coefficient is 0.87; we do observe instances wherein the BWC values could vary appreciably even among vertices with the same degree centrality.

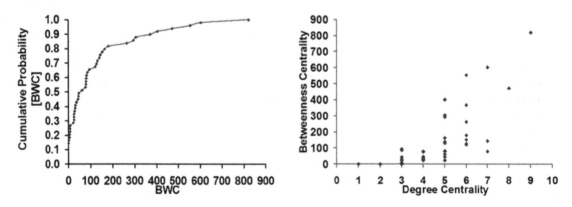

(a) Cumulative Probability Distribution of BWC (b) Degree Centrality vs. Betweenness Centrality

Figure 4. Betweenness Centrality of the Vertices in the US States Graph

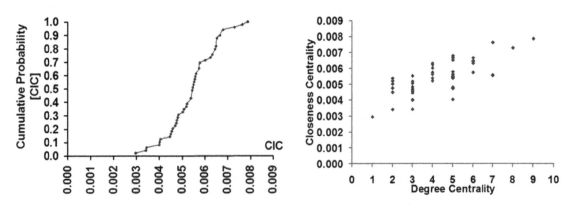

(a) Cumulative Probability Distribution of ClC (b) Degree Centrality vs. Closeness Centrality

Figure 5. Closeness Centrality of the Vertices in the US States Graph

Table 5. Ranking of the Vertices in the US States Network Graph based on Closeness Centrality (ClC)

Rank	ID	ClC	Rank	ID	ClC	Rank	ID	ClC	Rank	ID	ClC
1	24	0.00787	10	15	0.00625	20	43	0.00543	29	2	0.00474
2	16	0.00763	11	32	0.00602	21	8	0.00538	30	29	0.00469
3	41	0.00730	12	19	0.00578	21	30	0.00538	31	25	0.00459
4	12	0.00680	13	23	0.00575	21	42	0.00538	32	4	0.00455
5	45	0.00667	13	37	0.00575	22	21	0.00521	33	9	0.00450
5	47	0.00667	14	1	0.00562	22	22	0.00521	34	33	0.00446
6	34	0.00654	14	10	0.00562	23	17	0.00518	35	20	0.00405
7	3	0.00649	15	5	0.00559	24	36	0.00508	36	44	0.00402
7	11	0.00649	16	40	0.00556	25	46	0.00503	37	6	0.00400
7	26	0.00649	17	48	0.00552	26	7	0.00483	38	28	0.00344
8	14	0.00645	18	49	0.00549	27	31	0.00481	39	38	0.00341
9	13	0.00633	19	27	0.00546	28	39	0.00476	40	18	0.00296
9	35	0.00633									

2.4 Closeness Centrality

The Closeness Centrality (ClC) of a vertex is a measure of the number of hops on the shortest paths from the vertex to every other vertex in the graph. The ClC of a vertex is the inverse of the sum of the lengths (hops) of the shortest paths from the vertex to the rest of the vertices in the graph (determined using the Breadth First Search algorithm (Cormen et al., 2009)). We observe the state of Missouri to have the largest ClC, followed by the states of Kentucky and Tennessee. The state of Maine has the lowest ClC indicating that the sum of the length of the shortest paths from this state to the rest of the states is the largest. From Table 5, a total of 40 unique values could be observed for the ClC of the vertices (there are several instances where two or three states have the same values for the ClC). Figure 5-a captures the cumulative distribution of the ClC; we observe the values to be uniformly distributed albeit within a smaller range (unlike the EVC and BWC) resulting in a relatively steep curve. Figure 5-b captures the relationship between degree centrality and closeness centrality; vertices with a larger degree are likely to have a larger closeness centrality and the Spearman's rank-based correlation coefficient value is 0.75.

2.5 Ranking of Vertices Based on the Centrality Metrics

Figures 3-b, 4-b and 5-b respectively capture the relationship between degree centrality and each of the other three centrality metrics (EVC, BWC and ClC). Figures 6-a, 6-b and 6-c capture the relationship between EVC, BWC and ClC. We present the values for the Spearman's rank-based correlation coefficient between any two centrality metrics in Table 6. The larger the value of the correlation coefficient for any two metrics, the more the similarity in the ranking of the vertices with respect to the two metrics in consideration. We observe the ranking between DegC and BWC to have the highest correlation coefficient (0.87), whereas the ranking between EVC and BWC has the lowest correlation coefficient (0.52). The lower correlation coefficient values for EVC-BWC and BWC-ClC metrics indicate the rankings of the vertices with respect to each of the two combinations are quite different from each other. Nevertheless, the state of Missouri has the largest value for all the four centrality metrics.

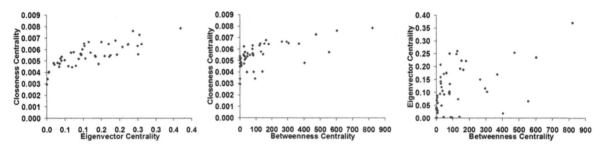

(a) EVC vs. ClC (b) BWC vs. ClC (c) BWC vs. EVC

Figure 6. Relationship between Eigenvector, Closeness and Betweenness Centrality Metrics for the US States Graph

Table 6. Spearman's Rank-based Correlation Coefficient among the Centrality Metrics for the US States Graph

	EVC	BWC	ClC
DegC	0.80	0.87	0.75
EVC		0.52	0.80
BWC			0.68

2.6 Maximum and Maximal Clique Size

A clique in a graph is a completely connected sub graph of the graph (Cormen et al., 2009); any two vertices within a clique are connected by an edge. The size of a clique is the number of vertices constituting the clique. The "maximum clique" is the clique of the largest size. However, not all vertices are likely to be part of the maximum clique (unless the graph is completely connected). In complex real-world networks, most of the vertices are likely to be part of cliques of size less than that of the maximum clique. The largest clique in which a vertex is part of is referred to as the maximal clique for the vertex and the corresponding clique size is referred to as the maximal clique size of the vertex. The problems of determining the maximum clique size for a graph as well as the maximal clique size for the individual vertices in a graph are NP-hard (Cormen et al., 2009) and one would need efficient heuristics to determine them. Pattabiraman et al (2016) proposed a branch-and-bound based heuristic to efficiently determine the maximum clique for complex network graphs and an extended version (Meghanathan, 2015b) of this heuristic could be used to determine the maximal clique size for the individual vertices in a graph. For the US States graph of 49 vertices, we observe the maximum clique size of the graph to be 4 comprising of the states of Arizona, Colorado, New Mexico and Utah (i.e., there is a shared boundary between any two of these four states), corresponding to the Four Corners Monument (Benson, 2008) and each of the remaining vertices (except Maine) have a maximal clique size of 3; the state of Maine has a maximal clique size of 2 as it has only one other state with which it shares a border. Table 7 lists the values for the centrality metrics for the four states constituting the maximum clique and the corresponding rank of these vertices with respect to these metrics is indicated in the parenthesis. We notice that the ranking of the vertices constituting the maximum clique is relatively higher with respect to the degree-based centrality metrics (DegC and EVC) compared to the shortest path-based centrality metrics (BWC and ClC). It appears that vertices constituting the maximum clique are not very critical to facilitate shortest path communication among the other vertices in the US States network graph.

Table 7. Centrality Metrics (Value and Rank) of the Vertices Constituting the Maximum Clique

State (ID)	DegC (Rank)	EVC (Rank)	BWC (Rank)	ClC (Rank)
Arizona (2)	5 (5)	0.1423 (17)	25.4 (33)	0.00474 (29)
Colorado (5)	7 (3)	0.2509 (4)	80.4 (21)	0.00559 (15)
New Mexico (30)	5 (5)	0.1720 (13)	45.5 (27)	0.00538 (21)
Utah (43)	5 (5)	0.1595 (15)	25.2 (34)	0.00543 (20)

2.7 Local Clustering Coefficient

The local clustering coefficient (LCC) of a vertex is a measure of the probability that any two neighbors of the vertex are connected. For a vertex v_i with k_i neighbors, the maximum number of links between any two neighbors of the vertex is $k_i(k_i-1)/2$. The LCC of a vertex is the ratio of the actual number of links connecting the neighbors of the vertex to that of the maximum possible number of links between the neighbors of the vertex. The smaller the LCC of a vertex, the more important is the vertex for facilitating shortest path communication among its neighbors (as there is a good chance that the neighbors of a vertex that are connected to each other go through the vertex for shortest path communication). Hence, we give a higher rank to vertices having a lower LCC.

Table 8. Ranking of the Vertices in the US States Network Graph based on Local Clustering Coefficient (LCC)

Rank	ID	LCC	Rank	ID	LCC	Rank	ID	LCC	Rank	ID	LCC
1	11	0.133	5	45	0.333	7	13	0.500	8	25	0.667
2	24	0.222	6	3	0.400	7	22	0.500	8	29	0.667
3	40	0.286	6	10	0.400	7	23	0.500	8	33	0.667
3	41	0.286	6	12	0.400	7	30	0.500	8	44	0.667
4	27	0.300	6	14	0.400	7	32	0.500	8	48	0.667
4	31	0.300	6	19	0.400	7	42	0.500	9	8	1.000
4	49	0.300	6	20	0.400	7	43	0.500	9	9	1.000
5	4	0.333	6	26	0.400	7	47	0.500	9	18	1.000
5	5	0.333	6	34	0.400	8	6	0.667	9	21	1.000
5	16	0.333	6	35	0.400	8	7	0.667	9	38	1.000
5	28	0.333	7	1	0.500	8	15	0.667	9	39	1.000
5	36	0.333	7	2	0.500	8	17	0.667	9	46	1.000
5	37	0.333									

Table 8 ranks the vertices in the US States graph in the increasing order of the values of the LCC. As the LCC values get larger, we observe a significant number of ties among the vertices. The state of Idaho (with a degree of 6) has the lowest LCC and hence is the top ranked with respect to the LCC metric. The state of Missouri (that was ranked first with respect to all the four centrality metrics) is ranked second with respect to LCC. There are only nine unique values for the LCC metric. Figure 7-a captures the cumulative probability distribution of the LCC metric and we observe that only about 15% of the vertices have a LCC of 0.3 or lower, and more than half of these vertices have the largest values for the BWC (as observed in Figure 7-b). We observe the Spearman's Rank-based correlation coefficient between LCC and BWC (computed based on the rankings in Tables 4 and 8) to be 0.82. Figure 7-c very well captures the inverse relationship between degree and LCC. Vertices having a larger degree are more likely to have a lower LCC as it would be difficult to expect any two neighbors of a high-degree node to be directly connected to each other and are more likely to go through the vertex for shortest-path communication. On the other hand, vertices having a lower degree are more likely to have a larger LCC as it is highly possible for any two neighbors of a low-degree vertex to be directly connected to each other and need not go through the vertex for shortest path communication. Thus, vertices with higher degree and lower LCC are more likely to have a larger BWC, and vertices with a lower degree and higher LCC are more likely to have a smaller BWC. A plot of Closeness Centrality (ClC) vs. LCC reveals that the two metrics are almost independent of each other (as vertices covering the entire range of values observed for the ClC have almost the same LCC), leading to a Spearman's rank-based correlation coefficient of 0.52.

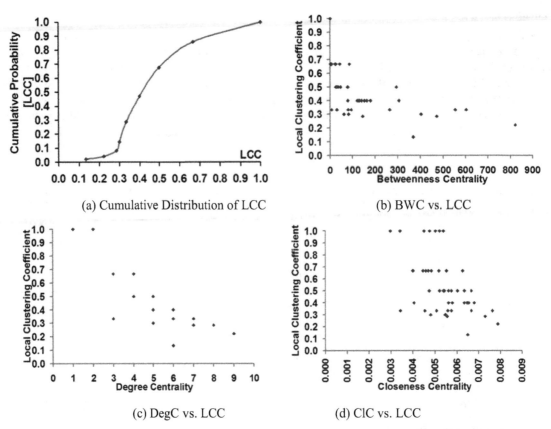

(a) Cumulative Distribution of LCC   (b) BWC vs. LCC

(c) DegC vs. LCC   (d) ClC vs. LCC

Figure 7. Cumulative Distribution of the Local Clustering Coefficient and its Relationship with the Degree Centrality, Betweenness Centrality and Closeness Centrality

2.8 Distance Metrics

We determine the distribution of the path length for any two vertices and eccentricity (Ecc) of the vertices in the US States network graph. The path length for a pair of vertices (u, v) is the number of hops in the shortest path (minimum hop path) between the two vertices. The eccentricity of a vertex is the maximum of the path lengths to any other vertex in the graph (Newman, 2010). In other words, the eccentricity of a vertex is the maximum of the minimum number of hops to any other vertex. The eccentricity of a particular vertex and the path lengths of the vertex to every other vertex are determined by running the Breadth First Search algorithm (Cormen et al., 2009) on the vertex. Figure 8 illustrates the distribution of the path length of the vertex pairs and eccentricity of the vertices in the US States graph. We observe the path length distribution to be Poisson in nature with a long tail (Kurtosis of 2.82) and mean value of 3.93 as well as a standard deviation of 1.98. The average path length value of 3.93 is close to the expected average path value (of 3.89) to exhibit the small-world property (path length of $\ln(n)$ for a graph of n vertices; Newman, 2010) for a graph of 49 vertices.

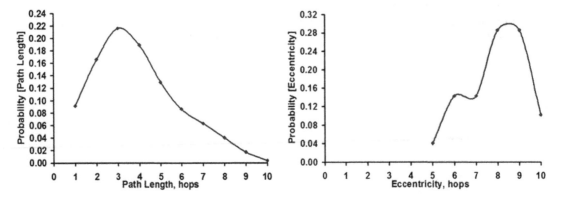

Figure 8. Distribution of Path Length and Eccentricity for the US States Graph

Table 9. Ranking of the Vertices in the US States Network Graph based on Eccentricity (Ecc)

Rank	ID	Ecc	Rank	ID	Ecc	Rank	ID	Ecc	Rank	ID	Ecc
1	34	5	3	31	7	4	35	8	5	42	9
1	47	5	3	32	7	4	39	8	5	43	9
2	8	6	3	41	7	4	44	8	5	46	9
2	13	6	4	1	8	4	48	8	5	49	9
2	16	6	4	3	8	5	5	9	6	2	10
2	19	6	4	6	8	5	9	9	6	4	10
2	21	6	4	10	8	5	17	9	6	18	10
2	37	6	4	11	8	5	22	9	6	25	10
2	45	6	4	14	8	5	27	9	6	33	10
3	7	7	4	15	8	5	28	9			
3	12	7	4	20	8	5	30	9			
3	24	7	4	23	8	5	36	9			
3	29	7	4	26	8	5	38	9			

The distribution of the eccentricity of the vertices shows that the minimum value (also called radius): 5 is half of the maximum value (also called diameter): 10. Nevertheless, we observe that more than 65% of the vertices have an eccentricity of 8 or above (i.e., more than 65% of the vertices have a maximum path length of 8-10 to one or more vertices) and only 4% of the 49 vertices (i.e., just 2 vertices) incur eccentricity values corresponding to the radius of the graph. The two states of West Virginia and Ohio (with an eccentricity corresponding to the radius) are said to form the "center" of the graph (Newman, 2010); each of these two vertices are within a maximum hop count of 5 on a shortest path to any other vertex in the graph. Note that neither of these two vertices are among the vertices that are ranked in the top 3 with respect to any of the centrality metrics and local clustering coefficient. There are five states (Arizona, California, Maine, Montana and North Dakota) that have an eccentricity corresponding to the diameter of the graph. Table 9 illustrates a ranking of the vertices based on eccentricity (the state with the smallest eccentricity is ranked first).

3. Network-Level Metrics

In this section, we evaluate the following network-level metrics for the US States graph: Bipartivity Index; Degree Metrics - Average, Standard Deviation, Kurtosis and Spectral Radius Ratio; Algebraic Connectivity; Assortativity Index and Modularity. We also determine the size of the Minimum Connected Dominating Set of vertices based on the four centrality metrics (DegC, BWC, EVC and ClC).

3.1 Bipartivity Index

A graph is bipartite (a.k.a. 2-colorable) if the vertices of the graph can be partitioned to two disjoint sets such that all the edges in the graph are those that connect a vertex from one partition to the other partition, and there are no edges between vertices within a partition (Cormen et al., 2009). The two partitions are determined using the sign of the entries in the eigenvector corresponding to the smallest eigenvalue of the binary adjacency matrix of the graph (Estrada & Rodriguez-Velazquez, 2005); the positive entries are grouped into one partition and the negative entries are grouped into another partition. Figure 9 displays the US States graph with the states colored in yellow or green to represent the two partitions.

A measure called bipartivity index (Estrada & Rodriguez-Velazquez, 2005) has been proposed in the literature to determine the extent of bipartivity for complex network graphs. The bipartivity index of a graph is computed using the eigenvalues of the binary adjacency matrix of the graph. The bipartivity index values could range from 0 to 1; if a graph has bipartivity index of 1, it implies all the edges in the graph are only those that connect the vertices across the two partitions. However, there exist several real-world network graphs for which there are few edges (called frustrated edges) that connect the vertices within each partition (though a majority of the edges connect the vertices across two partitions; Estrada & Rodriguez-Velazquez, 2005). Graphs with one or more frustrated edges have bipartivity index less than 1 and graphs with no frustrated edges have bipartivity index equal to 1 (Estrada & Rodriguez-Velazquez, 2005). While graphs with no frustrated edges have been referred to as *truly bipartite*, graphs with frustrated edges have been referred to as *close-to-bipartite* (Estrada & Rodriguez-Velazquez, 2005). The bipartivity index of the US States graph has been observed to be 0.66 and the fraction of frustrated edges in the network is 0.32. Though the bipartivity index value is not that close to 1, it is still larger than the values observed for several of the real-world networks in the literature (Estrada & Rodriguez-Velazquez, 2005).

Figure 9. On the Bipartivity of the US States Network Graph (48 Contiguous States and DC)

Bipartivity Index: 0.66

3.2 Degree Metrics

From Figure 2, we observe that the degree distribution of the vertices is Poisson and bi-modal in nature. To corroborate this assertion, we observe the average degree of the vertices to be 4.37 (roughly close to the average of the two peak degree values of 3 and 5), with a standard deviation and Kurtosis of 1.72 and 2.75 respectively (all indicating that the degree distribution is close to being a normal/Poisson distribution; Balakrishnan & Nevzorov, 2003). Kurtosis is a measure of the "tailedness" of a probability distribution (Balanda & MacGillivray, 1998). For normal distribution, the expected value for the Kurtosis is 3; distributions with Kurtosis values above or below 3 are said to be fat-tailed and thin-tailed respectively (Balanda & MacGillivray, 1998). Further, the spectral radius ratio for node degree (defined as the ratio of the principal eigenvalue of the adjacency matrix of the graph and the average node degree; Meghanathan, 2014a) is observed to be 1.24. The spectral radius ratio for node degree is a measure of the variation in node degree of the vertices; the minimum possible value for this metric is 1.0 and farther the value of the spectral radius ratio for node degree from 1, the larger is the variation in node degree. Though the spectral radius ratio for node degree value of 1.24 is not much larger than 1, the value is not as close to 1 (Meghanathan, 2014a) as observed for the US Football network (Girvan & Newman, 2002): a network with a unimodal Poisson degree distribution of the vertices; the value of 1.24 could be attributed to the variation due to the bi-modal degree distribution of the vertices.

3.3 Algebraic Connectivity

The algebraic connectivity of a graph is a measure of the robustness of the graph (Fiedler, 1973). The farther the value of this metric from 0, the larger is the robustness of the graph with respect to the overall connectivity of the network. The algebraic connectivity of a graph is computed as the second smallest eigenvalue of the Laplacian matrix of the graph [24]. We determine the algebraic connectivity of the US States graph to be 0.0973. Such a low value indicates that (though the entire graph is connected), the robustness of the graph is very low. The entries in the Laplacian matrix of a graph are defined (Fiedler, 1973) as follows:

$$L(i,j) = \begin{cases} degree(i) & if\ i=j \\ -a_{ij} & if\ i \neq j \end{cases}$$ where a_{ij} is an entry (0 or 1) in the adjacency matrix for vertices i and j.

3.4 Assortativity

The assortative index of the edges (with respect to a particular node-level metric like centrality metrics) in a graph is a measure of the extent of similarity (with respect to the metric) between the end vertices of the graph (Newman, 2010). Assortative index with respect to a particular metric is computed as the Pearson's product-moment correlation coefficient values (with respect to the metric in consideration) for the end vertices of the edges in the graph. Like correlation coefficient, the values for the Assortative index could range from -1 to 1 (Newman, 2010). If the Assortative index value is close to 1 (or -1), it implies the end vertices of the edges in the graph have similar values (or dissimilar values) for the particular metric in consideration. Networks with assortative index value closer to 1 are said to be more assortative and value closer to -1 are said to be more dissortative with respect to the node-level metric in consideration (Meghanathan, 2016a). If the Assortative index value is closer to 0, it implies the values for the end vertices of the edges are independent of each other with respect to the particular metric in consideration. Random networks are expected to have an Assortative index closer to 0 for any node-level metric (Meghanathan, 2016a).

We conduct an assortativity analysis of the edges in the US States graph with respect to the four centrality metrics (DegC, EVC, BWC and ClC) and local clustering coefficient (LCC) and observe the following values: (i) DegC-based Assortativity index: 0.23; (ii) EVC-based Assortativity index: 0.62; (iii) BWC-based Assortativity index: 0.23; (iv) ClC-based Assortativity index: 0.65 and (v) LCC-based Assortativity index: -0.03. We thus observe the US States graph to be relatively more assortative with respect to EVC and ClC and less assortative with respect to DegC and BWC; also, the US States graph is neither assortative nor dissortative with respect to LCC.

Table 10. Partitioning of the Vertices of the Contiguous States Graph (48 States and DC) into Communities (using the Louvain Algorithm; Blondel et al., 2008)

1		2		3		4		5		6	
ID	State	ID	State	ID	State	ID	State	ID	State	ID	State
1	AL	2	AZ	25	MT	6	CT	7	DE	12	IL
3	AR	4	CA	26	NE	18	ME	8	DC	13	IN
9	FL	5	CO	33	ND	20	MA	19	MD	14	IA
10	GA	11	ID	40	SD	28	NH	29	NJ	16	KY
17	LA	15	KS	49	WY	31	NY	37	PA	21	MI
23	MS	27	NV			38	RI	45	VA	22	MN
32	NC	30	NM			44	VT	47	WV	24	MO
39	SC	35	OK							34	OH
41	TN	36	OR							48	WI
42	TX	43	UT								
		46	WA								

3.5 Modularity

We used the Louvain algorithm (Blondel et al., 2008) to determine an optimal partitioning of the US States graph into communities. The modularity score (in a scale of 0 to 1; Newman, 2006) was observed to be 0.586 and there were a total of 6 communities of the vertices (see Table 10 and Figure 10). We observe the vertex communities to closely resemble the nine regional divisions used by the United States Census Bureau (http://www2.census.gov/geo/pdfs/maps-data/maps/reference/us_regdiv.pdf). Figure 10 displays the six communities with different colors (one color per community) using the map from http://www.thecolor.com.

Figure 10. Communities of Vertices in the US States Graph (48 Contiguous States and DC) Detected using the Louvain Algorithm (Modularity Score: 0.586)

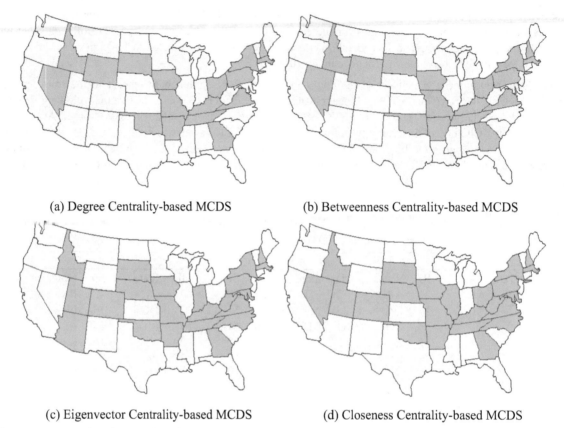

(a) Degree Centrality-based MCDS   (b) Betweenness Centrality-based MCDS

(c) Eigenvector Centrality-based MCDS   (d) Closeness Centrality-based MCDS

Figure 11. Approximations to the Minimum Connected Dominating Set (MCDS) based on Centrality Metrics for the US States Graph (48 Contiguous States and DC)

3.6 Connected Dominating Set

A connected dominating set (CDS) of a graph is a subset of the vertices such that every vertex in the graph is either in the CDS or is a neighbor of a node in the CDS (Cormen et al., 2009). The problem of determining a minimum connected dominating set (MCDS) is NP-hard (Cormen et al., 2009) and there are several heuristics (e.g., Newman, 2006; Meghanathan, 2014b) available in the literature to approximate a MCDS. We use the heuristic proposed by Meghanathan (2014b) to determine an approximate MCDS with respect to a chosen node-level metric. The idea behind the MCDS-heuristic is to prefer to include nodes with the largest value for the node-level metric in consideration to be part of the CDS; once a node is included is to the CDS, all its neighbor nodes are said to be covered and are considered for possible inclusion to the CDS. The heuristic proceeds in iterations; in each iteration, a covered node with the largest value for the node-level metric is included to the CDS as long as the covered node has at least one uncovered neighbor node that is not yet covered by nodes already included to the CDS. The iterations are continued until all nodes are covered (i.e., a node is either in the CDS or is covered by a node in the CDS).

Any node-level metric could be used to approximate a MCDS; however, the size of the MCDS varies with the node-level metric used. Traditionally, the degree centrality metric has been observed to return CDSs of the smallest size (Newman, 2006; Meghanathan, 2014b) as a high-degree node included to the CDS is more likely to cover several other nodes. In this paper, we indeed observe the above assertion to be true as a degree-based MCDS of the US States graph of 49 vertices has only 17 vertices; we also observe the BWC-MCDS of the US States graph to comprise of the same minimum number of vertices (i.e., 17 vertices) and the constituent states for both the MCDSs are the same. We observe the EVC and ClC-based MCDSs to incur a relatively larger number of vertices (22 and 23 vertices respectively). Figures 11-(a) through 11-(d) present the MCDSs of the US States network graph (vertices that are part of the MCDS are colored in green and vertices that are not part of the MCDS, but covered by at least one node in the MCDS are colored in yellow).

4. Normalization-based Comprehensive Centrality Scores

As there are ties among the vertices when ranked with respect to a particular centrality metric, we propose a normalization-based approach to obtain a potentially tie-free comprehensive ranking of the vertices in the US states network graph. In addition to the above objective, we seek to identify the centrality metric whose normalized values are relatively the closest to the NCC values as well as we intend to identify the centrality metric whose ranking of the vertices matches relatively closest to the ranking based on the NCC values. If we could identify such centrality metrics with a lower root mean square difference (RMSD) value, we could just compute these centrality metric(s) and consider the ranking based on these metric(s) as a comprehensive measure of ranking the vertices rather than individually computing the various centrality metrics. A similar approach could be applied for any real-world network or synthetic networks generated from theoretical models (Erdos & Renyi, 1959; Barabasi & Albert, 1999).

Table 11. Normalized Comprehensive Centrality (NCC)-based Ranking of Vertices in the US States Graph

Rank	ID	NCC	Rank	ID	NCC	Rank	ID	NCC	Rank	ID	NCC
1	24	0.3454	14	34	0.1556	26	32	0.1062	38	44	0.0639
2	16	0.2595	15	12	0.1555	27	42	0.1032	39	7	0.0624
3	41	0.2485	16	31	0.1394	28	23	0.1027	40	28	0.0608
4	11	0.1900	17	49	0.1272	29	1	0.0974	41	8	0.0601
5	37	0.1896	18	15	0.1266	30	22	0.0965	42	29	0.0594
6	26	0.1732	19	30	0.1230	31	20	0.0884	43	21	0.0582
7	14	0.1721	20	27	0.1197	32	48	0.0856	44	46	0.0576
8	45	0.1692	21	43	0.1169	33	17	0.0789	45	6	0.0568
9	35	0.1684	22	19	0.1151	34	25	0.0731	46	39	0.0546
10	3	0.1681	23	10	0.1107	35	36	0.0728	47	9	0.0527
11	5	0.1649	24	13	0.1099	36	33	0.0691	48	38	0.0376
12	40	0.1606	25	2	0.1082	37	4	0.0682	49	18	0.0267
13	47	0.1578									

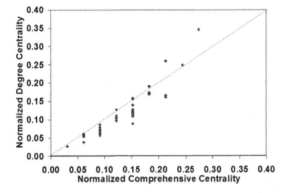
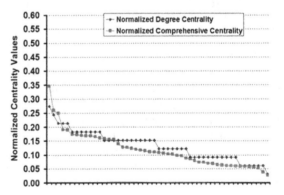

12-(a): Node-Level Distribution and Distribution of the Sorted Values for Degree and NCC (RMSD = 0.027)

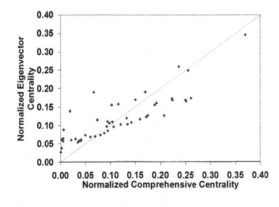
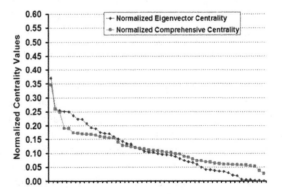

12-(b): Node-Level Distribution and Distribution of the Sorted Values for EVC and NCC (RMSD = 0.047)

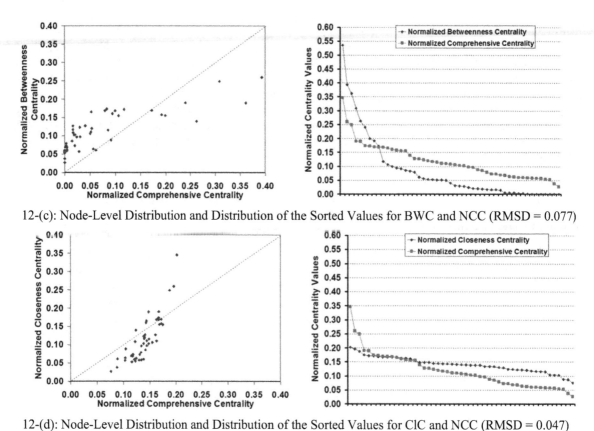

12-(c): Node-Level Distribution and Distribution of the Sorted Values for BWC and NCC (RMSD = 0.077)

12-(d): Node-Level Distribution and Distribution of the Sorted Values for ClC and NCC (RMSD = 0.047)

Figure 12. Node-Level Distribution of the Normalized Comprehensive Centrality Scores and the Normalized Centrality Scores for the Individual Metrics: (a) Degree, (b) EVC, (c) BWC and (d) ClC

We normalize the centrality values for each of the four metrics: degree, eigenvector, betweenness and closeness, and compute a normalized comprehensive centrality (NCC) of the vertices as a weighted average of the normalized values of the centrality metrics. There could be a tie between two or more vertices with respect to the NCC values if and only if the corresponding vertices incur identical values for the four centrality metrics that are part of the NCC formulation. In this paper, we assign equal weights (0.25 each) for the four centrality metrics that are used to compute the NCC values. In general, this idea could be used to compute a normalized comprehensive centrality score involving any number of centrality metrics and with different weight for each metric as long as the sum of the weights is 1.0. Since larger the value for an individual centrality metric (for all the four centrality metrics that we use to compute the NCC), the higher is the ranking of the vertex with respect to the centrality metric, we propose that the larger the NCC value for a vertex, the higher is the overall ranking of the vertex. One can observe in Table 11: the NCC values are unique for the vertices and the ranking of the vertices could be done without any ties. ThisWe observe the states of Missouri, Kentucky and Tennessee to obtain the top three ranking with respect to NCC. At least two of these three states obtain the top three ranking with respect to each of the four centrality metrics. We observe the state of Maine to obtain the bottommost ranking with respect to the NCC scores and this state also obtained the bottommost ranking for three of the above four centrality metrics.

In Figures 12-(a) through 12-(d), we compare the normalized comprehensive centrality values to that of the individual normalized centrality values as well as illustrate the distribution of the normalized values for each of the four centrality metrics vis-a-vis the normalized comprehensive centrality value (each shown in the order of the largest to the smallest). For a majority of the vertices: we observe the normalized comprehensive centrality values to be lower than that of normalized degree (see Figure 12-a) and closeness centrality metric values (see Figure 12-d); whereas, we observe the normalized comprehensive centrality values to be larger than that of the normalized betweenness centrality values (see Figure 12-b). On the other hand, we observe the data points for the normalized comprehensive centrality and the normalized eigenvector centrality to be evenly distributed above and below the diagonal line (see Figure 12-b).

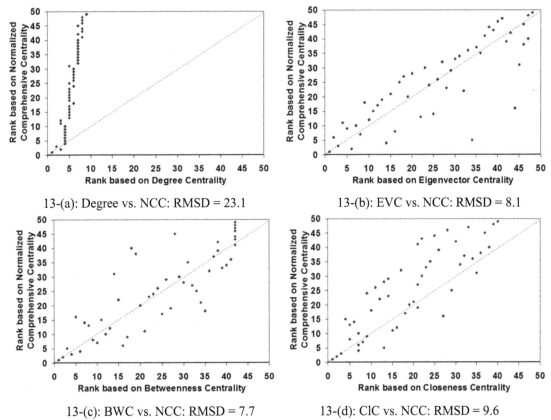

13-(a): Degree vs. NCC: RMSD = 23.1   13-(b): EVC vs. NCC: RMSD = 8.1

13-(c): BWC vs. NCC: RMSD = 7.7   13-(d): ClC vs. NCC: RMSD = 9.6

Figure 13. Distribution of the Ranking of the Vertices based on the Normalized Comprehensive Centrality Scores and the Normalized Centrality Scores for the Individual Metrics: (a) Degree, (b) EVC, (c) BWC and (d) ClC

We computed the root mean squared difference (RMSD) between the NCC values and the values for each of the four centrality metrics. The RMSD values are shown along with the charts in Figures 12-(a) through 12-(d). We observe the degree centrality-NCC combo to have relatively the lowest RMSD value (0.027), while the BWC-NCC combo incur relatively the largest RMSD value (0.077). The EVC-NCC combo and ClC-NCC combo incur RMSD value of 0.047 each. Thus, for the US States network graph, the degree centrality appears to be the centrality metric whose normalized values are relatively the closest to the NCC values.

Similar to the approach taken above, we identify the centrality metric whose ranking for the vertices matches relatively the closest to the ranking of the vertices based on NCC. In Figures 13-(a) through 13-(d), we show plots of the numerical ranking of the vertices based on each of the four centrality metrics vis-a-vis the NCC. For all the four centrality metrics, we notice vertices that were ranked high (i.e., lower numerical value for the rank) are also more likely to receive a higher rank with respect to NCC. We computed the RMSD values for the ranking obtained with NCC and each of the four centrality metrics. We observe the BWC-NCC combo to incur the lowest RMSD value of 7.7, closely followed by the EVC-NCC combo (with a RMSD value of 8.1). The degree centrality-NCC combo incurred the largest RMSD value of 23.1, primarily attributed to the narrow range of values [1...9] for node degree and the broader range of values [1...49] for the NCC.

Table 12 summarizes the RMSD values obtained for the ranking of the vertices based on the normalized individual centrality scores and the normalized comprehensive centrality scores (Figures 13-a through 13-d) and the actual scores themselves (Figures 12-a through 12-d). The degree cenntrality metric incurs the lowest RMSD value based on the normalized centrality scores and the largest RMSD value based on the ranking of the vertices. On the other hand, the betweenness centrality metric incurs the lowest RMSD value based on the ranking of the vertices and the largest RMSD value based on the normalized centrality scores. The closeness centrality metric incurs the second largest RMSD value based on the ranking of the vertices. Considering all of the above, the eigenvector centrality metric (EVC), which incurs the second lowest RMSD value with respect to both the normalized centrality scores and the ranking of the vertices, could be claimed as the centrality metric that closely matches to the normalized comprehensive centrality (NCC) values computed for the vertices of the US States network graph.

Table 12. Root Mean Square Difference (RMSD) Values obtained for the Node-Level Distribution of the Normalized Centrality Scores and the Ranking of the Vertices based on the Normalized Scores vis-a-vis the Normalized Comprehensive Centrality (NCC) Scores

Centrality Metric-NCC Combo	Node-Level Distribution of the Normalized Values	Ranking of the Vertices based on the Normalized Values
Degree-NCC	0.027	23.1
Eigenvector-NCC	0.047	8.1
Betweenness-NCC	0.077	7.7
Closeness-NCC	0.047	9.6

5. Configuration Model-Based Analysis

Given the degree sequence of a real-world network, the Configuration model could be used to generate a random network whose degree sequence is also the same as that of the real-world network (i.e., the random network could even have a non-Poisson degree distribution if the corresponding real-world network has one; Meghanathan, 2016c). In this paper, we use the Configuration model to study whether the degree sequence of the US States network graph (a real-world network) would be sufficient to generate a random network whose node-level metrics and network-level metrics exhibit strong correlation or proximity with the values incurred for these metrics in the corresponding real-world network.

Let N and L be respectively the number of nodes and edges in the chosen real-world network of study (like the US States network graph). Given the degree sequence (D) for the chosen real-world network, we simulate the generation of a random network per the configuration model as follows: We create a list LD (of length corresponding to the sum of the node degrees): the list is initialized with node IDs and the number of instances a node ID appears in the list corresponds to the degree of the node in D. The list LD is shuffled. We then proceed in iterations (to generate the random network), traversing the list LD in the reverse direction (i.e., with index j from |LD| to 2). In each iteration: we generate an edge (for the random network) involving the vertex at index j in the list LD to a vertex at a randomly chosen index i ($i < j$) when the following conditions are met: (i) the two entries are not -1, (ii) the two vertices are not the same (to avoid self-loop) and (iii) there does not exist already an edge involving the two vertices in the random network. The entries at both the indexes i and j are then set to -1.

Table 13. Correlation of the Node-Level Metrics for the US States Network Graph and its 100 Instances of Random Networks (with the same Degree Sequence) Generated using the Configuration Model

Node-Level Metric	Correlation Coefficient Value	Level of Correlation
Degree Centrality	0.99	Very Strongly Positive
Closeness Centrality	0.99	Very Strongly Positive
Eigenvector Centrality	0.76	Strongly Positive
Betweenness Centrality	0.72	Strongly Positive
Eccentricity	0.48	Moderately Positive
Maximal Clique Size	0.38	Weakly Positive
Local Clustering Coefficient	0.33	Weakly Positive

Table 14. Correlation of the Node-Level Metrics for the US States Network Graph and its 100 Instances of Random Networks (with the same Degree Sequence) Generated using the Configuration Model

Network-Level Metric	Real-World Network (US States Network Graph)	Random Network (Configuration Model)
Average Path Length	3.93	2.61
Diameter	10.00	5.28
Bipartivity Index	0.66	0.85
Algebraic Connectivity	0.097	0.645
Spectral Radius	1.24	1.19
Modularity Score	0.58	0.88
Edge Assortativity (Degree)	0.23	0.23
Edge Assortativity (EVC)	0.63	0.17
Edge Assortativity (BWC)	0.23	0.16
Edge Assortativity (ClC)	0.65	0.18

We generate 100 instances of random networks for the US States network graph according to the Configuration model and measure the following node-level metrics: (i) Degree Centrality, (ii) Eigenvector Centrality, (iii) Betweenness Centrality, (iv) Closeness Centrality, (v) Maximal Clique Size, (vi) Local Clustering Coefficient and (vii) Eccentricity; and network-level metrics: (i) Assortativity Index of the edges based on each of the four centrality metrics, (ii) Spectral Radius Ratio for Node Degree, (iii) Average Path Length, (iv) Diameter, (v) Bipartivity Index, (vi) Algebraic Connectivity and (vii) Modularity score determined using the Louvain algorithm. In the case of the node-level metrics, we measured the Pearson's product-moment correlation coefficient (Triola, 2012) between the values incurred for the nodes in each of the 100 instances of the random networks and the actual real-world network and averaged the correlation coefficient values (shown in Table 13 in the decreasing order of the correlation coefficient values).

We adapt the range of correlation coefficient values (rounded to two decimals) proposed in the literature (Evans, 1995) to decide on the level of correlation. We observe a very strong positive correlation (range: 0.80...1.00) in the case of the degree centrality (as expected) and closeness centrality metrics, and a strongly positive correlation (range: 0.60...0.79) in the case of the eigenvector centrality and betweenness centrality metrics. On the other hand, we observe a moderately positive correlation (range: 0.40...0.59) in the case of eccentricity, and a weakly positive correlation (range: 0.20...0.39) in the case of maximal clique size and local clustering coefficient.

For each network-level metric, we averaged the results obtained with the 100 instances of the random networks and compared this average value with the value incurred for the actual US States network graph (shown in Table 14). For none of the network-level metrics (other than degree-based edge assortativity and spectral radius ratio for node degree), we observe the average values obtained for the random networks generated using the configuration model to be closer to the values obtained for the actual US States network graph. We observe the random network instances to be relatively more bipartite, more robust to disconnection and more modular. We also observe the random network instances to have a relatively smaller diameter and a smaller average path length between any two nodes. As expected of a random network, we also observe the edges to be very weakly assortative with respect to all the four centrality metrics for the random networks generated using the configuration model; on the other hand, we observe the edges to be strongly assortative with respect to the eigenvector and closeness centrality metrics for the actual US States network graph.

Thus, based on the results obtained for the node-level metrics, we could conclude that the degree sequence of the US States network graph would be sufficient to generate random network instances that exhibit strong-very strong positive levels of correlation with respect to all the four centrality metrics. On the other hand, with respect to the other node-level metrics (like Eccentricity, Maximal Clique Size and Local Clustering Coefficient) as well as for all the network-level metrics (other than Degree centrality and Spectral radius ratio for node degree), we could conclude that the degree sequence of the US States network graph would alone not be sufficient to generate random network instances that exhibit comparable values for these metrics.

6. Related Work

Very few works have been conducted on network graphs related to the US. We review these works below: Fogarty et al. (2008) conducted a network analysis-based study on the hurricanes that made landfalls in the US from 1851 to 2008. A set of 23 non-overlapping regions (nodes) of the US that were affected with at least one hurricane were identified; two nodes were linked with an edge if at least one hurricane impacted the regions corresponding to both of them. One of the interesting conclusions from this study was that regions (like Louisiana) with a high occurrence rate of hurricanes had a low connectivity with the rest of the regions; on the other hand, regions with high connectivity (like Virginia) had a low occurrence rate. Several similarities have been observed between the hurricane landfall network by Fogarty et al (2008) and the US states network graph studied in this paper. For both the networks, the betweenness centrality metric exhibited a power-law distribution and the closeness centrality metric exhibited a uniform distribution with narrow range of values. While the average local clustering coefficient of the nodes in the landfall network was 0.46, the average local clustering coefficient of the nodes in the US states network graph is slightly larger (0.52). The diameter values for the network graphs are proportional: we observe a diameter of 10 for the US states network graph of 49 nodes and a diameter of 5 for the landfall network of 23 nodes. However, the two networks differ with respect to the degree centrality metric: we observe a clear bi-modal degree distribution for the US states network graph and no such distinct distribution could be attributed for the degree centrality metric in the landfall network. Though the hurricane landfall network and the US States network shared several similarities (as mentioned above), it must be remembered that the hurricane landfall network was constructed by cumulatively considering the landfall of hurricanes over a longer period of time (for about 150 years). We anticipate the results for the node-level and network-level metrics to appreciably differ for the two networks if the landfall network is constructed for a particular year or over a shorter time period.

Lin et al. (2014) conducted a network analysis of food flows within the US and had the following results: The distributions for the degree centrality and betweenness centrality were observed to be normal and Weibull (Balakrishnan, & Nevzorov, 2003) in nature. A power-law relationship (Balakrishnan, & Nevzorov, 2003) existed between the degree centrality and betweenness centrality metrics, indicating a vulnerability to the disturbance of key nodes. On the other hand, we did not observe a power-law relationship between degree and betweenness centrality for the US States network graph; even vertices with moderate-high degree had a low betweenness centrality. Lyte et al. (2015) conducted a citation network-based analysis of the different sections that fall under the 52 titles of United States Code; each section is a node and there exists a directed edge from one section to another section if the former cites the latter. The betweenness and eigenvector centrality metrics were used in this study to identify major pathways of references from one section to another. The modularity-based Louvain community detection algorithm (Blondel et al., 2008) was used to identify communities of sections that had similarities with respect to concepts and codes. It was observed that though sections under two or more related titles formed a single community, most of the communities detected were a collection of sections under a particular title. For the US States network graph, the communities detected using the Louvain algorithm were similar to the regional divisions used by the United States Census Bureau.

Cheung and Gunes (2012) conducted a complex network analysis study of the US air transportation network as of 2011 and compared it with the networks that existed in 1991 and 2001. Their study revealed no major changes in the features (like centrality and connectivity of the airports) of the air transportation networks that evolved with time (with increase in the number of airports and flight connections). A critical finding from the study was that the US air transportation network of 2011 has been identified to be more vulnerable to airport closures than it was in the past. The degree distribution of the 2011 US air transportation network only follows a partial Power-law (i.e., the distribution exhibited Power-law only after a degree value > 1), unlike the world-wide air transportation network that follows Power-law starting from degree value of 1 (Guimera, 2005). Random network instances (generated using the configuration model) of the US States network graph exhibited strong positive correlation with respect to the centrality metrics, but were observed to be relatively more bipartite, modular and robust to disconnection.

7. Summary and Conclusions

Our high-level contribution in this paper is to illustrate complex network analysis of a connected graph of the states within a country at node-level and network-level as well as propose a normalization-based approach to comprehensively rank the vertices (more likely to be tie-free) in a network graph based on the centrality metrics. We implemented the algorithms to compute a suite of node-level and network-level metrics and ran them on the US States network graph. We summarize the results and key observations as follows: (i) The state of Missouri is the top-ranked node with respect to all the commonly studied centrality metrics such as degree, betweeenness, closeness and eigenvector centralities. This is vindicated with several airlines (like American Airlines, Southwest Airlines, etc) choosing the city of Missouri as one of their primary hubs over the past two decades. (ii) The degree distribution appears to mimic a bi-modal Poisson distribution, while the betweenness centrality (BWC) exhibits a Power-law style distribution. (iii) There exists a maximum clique of size 4 involving the states of Arizona, Colorado, New Mexico and Utah; the rest of the states (except Maine) are part of maximal cliques of size 3. (iv) The state of Idaho has the lowest non-zero local clustering coefficient, indicating that the state is the most critical state with respect to facilitating communication between its neighboring states. (v) The radius, diameter and average path length are 5, 10 and 3.94 respectively. The states of Ohio and West Virginia form the "center" of the graph with an eccentricity corresponding to the radius of the graph (these states are at most 5 hops away from any other state in the graph). The states of Arizona, California, Maine, Montana and North Dakota have an eccentricity corresponding to the diameter of the graph (these states could be as large as 10 hops away to one or more states in the graph). More than 65% of the vertices have an eccentricity of 8 or above. (vi) The bipartivity index of the graph is 0.66 with 32% frustrated edges. (vii) The algebraic connectivity of the network graph is 0.0973 (indicating low robustness) and the spectral radius ratio for node degree is 1.24 (moderately high for a Poisson network, vindicating the bi-modal degree distribution of the vertices). (viii) The modularity score of the graph is 0.58 with a total of six non-overlapping communities of states, closely resembling the regional classification of the states. (ix) The network has been observed to be relatively more assortative with respect to eigenvector and closeness centralities; whereas the degree-based and BWC-based approximations to the minimum connected dominating sets are of the smallest size. (x) The Configuration model-based study of the US States network graph indicated that the degree sequence alone was sufficient to generate random network instances that exhibited strong-very strong levels of positive correlation for the centrality metrics, but the degree sequence was not sufficient to observe such a strong correlation for the other node-level metrics and comparable values for the network-level metrics. The random network instances of the US States network graph were observed to be relatively more robust to network disconnection, more bipartite and more modular. Thus, even though it might look like some states may have a common border by chance (especially, if the common border is over a smaller area), the above results (especially those from assortativity analysis and the configuration model-based study) indicate that the network of US states is very much different from a random network.

We have also proposed a normalization-based approach to arrive at a (possibly tie-free) ranking of the vertices based on their comprehensive centrality scores determined as a weighted average of the normalized scores of the individual centrality metrics. We also show how to identify the centrality metric whose normalized individualized scores and ranking of the vertices is relatively the closest to the normalized comprehensive centrality (NCC) scores and the ranking of the vertices based on the NCC scores. Considering the results plotted in Figures 12-(a) through 12-(d) and Figures 13-(a) through 13-(d), it appears that the Eigenvector Centrality metric (that consistently incurs the second smallest RMSD values with respect to both the normalized centrality scores and the numerical ranking of the vertices) could be relatively the best metric that could be used to obtain a comprehensive centrality-based ranking of the vertices in the US States network graph. A similar approach could be used to identify a centrality metric that could be considered the candidate metric to claim a comprehensive centrality-based ranking of the vertices in other real-world network graphs and synthetic graphs generated from theoretical models.

To the best of our knowledge, we have not come across a paper that comprehensively analyzes a suite of node-level and network-level metrics for any real-world network and one especially based on the states within a country. The approach taken and the metrics evaluated in this paper could have several applications: For example, we could identify the states that are most the central states as well as identify the states that could form a connected backbone and geographically well-connected to the rest of the states within a country and use this information to design the road/rail transportation networks; we could identify the states that could be clustered to a particular geographical region within a country and use this information for region-based analysis and etc. For countries with a reasonably larger area and an appreciable number of states, each state (except those in the corners of the country) typically shares border with a similar number of states. Hence, we anticipate the distribution of values for the node-level metrics to be about the same for several other countries too. We thus opine the paper to serve as a model for anyone interested in analyzing a connected graph of the states within a country from a Network Science perspective.

Acknowledgments

The research is financed by the NASA EPSCoR sub award (#: NNX14AN38A) from University of Mississippi.

References

Balakrishnan, N., & Nevzorov, V. B. (2003). *A Premier on Statistical Distributions*. (1st ed.) Wiley-Interscience.

Balanda, K. P., & MacGillivray, H. L. (1998). Kurtosis: A Critical Review. *The American Statistician, 42*(2), 111-119. http://dx.doi.org/10.2307/2684482.

Barabasi, A. L., & Albert, R. (1999). Emergence of Scaling in Random Networks. *Science, 286*(5439), 509-512. http://dx.doi.org/10.1126/science.286.5439.509.

Benson, S. J. (2008). *Explorer's Guide The Four Corners Region: Where Colorado, Utah, Arizona & New Mexico Meet: A Great Destination*. (1st ed.) Countryman Press.

Blondel, V. D., Guillaume, J. L., Lambiotte, R., & Lefebvre, E. (2008). Fast Unfolding of Communities in Large Networks. *Journal of Statistical Mechanics: Theory and Experiment*, P10008, 1-11. http://dx.doi.org/10.1088/1742-5468/2008/10/P10008.

Brandes, U. (2001). A Faster Algorithm for Betweenness Centrality. *The Journal of Mathematical Sociology, 25*(2), 163-177. http://dx.doi.org/10.1080/0022250X.2001.9990249.

Cherven, K. (2015). *Mastering Gephi Network Visualization*. (1st ed.) Packt Publishing.

Cheung, D. P., & Gunes, M. H. (2012). *A Complex Network Analysis of the United States Air Transportation*. Paper presented at the IEEE/ACM International Conference on Advances in Social Networks Analysis and Mining, Istanbul, Turkey. http://dx.doi.org/10.1109/ASONAM.2012.116.

Chung, L. L. F. (2006). *Complex Graphs and Networks*. (1st ed.) American Mathematical Society.

Cormen, T. H., Leiserson, C. E., Rivest, R. L., & Stein, C. (2009). *Introduction to Algorithms.* (3rd ed.) MIT Press.

Daniel, W. W. (2000). *Applied Nonparametric Statistics.* (2nd ed.) Cengage Learning.

Ding, Y. (2011). Scientific Collaboration and Endorsement: Network Analysis of Coauthorship and Citation Networks. *Journal of Informetrics, 5*(1), 187-203. http://dx.doi.org/10.1016/j.joi.2010.10.008.

Erdos, P., & Renyi, A. (1959). On Random Graphs I. *Publicationes Mathematicae, 6,* 290-297.

Estrada, E., & Rodriguez-Velazquez, J. A. (2005). Spectral Measures of Bipartivity in Complex Networks. *Physical Review E, 72*(4), 046105. https://doi.org/10.1103/PhysRevE.72.046105.

Evans, J. D. (1995). *Straightforward Statistics for the Behavioral Sciences.* (1st ed.) Brooks Cole Publishing Company.

Fiedler, M. (1973). Algebraic Connectivity of Graphs. *Czechoslovak Mathematical Journal, 23*(2), 298-305.

Fogarty, E. A., Elsner, J. B., Jagger, T. H., & Tsonis, A. A. (2008). Network Analysis of U. S. Hurricanes. *Springer Hurricanes and Climate Change,* 153-167. http://dx.doi.org/10.1007/978-0-387-09410-6_9.

Fruchterman, T. M. J., & Reingold, E. M. (1991). Graph Drawing by Force-Directed Placement. *Software - Practice & Experience, 21*(11), 1129-1164.

Ghali, N., Panda, M., Hassanien, A. E., Abraham, A., & Snasel, V. (2012). Social Network Analysis: Tools, Measures and Visualization. *Computational Social Networks,* 3-23. http://dx.doi.org/10.1007/978-1-4471-4054-2_1.

Girvan, M., & Newman, M. E. J. (2002). Community Structure in Social and Biological Networks. *Proceedings of the National Academy of Sciences of the United States of America, 19*(12), 7821-7826. http://dx.doi.org/10.1073/pnas.122653799.

Guha. S., & Khuller, S. (1998). Approximation Algorithms for Connected Dominating Sets. *Algorithmica, 20*(4), 374-387. http://dx.doi.org/10.1007/PL00009201.

Guimera, R., Mossa, S., Turtschi, A., & Amaral, L. A. N. (2005). The World-Wide Air Transportation Network: Anomalous Centrality, Community Structure, and Cities' Global Roles. *Proceedings of the National Academy of Sciences, 102*(22), 7794-7799. http://dx.doi.org/10.1073/pnas.0407994102.

Lay, D. C., Lay, S. R., & McDonald, J. J. (2015). *Linear Algebra and its Applications.* (5th Ed.) Pearson.

Lin, X., Dang, Q., & Konar, M. (2014). A Network Analysis of Food Flows within the United States of America. *Environmental Science & Technology, 48*(10), 5439-5447. http://dx.doi.org/10.1021/es500471d.

Lyte, A., Slater, D., & Michel, S. (2015). Network Measures of the United States Code. Technical Report, MITRE.

Ma, X., & Gao, L. (2012). Biological Network Analysis: Insights into Structure and Functions. *Briefings in Functional Genomics, 11*(6), 434-442, November 2012. https://doi.org/10.1093/bfgp/els045.

Meghanathan, N. (2014a). Spectral Radius as a Measure of Variation in Node Degree for Complex Network Graphs. Paper presented at the 3rd International Conference on Digital Contents and Applications, Hainan, China. http://dx.doi.org/10.1109/UNESST.2014.8.

Meghanathan, N. (2014b). Centrality-based Connected Dominating Sets for Complex Network Graphs. *International Journal of Interdisciplinary Telecommunications and Networking, 6*(2), 1-19. http://dx.doi.org/10.4018/ijitn.2014040101.

Meghanathan, N. (2015a). Exploiting the Discriminating Power of the Eigenvector Centrality Measure to Detect Graph Isomorphism. *International Journal in Foundations of Computer Science and Technology, 5*(6), 1-13. http://dx.doi.org/10.5121/ijfcst.2015.5601.

Meghanathan, N. (2015b). Distribution of Maximal Clique Size of the Vertices for Theoretical Small-World Networks and Real-World Networks. *International Journal of Computer Networks and Communications, 7*(4), 21-41. http://dx.doi.org/10.5121/ijcnc.2015.7402.

Meghanathan, N. (2016a). Maximal Assortative Matching for Complex Network Graphs. *Journal of King Saud University: Computer and Information Sciences, 28*(2), 230-246. http://dx.doi.org/10.1016/j.jksuci.2015.10.004.

Meghanathan, N. (2016b). On the Conduciveness of Random Network Graphs for Maximal Assortative or

Maximal Dissortative Matching. *Computer and Information Science,* 9(1), 21-30. http://dx.doi.org/10.5539/cis.v9n1p21.

Meghanathan, N. (2016c). On the Sufficiency of using the Degree Sequence of the Vertices to Generate Random Networks Corresponding to Real-World Networks. *Polibits: Research Journal on Computer Science and Computer Engineering with Applications,* 53(1), 5-21. http://dx.doi.org/10.17562/PB-53-1.

Newman, M. (2006). Modularity and Community Structure in Networks. *Proceedings of the National Academy of Sciences,* 103(23), 8577-8582. http://dx.doi.org/10.1073/pnas.0601602103.

Newman, M. (2010). *Networks: An Introduction.* (1st ed.) Oxford University Press.

Pattabiraman, B., Patwary, M. A., Gebremedhin, A. H., Liao, W-K., & Choudhary, A. (2013). *Fast Problems for the Maximum Clique Problem on Massive sparse Graphs.* Paper presented at the 10th International Workshop on Algorithms and Models for the Web Graph, Cambridge, MA, USA. http://dx.doi.org/10.1007/978-3-319-03536-9_13.

Triola, M. F. (2012). *Elementary Statistics.* (12th ed.) Pearson.

Zhao, D., & Strotmann, A. (2015). *Analysis and Visualization of Citation Networks.* (1st ed.) Morgan & Claypool Publishers.

Permissions

All chapters in this book were first published in CIS, by Canadian Center of Science and Education; hereby published with permission under the Creative Commons Attribution License or equivalent. Every chapter published in this book has been scrutinized by our experts. Their significance has been extensively debated. The topics covered herein carry significant findings which will fuel the growth of the discipline. They may even be implemented as practical applications or may be referred to as a beginning point for another development.

The contributors of this book come from diverse backgrounds, making this book a truly international effort. This book will bring forth new frontiers with its revolutionizing research information and detailed analysis of the nascent developments around the world.

We would like to thank all the contributing authors for lending their expertise to make the book truly unique. They have played a crucial role in the development of this book. Without their invaluable contributions this book wouldn't have been possible. They have made vital efforts to compile up to date information on the varied aspects of this subject to make this book a valuable addition to the collection of many professionals and students.

This book was conceptualized with the vision of imparting up-to-date information and advanced data in this field. To ensure the same, a matchless editorial board was set up. Every individual on the board went through rigorous rounds of assessment to prove their worth. After which they invested a large part of their time researching and compiling the most relevant data for our readers.

The editorial board has been involved in producing this book since its inception. They have spent rigorous hours researching and exploring the diverse topics which have resulted in the successful publishing of this book. They have passed on their knowledge of decades through this book. To expedite this challenging task, the publisher supported the team at every step. A small team of assistant editors was also appointed to further simplify the editing procedure and attain best results for the readers.

Apart from the editorial board, the designing team has also invested a significant amount of their time in understanding the subject and creating the most relevant covers. They scrutinized every image to scout for the most suitable representation of the subject and create an appropriate cover for the book.

The publishing team has been an ardent support to the editorial, designing and production team. Their endless efforts to recruit the best for this project, has resulted in the accomplishment of this book. They are a veteran in the field of academics and their pool of knowledge is as vast as their experience in printing. Their expertise and guidance has proved useful at every step. Their uncompromising quality standards have made this book an exceptional effort. Their encouragement from time to time has been an inspiration for everyone.

The publisher and the editorial board hope that this book will prove to be a valuable piece of knowledge for researchers, students, practitioners and scholars across the globe.

List of Contributors

Sofyan M. A. Hayajneh and AbdulRahman Rashad
Faculty of Engineering, Isra Univeristy, Amman, Jordan

Obaida M. Al-hazaimeh
Faculty of Informatics, AlBalqa Applied University, Salt, Jordan

Omar A. Saraereh
Faculty of Informatics, AlBalqa Applied University, Salt, Jordan
Faculty of Engineering, The Hashemite University, Amman, Jordan

Hayel Khafajeh and Issam Jebreen
Faculty of Information Technology, Zarqa University, Jordan

Omar H. Alhazmi
Department of Computer Science, Taibah University, Medina, Saudi Arabia

Eman Fares Al Mashagba
Zarqa University, Jordan

Saed Tarapiah
Telecommunication Engineering Department, An-Najah National University, Nablus, Palestine

Shadi Atalla
College of Information Technology (CIT), University of Dubai, Dubai, UAE

Kamarul Faizal Bin Hashim
College of Information Technology (CIT), University of Dubai, Dubai, UAE

Motaz Daadoo
Computer Systems Engineering, Palestine Technical University (Kadoorie), Tulkarm, Palestine

Sanjay P. Ahuja and Jesus Zambrano
University of North Florida, USA

Mohamed S. Farag, M. M. Mohie El Din and H. A. El Shenbary
Department of Mathematics, Faculty of Science Al-Azhar University, Egypt

Francesco Di Tria, Ezio Lefons and Filippo Tangorra
Dipartimento di Informatica, Università Aldo Moro, Bari, Italy

Simon M Karume
Department of Computing and Informatics , Laikipia University, Nyahururu, Kenya

Aree Ali
School of Science, University of Sulaimani, Sulaimani, KRG, Iraq

Bayan Omer
College of Science and Technology, University of Human Development, Sulaimani, KRG, Iraq

Azadeh Nazemi, Chandrika Fernando and Iain Murray
Department of Electrical and Computer Engineering, Curtin University Perth, Western Australia

David A. McMeekin
Department of Spatial Sciences, Curtin University Perth, Western Australia

Qiuyun Miao and Yang Shen
School of Economics and Management, Nanjing University of Aeronautics and Astronautic, China

Xu Tingting and Zuo Yuxiu
College of Information Engineering, Taishan Medical University, Tai'an, China

Ma Cunhong
Enrollment and Employment Office, Taian Technician College, Tai'an, China

Asma Ali Mosa, Mohd. Naz'ri bin Mahrin and Roslina Ibrrahim
Advanced Informatics School, Universiti Teknologi Malaysia (UTM), Malaysia

Huda Elmogazy and Omaimah Bamasag
Department of Computer Science, Faculty of Computing and Information Technology, King AbdulAziz University, Saudi Arabia

Nedhal A. Al-Saiyd
Applied Science Private University, Jordan

Kenmogne Edith Belise
Faculty of Science, Department of Mathematics and Computer Science, Cameroon

Rodrigo da Rosa Righi, Vinicius F. Rodrigues, Cristiano A. Costa and Roberto Q. Gomes
Applied Computing Graduate Program, Universidade do Vale do Rio dos Sinos, Brazil

Natarajan Meghanathan
Department of Computer Science, Jackson State University, USA

Index